Prosecuting International Crimes in Africa

Chacha Murungu & Japhet Biegon (editors)

Pretoria University Law Press
PULP

2011

Prosecuting international crimes in Africa

Published by:

Pretoria University Law Press (PULP)

The Pretoria University Law Press (PULP) is a publisher at the Faculty of Law, University of Pretoria, South Africa. PULP endeavours to publish and make available innovative, high-quality scholarly texts on law in Africa. PULP also publishes a series of collections of legal documents related to public law in Africa, as well as text books from African countries other than South Africa. This book was peer reviewed prior to publication.

For more information on PULP, see www.pulp.up.ac.za

Printed and bound by:

ABC Press
Cape Town

To order, contact:
PULP
Faculty of Law
University of Pretoria
South Africa
0002
Tel: +27 12 420 4948
Fax: +27 12 362 5125
pulp@up.ac.za
www.pulp.up.ac.za

Cover:

Yolanda Booyzen, Centre for Human Rights

Cover image:

Angola landmine victims by Paul Jeffrey

ISBN: 978-0-9869857-8-2

Konrad Adenauer Stiftung

RWI

The financial assistance of Konrad Adenauer Stiftung and Raoul Wallenberg Institute is gratefully acknowledged.

TABLE OF CONTENTS

PART II: INTERNATIONAL COURTS AND THE PROSECUTION OF INTERNATIONAL CRIMES IN AFRICA

PART IV: THE IMPLEMENTATION OF THE ROME STATUTE IN AFRICA

FOREWORD

I write this foreword with great pride and pleasure – in my capacity as Director of the Centre for Human Rights and as Academic Coordinator of the LLM (Human Rights and Democratisation in Africa).

I say 'with pride' because all the contributors to this collection are graduates of the Centre for Human Rights. With the exception of one, they have all been students on the LLM (Human Rights and Democratisation in Africa programme). The single exception, George William Mugwanya, completed the Master's degree in human rights that preceded the LLM (Human Rights and Democratisation in Africa). It is immensely gratifying to follow these students' progress since their graduation. Many proceeded to do doctorates at a wide range of universities. Others now hold teaching positions at African universities. Some are actively involved in the practice of international criminal justice. The two editors are, at the time of writing, doctoral candidates at the Centre for Human Rights.

I say 'with pleasure' in appreciation of the breadth and depth of the contributions in this volume. Here, fourteen African voices are provided with a platform to participate in the on-going debate on issues pertaining to international criminal justice as they arise in respect of past, present or possible future prosecutions by domestic, international and hybrid tribunals in Ethiopia, Kenya, Malawi, Rwanda, Senegal, Sierra Leone, South Africa, Sudan, Uganda and Zambia. The topics they address, the issues they raise and the countries on which they focus reflect the diversity and demographic spread of alumni of the LLM programme. Quite clearly, this collection does not make a claim to provide a comprehensive picture. What it does, however, is to strengthen the contribution of African scholars and practitioners to an area of concern to Africa, in which African voices are often underrepresented.

As the editors indicate in their 'Introduction', this publication stems from a workshop held in May 2010. Authors were required to complete their chapters before the workshop, so as to allow critical discussion of their contributions. This intensive process, in addition to peer review by experts in the field, contributed significantly to ensuring that the potential of each contribution was fully explored. The Centre gladly acknowledges the role of the Konrad Adenauer Stiftung in supporting the process.

This book can be viewed as a gift to the Centre by (some of) its alumni. It celebrates two milestones of both the LLM programme and the Centre itself.

The first milestone that the book celebrates relates to 2009, which marked the 10-year existence of the LLM (Human Rights and Democratisation in Africa). Coinciding with the graduation of the 'Class of 2009', an Alumni Conference was held. It served as a forum to renew and strengthen the personal and professional bonds between graduates along the axes of year groups, professional interests and countries; but also across the divides of year groups and countries.At the event, graduates decided to launch an LLM (Human Rights and Democratisation in Africa)

Alumni Association (LLM (HRDA) Alumni Association), to fully exploit the potential of the multiple networks of alumni – most of whom are based somewhere on the African continent. The idea of this publication was conceived as a way of harvesting existing expertise and experience among members of the graduate network. It illustrates the intellectual potential of the network of graduates, and gives a concrete example of what may be achieved by the Alumni Association or other collective action by graduates.

The second milestone to which the book relates is the Centre's 25-year celebrations in 2011. While most of the work in the preparation of this publication was done in 2010, it is finally published in 2011, the year in which the Centre commemorates 25 years of existence.

If this book is a gift, thanks should go to the editors. They toiled enthusiastically, spent countless hours in following up contributors and persevered to the last in locating missing details and carefully proof-reading the text. Chacha Murungu deserves special mention for his role in initiating and conceptualising the idea that led to this publication. Annelize Nienaber assisted with copy-editing the text. Thanks also go to the Konrad Adenauer Stiftung and Raoul Wallenberg Institute, whose assistance made the publication and distribution of this book possible.

FransViljoen
Director, Centre for Human Rights

CONTRIBUTORS

Benson Olugbuo is a Solicitor and Advocate of the Supreme Court of Nigeria and a Doctoral Candidate and Teaching and Research Assistant at the University of Cape Town, South Africa

Bonolo Dinokopila is a Lecturer at the Department of Law, University of Botswana and a Doctoral Candidate at the Centre for Human Rights, Faculty of Law, University of Pretoria, South Africa

Chacha Murungu is an Advocate of the High Court of Tanzania and a Doctoral Candidate at the Centre for Human Rights, Faculty of Law, University of Pretoria, South Africa. He is also the Coordinator of the African Expert Study Group on International Criminal Justice

Christian Garuka is a Legal Researcher at the Centre for the Study of AIDS, University of Pretoria, South Africa

Christopher Mbazira is a Lecturer and Deputy Dean (Postgraduate & Administration), Faculty of Law, Makerere University, Uganda

Firew Tiba is a Lecturer at the University of Waikato, New Zealand

George Mugwanya is a Senior Appeals Counsel at the International Criminal Tribunal for Rwanda and an Advocate of Uganda's Courts of Judicature

Japhet Biegon is an Advocate of the High Court of Kenya and a Doctoral Candidate at the Centre for Human Rights, Faculty of Law, University of Pretoria, South Africa

Osogo Ambani is a Lecturer at the Faculty of Law, Catholic University of Eastern Africa, Kenya

Ken Obura is a Doctoral Candidate at Rhodes University, South Africa, and an Advocate of the High Court of Kenya

Lee Stone is an Attorney of the High Court of South Africa and a Senior Lecturer at the Faculty of Law, Howard College Campus, University of KwaZulu-Natal, South Africa

Mwiza Nkhata is a Lecturer at the Faculty of Law, University of Malawi, Malawi and a Doctoral Candidate at the Centre for Human Rights, Faculty of Law, University of Pretoria, South Africa.

Kameldy Neldjingaye is a Legal Officer at the Institute for Human Rights and Development in Africa, Banjul, The Gambia

Steve Odero is a Lecturer in Law and Political Science at Africa Nazarene University, Kenya

ABBREVIATIONS

AC	Appeals Chamber
AFRC	Armed Forces Revolutionary Council
AU	African Union
CAR	Central African Republic
CAT	Convention against Torture and other Cruel, Inhuman or Degrading Treatment or Punishment
CDF	Civil Defence Forces
CEAJ	Committee of Eminent African Jurists
CPA	Comprehensive Peace Agreement
DDS	Documentation and Security Directorate
DPP	Director of Public Prosecutions
DRC	Democratic Republic of Congo
ECCC	Extraordinary Chambers in the Courts of Cambodia
ECOWAS	Economic Community of West African States
ICC	International Criminal Court
ICCPR	International Covenant on Civil and Political Rights
ICJ	International Court of Justice
ICTR	International Criminal Tribunal for Rwanda
ICTY	International Criminal Tribunal for the former Yugoslavia
IDP	Internally Displaced Person
ILC	International Law Commission
JCE	Joint Criminal Enterprise
LRA	Lord's Resistance Army
NGO	Non Governmental Organisation
NRA	National Resistance Army
OAU	Organisation of African Unity
OTP	Office of the Prosecutor
PDO	Public Defenders Office
RAF	Rwandan Armed Forces
RPF	Rwandan Patriotic Front
RUF	Revolutionary United Front
SADC	Southern African Development Community
SCCED	Special Criminal Court for Events in Darfur
SCSL	Special Court for Sierra Leone
SPO	Special Prosecutor's Office
TC	Trial Chamber
TRC	Truth and Reconciliation Commission
UN	United Nations
UNCLOS	United Nations Convention on the Law of the Sea
UPDF	Uganda People's Defence Forces
WCD	War Crimes Division

INTRODUCTION

Chacha Murungu & Japhet Biegon***

Prosecuting International Crimes in Africa presents contributions by African-based scholars and international criminal law practitioners who are alumni of the Centre for Human Rights, that has been responsible for the Master's degree programme in Human Rights and Democratisation in Africa since 2000. The programme produced graduates with skills in human rights in Africa. This book is a product of the concerted efforts by some of these graduates.

Contributions are on different topics of importance to persons interested in international criminal justice as it applies in Africa. This book is aimed at a range of stakeholders in the field of international law and human rights in Africa. Specifically, it is relevant to persons involved in post-graduate studies, researchers, members of national and international judicial bodies and international criminal law practitioners. The book is divided into four parts. Part I deals with general issues in the prosecution of international crimes. Part II focuses on the prosecution of international crimes before international courts: the ICTR, ICC, and the SCSL. Part III examines the prosecution of international crimes before national courts, particularly Ethiopia, Kenya, Senegal, Rwanda, and Uganda. Part IV deals with the implementation of the Rome Statute in African states. The states covered in this regard are Malawi, Zambia and South Africa. The issue of positive complementarity is covered in respect of Uganda, the Democratic Republic of the Congo and Sudan.

Consisting of 14 chapters, the book contributes to the rule of law and respect for human rights in Africa. The ultimate goal is to contribute to the eradication of the culture of impunity in Africa. All contributions deal with

* LL.B (Hons) (Dar es Salaam); LL.M; LL.D Candidate (Pretoria); Advocate of the High Court of Tanzania.

** LL.B (Hons) (Moi); PGDL (Kenya School of Law); LL.M; LL.D Candidate (Pretoria); Diploma (International Protection of Human Rights) (Åbo Akademi University); Advocate of the High Court of Kenya.

prosecution of international crimes in Africa. The focus of the chapters is on how international crimes have been prosecuted by national courts from some African jurisdictions and international courts.

Contributions are on specific aspects of international criminal justice. Some chapters present the contribution by international courts and tribunals to the development of international law in Africa. Particularly, a few contributions deal with the jurisprudence of the International Criminal Tribunal for Rwanda (ICTR) and the Special Court for Sierra Leone (SCSL). Undoubtedly, all these courts have contributed to the development of international law. Other chapters address specific aspects of international criminal justice in Africa.

International law imposes on states the duty to prosecute or extradite persons responsible for international crimes. Obura's contribution in chapter 1 focuses on this, presenting an analysis of the position of international law on the question whether and to what extent states are under a legal obligation to prosecute international crimes. It reviews this question in relation to the concepts of *jus cogens* and the obligation *erga omnes*. It also addresses the controversial question of amnesty for international crimes. Obura concludes that principles of international law, both customary and conventional, impose on states the duty to prosecute and punish international crimes and that amnesty does not bar the prosecution of persons responsible for international crimes. A similar conclusion is drawn by Murungu in his contribution on the Special Court for Sierra Leone (chapter 4) in which he argues that amnesty is not a defence to the prosecution of perpetrators of international crimes.

International crimes are committed by individuals, including senior state officials. When state officials are accused of international crimes, they tend to put forward the defence of their official position or immunity attaching to them. The issue of immunity of state officials in relation to the prosecution of international crimes is addressed by Murungu (chapter 2). It is argued that while immunity is a norm under customary international law, it does not prevail over the other higher *jus cogens* norms imposing the duty to prosecute and punish individuals, including state officials responsible for international crimes. Hence, Murungu argues that immunity is not a bar to prosecution of perpetrators of international crimes because immunity has long been outlawed by customary and conventional international law, in addition to statutes establishing the ICC and other tribunals. Although immunity is not a defence to the prosecution of international crimes, different international criminal tribunals or courts have given conflicting decisions on whether state officials are immune from being subpoenaed to testify or submit evidence in international courts. Murungu concludes that immunity does not exist in respect of prosecution and subpoenas against state officials.

The commission of international crimes in Africa has led to the establishment of international criminal tribunals to prosecute and punish persons responsible for such crimes. The 1994 genocide in Rwanda led to the establishment of the ICTR. Mugwanya's chapter is on the ICTR's contribution to the development of international criminal law. Mugwanya relates his first-hand experience of the ICTR. Specifically, his chapter highlights the jurisprudence of the tribunal on a range of issues, including the definition of genocide, crimes against humanity and war crimes and their constitutive mental and physical elements. His chapter addresses a few substantive, procedural and evidentiary areas of international criminal justice, with particular focus on instances where the ICTR has pioneered the development of international law, breaking new ground and moving the law forward. Further, the chapter addresses instances where the ICTR has offered important clarification or elaboration of existing jurisprudence, or applied it to novel or challenging factual circumstances.

Closely related but distinct from the ICTR is the SCSL which was established in 2002 to prosecute and punish persons bearing the greatest responsibility for crimes against humanity and war crimes committed in Sierra Leone during the decade-long internal armed conflict. Undoubtedly, the SCSL has contributed to the development of international law principles. In chapter 4, Murungu highlights key areas in which the legacy of the Court is observed. He argues that the SCSL is in its final phase after having prosecuted nine cases. In addition to creating jurisprudence on war crimes and crimes against humanity, other significant contributions advanced by the SCSL include the clarification of international law concepts, particularly, 'persons bearing the greatest responsibility for international crimes', the status of the SCSL in international law, 'forced marriage at the time of armed conflict', the official position of individuals charged with international crimes – including state officials, the relationship between the Truth and Reconciliation Commission and the SCSL in prosecuting international crimes and the illegality of amnesty for individuals charged with international crimes. The chapter concludes that the SCSL has made a meaningful contribution to certain areas of international law, and that its jurisprudence will serve a meaningful purpose to international courts dealing with international crimes.

Following the discussion on the substantive contribution by the SCSL as presented by Murungu above, it is important to note that the SCSL has made immense contributions to international law through its sentencing practice. Dinokopila's chapter looks at the sentencing practices of the SCSL and examines the manner in which it has approached the issue of sentencing. It does so by revisiting the debate as to the purpose of sentencing at the international level and examines how various theories of punishment are applied by international criminal tribunals. Most importantly, Dinokopila assesses whether the jurisprudence of the SCSL has added value to the existing jurisprudence on the subject and how the jurisprudence could be of future use.

The African continent has been beset by armed conflicts. Most of the conflicts are non-international in character. These have occurred, for example, in the Democratic Republic of the Congo (DRC), the Central African Republic, the Sudan and Uganda. It is inevitable that when armed conflicts occur, international crimes, especially war crimes, crimes against humanity or genocide are committed by individuals. International criminal justice and humanitarian law require that perpetrators of international crimes should be brought to justice. The international community has agreed to put an end to impunity by, among other things, establishing the ICC. The ICC was established by the Rome Statute of the International Criminal Court of 1998 which entered into force on 1 July 2002. Following the establishment of the ICC, situations needing attention were referred to the Prosecutor of the ICC. The DRC, Uganda and Central African Republic did such referrals. The Darfur situation in Sudan was a referral by the Security Council of the United Nations in 2005. Self referrals, a referral by the Security Council and a *proprio motu* investigation by the Prosecutor of the ICC in respect of crimes against humanity committed in Kenya during the post-election violence between 2007 and 2008 triggered investigations and subsequent indictments against individuals allegedly responsible for crimes committed in such states.

It is apparent that the indictment of the Sudanese head of state, President Omar Hassan Al Bashir, has created tensions between the African Union (AU) and the ICC. The AU contends that indicting President Omar Al Bashir jeopardises the peace processes in Darfur. This seems contrary to the duty to prosecute persons responsible for international crimes, a duty imposed by customary international law, and arising from obligations to cooperate with the ICC in arresting and surrendering suspects of international crimes as envisaged under the Rome Statute. Odero writes in chapter 6 about the politics of international criminal justice in respect of the warrants of arrest issued by the ICC against President Omar Al Bashir of Sudan. He emphasises the need for lawyers and political scientists to make an attempt at synchronising their work. The analysis is unusual, drawing from the disciplines of law and political science and therefore is a challenge to lawyers, calling on them to unpack controversial factual issues and in so doing, adding to their understanding of the complex and non-legal factors that are at play in international criminal justice. Likewise, it is a challenge to political scientists to pay more attention to legal phenomena that are often at play and likely to influence political processes. Odero argues that it is only through a meeting of minds by scholars, practitioners and policy makers from these two fields, that sound judgments grounded in law and political reality may be reached and successfully implemented.

Apart from international criminal prosecutions, national courts in some African states have done a tremendous job in prosecuting and possibly punishing perpetrators of international crimes, or are in the process of doing so. In this regard, we present efforts by national courts to prosecute international crimes of concern to the international community. The Ethiopian courts have been able to punish individuals responsible for genocide and crimes against humanity. Tiba's contribution in chapter 7 is on the Trial of Mengistu Haile-Mariam, former state official of Ethiopia and other members of the then government for genocide, torture and summary executions. His chapter examines the trials by the Federal Courts and their contribution to post-conflict justice in Ethiopia. Tiba concludes that Ethiopian courts have rendered an important contribution to the law on genocide, especially at the domestic level by going beyond the Genocide Convention, by including a 'political group' as a protected group. Further, the Ethiopian courts have also stressed their rejection of the official status of accused persons responsible for genocide. He criticises the trials for representing victors' justice, their lack of fairness, disregard of the rights of accused and the inherent problems associated with trials *in absentia.*

In chapter 8, Neldjingaye discusses the trial of Hissène Habré in Senegal. Habré is allegedly responsible for crimes against humanity, particularly torture committed in Chad during his term in office as the President of Chad. Neldjingaye analyses the relevance in international law of the trial of Hissène Habré in Senegal. He provides the background of the Habré case by examining the Hissène Habré's human rights legacy and discusses the Belgium extradition request as well as the role played by the Committee against Torture in the case. He highlights that the trial is likely to contribute to the development of international law in aspects of the immunity of state officials, the principles of universal jurisdiction, territoriality and passive personality, and the duty to prosecute and punish individuals responsible for international crimes despite the principle of the non-retroactivity of punishment and law.

Although Uganda referred the situation to the Prosecutor of the ICC for investigation and prosecution of the leaders of the Lord's Resistance Army (LRA), there subsequently emerged the need for domestic prosecutions in Uganda especially after the establishment of the War Crimes Division of the High Court of Uganda. Parallel to this was the need for traditional justice system in Uganda. In chapter 9, Mbazira looks at the genesis and causes of the LRA war, the different attempts to end the war and mechanisms that have been put in place to deliver justice and end impunity in Uganda. Mbazira's chapter also reviews some of the important provisions of the International Criminal Court Act, 2010 which allows cooperation between the ICC and Uganda. Further, he reviews a constitutional petition which has been filed challenging the consistency of the ICC Act to the Constitution of Uganda, 1995. The conclusion reached is that the situation in Uganda illustrates some of the challenges African countries face in trying to punish international crimes: dealing with impunity and finding lasting peace in armed conflict situations. One of the challenges is balancing traditional mechanisms of dispute resolution based on restorative justice, on the one hand, and formal retributive and punitive justice mechanisms, on the other.

In chapter 10, Garuka presents a discussion on the domestic criminal prosecutions of the perpetrators of genocide in Rwanda. He discusses them in comparison with the ICTR-based prosecutions. He analyses the prosecution of genocide in ICTR and *Gacaca* courts. Both the ICTR and *Gacaca* have jurisdiction on genocide but the main difference lies in the lack of definition by the *Gacaca* law. He argues that the nature of the two jurisdictions is more visible: judges from the ICTR are trained judges whereas *Gacaca* judges do not have any formal legal training and therefore they cannot develop jurisprudence in terms of genocide since their understanding of genocide is limited as far as case law is concerned. Furthermore, he argues that *Gacaca* courts provide for community service as a sentence for some accused belonging to the second category whereas the ICTR Statute has no such provision.

Although it is sometimes contested that piracy is not an international crime, we nevertheless think that piracy deserves to be included in the category of international crimes affecting the international community. This crime has persisted in the Indian Ocean and the Coast of Somalia in Africa. In chapter 11, Ambani deals with the prosecution of piracy in Kenya. His chapter studies the international legal framework regulating piracy and Kenya's domestic system, which has been singularly entrusted with the task of prosecuting pirate cases off the coast of Somalia. He concludes that, although Kenya has prosecuted piracy, it has faced several challenges including inadequate international and municipal legislative frameworks, jurisdictional problems and a lack of capacity.

The final part of the book is devoted to the implementation of the Rome Statute of the ICC in African jurisdictions. However, only selected jurisdictions are presented. In chapter 12, Olugbuo presents a contribution on positive complementarity and the fight against impunity in Africa, with particular reference to Uganda and Sudan. The chapter echoes the principle that the Rome Statute operates on complementarity. This principle places the primacy of the investigation and prosecution of international crimes in the domain of national jurisdictions. The Court is meant to complement and not supplant national judicial systems. Olugbuo argues that the effective application of the principle of positive complementarity would ensure the development of synergies of cooperation that would be mutually beneficial to states and the court in the fight against impunity. It is argued that positive complementarity is achievable. The ICC can support national jurisdictions in efforts aimed at judicial reforms that will enable states to build capacities to prosecute international crimes and ensure that the ICC plays its role as a court of last resort. The conclusion reached is that the ICC and African states need to do more to reassure each other that they are willing and able to work together to end impunity in Africa. The ICC cannot go it alone in ensuring that those who are responsible for international crimes are held accountable. Further, it is argued that the principle of complementarity applies even when the case is before the ICC.

Nkhata's contribution (chapter 13) is on the implementation of the Rome Statute in Malawi and Zambia. Bearing in mind that the two states have not yet enacted implementing laws, Nkhata explores the challenges these countries are facing in implementing the Rome Statute. He also provides an indication of the prospects for the domestication of the treaty in the two states. The conclusion reached is that the case for domestication of the Rome Statute is highly compelling and flows, principally, from a state party's ratification of the treaty. He urges that Malawi and Zambia need to take urgent steps to domesticate the Rome Statute.

Stone's contribution (chapter 14) is on the implementation of the Rome Statute in South Africa. She elucidates the role played by South Africa in the drafting and adoption of the Rome Statute and analyses the way the Rome Statute has been domesticated by South Africa. The mechanisms employed by the South African authorities to give effect to the principle of complementarity and to provide the requisite co-operation and assistance to the ICC in pursuit of achieving its objectives are dealt with in-depthly. Stone highlights some of the major weaknesses of the ICC Act and recommends amendments to the Act. She also examines recent developments reflecting on South Africa's adherence to the obligations it has voluntarily assumed under the Rome Statute.

The book is limited in two respects. Firstly, although we have tried to present a wide range of aspects of international criminal justice as they apply in Africa, the book is not exhaustive. Secondly, the issues covered only relate to developments as of December 2010. We hope that further developments in the field will be covered in the next issue of the book. With the above caveats, we hope we have contributed to the understanding of international criminal justice in Africa and that it will serve as an impetus to the realisation of human rights in Africa through the prosecution of persons responsible for international crimes.

We are most grateful to the contributors of the various chapters in this book. The chapters were initially presented at a workshop organised by the Centre for Human Rights on 21 and 22 May 2010. The workshop was made possible through the generous financial support of the Konrad Adenauer Stiftung (KAS) and the Raoul Wallenberg Institute of Human Rights and Humanitarian Law. Particularly, we are grateful for the support we received from Marlize van den Berg and Werner Bohler from KAS.

We wish to thank Christof Heyns, Johan Van der Vyver, Charles Fombad, Frans Viljoen and Michelo Hansungule who stimulated the discussions at the workshop. From these discussions, authors incorporated the comments given by participants in the workshop. Comments that emanated from the workshop discussions were additional to the independent peer-reviewers' reports by internationally-acclaimed experts in the field of international criminal justice. In this regard, we wish to acknowledge the immense support we received from independent peer-reviewers of the chapters. We acknowledge the critical and constructive comments from different experts especially William Schabas, Christo Botha, Philippe Sands, Nsongurua Udombana, Curtis Doebbler, Charles Fombad, Henry Mutai, Cecil Aptel, Ramuold Haule, Jesse James, Robert Turyahebwa, Charles Majinge, Anton du Plessis and Adem Abebe.

The kind assistance of Annelize Nienaber in the editing process is much appreciated. We also gratefully acknowledge the role of Lizette Besaans and Yolanda Booyzen in the production process of the book. We thank Emily Laubscher and Harold Meintjies for their assistance.

PART I: GENERAL ISSUES IN THE PROSECUTION OF INTERNATIONAL CRIMES

CHAPTER 1

DUTY TO PROSECUTE INTERNATIONAL CRIMES UNDER INTERNATIONAL LAW

*Ken Obura**

> No man is an island, entire of itself; every man is a piece of the continent, a part of the main ... Any man's death diminishes me because I am involved in mankind, and therefore never send to know for whom the bell tolls; it tolls for thee.[1]

1 Introduction

Questions related to the international legal obligation to prosecute and punish international crimes have generated rich discussion.[2] While most commentators agree that international crimes should be prosecuted and punished pursuant to international law,[3] the content of the duty to prosecute and punish these crimes under the substantive body of international law remains contentious.[4] Many analysts argue that international law places hardly any restraints on a state's discretion in the punishment of international law crimes.[5] A principal reason for this is that key sources of the duty to prosecute international crimes fail to expressly

* LL.B (Nairobi); LL.M (Pretoria); Doctoral Candidate (Rhodes).

1 J Donne *Devotions upon emergent occasions* XVII (1624) quoted in MC Bassiouni 'Searching for peace and achieving justice: The need for accountability' (1996) 9 *Law & Contemporary Problems* 10.

2 Human rights professionals have figured most prominently in the debate. Other participants include journalists, academics and political leaders.

3 For a discussion see eg DF Orentlicher 'Settling accounts The duty to prosecute human rights violations of a prior regime' (1991) 100 *Yale Law Journal* 2537; M Scharf 'Swapping amnesty for peace' (1996) 31 *Texas International Law Journal* 1; R Boed 'The effect of a domestic amnesty' (2000) 33 *Cornell International Law Journal* 297; C Edelenbos 'Human rights violations: A duty to prosecute?' (1994) 7 *Leiden Journal of International Law* 5; Amnesty International *Universal jurisdiction – The duty of states to enact and implement legislation* (2001).

4 See the various sources in n 3 above.

5 See generally A Henkin 'Conference Report' in *Justice and Society Program of the Aspen Inst, State Crimes: Punishment or Pardon* 92 (1989) (*Aspen Institute Report*).

oblige states to prosecute and punish violations.[6] A further argument is that state practice so far is inconsistent.[7]

This chapter identifies and analyses the applicable international legal standards with regard to the duty to prosecute and punish international crimes in international law, arguing that existing law does in fact impose a legal duty on states to prosecute and punish atrocious crimes.

2 Delineating the concept of international crimes

There is no unanimously agreed upon definition of 'international crimes' in international law.[8] The International Law Commission's Draft articles on State Responsibility, for example, use the term 'international crime' to refer to crimes of a state.[9] The judgment of the International Military Tribunal at Nuremberg, on the other hand, asserts that '... crimes against international law are committed by men, not by abstract entities ...'.[10] Similarly, the corpus of conduct that falls within the category of international crimes is not definitively settled.[11] For example, Ian Brownlie notes a distinction drawn between breaches of international law that may be punished by any state, such as violations of the laws of war;

6 Orentlicher (n 3 above) 2537 (arguing that international human rights undertakings have typically emphasised 'obligation of result' leaving to states the determination of the mean for protecting rights); see also O Schachter 'The obligation to implement the Covenant in domestic law' in L Henkin (ed) *The international bill of rights* (1981) 311; Y Dinstein 'International criminal law' (1985) 20 *Israel Law Review* 206 225.

7 See eg MM Jackson 'The customary international law duty to prosecute crimes against humanity: A new framework' 16 *Tulane Journal of International & Comparative Law* 117 124 (arguing that the pervasive state practice of granting amnesties to perpetrators of international crimes negates the assertion that this duty has evolved into customary international law).

8 Compare PQ Wright 'The law of the Nuremberg trial' (1947) 41 *American Journal of International Law* 38 56 (a crime against international law is 'an act committed with intent to violate a fundamental interest protected by international law or with knowledge that the act will probably violate such an interest, and which may not be adequately punished by the exercise of the normal criminal jurisdiction of any state') with Dinstein (n 6 above) 221 (while international crimes typically are grave offences that 'harm fundamental interests of the whole international community', an offence becomes an international crime only when defined as such by positive international law).

9 Art 19 Draft Articles on State Responsibility UN Doc A/CN 4/SER A/1976/Add 1.

10 *International Military Tribunal* Judgment, reprinted in (1947) 41 *American Journal of International Law* 172 220-221. See also *Tel-Oren v Libyan Arab Republic* 726 F 2d 774, 795 (DC Cir 1984) (noting 'the handful of crimes to which the law of nations attributes individual responsibility').

11 See MJ Kelly 'Cheating justice by cheating death: The doctrinal collision for prosecuting foreign terrorists – passage of *aut deder judicare* into customary law & refusal to extradite based on the death penalty' (2003) 20 *Arizona Journal of International & Comparative Law* 491 497 (pointing out that it has been widely accepted that there is no customary obligation to prosecute and punish perpetrators of all international offences).

and other offences, such as piracy, established by municipal law, which international law authorises states to punish.[12]

This chapter focuses on crimes under international law – that is, conduct that infringes international law and which is punishable as such by the imposition of individual criminal liability – rather than all crimes that have an international aspect. Furthermore, it does not analyse all conduct that may constitute a crime under international law but rather deliberates on those crimes that constitute *jus cogens*[13] violations of international law, especially war crimes, crimes against humanity, genocide, and torture.[14]

12 I Brownlie *Principles of public international law* (1990) 305. See also Amnesty International (n 3 above) 1 (distinguishing crimes under international law (such as war crimes, crimes against humanity, genocide, and torture), crimes under national law of international concern (such as hijacking or damaging aircraft, hostage taking and attacks on diplomats), and ordinary crimes under national laws (such as murder, abduction, assault and rape).

13 *Jus cogens* is formally defined by the Vienna Convention on the Law of Treaties as a body of 'peremptory norm[s] of general international law ... from which no derogation is permitted' (art 53 Vienna Convention on the Law of Treaties, 23 May 1969). *Jus cogens* crimes impose duties on all states notwithstanding their ratification of relevant treaty laws.

14 There is a division of opinion on how a given international crime achieves the status of *jus cogens*. As one author notes, 'there is no scholarly consensus on the methods by which to ascertain the existence of a *jus cogens* norm, nor to assess its significance or determine it content'; see MC Bassiouni 'International crimes: *jus cogens* and *obligatio erga omnes*' (1996) 59 *Law & Contemporary Problems* 67. However, there is some consensus as to specific crimes which are *jus cogens*: aggression, genocide, crimes against humanity, war crimes, piracy, slavery and slave-related practices, and torture. Sufficient legal basis exists to reach the conclusion that all these crimes are part of *jus cogens*. The ICJ, for example, states that '[*jus cogens*] obligations derive, for example, in contemporary international law, from the outlawing of acts of aggression, and of genocide, as also from the principles and rules concerning the basic rights of the human person, including protection from slavery and racial discrimination. Some of the corresponding rights of protection have entered into the body of general international law; others are conferred by international instruments of a universal or quasi-universal character'. See *Barcelona Traction Light and Power Co Ltd (Belgium v Spain)* 1970 ICJ 32. The Nuremberg and Tokyo Charters included the crime of aggression while modern international criminal law – as embodied in the Statutes of the ICTY, ICTR, ICC and other international and internationalised tribunals and developed in their jurisprudence – tends to focus exclusively on the three core categories of crimes: crimes against humanity, genocide and war crimes. Aggression also labelled 'crimes against peace' is included in the Rome Statute of the ICC and the International Law Commission's Draft Code of Crimes Against the Peace and Security of Mankind. See art 16 Draft Code of Crimes Against Peace and Security of Mankind *Report of the International Law Commission on the Work of Its Forty-eighth Session* UN Doc A/51/10 (1996); art 5(2) Rome Statute of the International Criminal Court, 17 July 1998, entered into force 1 July 2002, UN Doc A/CONF 183/9 (providing that the ICC 'shall exercise jurisdiction over the crime of aggression once a provision adopted in accordance with articles 121 and 123 defining the crime and setting out the conditions under which the Court shall exercise jurisdiction with this crime').

3 The obligation to prosecute and punish international crime

Once a crime has been identified as having *jus cogens* status, it inevitably imposes obligations *erga omnes*, or obligations owed to all mankind.[15] These obligations include the duty to prosecute accused perpetrators and to punish those found guilty.[16] These *erga omnes* duties are legally enforceable, at least in theory, are non-derogable and are binding as such on all members of the international community.[17] It is therefore possible to argue that, by stating a duty and allowing no derogation from it, international law may serve as persuasive evidence of the existence of an *erga omnes* duty, although it is not sufficient.[18] The actual law and practice of nations, as well as the decisions by international tribunals, must uphold the duty as 'an obligatory rule of higher standing' before it will be accepted as *erga omnes*.[19] It is to these laws, practices and decisions of courts and tribunals that we now turn.

4 Sources of the obligation to punish or extradite perpetrators of international crimes

4.1 International conventions

The obligation of a state to punish or extradite the perpetrators of international crimes may be provided for by treaties to which the state is a party. In such a case, the failure to prosecute and punish persons

15 See *Presbyterian Church of Sudan v Talisman Energy Inc* 244 F Supp 2d 289, 306 (SDNY 2003) (holding that 'violations of *jus cogens* norms constitute violations of obligations owed to all' ('*erga omnes*')).

16 Bassiouni (n 14 above) 63 (pointing out that other duties include 'the non-applicability of statutes of limitations for such crimes, the non-applicability of any immunities up to and including heads of state, the non-applicability of the defense of "obedience to superior orders" (save as mitigation of sentence), the universal application of these obligations whether in time of peace or war, their non-derogation under "states of emergency", and universal jurisdiction over perpetrators of such crimes').

17 Bassiouni (n 14 above) 65-68 (taking the position that 'the implications of *jus cogens* are those of a duty and not of optional rights ... Consequently, these obligations are non-derogable', but noting that the question of these implications 'has neither been resolved in international law nor addressed by ICL doctrine'.) For a more sceptical view of the legal force of *jus cogens*, see AP Rubin '*Actio popularis, jus cogens*, and offences *erga omnes*?' (2001) 35 *New England Law Review* 265.

18 DS Mitchel 'The prohibition of rape in international humanitarian law as a norm of *jus cogens*: Clarifying the doctrine' (2005) 15 *Duke Journal of Comparative & International Law* 219 233.

19 *Barcelona Traction* case (n 14 above, 32); MC Bassiouni 'A functional approach to general principles of international law' (1990) 11 *Michigan Journal of International Law* 768 801-809.

responsible for committing crimes defined in the treaty would constitute a breach of the state's treaty obligations.[20]

There are several treaties that provide for the duty to prosecute and punish international crimes. The obligation in some of these treaties has distilled into custom over time due to widespread and representative participation.[21] A number of these treaties are discussed below.

4.1.1 1949 Geneva Conventions and 1977 Additional Protocols

Under the 1949 Geneva Conventions and the 1977 Additional Protocols, member states[22] are obliged to put to an end to all 'grave breaches' set out therein.[23] These 'grave breaches' (which are war crimes under international law) are listed under the Geneva Conventions and Additional Protocol I as willful killing; torture or inhuman treatment, including biological experiments; willfully causing great suffering or serious injury to body or health; extensive destruction of property not justified by military necessity; willfully depriving a civilian of the rights of a fair and regular trial; and the unlawful confinement of a civilian.[24]

The Conventions and Additional Protocols place particular obligations on state parties to search for, prosecute, and punish

20 As art 27 of the Vienna Convention on the Law of Treaties provides '[a] party may not invoke the provisions of its internal law as justification for failure to perform a treaty' Vienna Convention on the Law of Treaties, 23 May 1969, UN Doc A/CONF39/27. See also L Oppenheim 'International law' in H Lauterpacht (1995) 45 ('If a state ... possess[es] such rules of municipal law as it is prohibited from having by the Law of Nations, it violates an international legal duty'). See also the *Greco-Bulgarian Communities* case 1930 PCIJ (Ser B) 17 23; and the *Polish Nationals in Danzig* case 1931 PCIJ (Ser A/B) 44 24.

21 Indeed, it has been recognised by the ICJ that this process constitutes 'one of the recognized methods by which new rules of customary international law may be formed' *North Sea Continental Shelf* cases 1969 ICJ 41; N Roht-Arriaza 'Sources in international treaties of an obligation to investigate, prosecute, and provide redress' in N Roht-Arriaza (ed) *Impunity and human rights in international law and practice* (1995) 41.

22 As of 2010, 194 states are party to the Geneva Conventions, 170 states to Optional Protocol 1, and 165 states to Optional Protocol II. See ICRC website http://www.icrc.org/Web/Eng/siteeng0.nsf/html/party_main_treaties (accessed 1 January 2010).

23 See V Morris & MP Scharf *An insider guide to the International Criminal Tribunal for former Yugoslavia* (1995) 64-65.

24 See art 50 Geneva Convention for the Amelioration of the Condition of the Wounded and Sick in Armed Forces in the Field, 12 August 1949, (Geneva Convention I); art 51 Geneva Convention for the Amelioration of the Condition of the Wounded, Sick, and Shipwrecked Members of the Armed Forces at Sea, 12 August 1949, (Geneva Convention II); art 130 Geneva Convention Relative to the Treatment of Prisoners of War, 12 August 1949 (Geneva Convention III); and art 147 Geneva Convention Relative to the Protection of Civilian Persons in Time of War, 12 August 1949 (Geneva Convention IV); art 4 Protocol 1 Additional to the Geneva Conventions of Aug. 12, 1949 and Relating to the Protection of Victims of International Armed Conflicts, opened for signature 12 December 1977 (Protocol I). See especially arts 11, 85, 86 Protocol II Additional to the Geneva Conventions of Aug 12, 1949, and Relating to the Protection of Victims of Non-International Armed Conflicts, opened for signature 12 December 1977 (Protocol II).

perpetrators of these 'grave breaches' unless they opt to hand over such persons for prosecution by another state party.[25] The Commentary to the Conventions, which is the official account of the negotiations preceding their adoption,[26] holds that the duty to prosecute and punish is 'absolute' - implying that state parties would be in breach of the treaty obligation if they fail or refuse to prosecute these grave breaches.[27] However, the duty to prosecute is limited to the context of international armed conflict.[28]

The international conflict requirement is derived from article 2 of the four Conventions. Article 2 describes such conflicts as cases of a declared state of war or any other armed conflict that may arise between two or more of the contracting powers, even if a state of war is not acknowledged by one of them; and cases of partial or total occupation of the territory of the contracting party, even if such occupation meets no armed resistance.[29] There is a high threshold of violence required to constitute a genuine armed conflict, as distinct from lower-level disturbances such as riots or isolated and sporadic acts of fighting.[30]

4.1.2 Convention on the Crime of Genocide

The Convention on the Crime of Genocide (Genocide Convention) entered into force on 12 January 1952 and was intended to prevent genocide by ensuring its punishment.[31] Article II of the Genocide Convention defines genocide as any of the following acts if committed 'with intent to destroy, in whole or in part, a national, ethnical, or religious group, as such':

25 Art 51 Geneva Convention I; art 52 Geneva Convention II; art 131 Geneva Convention III; art 148 Geneva Convention IV.

26 According to art 32 of the Vienna Convention on the Law of Treaties, '[r]ecourse may be had to supplementary means of interpretation, including the preparatory work of the treaty and the circumstances of its conclusion, in order to ... determine the meaning' when the text of a treaty provision 'leaves the meaning ambiguous or obscure' UN Doc A/Conf 39/27 (23 May 1969).

27 See Morris & Scharf (n 23 above) 114; see also T Meron *Human rights and humanitarian norms as customary law* (1989) 215 (finding the Geneva Conventions are not subject to derogation).

28 See *Prosecutor v Tadic* (Case IT-94-1-T) Decision on jurisdiction para 68; M Scharf (n 3 above) 54, 64-65, 114 n 356; but see JJ Paust 'Applicability of international criminal laws to events in the former Yugoslavia' (1994) 9 *American Journal of International Law & Policy* 499 511-512; ICRC *Customary International Humanitarian Law* (2005) 603.

29 See art 2 Geneva Conventions I, II, III; n 24 above.

30 Meron (n 27 above) 46. For a discussion of the historical development of the notions of 'war' and 'armed conflict' see W Meng 'War' in (1982) 4 *Encyclopedia of Public International Law* 282; KJ Partsch 'Armed conflict' in (1992) 1 *Encyclopedia of Public International Law* 249.

31 See UNGAOR 178th, 179th, Plen Mtg 825 (remarks of Soviet delegate); 819 (remarks of delegate from Pakistan); 820 (remarks from US delegate); 823 (remark from Australian delegate); 840 (remarks of Polish delegate) (indicating that the prevailing purpose was to prevent genocide by guaranteeing punishment of offenders.

(a) Killing members of the group;

(b) Causing serious bodily or mental harm to members of the group;

(c) Deliberately inflicting on the group conditions of life calculated to bring about its physical destruction in whole or in part;

(d) Imposing measures intended to prevent births within the group; or

(e) Forcibly transferring children of the group to another group.[32]

Pursuant to article I, contracting parties 'confirm that genocide ... is a crime under international law which they undertake to prevent and to punish'.[33] Article IV provides for an absolute obligation to prosecute persons responsible for genocide as defined in the Convention.[34]

The International Court of Justice (ICJ) has held in an advisory opinion that the principles underlying the Genocide Convention 'are recognised by civilized nations as binding on States, even without any conventional obligation'.[35] Though the ICJ did not indicate which provisions reflect customary law, most commentators hold that those requiring the prosecution and punishment of offenders are included.[36] The upshot of this view is that all states, whether a contracting party to the Genocide Convention or not, have a duty to prosecute and punish perpetrators of genocide.[37]

However, the Genocide Convention applies only to people with specific intent to destroy in whole or in part the population of a target group;[38] and when the victims constitute one of the groups enumerated

32 Convention on the Crime of Genocide, 9 December 1948.

33 Art I Genocide Convention.

34 Art IV states 'Persons committing genocide or any of the other acts enumerated in article 3 shall be punished, whether they are constitutionally responsible rulers, public officials or private individuals'. Art V requires states to 'provide effective penalties' for persons guilty of genocide. The *travaux preparatoires* indicate that while delegates to the drafting committee doubted states willingness to prosecute acts of genocide committed in their territory, there was no question of contracting parties' duty to do so. A proposal to include a provision contemplating reparations for genocide was defeated because some delegates feared that the draft provision would dilute the Convention's emphasis on criminal punishment. For a discussion see L Kuper *Genocide: Its political use in the twentieth century* (1982) 38.

35 *Reservation to the Convention on the Prevention and Punishment of the Crime of Genocide*, 1951.

36 The ICJ observed that 'it was the intention of the United Nations to condemn and punish genocide as a 'a crime under international law ...' *Reservation to the Convention on the Prevention and Punishment of the Crime of Genocide* (n 35 above); see also Restatement (Third) of the Foreign Relations Law of the United Nations & 702 (1987) (stating that a 'state violates customary law if it practices or encourages genocide, fails to make genocide a crime or to punish persons guilty of it, or otherwise condones genocide').

37 See Restatement (Third) (n 36 above).

38 See JS Abrams & SR Ratner *Striving for justice: Accountability and the crimes of the Khmer Rouge* (1995) 39 (conclude that 'most commentators assert that the number of individuals intended to be destroyed must be substantial, in light of the Convention's emphasis on acts against large numbers, rather than individuals).

namely, national, ethnic, racial, or religious.[39]

4.1.3 Convention Against Torture and Other Cruel, Inhuman or Degrading Treatment or Punishment

The Convention Against Torture and Other Cruel, Inhuman, or Degrading Treatment or Punishment (Torture Convention)[40] imposes an unequivocal duty on state parties to prosecute acts it defines as criminal.[41] It requires each state party to ensure that all acts of torture are criminalised under its municipal laws,[42] and to establish its jurisdiction over such offences in cases where, *inter alia*, the alleged offender is its national.[43] Article 7 requires state parties either to prosecute or extradite alleged offenders.[44] Because of this latter requirement several commentators have argued that the Torture Convention 'does not explicitly require that a prosecution takes place, let alone that punishment be imposed and served'.[45] On the contrary, this formulation was designed to ensure that 'no offender would have the opportunity to escape the consequences of his acts of torture'.[46]

39 The part interestingly does not include political groups. This was due mainly to the fact that the Convention was negotiated during the Cold War, when the Soviet Union and other totalitarian governments feared that they would face interference in their internal affairs if genocide were defined to include acts committed to destroy political groups. According to Kuper, 'one may fairly say that the delegates, after all, represented governments in power, and that many of these governments wished to retain an unrestricted freedom to suppress political opposition' Kuper (n 34 above) 30.

40 Convention Against Torture and Other Cruel, Inhuman or Degrading Treatment or Punishment, UN Doc A/39/51, entered into force 26 June 1987, article 4.

41 Similarly, articles 6 and 12 of the Inter-American Convention to Prevent and Punish Torture (OEA/ser A /42 (1986), entered into force 1987) require state parties to criminalise torture and to punish violations.

42 Art 1 defines 'torture' as 'any act by which severe pain or suffering, whether physical or mental, is intentionally inflicted on a person for such purposes as obtaining from him or a third person information or a confession, punishing him for an act he or a third person has committed or is suspected of having committed, or intimidating or coercing him or a third person, or for any reason based on discrimination of any kind, when such pain or suffering is inflicted by or at the instigation of or with the consent or acquiescence of a public official or other person acting in an official capacity. It does not include pain or suffering arising only from, inherent in or incidental to lawful sanctions'.

43 Art 5 Torture Convention. Art 4 requires parties to criminalise acts which 'constitute complicity or participation in torture'.

44 In the view of the drafters of the Torture Convention, 'in applying article 4 (which requires states to make torture 'punishable by appropriate penalties which take into account their grave nature,') it seems reasonable to require that the punishment for torture should be close to the penalties applied to the most serious offences under the domestic legal system'. See JH Burgers & H Danelius *The United Nations Convention against Torture: A handbook on the Convention against Torture and other Cruel, Inhuman or Degrading Treatment or Punishment* (1988) 129.

45 See Orentlicher (n 3 above) 2604.

46 Report of the Working Group on a Draft Convention Against Torture and Other Cruel, Inhuman or Degrading Treatment or Punishment, 36 UN ESCOR Comm'n on Hum Rts 11 para 61, UN Doc E/CN 4/1367 (1980). In contrast to the analogous provision in the Genocide Convention, the duty established by art 7 was understood to be a practical and effective means of suppressing torture. This much is evident both from

Article 5(2) of the Convention provides for a form of universal jurisdiction to ensure punishment in the event a state party fails to prosecute torture.[47] This provision was intended to address situations where a complicit government is unwilling to prosecute its officials[48] and to ensure that '[n]o one guilty of torture [would] feel safe from prosecution.'[49] However, as has been held by the Committee established to monitor compliance with the Torture Convention,[50] the duty to prosecute or extradite arises only when the alleged torture occurs after the Convention had entered into force with respect to the state party.[51]

4.1.4 Rome Statute of the International Criminal Court

An obligation on the part of states to investigate and prosecute 'core international crimes'[52] arguably also emanates from the Rome Statute of

statements of the drafting committee (See Summary Prepared by the Secretary-General in accordance with Commission Resolution 18 (XXXIV) 35 UN ESCOR Comm'n on Hum Rts 16, UN Doc E/CN 4/1314 (1978)) and from the text of the Convention which establishes an array of domestic measures designed to assure freedom from torture (see arts 14 and 10 of the Convention Against Torture). See also M Scharf 'The letter of the law: The scope of the international legal obligation to prosecute human rights crimes' (1996) 59 *Law & Contemp Problems* 41 46 (pointing out that this formulation was shaped by the developments in international standards of due process that had occurred in the nearly 40 years since the Genocide Convention). Because of the development alluded to by Scharf, subsequent international conventions have reproduced verbatim the formulation 'prosecute or extradite.' See, eg, Convention for the Suppression of Unlawful Seizure of Aircraft, entered into force 14 October 1971; Convention for the Suppression of Unlawful Acts Against the Safety of Civil Aviation, entered into force 26 January 1973); Convention on the Prevention and Punishment of Crimes Against Internationally Protected Persons, including Diplomatic Agents, entered into force 20 Febuary 1977); International Convention Against the Taking of Hostages, GA Res 34/146, UN Doc A/34/146, entered into force 4 June 1983); Convention for the Suppression of Unlawful Acts Against the Safety of Maritime Navigation, Rome, 10 March 1988; and the Protocol for the Suppression of Unlawful Acts Against the Safety of Fixed Platforms Located on the Continental Shelf, Rome, 10 March 1988.

47 Art 5(2) Torture Convention.

48 See Report of the Working Group on the Draft Convention Against Torture, 38 UN ESCOR Comm'n on Hum Rts 7 para 40, UN Doc E/CN 4/1982/L 40.

49 Summary Records of the 32nd Meeting, 40 UN ESCOR Comm'n on Hum Rts (32d mtg) 16, para 85, UN Doc E/CN 4/1984/SR 32 (delegate from Germany). Even though some delegates were initially hesitant to accept a provision establishing universal jurisdiction, no state fought its insertion into the draft convention. See Question of the Human Rights of All Persons Subjected to any Form of Detention or Imprisonment, Torture and Other Cruel, Inhuman or Degrading Treatment or Punishment, 40 UN ESCOR Comm'n on Hum Rts (32d mtg) 5 para 26, UN Doc E/CN 4/1984/72.

50 Art 17 Torture Convention.

51 Decision on Admissibility, dated 23 November 1989, Regarding Communications 1/1988, 2/1988 and 3/1988 (*OR,, MM and MS v Argentina*), Report of the Committee Against Torture, UN GAOR, 45th Sess, Supp 44, annex VI, UN Doc A/45/44 (1990). However, the Committee stated that even 'Even before the entry into force of the Convention against Torture, there existed a general rule of international law which should oblige all states to take effective measures to prevent torture and to punish acts of torture' (above, 111).

52 Art 5 Rome Statute defines these crimes as crimes against humanity, genocide, war crimes, and aggression.

the International Criminal Court (ICC),[53] as state parties risk an intervention by the ICC if there is no investigation or prosecution.[54] The ratification of the Rome Statute by more than 110 states[55] constitutes significant evidence of an acknowledgement of the duty to prosecute and punish these crimes.[56] Furthermore, the Rome Statute makes no provision for amnesty.[57] The Statute defines crimes against humanity for the first time and provides for their prosecution and punishment.[58]

4.1.5 Human rights conventions

At first glance international human rights conventions such as the International Covenant on Civil and Political Rights (ICCPR),[59] the European Convention for the Protection of Human Rights and Fundamental Freedoms (European Convention),[60] the American Convention on Human Rights (Inter-American Convention),[61] and the African Charter on Human and Peoples' Rights (African Charter),[62] appear silent about a duty to prosecute and punish violations of the rights they are to protect.[63] Nevertheless, some commentators argue that the

53 For a discussion of the Rome Statute and the duty to prosecute and punish, see eg, MP Scharf 'The amnesty exception to the jurisdiction of the International Criminal Court' (1999) 32 *Cornell International Law Journal* 507; J Gavron 'Amnesties in light of developments in international law and the establishment of the International Criminal Court' (2002) 51 *International & Comparative Law Quarterly* 91; D Robinson 'Serving the interest of justice: Amnesties, truth commissions and the International Criminal Court' (2003) 14 *European Journal of International Law* 481; T Clark 'The prosecutor of the International Criminal Court, amnesties, and the "interests of justice": Striking a delicate balance' (2005) 4 *Washington University Global Studies Law Review* 389.

54 In its Preamble, the Rome Statute insists that 'it is the duty of every state to exercise its criminal jurisdiction over those responsible for international crimes'. The statute also adopts the principle of 'complementarity' which gives national courts and the ICC jurisdiction of over war crimes, crimes against humanity, and genocide (art 17(1)(a)).

55 As of March 2010, 111 states had ratified the Rome Statute.

56 The Rome Statute requires states to either prosecute and punish the enshrined crimes domestically or submit the suspects to ICC prosecution (art 17(1)(a)–(b) Rome Statute).

57 In the *travaux preparatoires*, amnesty and pardon were both considered and rejected in the context of the defence of *neb is in idem*. See Report of the Preparatory Committee on the Establishment of an International Criminal Court 40 (para 174) (Proceedings of the Preparatory Committee during March-April and August 1996) GAOR, 51st Session, Supplement 22 (UN Doc A/51/22); UN Doc A/CONF/283/2/Add 1 (1998) art 19. See also R Wedgwood 'The International Criminal Court: An American view' (1999) 10 *European Journal of International Law* 108 109-113 (reporting that in August 1997 the United States circulated a 'non-paper' to the Preparatory Committee suggesting that a responsible decision by a democratic regime to allow an amnesty should be taken into account in judging the admissibility of a case).

58 Art 7.

59 Adopted 19 December 1966 and entered into force 23 March 1976.

60 Signed 4 November 1950 and entered into force 3 September 1953).

61 Adopted 7 January 1970, OAS Official Records, OEA/Ser K/XVI/1.1, doc 65 rev 1, corr 1 (1970).

62 Adopted 26 June 1981, OAU Doc CAB/LEG/67/3 Rev 5 (entered into force 21 October 1986), art 22.

63 Human rights instruments usually impose a general duty to respect, protect, promote, and fulfil the rights enshrined therein; see H Shue *Basic rights: Substance, affluence and US foreign policy* (1980).

duty to protect rights implies a duty to prosecute violators.[64] Authoritative interpretations of these treaties also hold that a state party fails in its duty to respect, protect, promote, and fulfil the rights enshrined therein if it does not investigate, prosecute and punish those who are responsible for serious violations of physical integrity rights – such as torture, extrajudicial executions and forced disappearances.[65]

The Human Rights Committee, established to monitor compliance with the ICCPR,[66] has held that state parties must investigate, prosecute and punish those responsible for summary executions,[67] torture[68] and unresolved disappearances.[69] The Committee has further held that

64 See N Roht-Arriaza 'State responsibility to investigate and prosecute grave human rights violations in international law' (1998) 78 *California Law Review* 451 467; Orentlicher (n 3 above) 2568; T Buergenthal 'To respect and to ensure: State obligations and permissible derogations' in Henkin (n 6 above) 77 (noting that the 'obligation to ensure rights creates affirmative obligations on the state- for example-to discipline its officials'); Y Dinstein 'The right to life, physical integrity, and liberty' in Henkin (n 6 above) 119 (noting that parties to the Covenant arguably must exercise due diligence to prevent intentional deprivation of life by individuals, 'as well as to apprehend murderers and to prosecute them in order to deter future takings of life').

65 Cf Scharf (n 46 above) 41 (arguing that during the negotiation of the Covenant, the delegates specifically considered and rejected a proposal that would have required states to prosecute violators).

66 The Committee is empowered to 'receive and consider' communications from individuals who are subject to the jurisdiction of states that have ratified an Optional Protocol and who claim to have suffered a violation of any of the rights protected by ICCPR. See art 1 Optional Protocol to the International Covenant on Civil and Political Rights, GA Res 2200A, UN Doc A/6316 (1966).

67 *Baoboeram v Surinam* Comm 146/1983 and 148-154/1983 para 13.2, UN Doc A/40/40 (1985). In General Comment on art 6 of ICCPR providing for right to life, the Committee alluded to a duty to punish when it said 'The Committee considers that States Parties should take measures not only to prevent and punish deprivation of life by criminal acts, but also to prevent arbitrary killing by their own security forces' Report of the Human Rights Committee para 3, UN Doc E/CN 4/Sub 2/Add 1/963 (1982). Similarly, in *Dermit v Uruguay* the Committee expressed the view that 'the State Party is under an obligation to take effective steps ... to establish the facts of Hugo Dermit's death, to bring to justice any person found to be responsible for his death and to pay appropriate compensation to his family' Comm 84/1981 para 11, UN Doc A/ 38/40 (1983).

68 *Muteba v Zaire* Comm 124/1982, UN Doc A/39/40 (1984). In General Comments interpreting art 7 of ICCPR which prohibits torture and cruel, inhuman or degrading treatment or punishment, the Committee asserted that '... Complaints about ill-treatment must be investigated effectively by competent authorities. Those found guilty must be held responsible, and the alleged victims must themselves have effective remedies at their disposal, including the right to obtain compensation'; see Report of the Human Rights Committee, General Comment 7(16) para 1, UN Doc E/CN 4/Sub 2/Add 1/963 (1982). Whether the requirement that offenders 'be held responsible' connotes a criminal penalty is unclear, but the UN Declaration on the Protection of All Persons from being Subjected to Torture and Other Cruel, Inhuman or Degrading Treatment or Punishment suggests that criminal punishment would be appropriate with respect to torture, while other disciplinary action might be appropriate for less serious forms of ill treatment (GA Res 3452, UN Doc A/10034 (1975) art 10).

69 In General Comments on art 6, the Committee observed that '... States should establish effective facilities and procedures to investigate thoroughly cases of missing and disappeared persons in circumstances which may involve a violation of the right to life'; see Report of the Human Rights Committee para 3, UN Doc E/CN 4/Sub 2/Add 1/963 (1982). Although not proscribed as such by the ICCPR, the Committee has

amnesties for serious violations of human rights are incompatible with duties of states under the ICCPR.[70] Such constructions by the Committee have been described as 'authoritative'[71] on the basis that parties to the Covenant, having agreed to be bound by the treaty obligations contained therein, are bound to accept, the interpretations rendered by the Committee.[72]

The Inter-American Convention, like the ICCPR, has been interpreted by the Inter-American Court of Human Rights[73] and the Inter-American Commission of Human Rights[74] to require state parties to investigate and punish serious violations of physical integrity rights – such as torture, extrajudicial executions and forced disappearances.[75] In the *Velasquez Rodriquez* case which concerns the unresolved disappearance of Manfredo Valasquez in September 1981, the Court interpreted article 1(1) of the Inter-American Convention to impose on state parties a legal duty to '... use the means at its disposal to carry out a serious investigation of violations committed within its jurisdiction, to identify those responsible, to impose the appropriate punishment and to ensure the victim adequate

interpreted the ICCPR to impose a duty to 'investigate, punish and compensate' when disappearance occur. In a case involving disappearances (forced abductions by state agents followed by denials of knowledge of the victims whereabouts) in Uruguay, the Committee concluded that the government of Uruguay should take effective steps to bring to justice any persons found responsible. *Quinteros v Uruguay* Comm 107/1981, UN Doc A/38/40 (1983); See also *Bleir v Uruguay* Comm 107/1981, UN Doc A/38/40 (1983).

70 In 1992 the Committee issued a General Comment asserting that amnesties covering acts of torture 'are generally incompatible with the duty of States to investigate such acts; to guarantee freedom from such acts within their jurisdiction; and to ensure that they do not occur in the future' General Comment 20 (44) (art 7), UN Doc CCPR/C21/Rev 1/Add 3, para 15 (April 1992).

71 Orentlicher (n 3 above) 2568; Roht-Arriaza (n 21 above) 28-30.

72 Cf B Simma *International human rights and general international law: A comparative analysis* (1995) 223.

73 Arts 62 and 64 respectively empower the Court to consider 'contentious cases' alleging a violation of the Convention and to render advisory opinions interpreting the Convention (as well as other treaties concerning the protection of human rights in the Americas). On the Court see generally, T Buergenthal 'The Inter-American Court of Human Rights' (1982) 76 *American Journal of International Law* 231.

74 The Commission was created to promote observance of human rights among the member states of the Organisation of America states (OAS); arts 4 – 6 Declaration at the Fifth Meeting of Consultation of Ministers of Foreign Affairs, Santiago, Chile, 12-18 August 1959, Final Act, OAS Official Records, OEA/ser C/II.5, (1959). The Commission also has powers to examine individual and inter-state communications alleging human rights violations. See Resolution XXII 'Expanded Functions of the Inter-American Commission on Human Rights' Final Act of the Second Special Inter-American Conference, OAS/serE/XIII 1, 45-46 (1965). For a general discussion on the Commission see JE Mendez & JM Vivanco 'Disappearances and the Inter-American Court: Reflection on a litigation experience' (1990) 13 *Hamline Law Review* 507 519-27.

75 See Orentlicher (n 3 above) 2537 (pointing out that the *travaux preparatoires* of the American Convention contain little indication that punishment was contemplated as a necessary means of enforcing the American convention).

compensation'.[76] Similarly, the Commission has held that state parties to the Inter-American Convention must investigate and 'try to punish those responsible' for the occurrence of serious violations of physical integrity rights.[77] The Court and the Commission have in addition held that amnesties are incompatible with the American Convention on Human Rights.[78]

The European Court of Human Rights and the European Commission of Human Rights have made it clear that state parties have a duty to prosecute and punish serious violations of certain rights under the European Convention.[79] In *X and Y v Netherlands*[80]the Court found the Netherlands in violation of the European Convention for failing to provide for the prosecution of Miss Y's rape assailant.[81] Likewise, in their decisions on the admissibility requirement of exhaustions of local remedies, the Court and the Commission both have held, albeit indirectly, that punishment plays a necessary part in the contracting state's duty to secure certain rights in the European Convention.[82] In *Tas v Turkey*,[83] on dealing with the disappearance of Muhsin Tas, a Turkish national, after being taken into custody by Turkish security forces, the European Court discussed that state's remedial obligations. Article 13 – the right to an effective remedy – was found by the Court to require: '[I]n addition to the

76 *Velasquez Rodriquez* case, Inter-Am CHR (Ser C) 4 para 174 (1998) (judgment). See also *Gary Hermosilla et al* case 10.843, Inter-Am CHR (1988) para 77, holding that the state 'has the obligation to investigate all violations that have been committed within its jurisdiction for the purpose of identifying the persons responsible, imposing appropriate punishment on them, and ensuring adequate reparations for the victims'. But see Orentlicher (n 69 above) 2578 (pointing out that although the judgment suggested that a duty to punish applies to 'every' violation of the American Convention, it is unlikely that the Court intended the obligation to extend to all violations regardless of the severity of the breach).

77 See Case 10.150, Informe 3/90 (Suriname), OEA/Ser L/V/II 77, doc 23, 14 (1990).

78 Inter-American Commission on Human Rights, Report 29/92 (Uruguay) 82nd Session OEA/LV/II.82 Doc25 (2 Oct 1992); Inter-American Commission on Human Rights, Report 29/92 (Argentina) 82nd Session OEA/LV/II.82 Doc24 (2 Oct 1992).

79 The European Commission has a mandate to receive and consider both individual and inter-state complaints alleging violation of the European Convention. See arts 24 and 25 European Convention. For a discussion on the European human rights system, see generally R Higgins 'The European Convention on Human Rights' in Meron (n 27 above) 505 - 511.

80 91 Eur Ct H R (ser A) (1985) (judgment).

81 The relevant provision of the Netherlands Criminal Code could only be invoked by a victim who was mentally sound. In this case the victim, Miss Y, was mentally handicapped and could therefore not initiate a criminal complaint. The court found this gap in breach of Netherlands duty to ensure the right for private life (n 80 above) paras 9 - 10.

82 See, eg, *Ireland v United Kingdom* 25 Eur Ct H R (ser A) 64 para 159 (1978) (holding that applicants need not exhaust local remedies if their complaint arises out of 'an administrative practice' characterised by 'repetition of acts, and official tolerance'). See also the Commission's report in the case of *France, Norway, Denmark, Sweden and The Netherlands v Turkey* 8 *Eur Hum Rts Rep* 205, 213 (1985) where the Commission seemingly assumed that criminal prosecution plays a necessary part in State Parties fulfillment of the Covenant duties when it noted that measures taken by Turkey to respond to allegation of torture included 'criminal prosecution and convictions concerning cases of torture'.

83 33 *Eur Hum Rts Rep* 15 PPHI-H3 (2000).

payment of compensation where appropriate, a thorough and effective investigation capable of leading to the identification and punishment of those responsible and including effective access for the relatives to the investigatory procedure'.[84]

In interpreting the African Charter, the African Commission on Human and Peoples' Rights (African Commission) has held that state parties have a duty to prosecute and punish serious violations of certain rights under the African Charter.[85] These serious violations attracting the duty to prosecute and punish include extrajudicial executions,[86] torture,[87] slavery,[88] and disappearances.[89] The Commission has also held that amnesties covering serious violations of human rights are incompatible with the duty of states to prosecute and punish these violations under the African Charter.[90]

4.2 Customary international law

Customary international law, which, unlike convention law, is binding on all states and cannot be derogated from,[91] arises from 'a general and consistent practice of states followed by them from a sense of legal obligation'.[92] Customary international law is composed of (1) *opinio juris*, that is, what states say they think is the law; and (2) state practice.[93]

84 Above, 91.

85 The African Commission is an eleven-member independent Commission, whose mandate includes a communication procedure, which examines complaints from states, individuals, NGOs, and others (see arts 47-59 African Charter).

86 See *Amnesty International and Others v Sudan* (2000) AHRLR 296 (ACHPR) para 56; see also *Commission Nationale des Droits de l'Homme et des Libertes v Chad* (2000) AHRLR 66 (ACHPR) para 22.

87 *Amnesty International and Others v Sudan* para 52.

88 *Malawi African Association and Others v Mauritania* (2000) AHRLR 149 (ACHPR 2000) para 134.

89 *Commission Nationale des Droits de l'Homme et des Libertes v Chad* (2000) AHRLR 66 (ACHPR); *Malawi African Association and Others v Mauritania* (2000) AHRLR 149 (ACHPR 2000).

90 See *Malawi African association and Others v Mauritania* (2000) AHRLR 149 (ACHPR 2000) paras 82 & 83 (the Commission held that amnesty laws having 'the effect of leading to the foreclosure of any judicial actions that may be brought before local jurisdictions' is in breach of State Parties duty to ensure rights under the African Charter').

91 In *Right of Passage Over Indian Territory (Portugal v India)* 1960 ICJ 123, 135 (12 April) Fernandes J stated: 'It is true that in principle special rules will prevail of general rules, but to take it as established that in the present case the particular rule is different from the general rule is to beg the question. Moreover, there are exceptions to this principle. Several rules *cogestes* prevail over any special rules. And the general principles to which I shall refer later constitute true rule of jus cogens over which no special practice can prevail.' See also *Legal Consequences for States of the Continued Presence of South Africa in Namibia (South West Africa) notwithstanding Security Council Resolution* 276, 1971 ICJ 66 (21 June).

92 Restatement (Third). See also art 38(1)(b) Statute of the International Court of Justice (sources of international law applied by Court include 'international custom, as evidence of a general practice accepted as law').

93 See generally L Mallinder *Amnesty, human rights and political transitions* (2008).

The establishment and operations since the beginning of the 90s of several international and hybrid criminal tribunals, such as the International Criminal Tribunals for the former Yugoslavia[94] and Rwanda,[95] the Special Court for Sierra Leone,[96] hybrid tribunals in Kosovo[97] and East Timor,[98] Lebanon,[99] Bosnia and Herzegovina,[100] and the Extraordinary Chambers of the Criminal Court in Cambodia,[101] are cited as evidence of an international resolve to ensure that those most responsible for core international crimes do not escape punishment.[102] The ICC Statute is often construed as imposing (or at least assuming) an obligation on the part of the states that negotiated it to investigate and prosecute core international crimes.[103]

Various international documents refer to a duty to prosecute and punish serious crimes, including war crimes, crimes against humanity and genocide.[104] While not conclusive, the frequent reiteration of a duty to

94 Statute of the International Criminal Tribunal for the Former Yugoslavia, SC Res 827, UN SCOR 48th Sess, 3217th mtg, UN Doc S/RES/827 (25 May 1993).

95 Statute of International Criminal Tribunal for Rwanda, SC Res 955, UN SCOR, 49th Sess, 3453d mtg, UN Doc S/RES/955 (8 November 1994).

96 Agreement Between the United Nations and the Government of Sierra Leone on the Establishment of a Special Court for Sierra Leone, 16 January 2002. The Special Court was endorsed by the UN Security Council in SC Res 1400, UN Doc S/RES/1400 (28 March 2002).

97 SC Res 1244, UN Doc S/RES/1244 (10 June 1999); see also UN Transitional Administration Mission in Kosovo, on the Authority of the Interim Administration in Kosovo, UN Doc UNMIK/REG/1999/1 (25 July 1999).

98 SC Res 1272, UN Doc S/RES/1272 (25 October 1999); See also UN Transitional Administration Mission in East Timor, on the Organization of Courts in East Timor, UN Doc UNTAET/REG/REG/2000/11 (6 March 2000).

99 SC Res 1757, UN Doc S/RES/1757 (30 May 2007); see also the Secretary-General, Report of the Secretary-General on the Establishment of a Special Tribunal for Lebanon, delivered to the Security Council, UN Doc S/2006/893 (15 November 2006).

100 The War Crimes Chambers was created in 2003 at the Peace Implementation Council Steering Board Meeting and underwent extensive negotiations until its adoption on 6 January 2005. See PP Singh *Human Rights Watch, narrowing the impunity gap: Trials before Bosnia's War Crimes Chamber* (2007).

101 Law on the Establishment of the Extraordinary Chambers in the Courts of Cambodia for the Prosecution of Crimes Committed During the Period of Democratic Kampuchea, Royal Decree NS/RKM/1004/006 (2004) (Cambodia).

102 For a discussion see MC Bassiouni 'From Versailles to Rwanda in seventy-five years: The need to establish a permanent international criminal court' (1997) 10 *Harvard Human Rights Journal* 11 13.

103 Wedgwood (n 57 above) 108.

104 The Declaration on the Protection of All Persons from Enforced Disappearances states that those who have or are alleged to have committed acts of enforced disappearance shall not benefit from any special amnesty law or similar measures that effectively might exempt them from any criminal proceedings or sanction. It also makes clear that in the exercise of the right of pardon, the extreme seriousness of acts of enforced disappearance shall be taken into account. GA Res 47/133 UN Doc A/47/49 (1992) adopted by General Assembly Resolution 47/133 of 18 December 1992; Principle 18 Basic Principles and Guidelines on the Right to a Remedy and Reparation for Victims of Gross Violations of International Human Rights Law and Serious Violations of International Humanitarian Law, adopted by the General Assembly in 2005 (Res 60/147) (which emphasised that true reconciliation requires accountability and measures of transnational justice, including investigation and prosecution, truth seeking, reparations and institutional reform); Updated Set of Principles for the Protection and

punish international crimes in international instruments is evidence that the duty already exists or is emerging as a customary norm.[105]

Additionally, a number of activities of the United Nations and other intergovernmental organisations reinforce the view that the prosecution and punishment of war crimes, torture, disappearances, extrajudicial executions, crimes against humanity, slavery, piracy and genocide are duties of states under customary law.[106] For example, reports prepared by special rapporteurs, special representatives and working groups appointed by the Commission on Human Rights of the United Nations (UN) to report on human rights conditions in particular countries[107] or on particular types of human rights violations,[108] have repeatedly condemned

Promotion of Human Rights Through Action to Combat Impunity (2005), Security Council Res 1674 (2006) (emphasised 'the responsibility of states to comply with their relevant obligations to end impunity and to prosecute those responsible for war crimes, genocide, crimes against humanity and serious violations of international humanitarian law…' UN Secretary-General's Report on the Rule of Law and Transnational Justice in Conflict and Post-Conflict Situations, s/2004/616. In 1971 the United Nations General Assembly adopted the Resolution on War Criminals affirming that a State's refusal 'to cooperate in the arrest, extradition, trial and punishment' of persons accused or convicted of war crimes and crimes against humanity is 'contrary to the United Nation's Charter and to generally recognized norms of international law.' GA Res 2840 (XXVI) UNDoc A/8429 (1971). See also the 1973 Principles of International Cooperation in the Detention, Arrest, Extradition, and Punishment of Persons Guilty of War Crimes and Crimes against Humanity (it declares that 'war crimes and crimes against humanity, wherever they are committed, shall be subject to investigation[,] and the persons against whom there is evidence that they have committed such crimes shall be subject to tracing, arrest, trial and, if found guilty, to punishment') GA Res 3074 (XXVIII) UN Doc A/9030 (1973).

105 As Meron points out, the 'repetition of certain norms in many human rights instruments is [in] itself an important articulation of state practice' (n 27 above) 92. See also *Filartiga v Pena Irala* 630 F 2d 876, 882-884 (2d Cir 1980).

106 Indeed, while there is disagreement among commentators on which human rights are protected by customary law, most agree that customary law prohibits torture, disappearances, extrajudicial executions, war crimes, crimes against humanity, slavery, piracy and genocide and that these prohibitions are *jus cogens* norms. See Meron (n 27 above) 210 (discussing the different human rights protected by customary law). For general discussion of *jus cogens* norms (rules that have peremptory status) see M McDougal *et al Human rights and world public order* (1980) 338-350.

107 See eg Report on Guatemala by the Expert, Mr Hector Gros Espiell, prepared in accordance with para 9 of UN Commission on Human Rights Resolution 1989/74, 46 UN ESCOR Comm'n on Hum Rts, paras 48, 49, 57, 66(c) UN Doc E/CN 4/1990/45; Report on Haiti by the Expert, Mr Philippe Texier, prepared in conformity with UN Commission on Human Rights Resolution 1989/73, 46 UN ESCOR Comm'n on Hum. Rts, paras 55, 61, 67, 87, 91, 102, 106(c) & (e), UN Doc E/CN 4/1990/44; Report prepared by the Special Rapporteur on the situation of human rights in Chile in accordance with para 11 of the Commission on Human Rights Resolution 1983/38 of 8 March 1983, UN Doc A/38/385 para 341 (1983); Final Report on the situation of human rights in El Salvador submitted to the Commission on Human Rights by Mr Jose Antonio Pastor Ridruejo in fulfilment of the mandate conferred under Commission resolution 1986/39, 43 UN ESCOR Comm'n on Hum Rts 13 para 60, UN Doc E/CN4/1987/21.

108 Eg, Report of the Working Group on Enforced or Involuntary Disappearances, 45 UN ESCOR Comm'n on Hum Rts 85 para 312, UN Doc E/CN 4/1989/18; Report of the Working Group on Enforced or Involuntary Disappearances, 47 UN ESCOR Comm'n on Hum Rts 86 para 406. For an exposition, see DS Wessbrodt 'The three "theme" special rapporteurs of the UN Commission on Human Rights' (1986) 80 *American Journal of International Law* 685.

governments' failure to punish serious violations of human rights such as torture, disappearances, and extra-legal violations.[109] Although not authoritative interpretations of international law, resolutions of the UN General Assembly have endorsed many of their reports' conclusions regarding the punishment of persons responsible for serious violations of human rights.[110]

Similarly, decisions of international and national courts support the position that the duty to prosecute and punish international crimes is part of customary international law. In his dissenting judgment in the *Lockerbie* case at the ICJ, Judge Weeramantry asserted that the duty to prosecute or extradite international crimes constitutes a well-established principle of customary law.[111] In *Prosecutor v Gbao,* the Appeals Chamber of the Special Court for Sierra Leone stated that 'under international law, states are under a duty to prosecute crimes whose prohibition has the status of jus cogens.'[112] The South African Constitutional Court in *State v Wouter Basson* has also stated that the international law obliges states to prosecute and punish crimes against humanity and war crimes.[113]

Respected authors in the field of international criminal law contend that the duty to prosecute and punish international law crimes is well-established in international law.[114] They argue that states' general obligation to ensure the enjoyment of fundamental rights is incompatible with impunity or blanket amnesties for international crimes.[115] In their view, a state's failure to investigate, prosecute and punish repeated or

109 See the two reports in n 108 above.

110 Eg, GA Res 37/185 para 10 (1982) (urging Salvadoran Judiciary to 'assume its obligation to ... prosecute and to punish those found responsible for assassinations, acts of torture and other forms of cruel, inhuman or degrading treatment'); GA Res 36/157, para 4(e) (1981) (urging Chilean authorities to 'investigate and clarify the fate of persons who have disappeared for political reasons, to inform the relatives of those persons of the outcome of the investigation and to prosecute and punish those responsible for such disappearances'); GA Res 33/173 para 1(b) (1978) (calling upon governments to 'ensure that law enforcement and security authorities or organizations are fully accountable, especially in law, in the discharge of their duties, such accountability to include legal responsibility for unjustifiable excesses which might lead to enforced or involuntary disappearances ...').

111 He based this position on the widespread use of the principle in international conventions; *Case Concerning Questions of Interpretation and Application of the 1971 Montreal Convention Arising from the Aerial Incident at Lockerbie (Libyan Arab Jamahiriya v United States)* 1992 ICJ 114, 160-181.

112 *Prosecutor v Gbao,* Decision on Preliminary Motion on the Invalidity of the Agreement Between the United Nations and the Government of Sierra Leone on the Establishment of the Special Court, Appeals Chamber, SCSL-04-15-PT-141, 25 May 2004, 10. Though bounds of *jus cogens* are still contested, the Appeals Chamber referred to crimes against humanity, genocide, war crimes, and 'other serious violations of international humanitarian law'.

113 *The State v Wouter Basson* 2005 SA 30/03 (CC) para 37.

114 See Orentlicher (n 3 above) 2537-2618; MC Bassiouni 'Searching for peace and achieving justice: The need for accountability' (1996) 59 *Law and Contemporary Problems* 9. See also A Cassese *International criminal law* (2003) 313.

115 See Orentlicher (n 3 above) 2537-2618; Cassese (n 114 above).

notorious violations of *jus cogens* norms breaches the customary obligation to respect the same set of peremptory rights.[116]

5 Duty to prosecute and amnesties

Amnesties adopted by a state party for any one of the above-discussed international crimes for which a duty to prosecute exists would generally be inconsistent with its international obligations.[117] To the extent that they exclude prosecution and punishment of certain internationally-defined crimes, amnesties are indeed incompatible with the obligation to prosecute and punish under conventional law or customary international law.[118] As the International Criminal Tribunal for Former Yugoslavia stated in the *Furundzija* case:[119]

> It would be senseless to argue, on the one hand, that on account of the *jus cogens* value of the prohibition against torture, treaties or customary rules providing for torture would be null and void *ab initio*, and then by unmindful of a State say, taking national measures authorizing or condoning torture or absolving its perpetrators through amnesty law.

The jurisprudence of the human rights treaty bodies also shows that amnesty for gross human rights violations – such as torture, disappearances, and extra judicial killings – is contrary to these 'non-derogable rights'[120] provided for under international law.[121] Four Latin

116 But see Scharf (n 46 above) 41 58 (noting the problems relating to the argument that there is a customary duty to prosecute for crimes against humanity); E Schabacker 'Reconciliation of justice and ashes: Amnesty commissions and the duty to punish human rights offenses' (1999) 12 *New York International Law Review* 1 37 (noting problems of divergent state practice); Orentlicher (n 3 above) 2582 (noting scholarly disagreements about the range of protected human rights under customary law).

117 But see Jackson (n 7 above) 120 (arguing that amnesty is consistent with the duty to prosecute).

118 The Office of the High Commissioner for Human Rights have defined amnesty as legal measures that have the effect of (a) prospectively barring criminal prosecution and, in some cases, civil actions against certain individuals or categories of individuals in respect of specific criminal conduct committed before the amnesty's adoption; or (b) retroactively nullifying legal liability previously established. Amnesties do not prevent legal liability for conduct that has not yet taken place, which would be an invitation to violate the law; see OHCHR *Rule of law tools for post-conflict states: Amnesties* HR/PUB/09/1 (2009) 41.

119 Case IT-95-17/1-T (10 December 1998) paras 151-157.

120 Under most international human rights regimes, states may not derogate from certain obligations therein. In General Comment 29, the HRC asserted that the list of non-derogable provision in art 4.2 of ICCPR was not exhaustive, opening the door for other non-enumerated, non-derogable rights, which it called 'peremptory norms' (2001). The African Commission has also held that all rights under the African Charter are non-derogable - see *Commission Nationale des Droits de l'Homme et des Libertes v Chad* (2000) AHRLR 66 (ACHPR 1995); *Media Rights Agenda and Others v Nigeria* (2000) AHRLR 200 (ACHPR 1998); *Constitutional Rights Project and Others v Nigeria* (2000) AHRLR 227 (ACHPR 1999); *Amnesty International and Others v Sudan* (2000) AHRLR 297 (ACHPR 1999); and *Malawi African Association and Others v Mauritania* (2000) AHRLR 149 (ACHPR 2000).

121 See section 4.1.4 above. Some of the Latin American amnesties of the 1970 and 1980s have been considered by the Inter-American Commission.

American amnesties of the 1970s and 1980s issued by Argentina,[122] Uruguay,[123] El Salvador,[124] and Chile[125] were considered by the Inter-American Commission and in all the cases the Commission found them in violation of the Inter-American Convention.[126] Scholars have argued that where the substantive right is non-derogable, it carries attendant remedial obligations that are equally non-derogable.[127] This obligation survives a change in government.[128]

However, state practice shows that the number of amnesty laws issued by states and the truth commissions formed after a given conflict far exceeds the number of prosecutions.[129] Similarly, some national courts, as

122 For a discussion, see CS Nino 'The duty to punish past abuses of human rights put into context: The case of Argentina' (1991) 100 *Yale Law Journal* 2619.

123 For a discussion see D Pion-Berlin 'To Prosecute or pardon? Human rights decisions in the Latin American Southern Cone (1993) 15 *Human Rights Quarterly* 105.

124 For a discussion see N Roht-Arriaza 'Case studies: Latin America, overview' in Roht-Arriaza (n 21 above) 148.

125 For a discussion see WW Burke-White 'Protecting the minority: A place for impunity? An illustrated survey of amnesty legislation, its conformity with international legal obligations, and its potential as a tool for minority-majority reconciliation, ethnopolitics & Minority Issues in *Europe* (2000) available at http://www.ecmi.de/jemie/download/JEMIE03BurkeWhite30-07-01.pdf (accessed on 25 December 2010).

126 See *Mendoza et al v Uruguay* Cases 10.029, 10.036, 10.145, 10.305, 10.373, 10.374 and 10.375, Report 29/92, Inter-Am CHR, OEA/SerL/V/II 83 doc 14 P154 (1993); *Mascre Las Hojas v El Salvador* Case 10.287, Report 26/92, Inter-Am CHR, OEA/SerL/V/II 83, doc 14 83, conclusion 5c (1993); *Consuelo et al v Argentina* Case 10.147, 10.181, 10.240, 10.262, 10.309, 10.311, Inter-Am CHR, Report 28/92, OEA/SerL/V/II 83, doc 14 P1 (1993); *Gary Hermosilla et al v Chile* Case 10.843 Inter-Am CHR, Report 36/96, OEA/SerL/V/II 95, doc 7 rev 46 (1997).

127 Eg, Roht-Arriaza asserts that '[c]ertain actions - torture, for example - are prohibited by a non-derogable right because such actions are so repugnant to the international community that no circumstances, no matter how exigent, can justify them. Thus, when these underlying rights are at issue, the right to state-imposed sanction and remedy by the state must also be non-derogable. The non-derogable nature of the underlying right would be meaningless if the state were not required to take action against those who violate the rights' (Roht-Arriaza (n 21 above) 57 63).

128 It is well established that a change in government does not relieve a state of its duties under international law. See L Henkin *et al International law: Cases and materials* (1987) 266.

129 See generally MC Bassiouni *The pursuit of international criminal justice: A world study on conflicts, victimization, and post conflict justice* (2009). Since 1974 some seventeen truth commissions have been established to enquire into the past of particular societies, to 'tell the truth' of what happened (P Hayner 'Fifteen truth commission – 1974 to 1994: A comparative study' (1994) 16 *Human Rights Quarterly* 600). While in theory, truth commission are not antithetical to prosecution (thus Louis Joinet in his 1997 Report on the 'Questions of the Impunity of Perpetrators of Human Rights Violations' to the Sub-Commission on Prevention of Discrimination and Protection of Minorities recommends that an extra judicial commission of inquiry into the events of the past should go hand in hand with prosecution and punishment of human rights violators - UN Doc E/CN 4/sub2/1997/20/Rev1 (1997)), in practice where truth commissions have been established prosecution have been very rare. As aptly captured by Priscilla Hayner in her study of fifteen truth commission: "[i]n only a few of the fifteen cases looked at [...] was there an amnesty law passed explicitly preventing trials, but in most other cases there was in effect a defacto amnesty –prosecutions were never seriously considered' (Hayne (above, at fn 4). Ratner also document that since the 70s, sixteen nations have granted amnesty to individuals accused of committing international war crimes (S Ratner 'New democracies, old atrocities: An inquiry in international law' (1999) 87 *Georgetown Law Journal* 707 722-23).

in the case of the courts of South Africa[130] and El Salvador,[131] express the view that international law not only fails to prohibit amnesty but rather encourages it.[132] These courts cite article 6(5) of Additional Protocol II of 1977 which on the face of it encourages amnesty by providing that at the end of hostilities in internal conflicts the authorities shall endeavor to grant the broadest possible amnesty to persons who have participated in the conflict'.[133]

The reality presented by these states practices on amnesties has made some scholars question the existence of the *erga omnes* duty to prosecute and punish international crimes.[134] It is our argument, however, that the granting of amnesties by states cannot negate the existence of this duty which, as we have demonstrated, exists both in treaty and customary law. As Carla Edelenbos aptly notes:[135]

> [e]ven those states which have adopted amnesty law and thereby allowed impunity do not deny the existence, in principle, of an obligation to prosecute, but invoke counterveiling considerations, such as national reconciliation or the instability of democratic process.

It is acknowledged that in some situations, such as in the aftermath of massive atrocities, states parties may not be in a position to prosecute every offender.[136] Both treaty and customary obligations to punish atrocious

130 *Azanian Peoples Organization (AZAPO) v President of the Republic of South Africa* 1996 (4) SA 671 (CC) 691 para 32.

131 Proceedings 10-93 (May 20, 1993); reprinted in NJ Kritz (ed) *Transitional Justice* (1995) 549 555.

132 Similarly, in the *Pinochet* case Lord Lloyd commenting on the question of amnesty stated: 'Further light is shed on state practice by the widespread adoption of amnesties for those who have committed crimes against humanity including torture. Chile was not the firs in the field. There was an amnesty at the end of the Franco-Algerian War in 1962. In 1971 India and Bangladesh agreed not to pursue charges of genocide against Pakistan troops accused of killing about one million East Pakistanis. General amnesties have also become common in recent years, especially in South America, covering members of former regimes accused of torture and other atrocities. Some of these have had the blessing of the United Nations, as a means of restoring peace and democractic government [...] it has not been argued that these amnesties are as such contrary to international law by reason of failure to prosecute the individual perpetrators' *R v Bow Street Metropolitan Stipendiary Magistrate. Ex Parte Pinochet* (1998) 4 All ER 897 (HL) 929 h-i.

133 This position is, however, disputed by the International Committee of the Red Cross. See D Cassel 'Lessons from the Americas: Guidelines for international response to amnesties for atrocities' (1996) 59 *Law & Contemporary Problems* 196 212.

134 See eg PA Schey *et al* 'Addressing human rights abuses: Truth commissions and the value of amnesty' (1997) 19 *Whittier Law Review* 325.

135 C Edelenbos 'Human rights violations: A duty to prosecute?' (1994) 7 *Leiden Journal of International Law* 5 21.

136 This has been true for countries such Philippines, Chile, Argentina and Uruguay: see J Zalaquett 'Confronting human rights violations committed by former governments: Principles applicable and political constraints' in *Aspen Institute Report* (n 5 above) 46-47. He points out that a government's ability to prosecute a prior regime's abuses is partly a function of the circumstances of the political transition. The widest scope for punishment exists when the transition was brought about by external conquest, as

crimes recognise this and are consistent with a limited program of prosecutions, but would be breached by wholesale impunity.[137] This means states could satisfy their *erga omnes* obligations through a limited number of prosecutions focusing, for example, on those who bear the greatest responsibility.[138]

6 Conclusion

An examination of international law confirms that international obligation to prosecute and punish international crimes exists. Though state practice shows a preponderant use of amnesties by states transitioning from conflicts, this does not in any way negate the existence of the duty to prosecute. In this regard, use of blanket amnesties where international crimes have been committed would be a breach of the international obligation to prosecute.

happened in post-war Germany and Japan. Less latitude for punishment exists if a retreating military has been discredited but still retains autonomous power, and still less if the military relinquishes power to civilians when it could remain in power indefinitely, and thus is in a position to dictate the terms of a transition. See also AC Stepan 'Paths toward redemocratization: Theoretical and comparative considerations' in G O'Donnell *et al* (eds) *Transitions from authoritarian rule: Comparative perspectives* (1986) 64.

137 OHCHR has similarly stated that blanket amnesties are contrary to the duty to prosecute as they 'exempt broad categories of serious human rights offenders from prosecution and/or civil liability without the beneficiaries having to satisfy preconditions, including those aimed at ensuring the full disclosure of what they know about the crimes covered by the amnesty, on an individual basis (OHCHR (n 118 above) 41).

138 This practice is emerging although none of the treaty instruments nor general human rights obligations explicitly make such a distinction. For example, in the *Velasquez Rodriquez* case, the Inter-American Court repeatedly asserts that a state party to the American Convention must investigate and punish 'any' and 'every' violation of the rights protected by the Convention. For a discussion on this point, see N Roht-Arriaza *Transnational justice and peace agreements* (2005) 53 (pointing out that prosecutions of those most responsible for designing and implementing a past system of state violence or for the most notorious violations would best comport with common standards of justice).

CHAPTER 2 IMMUNITY OF STATE OFFICIALS AND THE PROSECUTION OF INTERNATIONAL CRIMES

*Chacha Murungu**

1 Introduction

The literature on the subject of immunity is diverse and confusing.[1] The large body of literature on the topic does not share a common and consistent definition on immunity of state officials. There are a number of terms that have been used interchangeably with 'immunity of state officials'.[2] Sinclair writes that sovereign immunity in the strict sense of the term has to be taken to refer to the 'immunity which a personal sovereign or head of state enjoys when present in the territory of another state'.[3] This definition equates state immunity with immunity of state officials and as such is confusing. It is this confusion that makes it necessary to explain what 'immunity of state officials' means. State immunity and immunity of state officials – though akin to each other – are distinct from each other. A meaningful distinction is provided by Broomhall. He writes: '[i]mmunities

* LL.B (Hons) (Dar es Salaam); LL.M; LL.D Candidate (Pretoria); Advocate of the High Court of Tanzania.

1 See eg G Robertson *Crimes against humanity: The struggle for global justice* (2002) 403-426; SK Kapoor *International law and human rights* (2007) 216-223; MN Shaw *International law* (2003) 621-692; J Dugard (2005) 238-265; I Detter *International legal order* (1994) 456-463; H Leuterpacht 'The problem of jurisdictional immunities of foreign states' (1951) 28 *British Yearbook of International Law* 265; R Higgins 'Certain unresolved aspects of the law of state immunity' (1982) 29 *Netherlands International Law Review* 265; H Fox 'State immunity and the international crime of torture' (2006) 2 *European Human Rights Law Reports* 142; L McGregor 'State immunity and *jus cogens*' (2006) 55 *International and Comparative Law Quarterly* 437-445; A Orakhelashvili *Peremptory norms in international law* (2006) 320.

2 Upon a thorough reading on immunities, one finds terms such as 'sovereign immunity', 'sovereignty', 'foreign sovereign immunity', 'foreign state immunity', 'state immunity', 'state sovereign immunity', 'act of state', 'state responsibility', 'diplomatic and consular immunity', 'impunity', 'amnesty', 'immunity of international organisations', 'immunity attaching to multilateral forces abroad', 'jurisdictional immunity', 'inviolability', 'immunity from procedural enforcement', 'immunity from execution' and 'immunity from prosecution'.

3 I Sinclair 'The law of sovereign immunity: Recent developments' (1980) II *Hague Recueil des Cours* 113, 167.

attaching to diplomats, heads of state, and other officials are distinct from the State immunity that attaches to the state as such'.[4] In this chapter, the discussion centres solely on immunity attaching to state officials in relation to international crimes before international and national courts.

The Rome Statute of the International Criminal Court, 1998 (Rome Statute) uses the term 'official capacity' in article 27 to describe 'immunity' or 'special procedural rules' attaching to the state officials under national and international law. The use of 'immunity of state officials' in this chapter is preferred for convenience and inclusive reasons. It is used interchangeably with the 'official position' or 'official capacity' of a person as a state official.

The phrase 'state officials' is meant to cover the meaning attached by contemporary international law to state leaders or representatives. The wide description of state officials is taken from article 27 of the Rome Statute. Although article 27(1) of the Rome Statute does not define the meaning of a state official, it nevertheless gives a classification of who ideally would qualify as state officials. These persons range from heads of state or governments; a member of a government or parliament; an elected representative; or a government official. Hence, in this chapter these persons are called 'state officials.' The term is also employed by the International Law Commission (ILC) in its current study on immunity of state officials from foreign criminal jurisdiction.[5] However, one must note the difference between state officials under national and international jurisdictions. While there is no difference under international law between state officials as per article 27(1) of the Rome Statute, municipal law does not equate, for example, a president with the position of a prime minister or any other government official. Under municipal law, a president sits at the apex of the hierarchy of state officials. It is not necessary to deal with the classification of state officials under municipal law; rather, the international practice is adopted as found in article 27(1) of the Rome Statute.

A definition of 'immunity' is attempted here. *Immunity* is defined by the *Oxford Advanced Learner's Dictionary* as 'the state of being protected from something'.[6] The word immunity originates from the late Middle-English, and denotes 'exemption from liability'. It derives from the Latin word '*immunitas*' meaning 'exempt from public service or charge'. In Kiswahili,

4 B Broomhall *International justice and the International Criminal Court: Between sovereignty and the rule of law* (2003) 128-129 (citing J Brohmer *State immunity and the violation of human rights* (1997) 26-32).

5 ILC 'Provisional agenda for the Sixty-first Session' Geneva, 4 May- 5 June, and 6 July - 7 August 2009, UN General Assembly, UN Doc A/CN4/605 Agenda item 8 'Immunity of state officials from foreign criminal jurisdiction'.

6 *Oxford Advanced Learner's Dictionary* (2005) 776.

'immunity' is termed '*kinga dhidi ya mashtaka*,'[7] which refers to '*immunity from prosecution*'. In other words, immunity means exception, resistance, exemption, protection or invulnerability. It may also mean any exemption from a duty, liability or service of process; especially such an exemption granted to a public official. According to the *Concise Law Dictionary*, immunity is a

> personal favour granted by law contrary to the general rule. An immunity is a right peculiar to some individual or body; an exemption from some general duty or burden; a personal benefit or favour granted by law contrary to the general rule. Freedom from liability; exemption conferred by any law, from a general rule ... [It can also mean] freedom or exemptions from penalty, burden or duty.[8]

Thus, '*immunity from prosecution*' means withdrawal from prosecution. Immunity may be exercised at any time in the course of the trial, but before judgment is delivered.[9] Hence, it means an exception or a bar to prosecution for crimes. According to Schabas, immunity is 'a defence'[10] under international criminal law. This opinion is also shared by Van Schaack and Slye.[11] It therefore constitutes a defence to international criminal responsibility for individuals accused of international crimes. Whether this defence of immunity is enforceable under international law is a contentious subject. However, it suffices at this early point to regard it as a kind of defence or ground that is commonly raised by state officials when subjected to international criminal proceedings.

Immunity may also be characterised as a barrier to individual accountability.[12] It is a ground that excludes the criminal responsibility of an individual. It 'has the effect of rendering inadmissible any action brought against the person who invokes it'.[13]

After this attempt to clarify the terms 'immunity' and 'state officials', then we next examine developments regarding the immunity of state officials under international law.

7 See art 46 Constitution of the United Republic of Tanzania, 1977 (official version in Kiswahili (2005)).

8 PR Aiyar *Concise Law Dictionary: With legal maxims, Latin terms and words and phrases* (2005) 549-550; *Jashir Singh v Vipin Kumar Jaggi* AIR 2001 SC 2734.

9 Aiyar (as above).

10 WA Schabas *An introduction to the International Criminal Court* (2007) 231.

11 B van Schaack and RC Slye *International criminal law and its enforcement: Cases and materials* (2007) 865-874.

12 DP Stewart 'Immunity and accountability: More continuity than change?'(2005) 99 *American Society International Law Proceedings* 227 228.

13 See Dissenting Opinion of Judge Jean Yves De Cara in the *Case Concerning Certain Criminal Proceedings in France (Republic of the Congo v France) Provisional Measures* Order of 17 June 2003, ICJ Reports (2003) 102, 122.

2 Developments on the immunity of state officials

Recent developments regarding the immunity of state officials under customary international law and conventional international law are presented in this section.

2.1 Customary international law

For a principle to attain the status of customary international law it has to satisfy certain conditions. Customary international law is constituted through 'evidence of a general practice accepted as law.'[14] It consists of the 'rules which, as a result of state practice over a period of time, have become accepted as legally binding. A rule of customary law is created by widespread state practice *(usus)* coupled with *opinio juris*, namely, a belief on the part of the state concerned that international law obliges it, or gives it a right, to act in a particular way'.[15] State practice may be derived from official pronouncements of governments to form rules of customary international law. *Opinio juris* is an opinion of an existence of law.[16] The existence of a customary law rule is dependent on widespread – but not necessarily unanimous – state practice.

The immunity of state officials or persons in their 'official capacity'[17] from jurisdiction or prosecution – finds its origin in customary international law,[18] later developing into convention or treaty international law. Schabas rightly observes that 'customary international law recognises certain degrees of immunity from criminal prosecution for heads of state and other officials'.[19] Hence it 'exists by virtue of customary

14 Art 38(1) Statute of the International Court of Justice.

15 See UK Ministry of Defence *The Manual of the law of armed conflict* (2004) 5 (secs 1.12-1.12.2); *Asylum* case *(Colombia v Peru)* Judgment, 20 November 1950, ICJ Reports (1950) 126; *North Sea Continental Shelf (Federal Republic of Germany v Denmark; Federal Republic of Germany v Netherlands)* Judgment, 20 February 1969, ICJ Reports (1969) paras 70-78; *Case Concerning Military and Paramilitary Activities In and Against Nicaragua, (Nicaragua v USA)* Judgment, 27 June 1986, ICJ Reports (1986) paras 77; 183-186; JE Ackerman and E O'Sullivan *Practice and procedure of the International Criminal Tribunal for the Former Yugoslavia* (2000) 2-3; E Kwakwa *The international law of armed conflict: Personal and material fields of application* (1992) 30; T Maluwa *International law in Post-Colonial Africa* (1999) 5. But see ICTY's view in *Prosecutor v Kuperškić et al* (Case IT-95-16-T), Trial Chamber II, Judgment dated 14 January 2000 para 540.

16 M du Plessis *African guide to international criminal justice* (2008) vii.

17 Art 27 Rome Statute, 1998, uses the term 'official capacity'.

18 B Stern 'Immunities for heads of state: Where do we stand?' in M Lattimer and P Sands *Justice for crimes against humanity* (2003) 73-106, particularly 73 ('Some of the tenets used in order to grant immunity to heads of state have their origin in customary international law…'). But see G Mettraux *International crimes and the Ad hoc tribunals* (2005) 13 (arguing that identifying customary international law is a daunting task).

19 WA Schabas *Genocide in international law* (2000) 316; *Attorney-General of Israel v Adolf Eichmann* (1968) 36 ILR 18 (District Court of Jerusalem) para 28; *Attorney-General of Israel v Adolf Eichmann* (1968) 36 ILR 227 (Supreme Court of Israel) para 14; *Prosecutor v*

international law'[20] and it is largely a matter of custom. The customary nature of the immunity of state officials is justified and based on state and certain judicial practices.[21] The International Court of Justice (ICJ) has accepted that the immunity of state officials originates from customary international law.[22] The ICJ observed so despite the existence of certain international conventions imposing obligations on states to prosecute and punish individuals who commit international crimes, thereby outlawing the defence of immunity of state officials.

Historically, state officials were not subjected to criminal responsibility for their actions because of a merger of the 'sovereign' and the 'sovereignty of the state'.[23] Immunity followed in the first place from the divine right of kings: 'you could not put an infallible ruler on trial since, if you did, the verdict must always go in his favour'.[24] The king was deemed an infallible and could not do any wrong in his own state or be sued in his own courts. With the establishment of secular states, their rulers became less known as kings but as heads of state or governments, referred to as 'state officials'.

Orakhelashvili observes that 'historically, the original concept of immunity of high level state officials, such as heads of state arose from the fact that they represent their states and to sue [them] was tantamount to suing an independent state'.[25] This position is supported by Burns who argues that state officials 'have with few exceptions been able to avoid responsibility for their conduct by wrapping themselves up in the blanket of state sovereignty ...'.[26] But, the state and its officials are distinct and

Blaškić (Case IT-95-14-AR 108bis) Judgment on the Request of the Republic of Croatia for Review of the Decision of Trial Chamber II of 18 July 1997, 29 October 1997 para 41.

20 Schabas (n 11 above) 231.

21 See *Amicus Brief in the Matter of David Anyaele and Emmanuel Egbuna v Charles Ghankay Taylor and Others* A submission from the Open Society Justice Initiative to the Federal High Court of Nigeria, Abuja Division, November 2004 paras 41-44 (on immunities- stating that 'while the immunity of diplomats has always been regulated by its own regime, the immunity of heads of state appears to have been subsumed within state immunities until relatively recently, owing to the identification of the state with its ruler'); D Akande 'International law immunities and the International Criminal Court' (2004) 98 *American Journal of International Law* 407; A Watts 'The legal position in international law of heads of states, heads of governments and foreign ministers' (1994) III 247 *Hague Recueil des Cours* 35-81; JL Mallory 'Resolving the confusion over the head of state immunity: The defined right of kings' (1986) 86 *Columbia Law Review* 169, 177; SK Verma *An introduction to public international law* (1998) 155 (stating that this concept is imbibed in customary international law).

22 *The Case Concerning the Arrest Warrant of 11 April 2000 (The Democratic Republic of Congo v Belgium)*, 2002 ICJ Reports 14 February 2002 paras 58 – 59; *Case Concerning Certain Criminal Proceedings in France (Republic of the Congo v France) Provisional Measures* Order of 17 June 2003 ICJ Reports 2003 paras 1-39, particularly paras 1 and 28.

23 MC Bassiouni *Crimes against humanity in international criminal law* (1999) 505-508 (stating that this is particularly true with respect to monarchies as evidenced by Louis XIV's statement: *'L'etat c'est moi'* (meaning that 'the state is me', - my own translation).

24 Robertson (n 1 above) 403.

25 Orakhelashvili (n 1 above) 320; Y Simbeye *Immunity and international criminal law* (2004) 105-109.

26 P Burns 'An international criminal tribunal: The difficult union of principle and politics' (1994) 5 *Criminal Law Forum* 341 342.

must not be confused: the two are different because a state can claim its own immunity from jurisdiction and execution from courts of other states; state officials may claim their own personal and functional immunity from prosecution from such courts too, and even international courts or criminal tribunals.

Arguably, the traditional doctrine of immunity from jurisdiction enjoyed by the state and the head of state is based on the principle of state dignity. This is a notion that a sovereign must not degrade the dignity of his nation by submitting to the jurisdiction of another state.[27] Consequently, a head of state is not to subject himself to a jurisdiction incompatible with his dignity and the dignity of his nation.[28] Possibly, the moral comity of nations may have contributed to the development of immunity. This is expressed by 'do unto others as you would have them do to you'.[29] In this regard, each state upholds the concept of immunity in the hope that its own head of state will be protected when on foreign soil.

State officials are granted immunity in order to allow them to perform their duties effectively under customary international law and benefit from absolute criminal immunity before courts of a foreign state.[30] It is a common practice for states and national laws to allow immunity to their own state officials or to officials from foreign countries.[31] Van Schaack and Syle observe that state officials 'under both international and national law may claim immunity from accountability for acts they may commit while in office' and that 'such officials have enjoyed such immunity for centuries, due in large to the conflation of the head of state with the state itself'.[32] However, this rule seems too absolute: it would mean allowing state officials to commit crimes and getting away scot-free.

The rule on the immunity of state officials has undergone changes in recent times. What seemed to be impossible in the past – that a state official could not be prosecuted before national courts even for international crimes – has now become possible under contemporary international law. Nowadays, state officials are open to prosecution and punishment for their crimes – especially international crimes – before international and even national courts. In fact, international criminal law statutes require that all

27 See Dissenting Opinion of Judge Jean Yves De Cara in the *Case Concerning Certain Criminal Proceedings in France (Republic of the Congo v France), Provisional Measures*, Order of 17 June 2003, ICJ Reports 2003, 123.

28 *The Schooner Exchange v McFadden* (1812) 11 US 137-138; *Mighell v The Sultan of Johore* [1894] 1 QB 149.

29 D Aversano 'Can the Pope be a defendant in American courts? The grant of head of state immunity and the judiciary's role to answer this question' (2006) 18 *Pace International Law Review* 495, 506.

30 Stewart (n 13 above) 229.

31 R *v Bow Street Stipendiary Magistrate and Others, ex parte Pinochet Ugarte* [1998] 4 All ER 897; [1998] 3 WLR 1456 (HL). In contrast, see *United States v Noriega* 808 F Supp 791 (SD Fla 1992) – where Noriega – was not accorded immunity simply because the executive did not consider him entitled to such protection.

32 Van Shaack and Slye (n 11 above) 865-866.

individuals responsible for international crimes, including state officials, be prosecuted. States are steadily beginning to prosecute their own former state officials for international crimes. In Africa, Ethiopia is a good example. Ethiopian authorities prosecuted and sentenced former state official, Mengistu Haile-Mariam, for genocide and crimes against humanity. Both his prosecution and sentence to death were *in absentia*, thus lacking legitimacy under international human rights law. In other countries, the jurisprudence on the prosecution of state officials before national courts will take time to be compatible with international law obligations.

2.2 Codification of immunity of state officials under international law

There is no specific international treaty on the doctrine of immunity of state officials.[33] However, immunity is governed by international law as found in treaties and statutes of international courts and tribunals. The first international efforts to hold state officials responsible for international crimes came after the World War I.[34] This is evidenced by the signing of the Treaty of Peace between the Allied and Associated Powers and Germany at Versailles on 28 June 1919 (Versailles Treaty).[35] This was followed by a Report presented to the Preliminary Peace Conference by the Commission on Responsibility of the Authors of the War and on the enforcement of penalties at Versailles in March 1919.[36] In Chapter III, the Report provided for the responsibility of state officials for international crimes, particularly former Kaiser Wilhelm II, 'without distinction of rank, including chiefs of state'. Despite this call, Kaiser Wilhelm II was never prosecuted.[37]

The application of international criminal law to the prosecution of state officials was first witnessed after the World War II. State officials from Germany were prosecuted and punished by the Nuremberg

33 Stern (n 19 above) 83.

34 MC Bassiouni 'The time has come for an international criminal court' (1991) 1 *Indiana International and Comparative Law Review* 1, 2-4.

35 Art 227 of the Versailles Treaty called for the trial of the former head of state of Germany, Wilhelm II.

36 Conference of Paris 1919; reprinted in (1920) 14 *American Journal of International Law* 95 (Supp) quoted in MC Bassiouni *Crimes against humanity in international law* (1992) 553, 555.

37 See EJ Guilherme de Aragao 'Setting standards for domestic prosecutions of gross violations of human rights through the ICC: International jurisdiction for wilful killings in Brazil?' in European Inter-University Centre for Human Rights and Democratisation, *The International Criminal Court: Challenges and prospects,* Proceedings of an International Conference organized by the European Inter-University Centre for Human Rights and Democratisation (EIUC) (2005) 13-38 15; JF Willis *Prologue to Nuremberg – The politics and diplomacy of punishing war criminals of the First World War* (1982) 98.

Tribunal[38] which was established by the Charter of the International Military Tribunal, annexed to the London Agreement signed on 8 August 1945.[39] The Charter outlawed state officials' defence of immunity for crimes against peace (aggression), crimes against humanity and war crimes.[40] Therefore, the immunity of state officials has been rejected at least since the Nuremberg Trials.[41] Nevertheless, Adolf Hitler and Benito Mussolini were never indicted.

The Charter of the International Military Tribunal was followed by the Allied Control Council Law 10 on the Punishment of Persons Guilty of War Crimes, Crimes against Peace and Against Humanity,[42] which rejected the defence of immunity attaching to state officials.[43] The Proclamation by the Supreme Commander for the Allied Powers issued on 19 January 1946 at Tokyo further called for the establishment of an International Military Tribunal for the Far East.[44] The Tribunal was established by the Charter of the International Military Tribunal for the Far East (the Tokyo Charter) in 1946.[45] The Tokyo Charter outlawed the defence of immunity of state officials in relation to international crimes.[46]

Subsequent to World War II, international law on the doctrine of immunity of state officials developed further. Different international conventions, principles and statutes of international criminal tribunals and courts rejected the defence of immunity of state officials before international courts and tribunals. In fact, international law (both conventional and customary international law) outlaws the defence of immunity of a head of state in respect of international crimes.[47] In all these

38 MP Scharf *Balkan justice: The story behind the first international war crimes trial since Nuremberg* (1997) 9-11. On the disposition and outcome of the Nuremberg Trials, see E de Aragao (n 38 above) 16; MC Bassiouni *Crimes against humanity in international law* (1992) 586-589.

39 Art 1 Agreement by the Government of the United States of America, the Provisional Government of the French Republic, the Government of the United Kingdom of Great Britain and Northern Ireland and the Government of the Union of Soviet Socialist Republics for the Prosecution and Punishment of the Major War Criminals of the European Axis.

40 Art 7 Charter of the International Military Tribunal, 1945.

41 K Kittichaisaree *International criminal law* (2001) 259.

42 *Official Gazette of the Control Council for Germany* Berlin, 31 January 1946.

43 Arts II (4)(a) & (5) Allied Control Council Law 10 on the Punishment of Persons Guilty of War Crimes, Crimes against Peace and Against Humanity.

44 Art 1 Proclamation by the Supreme Commander for the Allied Powers, Tokyo, 19 January 1946. The proclamation was ordered and signed by Douglas MacArthur (the Supreme Commander for the Allied Powers).

45 On the Tokyo Tribunal, see U Kei *Beyond the judgment of civilization: The intellectual legacy of the Japanese war crimes trials 1946-1949* (2003) 1-336; C Hosoya *et al The Tokyo war crimes trial* (1986) 1-226.

46 Art 6 Charter of the International Military Tribunal for the Far East, 1946.

47 See, generally, Principle III Principles of International Law Recognized in the Charter of the Nuremberg Tribunal and in the Judgment of the Tribunal, 1950 (1950) 82 *Yearbook of the International Law Commission* 374-378; Report of the International Law Commission Covering its Second Session 5 June-29 July 1950 Doc A/1316 11-14; art 1

instruments, the official capacity of a person is neither a defence for prosecution nor a mitigating factor in their punishment. The contemporary law on non-recognition of the immunity of state officials for international crimes is article 27 of the Rome Statute, 1998, which sets out the position in international law for the prosecution of individuals for international crimes before international courts.

Recognising the increasing problem of the immunity of state officials before national courts, the International Law Commission (ILC) has embarked on a study on the immunity of state officials from foreign criminal jurisdiction. At its fifty-eighth session in 2006, the ILC considered the topic in its long-term programme of work. The General Assembly of the United Nations (UN) noted the decision of the ILC during its fifty-eighth session of 2006 in Resolution 62/66 of 6 December 2007. At its fifty-ninth session in 2007, the ILC decided to include the topic 'Immunity of State Officials from foreign criminal jurisdiction' in its programme of work and appointed Roman Kolodkin as Special Rapporteur on the question of immunity.[48] The Special Rapporteur submitted his preliminary report on immunity at the sixtieth session of the ILC in 2008 whereby the ILC considered the preliminary report. At its sixty-third session, the General Assembly of the United Nations adopted a resolution on the report of the ILC on the work of its sixtieth session on 15 January 2009.[49] During the ILC's sixty-first session, the topic of immunity of state officials from foreign criminal jurisdiction was included in the provisional agenda for the sixty-first session convened at Geneva on 4 May 2009. However, at this session, the ILC did not consider the topic of immunity.[50] It is expected that the ILC will discuss it in subsequent sessions. Perhaps the ILC would not detract from the position already stated in the Rome Statute so as to

1954 Draft Code of Offences Against the Peace and Security of Mankind (1954) *Yearbook of the International Law Commission* II, ii; art 7 1996 Draft Code of Offences Against the Peace and Security of Mankind (1996) 2 *Yearbook of the International Law Commission* ii; art 6 Statute of International Criminal Tribunal for Rwanda, 1994; art 7 Statute of International Criminal Tribunal for the former Yugoslavia 1993; art 27 Rome Statute of the International Criminal Court, 1998; art 6 Statute of the Special Court for Sierra Leone; art 29 Law on the Establishment of Extra-ordinary Chambers in the Courts of Cambodia for the Prosecution of Crimes Committed during the period of Democratic Kampuchea, 2001; art 15(3) Statute of the Supreme Iraqi Criminal Tribunal, 2005; Principles 5 and 14 Princeton Project on Universal Jurisdiction; art 11(1)(a)-(b) Resolution on Immunities from Jurisdiction and Execution of Heads of State and of Government in International Law, 2001; art II Convention on Non-Applicability of Statutory Limitations to War crimes and Crimes against Humanity, 1968; art IV Genocide Convention, 1950; art 2(1)-(3) Convention against Torture, 1984; art 2 International Convention on the Suppression and Punishment of the Crime of Apartheid, 1973; art 12 Protocol for the Prevention and Punishment of Genocide, Crimes against Humanity, War Crimes and All forms of Discrimination, 2006.

48 At its 2940th meeting on 27 July 2007 Official Records of the General Assembly Sixty-second Session, Supplement 10 (A/62/10) para 376.

49 See Official Records of the General Assembly Sixty-third Session Suppl 10 (A/63/10) UN Doc A/RES/63/123 Agenda item 75.

50 See International Law Commission Provisional Agenda for the Sixty-first Session, Geneva, 4 May-5 June, and 6 July-7 August 2009 UN Doc A/CN 4/605 Agenda item 8 'Immunity of State officials from foreign criminal jurisdiction'.

avoid contradiction on the question of immunity attaching to state officials who commit international crimes.

The preceding section demonstrated the origin of immunity of state officials and its relationship with the state. Next, we address the scope of the immunity of state officials.

3 Scope of immunity of state officials

There are two aspects to state officials' immunity considered in international law: functional immunity and personal immunity. Functional immunity is commonly referred to as 'immunity *ratione materiae'* while personal immunity is called 'immunity *ratione personae'*. The question of immunity *ratione personae* arises particularly and most strongly with regard to international courts or tribunals, and even domestic courts. Serving state officials may be rendered susceptible to the jurisdiction of international tribunals depending on the terms of the statutes of such tribunals.[51] Shaw observes that in domestic courts, the situation is more complex because of the 'status of head of state before domestic courts' and that 'international law has traditionally made a distinction between official and private acts of a head of state'.[52] Thus, immunity only exists for official acts done while a person is in office.

Personal immunity or *ratione personae* attaches to senior state officials while they are still in office. State as well as judicial practice indicate that this form of immunity applies even to international crimes, as held by domestic courts in cases involving Muammar Qaddafi[53] and Robert Mugabe.[54] As observed by Dapo Akande, '[j]udicial opinion and state practice on this point are unanimous and no case can be found in which it was held that a state official possessing immunity *ratione personae* is subject to the criminal jurisdiction of a foreign state where it is alleged that he or she has committed an international crime'.[55]

51 Shaw (n 1 above) 655-656.
52 As above.
53 French *Cour de Cassation* 13 March 2001 Judgment 1414 (2001) 105 *Revue Generale de Droit International Public* 437.
54 See *Tachiona v Mugabe* 169 F Supp 2d 259, 309 (SDNY 2001); see generally the opposition submission in the 'Brief for the United States, in Tachiona, on her own behalf and on behalf of her late Husband Tapfuma Chiminya Tachiona *et al' Petitioners v United States of America On Petition for a Writ of* Certiorari *to the United States Court of Appeals for the Second Circuit* In the Supreme Court of the United States 05-879, April 2006. In n 9: 'The assertion of head-of-state immunity on behalf of Foreign Minister Mudenge is consistent with international practice [citing also *Case Concerning the Arrest Warrant of 11 April 2000*], paras 20-21, 22'.
55 Akande (n 22 above) 407; Dugard (n 1 above) 252; C Bhoke 'The trial of Charles Taylor: Conflict prevention, international law and an impunity-free Africa' *Institute for Security Studies Occasional Paper 27* (2006) 8-10.

Functional Immunity or *ratione materiae* attaches to the official acts or functions of senior state officials. This type of immunity may be invoked not only by serving state officials but also by former state officials in respect of their official acts while they were in office. Such immunity cannot exist when a person is charged with international crimes either because such acts can never be 'official' or because they violate norms of *jus cogens*,[56] and such peremptory norms must prevail over immunity.[57] In this connection, if indeed state officials should ever be shielded from arrest and prosecution by the doctrine of immunity, 'immunity would allow states to choose whether or not their agents would be responsible under international law'.[58]

An incumbent or former state official may be subject to criminal proceedings before properly constituted international criminal courts.[59] Contemporary international law no longer accepts a state official committing crimes which go unpunished. As Dugard argues, 'some human rights norms enjoy such a high status that their violations, even by state officials, constitute an international crime. The doctrine of immunity cannot stand aloof from these developments.'[60] Nowadays, 'it is well established that the official position of individuals does not exempt them from individual responsibility for acts that are crimes under international law, and thus does not constitute a substantive defence'.[61] The preceding remains the position in respect of international crimes within the jurisdiction of international courts.

The following section presents the controversy related to the immunity of state officials under international law, and demonstrates how international courts have approached their immunity from prosecution and subpoenas in relation to international crimes.

4 International courts and the controversy on immunity of state officials

This section demonstrates how international courts have developed the jurisprudence on the immunity of state officials from prosecution and punishment for international crimes, reflecting their uncertainty regarding the concept in relation to the prosecution of international crimes. The key question here is whether state officials are immune from the issuance of subpoenas by international courts to appear and testify or to produce

56 On *jus cogens*, see NHB Jorgensen *The responsibility of states for international crimes* (2000) 85-92.
57 Bhoke (n 55 above).
58 Broomhall (n 4 above) 128.
59 *Arrest Warrant* case (n 24 above) para 61.
60 Dugard (n 1 above) 249-250.
61 Akande (n 22 above) 415.

evidence. In other words, does immunity from prosecution extend to subpoenas issued against state officials?

4.1 Immunity of state officials is not a defence: A settled position

Should the immunity of state officials prevail over the duty to prosecute and punish individuals responsible for international crimes? Genocide, war crimes and crimes against humanity are committed not by the state but by individuals, including state officials. State officials do not necessarily personally or directly commit crimes – they do so by participating as co-perpetrators or tolerating, inciting, aiding or condoning the commission of international crimes. All states are obliged to prosecute and punish perpetrators of international crimes as this obligation has attained the status of customary international law and is a *jus cogens* norm which must not be subservient to the lower norm of immunity. When the prosecution and punishment of individuals responsible for international crimes are weighed against the immunity of state officials, the duty to prosecute and punish international crimes must prevail over immunity. This is so because humanity requires that individuals who commit egregious crimes must be held responsible for their acts.

Generally, international courts have held that state officials do not benefit from immunity accorded to them by national or international law, especially where such officials have been charged with international crimes. The International Court of Justice (ICJ),[62] the International Criminal Court (ICC),[63] the International Criminal Tribunal for the former Yugoslavia (ICTY),[64] and the International Criminal Tribunal for Rwanda (ICTR)[65] have held that the official position of individuals is not a defence for prosecution nor is it a mitigating factor in the punishment of such persons. The position has remained so since the Nuremberg and Tokyo trials.[66] The Appeals Chamber of the Special Court for Sierra Leone (SCSL) held in the case against Charles Taylor that the official

62 *Arrest Warrant* case (n 24 above) para 61.

63 *Prosecutor v Al Bashir* Decision on the Prosecution's Application for a Warrant of Arrest against Omar Hassan Al Bashir (Case ICC-02/05-01/09) Public Reducted Version, Pre-Trial Chamber I, 4 March 2009 15, paras 41-43.

64 *Prosecutor v Milošević* Decision on Preliminary Motions, Trial Chamber, Decision of 8 November 2001, paras 26-34; *Prosecutor v Kunarać, Kovać and Vuković* (Cases IT-96-23 –T and IT-96-23/1-T) Trial Chamber, Judgment 22 February 2001, para 494; *Prosecutor v Karadžić* (Case IT-95-5/18-PT) Decision on the Accused's Holbrooke Agreement Motion, 8 July 2009, Trial Chamber, para 5; *Prosecutor v Karadžić* Case (IT-95-5/18-PT) Appeal of the Decision Concerning Holbrooke Agreement Disclosure, 28 January 2009, Appeals Chamber, paras 8-12; Decision on Appellant Radovan Karadžić's Appeal Concerning Holbrooke Agreement Disclosure, Appeals Chamber, 6 April 2009, para 17.

65 *Prosecutor v Kambanda* (Case ICTR 97-23-S) Judgment and Sentence, 4 September 1998.

66 Nuremberg Judgment *International Military Tribunal*, 1946, reprinted in (1947) 41 *American Journal of International Law* 172, 221.

position of a person – whether a state official or not – does not bar prosecution before international courts. The Chamber emphasised that the official position of Charles Taylor 'as an incumbent Head of State at the time when [...] criminal proceedings were initiated against him is not a bar to his prosecution by this court'. As such, Charles Taylor 'was and is subject to criminal proceedings before the Special Court for Sierra Leone'.[67] The case against Taylor represents an interesting scenario. It touches on the immunity of a state official from a state not party to the agreement establishing the SCSL. The decision of the SCSL rejecting immunity has the effect that even if the immunity in question relates to an official from a state not party to an instrument establishing an international court, such immunity does not prevail. This is a great development outlawing immunity regardless of whether a state is a party to an instrument creating the court or not.

The Extra-ordinary Chambers in the Courts of Cambodia (ECCC)[68] and the Iraqi Supreme Criminal Tribunal[69] have held the same regarding immunity of state officials. Hence, international criminal courts or tribunals have jurisdiction to prosecute persons responsible for international crimes, including state officials.

New developments in international criminal law indicate that a serving state official of a state not a party to the Rome Statute may be prosecuted by the ICC after the UN Security Council refers a case or situation to the Prosecutor of the ICC.[70] The ICC decided on this matter in the case against the President of Sudan who was charged with crimes against humanity, war crimes and genocide. In this regard, regardless of whether an individual is a former or serving state official, such person may be prosecuted for international crimes by international courts vested with criminal jurisdiction over such a person. However, the ICJ has held that under customary international law, serving state officials enjoy immunity

67 *Prosecutor v Taylor* (Case SCSL-03-01-I) Decision on Immunity from Jurisdiction, Appeals Chamber, 31 May 2004, paras 45-53.

68 Arts 2 and 29 Law on the Establishment of Extra-ordinary Chambers in the Courts of Cambodia for the Prosecution of Crimes committed during the Period of Democratic Kampuchea, 27 October 2004, as revised on 23 November 2004, (NS/RKM/1004/006); Criminal Case File 002/14-08-2006, Investigation 002/19-2007-ECCC/OCIJ (Khieu Samphan) *Provisional Detention Order* 19 November 2007; Criminal Case File 002/14-08-2006, Investigation 002/19-09-2007 *Provisional Detention Order*, ECCC-OCIJ, 19 September 2007 1-5 paras 1-6; Extra-ordinary Chambers in the Courts of Cambodia, Criminal Case File 002/14-08-2006, Investigation 002/19-09-2007, ECCC-OCIJ, *Police Custody Decision* 12 November 2007 1-2; Extra-ordinary Chambers in the Courts of Cambodia, Criminal Case File 002/14-08-2006, Investigation 002/19-09-2007, ECCC-OCIJ, *Provisional Detention Order* 14 November 2007 1-5, paras 1-11.

69 *Prosecutor v Saddam Hussein Al-Majid et al,* Defendants' Preliminary Submission Challenging the Legality of the Special Court 21 December 2005, 1-24 paras 1-121.

70 *Prosecutor v Al Bashir* Decision on the Prosecution's Application for a Warrant of Arrest against Omar Hassan Al Bashir (Case ICC-02/05-01/09) Public Reducted Version, Pre-Trial Chamber I, 4 March 2009 15 para 41.

from prosecution before foreign national courts.[71] Arguably, the decision of ICJ disregards the customary international law duty of states to prosecute and punish perpetrators of international crimes, regardless of their official capacity.

The next section examines the uncertainty regarding the immunity of state officials who are subpoenaed to testify (*subpoena ad testificandum*) or produce evidence (*subpoena duces tecum*) before international courts.

4.2 Immunity of state officials and the question of subpoenas

When state officials are required to appear before international courts to testify or produce evidence, international courts have not been consistent in granting the applications of accused persons or prosecutors to compel state officials to appear before such courts. The appearance of individuals may be sought by voluntary attendance or appearance as envisaged under the Rome Statute.[72] When a person fails to voluntarily appear in court, the prosecutor may apply for an order of the court to compel such a person to appear under article 64(6)(b) of the Rome Statute. Subpoenas are also recognised by the Rules of Procedure and Evidence of the ICTY and ICTR respectively.[73] If persons do not comply with such court orders they may be held in contempt of court.

If individuals voluntarily appear before court they waive their immunity by means of the operation of estoppel. The question of immunity would not arise in the case of these individuals. The position is different when individuals refuse to appear before international courts on the ground of immunity. The concern here is non-compliance with voluntary appearance leading to compulsory court orders summoning individuals, including state officials to appear and testify or produce evidence in court. The question is now raised: *does immunity extend to subpoenas and other court processes?* The issue of subpoenas arise especially when state officials are required to testify against their subordinates or other accused persons before international courts, or when state officials are to produce evidence in courts to assist the court in conducting or expediting trials.

International courts have arrived at different interpretations on whether the immunity of state officials extends to the issuance of a subpoena to testify or produce evidence.[74] The Trial and Appeals

71 *Arrest Warrant* case (n 23 above) para 61; *Congo v France* (n 22 above) 102 paras 1 and 28; *Case Concerning Questions Relating to the Obligation to Prosecute or Extradite (Belgium v Senegal)* Request for the Indication of Provisional Measures Order of 28 May 2009, ICJ General List 144.

72 Art 58(1) and (7) Rome Statute.

73 Rule 54 Rules of Procedure and Evidence of the ICTY and ICTR; Rule 54 Rules of Procedure and Evidence of the SCSL; Rule 84 Internal Rules of the ECCC.

74 On subpoenas, see A Cassese *International criminal law* (2008) 308-313.

Chambers of the SCSL both surprisingly held that the immunity of state officials from prosecution for international crimes extends to protecting them (particularly the serving president of Sierra Leone) from testifying before the SCSL. The two Chambers of the SCSL contended that section 48(4) of the Constitution of Sierra Leone protected the president from testifying.[75]

The only notable position in contemporary international law on the prosecution of international crimes is that stated in the dissenting opinions of the Judges in the Trial and Appeals Chambers of the SCSL in the cases of *Norman, Fofana* and *Kondewa*. Judge Bankole Thompson (Trial Chamber) held that the sitting president of Sierra Leone does not enjoy immunity from testifying before the SCSL in respect of international crimes.[76] The same position was followed by Justice Geoffrey Robertson of the Appeals Chamber.[77]

The SCSL Trial Chamber has however held that a subpoena *ad testificandum* may be issued against a former president. The Chamber's position is found in the case of *Sesay*, decided in 2008, whereby the Chamber ordered former president Ahmad Tejan Kabbah to testify.[78] In this regard, the court echoed that former state officials enjoy no immunity from being subpoenaed.

The position that state officials do not enjoy immunity – not only from prosecution but also from *subpoenas ad testificandum* – is the right interpretation of the scope of immunity, and should be followed in respect of international crimes. Granting applications for subpoenas of state officials ensures transparency, equality of arms and a fair trial, and is necessary for the preparation and conduct of trials, especially in complex international cases.

Differences in opinion regarding the immunity of state officials to *subpoena ad testificandum* and *subpoena duces tecum* are observed in the decisions of the ICTR and ICTY. These are examined below, but it is necessary to first state the conditions for the issuance of subpoenas as

75 *Prosecutor v Norman, Fofana and Kondewa* (Case SCSL-04-14-T) Decision on Motions by Moinina Fofana and Sam Hinga Norman for the Issuance of a Subpoena Ad Testificandum to HE Alhaji Dr Ahmad Tejan Kabbah, President of the Republic of Sierra Leone, Trial Chamber I, 13 June 2006, see the Separate Concurring Opinion of Hon Justice Benjamin Mutanga Itoe on the Chamber Majority Decision on Motions, especially paras 57-58, 83-93, 94-180. The majority in the Appeals Chamber of the Special Court for Sierra Leone confirmed the decision of the Trial Chamber.

76 Dissenting Opinion of Hon Justice Bankole Thompson on Decisions on Motions by Moinina Fofana and Sam Hinga Norman for the Issuance of a Subpoena Ad Testificandum to H.E Alhaji Dr Ahmed Tejan Kabbah, President of the Republic of Sierra Leone (Case SCSL-04-14-T) paras 8, 15-16.

77 Dissenting Opinion of Judge Geoffrey Robertson against the decision of the Appeals Chamber of SCSL, paras 10-50.

78 *Prosecutor v Sesay, Kallon and Gbao* (Case SCSL-04-15-T) Trial Chamber I, 30 June 2008, para 21.

developed by international courts. The applicant for a subpoena requiring a person to give testimony or submit to an interview must show that three conditions are satisfied: '(i) reasonable attempts have been made to obtain the voluntary cooperation of witnesses; (ii) the prospective witness has information which can materially assist the applicant in respect of clearly identified issues relevant to the trial; and (iii) the witness's testimony must be necessary and appropriate for the conduct and fairness of the trial'.[79] Subpoenas are not issued lightly.[80] Also, information sought from prospective witnesses must not be obtainable by other means except by subpoena.[81]

The ICTY and ICTR have taken inconsistent positions on subpoenas against serving state officials. In 2005, when Slobodan Milošević requested the ICTY to issue subpoenas for a pre-testimony interview against the then serving Prime Minister of the United Kingdom (Tony Blair) and former Chancellor of Germany (Gerhard Schroder),[82] the tribunal did not issue the subpoenas. The Governments of the United Kingdom and Germany had argued that such leaders enjoyed immunity from testifying before the ICTY.[83] The Trial Chamber of ICTY rejected the application and did not address the question of immunity because it had found that conditions had

79 *Prosecutors v Bagosora et al* (Case ICTR-98-41-T) Decision on Request for Subpoenas of United Nations Officials, Request for Subpoenas of Kofi Annan, Iqbal Riza, Shaharyar Khan and Michel Hourigan Pursuant to Rule 54 of 25 August 2006 Trial Chamber I Decision of 6 October 2006 para 3; *Prosecutor v Krstic* (Case IT-98-33-A) Decision on Application for Subpoenas, Appeals Chamber of ICTY 1 July 2003, para 10; *Prosecutor v Halilović* (Case IT-01-48-AR73) Decision on the Issuance of Subpoenas, Appeals Chamber of ICTY, 21 June 2004, para 7; *Prosecutor v Bagosora et al* Decision on Request for a Subpoena, Trial Chamber of ICTR, 11 September 2006, para 5; *Prosecutor v Karemera et al* (Case ICTR-98-44-T), Decision on Defence Motion for Issuance of Subpoena to Witness T, Trial Chamber of ICTR, 8 February 2006 para 4; *Prosecutor v Bagosora et al* (Case ICTR-98-41-T) Decision on Ntabakuze Motion for Information from the UNHCR and a Meeting with one of its Officials, Trial Chamber I, 6 October 2006 paras 6 and 9 and accompanying text in fn 7 and 8 of para 6; *Prosecutor v Bagosora et al* (Case ICTR-98-41-T) Decision on Request for Cooperation of the Government of France Trial Chamber I, 6 October 2006 para 2.

80 *Prosecutor v Halilović* (Case IT-01-48-AR73) Decision on the Issuance of Subpoenas, Appeals Chamber of ICTY, 21 June 2004 para 7.

81 *Prosecutors v Bagosora et al* Decision on Request for a Subpoena, Trial Chamber of ICTR, 11 September 2006 para 6; *Prosecutor v Karemera et al* Decision on Nzirorera's *Ex Parte* Motion for Order for Interview of Defence Witnesses NZ1, NZ2 Trial Chamber of ICTR, 12 July 2006 para 12; *Prosecutor v Milošević* (Case IT-02-54-T) Decision on Assigned Counsel Application for Interview and Testimony of Tony Blair and Gerhard Schroder Trial Chamber of ICTY, 9 December 2005 paras 30 and 33. See also para 9 referring to Rule 54*bis* of the Rules of Procedure and Evidence of the ICTY.

82 *Prosecutor v Milošević* (Case IT-02-54-T) Request for Binding Order to be Issued to the Government of the United Kingdom for the Cooperation of a Witness pursuant to Rule 54bis, 18 August 2005 para 19 which requested the Trial Chamber of ICTY to '(a) order the Government of the United Kingdom to arrange for the Assigned Counsel and an Associate of the Accused to interview the United Kingdom State Official: the Prime Minister the Right Hon. Mr. Anthony Blair MP; and, (b) order the Government of the United Kingdom to make arrangements with the Assigned Counsel and an Associate for the Accused for the Witness … to give evidence in the defence stage of the trial of Slobodan Milosevic if the Accused decides to call the same as a witness'.

83 *Prosecutor v Milošević* Decision on Assigned Counsel Application for Interview and Testimony of Tony Blair and Gerhard Schroder Trial Chamber of ICTY, 9 December 2005 para 2.

not been met for the issuance of the subpoenas.[84] However, in 1997 the Trial Chamber of the ICTY (Judge MacDonald) allowed motions for the issuance of *subpoena duces tecum* against the Government of Croatia and its Defence Minister, Gojko Šušak, directing the state and its official to comply with the order.[85] Judge MacDonald held that the ICTY had jurisdiction to issue subpoenas *duces tecum* against states and individual state officials as it is an international tribunal.[86] The Chamber held that subpoenas *duces tecum* were necessary for fairness and the expedition of the trial and in order to guarantee the rights of the accused.[87] It considered that states as well as individual state officials have the same way of complying with orders from international tribunals[88] and, therefore, the fact that the person identified by an international tribunal is a state official does not preclude the issuance of subpoenas *duces tecum*.[89] The decision of the Trial Chamber was in line with Rule 54 of the Rules of Procedure and Evidence of the ICTY which allows subpoenas to be issued against individuals for the preparation or conduct of a trial.

However, the Appeals Chamber of the ICTY reviewed the decision of the Trial Chamber in the *Blaškić* case and suspended the subpoenas *duces tecum* issued against Croatia and its Defence Minister. It held rather surprisingly that subpoenas *duces tecum* cannot be issued against states.[90] The Appeals Chamber relied on the principle of state sovereignty. In its conclusion, the Appeals Chamber held that 'both under general international law and the Statute itself, Judges or Trial Chambers cannot address binding orders to State officials'.[91] It dismissed the possibility of the ICTY 'addressing subpoenas to state officials in their official capacity'.[92] By so holding, the Chamber emphasised that such state officials cannot be subjects of subpoenas.

In my opinion the Appeals Chamber was wrong and created confusion on the issue. International tribunals have inherent powers[93] to issue

84 *Prosecutor v Milošević* paras 67 and 69(b) and (c).

85 *Prosecutor v Blaškić* (Case IT-95-14-PT) Decision on the Objection of the Republic of Croatia to the issuance of Subpoenae Duces Tecum, Trial Chamber II, 18 July 1997 paras 1 and 2.

86 *Prosecutor v Blaškić* paras 24 and 31; *Prosecutor v Blaškić* (Case IT-95-14-PT) Decision on the Admissibility of the Request for Review by the Republic of Croatia of an Interlocutory Decision of a Trial Chamber (Issuance of Subpoenae Duces Tecum) and Scheduling Order, 29 July 1997, Appeals Chamber para 2 (A)-(F).

87 *Prosecutor v Blaškić* para 32.

88 *Prosecutor v Blaškić* paras 33 and 34.

89 *Prosecutor v Blaškić* para 69.

90 *Prosecutor v Blaškić* (Case IT-95-14) *Judgment on the Request of the Republic of Croatia for Review of the Decision of Trial Chamber II of 18 July 1997*, 29 October 1997 Appeals Chamber reversing the decision of the Trial Chamber 18 July 1997 para 25.

91 *Prosecutor v Blaškić* paras 43 and 44.

92 *Prosecutor v Blaškić* para 38.

93 *Prosecutor v Tadić* (Case IT-94-1-AR72) Decision on the Defence Motion for Interlocutory Appeal on Jurisdiction, 2 October 1995, whereby the Appeals Chamber of ICTY decided that it had jurisdiction to determine the validity of its own establishment.

subpoenas against private individuals and state officials alike.[94] In this regard, the decision of the Trial Chamber in *Blaškić* case must be followed as authority on subpoenas against state officials. This is supported by the decision of the Appeals Chamber of the ICTY in the subsequent developments on the law in 2003 in which it departed from its own decision in the *Blaškić* case. In *Prosecutor v Krštić*,[95] the Appeals Chamber of the ICTY stated categorically that the ICTY may compel senior state agents to testify before it, whether or not such agents witnessed the relevant facts in their official capacity. Here, the Appeals Chamber clarified that the proper procedure to call the state official to be interviewed or testify as a witness before the Tribunal is by way of issuing a *subpoena ad testificandum* under Rule 54 of the Rules of Procedure and Evidence of the ICTY. Therefore, the Appeals Chamber gave an order that a subpoena be issued against the two state officials as prospective witnesses to attend a location in Bosnia and Herzegovina at a time to be nominated by the defence in order to be interviewed.[96]

Since the majority decision in the Appeals Chamber in *Krštić* case, a number of Trial Chambers have issued 'subpoenas to state officials for both testimony and pre-testimony-interviews'.[97] In this regard, the position by the Appeals Chamber of the ICTY in *Krštić* and subsequent cases as stated above must be followed as authoritative on the question of *subpoenas duces tecum*.

For its part, the ICTR has also contributed to the confusion on the issue of subpoenas against serving state officials as the Trial Chambers of the ICTR have issued conflicting decisions. On the one hand, the Chambers have accepted that state officials can be subpoenaed to appear and testify or produce evidence before the ICTR, and on the other hand, the Chambers have held that state officials cannot be subpoenaed before the ICTR. These two positions are examined here. Since the ICTR and

94 H Fox 'Some aspects of immunity from criminal jurisdiction of the state and its officials: The *Blaškić* case' in LC Vohrah *et al* (eds) *Man's inhumanity to man: Essays on international law in Honour of Antonio Cassese* (2003) 297-307, 298.

95 *Prosecutor v Krštić* ICTY Appeal Chamber, Decision on Application for Subpoenas para 27.

96 *Prosecutor v Krštić* para 29.

97 *Prosecutor v Milošević* para 16 (referring to *Prosecutor v Martić* (Case IT-95-11-PT) Decision on the Prosecution's Additional Filing Concerning 3 June 2005 Prosecution Motion for Subpoena, 16 September 2005; *Prosecutor v Halilović* (Case IT-01-48-T) Decision on Prosecution's Motion for Issuance of a *Subpoena Ad Testificandum* and Order for Lifting *Ex Parte* Status, 8 April 2005; *Prosecutor v Strugar* (Case IT-01-42-T) *Subpoena ad Testificandum* 28 June 2004; *Prosecutor v Blagojević* (Case IT-02-60-T Order In re Defence's Request for the Issuance of *Subpoenas ad Testificandum*, Orders for Safe Conduct and an Order for the Service and Execution of the Subpoenas and Orders for Safe Conduct, 5 May 2004; *Prosecutor v Brdanin and Talić* (Case IT-99-36-T) *Subpoena ad Testificandum*, 17 July 2003; *Prosecutor v Milošević* (Case IT-02-54-T) Decision on the Prosecution's Application for Issuance of a *Subpoena ad Testificandum* for Witness K33 and Request for Judicial Assistance Directed to the Federal Republic of Yugoslavia, 5 July 2002).

ICTY share the same Appeals Chamber, it is clear that the authority stated in *Krštić* is binding even on the ICTR.

When President Paul Kagame was called by the defence and required to submit himself for an interview before the ICTR regarding his role in the genocide in Rwanda, particularly the role of the Rwandan Patriotic Front (RPF) in the downing of a plane carrying former President Habyarimana of Rwanda who died in 1994 due to the incident,[98] the Tribunal held that Kagame could not testify before it.[99] The defence had argued that RPF was responsible for the downing of the plane and that it knew of no other person to testify other than President Kagame who could provide direct and conclusive evidence on the incident as he was leading the RPF at the time.[100] The defence demonstrated that it had attempted to secure the voluntary attendance and appearance of President Kagame but that Kagame refused. There was therefore no other way of getting evidence from him except by subpoena.[101]

The Trial Chamber denied the motion in its entirety without discussing whether the defence for Nzirorera had failed to demonstrate that there was a reasonable belief that President Kagame's testimony was likely to give the relevant information sought for the defence's case. Arguably, the decision of the Trial Chamber was unreasonable because the defence for Nzirorera had made attempts to obtain information and cooperation from President Kagame but to no avail. Besides, the requested information would have been of considerable assistance to the defence's case.

However, in other instances the Trial Chamber of ICTR accepted that state officials may be compelled to testify before international criminal tribunals, most notably in the cases against Theoneste Bagosora.[102] In the *Bagosora* cases, the Trial Chamber considered it necessary that '[g]overnment officials enjoy no immunity from a subpoena, even where the subject-matter of their testimony was obtained in the course of the government service'. Consequently, since the defence had made 'reasonable efforts to secure the witness's voluntary appearance, a subpoena *ad testificandum* is both necessary and appropriate for the fair

98 *Prosecutor v Karemera, Ngirumpatse and Nzirorera* (Case ICTR-98-44-T) Decision on Joseph Nzirorera's Motions for Subpoena to Leon Mugesera and President Paul Kagame, Trial Chamber III, 19 February 2008 para 3, quoting Joseph Nzirorera's Motion for Subpoena to President Paul Kagame, filed on 28 January 2008.

99 *Prosecutor v Karemera, Ngirumpatse and Nzirorera* paras 1-16.

100 *Prosecutor v Karemera, Ngirumpatse and Nzirorera* paras 3, 12 and 14.

101 *Prosecutor v Karemera, Ngirumpatse and Nzirorera* para 12.

102 *Prosecutor v Bagosora* (Case ICTR-98-41-T) ICTR Trial Chamber, Decision on request for a subpoena for Major J Biot para 4; *Prosecutor v Bagosora et al* Decision on Defence Request to Correct Errors in Decision on Subpoena for Major Biot, Trial Chamber I, 29 August 2006 paras 1-3.

conduct of trial'.[103] The ICTR has emphasised that states, as well as their officials, may be compelled to testify before international courts.[104] In fact, the ICTR has issued a subpoena against the Rwandan Defence Minister in which it held that '[g]overnment officials enjoy no immunity from the normal legal processes available to compel the testimony of private individuals. It makes no difference whether the official's knowledge was obtained in the course of official duties or not ...'.[105] In line with this position, the ICTR has also gone a step further in ordering state officials to appear before it. For example, in 2006 the Trial Chamber issued a subpoena for Mr Ami Mpungwe, a Tanzanian ambassador, to appear before it during a trial session.[106] It should be understood that the ICTR has even issued subpoenas to international organisations such as the UNHCR.[107] Hence it may be said that state officials are not immune from subpoenas before the ICTR, in line with the requirements under international criminal law.

It may therefore be concluded that the jurisprudence of international courts indicates that subpoenas may be issued against serving state officials. The decisions of the Appeals and Trial Chambers of ICTY in *Krštić* and *Blaškić*, the ICTR's emphatic position in the *Bagosora* cases, the dissenting opinions of judges of the SCSL in the *Norman, Fofana* and *Kondewa* cases, and the decision in *Sesay*, are useful authority for this. These decisions may be used by the ICC in interpreting article 64(6)(b) of the Rome Statute progressively, in line with demands of international criminal law. The ICC should adopt this approach in the cases before it because state officials have a duty to assist international courts prosecuting international crimes. Subpoenas against state officials would guarantee rights for accused persons, help in the preparation and conduct of trials expeditiously and ensure equality of arms for both the prosecution and the accused.

103 *Prosecutor v Bagosora* Decision on request for a subpoena for Major J Biot paras 3-4, citing *Prosecutor v Krštić* Appeal Decision of the ICTY Appeals Chamber para 27, quotations omitted.

104 *Prosecutor v Bagosora et al* Decision on Kabiligi Motion for Cooperation of the Government of France and Subpoena of Former Officers, Trial Chamber I, 31 October 2006 para 2 (quoting *Prosecutor v Bagosora et al* Decision on Bagosora Defence Request for Subpoena of Ambassador Mpungwe and Cooperation of the Government of the United Republic of Tanzania, Trial Chamber, 26 August 2006 para 2).

105 *Prosecutor v Bagosora et al* Decision on Request for a Subpoena, Trial Chamber I, 11 September 2006 para 4 (referring to *Prosecutor* v *Krštić* Decision on Application for Subpoenas (AC), 1 July 2003 para 27); *Prosecutor v Milošević* Decision on Assigned Counsel Application for Interview and Testimony of Tony Blair and Gerhard Schröder (TC) para 30).

106 *Prosecutor v Bagosora et al* Decision on Request for Subpoena of Ami R Mpungwe para 6.

107 *Prosecutor v Bagosora et al* Decision on Ntabakuze Motion for Information from the UNHCR and a Meeting with one of its Officials Trial Chamber I, 6 October 2006 para 6.

5 Immunity of state officials in Africa

Currently, there is no regional framework outlawing the immunity of state officials in Africa. There is similarly no regional treaty on immunity in relation to the prosecution of international crimes in Africa. However, it should be known that impunity is prohibited: the Constitutive Act of the African Union (AU) contains key principles that reject impunity in Africa. Such principles are reflected in article 4 of the Constitutive Act. Amongst them is the principle that allows the AU to have the right to intervene in a member state pursuant to a decision of the Assembly of Heads of State and Government of the Union in respect of grave circumstances, namely: war crimes, genocide and crimes against humanity.[108]

Apart from article 4(h) of the Constitutive Act, the AU does not have an express mandate to prosecute individuals who commit international crimes in Africa, particularly at the regional level. Further, it is difficult to infer that intervention would include prosecution of perpetrators of international crimes in Africa. None of the provisions of the Constitutive Act of the AU rejects immunity, except article 4(o) which rejects impunity (and by analogy, immunity of state officials) for international crimes. Despite the rejection of impunity, it is not specifically provided in the Constitutive Act of the AU whether an African state official may be prosecuted for international crimes and therefore, in grave circumstances of genocide, war crimes and crimes against humanity, a state official may not claim immunity from prosecution for such crimes in Africa. However, based on customary and conventional international law, it may be argued that such state officials cannot benefit from immunity for international crimes.

Short of any regional legal framework on the prosecution of international crimes in Africa, one must rely on sub-regional legal instruments. In Africa, the only express sub-regional treaty that calls for prosecution of individuals who commit international crimes and rejects immunity of state officials is the Protocol for the Prevention and the Punishment of the Crime of Genocide, War Crimes and Crimes against Humanity and all forms of Discrimination,[109] signed by the International Conference on the Great Lakes Region on 29 November 2006. This is a Protocol to the Pact on Security, Stability and Development in the Great Lakes Region.[110] The Protocol draws from the Genocide Convention and the Rome Statute and calls for the prosecution and punishment of international crimes in the sub-region. It requires states in the sub-region to

108 Art 4(h) Constitutive Act of the AU.

109 Protocol for the Prevention and the Punishment of the Crime of Genocide, War Crimes and Crimes against Humanity and all forms of Discrimination, signed by the International Conference on the Great Lakes Region on 29 November 2006.

110 Pact on Security, Stability and Development in the Great Lakes Region, International Conference on the Great Lakes 2006, signed at Nairobi, Kenya.

address impunity and to take appropriate measures to bring before competent courts the perpetrators of genocide, war crimes and crimes against humanity in accordance with the Genocide Convention and the Rome Statute. Relevant is article 12 of the Protocol which provides that:

> The provisions of this chapter shall apply to all persons suspected of committing the offences to which this Protocol applies, irrespective of the official status of such persons. In particular, the official status of a Head of State or Government, or an official member of a Government or Parliament, or an elected representative or agent of a State shall in no way shield or bar their criminal liability.

Since the Protocol was adopted with the provisions of the Rome Statute in mind, it is not surprising that article 12 of the Protocol replicates the contents of article 27 of the Rome Statute. The Protocol is the only strong legal instrument in Africa at present which specifically does not recognise the immunity of state officials from prosecution for international crimes, and calls for punishment of persons who commit international crimes. It is a major sub-regional effort to curb the rising trend of international crimes by state and private individuals in Africa.

Next I examine how national laws in Africa have addressed the question of immunity of state officials. Although immunity is addressed in many constitutions of African states,[111] the focus here is only on specific laws that have been enacted to proscribe and punish international crimes. In this regard, only laws implementing the Rome Statute at domestic level, and those which do not implement the Rome Statute but address international crimes in specific African states, are considered. Only a few African states have enacted laws implementing the Rome Statute; some have enacted other laws on international crimes thereby outlawing the defence of immunity of state officials.

Rwanda enacted Organic Law 08/96 of 30 August 1996 on the Organisation of Prosecutions for Offences constituting the Crime of Genocide or Crimes against Humanity committed since 1 October 1990. In 2003, Rwanda enacted Law 33 Repressing the Crime of Genocide, Crimes against Humanity and War Crimes. Section 18 outlaws the immunity of state officials for these international crimes. The Rwandan laws on international crimes were enacted after the aftermath of the genocide committed in Rwanda in 1994. Rwanda is not a state party to the Rome Statute.

111 Sec 30 Constitution of the Republic of Zimbabwe ('Presidential immunity'); art 46 Constitution of the United Republic of Tanzania, 1977 (as amended); art 98 Constitution of the Republic of Uganda, 1995; sec 34(1)-(5) First Schedule to the Constitution of the Republic of Ghana, 1992; Constitution of the Fourth Republic of Ghana (Promulgation) Law, 1992; secs 28(1), 34*bis* and 35(1)-(3) Constitution of the Kingdom of Swaziland; art 61 Constitution of Liberia; art 48(4) Constitution of the Republic of Sierra Leone, 1991.

In 2009, Burundi amended its Penal Code to include and punish international crimes such as genocide, crimes against humanity, torture and war crimes.[112] These crimes are defined as in the Rome Statute and the Convention against Torture, 1984. Article 10 of Law 1/5 of 22 April 2009 creates universal jurisdiction for these crimes, and for acts of terrorism committed outside Burundi. These crimes are punishable with life sentences. One must note here that the Constitution protects the President from prosecution, unless the National Assembly removes immunity.[113]

Article 10 of the Constitution of the Republic of Congo, 2001, proscribes international crimes of genocide, crimes against humanity and war crimes. Section 17 of the Constitution of Malawi, 1994, prohibits acts of genocide. In 2002, South Africa enacted a law to implement the Rome Statute, and outlawed the immunity of state officials for crimes recognised under the Rome Statute.[114] This law recognise apartheid as a crime against humanity. However, a state official, Adriaan Vlok, a former Minister of Law and Order who was prosecuted in 2007 for apartheid crimes,[115] was not prosecuted under this law, and was given a suspended sentence of 10 years imprisonment following a plea bargain with the National Prosecution Authority under the Prosecution Policy, 2005.[116]

Kenya has enacted the International Crimes Act, 2008, outlawing the immunity of state officials in section 27. However, section 27 provides that any request for arrest and surrender to the ICC may not be precluded by immunity. Section 27 of this law further accords state officials with immunity before courts in Kenya.[117] This is inconsistent with article 27 of the Rome Statute. Section 18 of the Act confers universal jurisdiction to the High Court of Kenya over any person responsible for international crimes, provided that after commission the person is found in Kenya. One wonders why Kenya did not use this provision to arrest President Omar Al Bashir who visited Kenya on 27 August 2010. The Constitution of Kenya, 2010, recognises customary international law as part of the law of Kenya. Article 2(5) of the Constitution of Kenya requires that the immunity of a state official should not prevail over Kenya's duty to prosecute arising from any ratified treaty outlawing immunity. Hence, immunity cannot exist for

112 Arts 195 -198 Law 1/5 of 22 April 2009, amending the Penal Code of Burundi.

113 Arts 117 and 118 Constitution of Burundi, 2004.

114 Art 4 Implementation of the Rome Statute of the International Criminal Court Act 27 of 2002.

115 *S v Johannes Velde van der Merwe, Adriaan Johannes Vlok, Christoffel Lodewikus Smith, Gert Jacobus Louis Hosea and Hermanus Johannes van Staden* Plea and Sentencing Agreement in Terms of Section 105A of Act 51 of 1977 (as amended) 17 August 2007.

116 National Prosecution Authority *Prosecution Policy* 1 December 2005, Appendix A 'Prosecution Policy and Directives Relating to the Prosecution of Offences Emanating from Conflicts of the Past and Which were Committed on or before 11 May 1994'.

117 Sec 27 International Crimes Act, 2008; A Okuta 'National legislation for prosecution of international crimes in Kenya' (2009) 7 *Journal of International Criminal Justice* 1063-1076, 1073.

any state official charged with international crimes recognised under the Rome Statute or under the International Crimes Act.

In Burkina Faso there is a law implementing the Rome Statute, thereby conferring jurisdiction to courts of Burkina Faso over international crimes.[118] Articles 16, 17, 18 and 19 of the law prohibit and punish genocide, crimes against humanity and war crimes as defined in the Rome Statute. Immunity of state officials in respect of these crimes is outlawed in article 7 compatible with article 27 of the Rome Statute. Additionally, article 39 requires that all persons arrested should be transferred to the ICC without distinction as to their official capacity. The law is very strongly against immunity of state officials and is therefore commendable.

In Niger, the Penal Code 61-27 of 15 July 1961 was amended in 2003 by Law 2003-025 of 13 June 2003 to introduce breaches of international humanitarian law. These include crimes against humanity, genocide and war crimes.[119] This law punishes genocide and crimes against humanity with the death sentence. War crimes may be punished by the death sentence or life imprisonment, depending on the number of persons killed. Immunity is outlawed in article 208.7. Further, the law empowers courts in Niger to punish these international crimes on the basis of universal jurisdiction, regardless of where the crime was committed or the nationality of the victims.

Uganda, which is a state party to the Rome Statute, enacted the International Criminal Court Act, 2010.[120] The Act was assented to by the President on 25 May 2010 and came into effect on 26 June 2010. The Act incorporates the Rome Statute into Ugandan law and gives effect to the Rome Statute.[121] It confers universal jurisdiction to Ugandan courts over international crimes recognised in the Rome Statute.[122] Such crimes include genocide, war crimes and crimes against humanity. These crimes are defined under sections 7, 8 and 9 of the Act in the same way as in the Rome Statute. Immunity of state officials is outlawed under section 25(1) and (2) of the Act in respect of the crimes within the ICC jurisdiction. However, one must also note the immunity provisions under article 98(5) of the Constitution of Uganda, 1995. Although immunity could be granted to the President under the Constitution, it is clear that the inconsistency between article 98(5) of the Constitution and sections 25(1) and (2) of the International Criminal Court Act, 2010, may be resolved by section 24(6)

118 Law 052-2009/AN of 31 December 2009 relating to the Determination of the Competence and Procedure in Implementing the Rome Statute of the International Criminal Court by Courts of Burkina Faso, Decree 2009-894/PRES 31 December 2009.
119 Arts 208.1, 208.2, 208.3 of Law 2003- 025 of 2003 amending the Penal Code of Niger, Law 61-27 of 15 July 1961.
120 International Criminal Court Act 11 of 2010 (Uganda).
121 Sec 2.
122 Secs 17 and 18.

of the Act which requires the Minister to consult the ICC and that it is the ICC which must decide whether there is any contradiction. Since the ICC has been given the power to determine this it is obvious that presidential immunity cannot prevail in respect of international crimes under the jurisdiction of the ICC and courts in Uganda.

Despite its monist nature, Senegal enacted a law implementing the Rome Statute. The country has also amended its Constitution in article 9 to confer jurisdiction to its courts to prosecute persons who commit international crimes, namely, genocide, war crimes and crimes against humanity.Senegal further amended its Code of Criminal Procedure in article 669 to allow universal jurisdiction for international crimes. The effect of these amendments in the Constitution and Code of Criminal Procedure is to allow for the retrospective application of Senegal's penal laws to persons who had in the past committed international crimes. This is due to the presence in Senegal of Hissène Habré, former president of Chad, who committed crimes against humanity in Chad and who enjoys asylum in Senegal. Following the new law courts in Senegal can prosecute Habré. This is contrary to what the Senegalese courts had held in 2005 when they decided that they could not prosecute Habré for crimes committed in Chad and that Habré enjoyed the immunity of a state official for acts of torture committed in Chad.[123]

Ethiopia became a state party to the Genocide Convention in 1949. It is not a state party to the Rome Statute. The Constitution of Ethiopia, 1995, prohibits and punishes the international crimes of genocide and crimes against humanity.[124] The Criminal Code of Ethiopia, 2005,[125] which repealed the Penal Code of Ethiopia of 1957[126] and came into force on 9 May 2005, prohibits and punishes genocide, crimes against humanity and war crimes.[127] The new law envisages the death penalty and rigorous punishment ranging from five years to life imprisonment in some cases.

Article 4 of the Criminal Code of Ethiopia, 2005, outlaws immunity for state officials who commit international crimes. It requires all accused persons to be treated equally regardless of their rank. It states that the immunity accorded by international law and Constitution apply to state officials of Ethiopia. Authorities in Ethiopia prosecuted former state official, Mengistu Haile-Mariam, for genocide and crimes against humanity[128] under the old law, the Penal Code of Ethiopia, 1957. They

123 *Belgium v Senegal* para 5.

124 Art 28 Constitution of Ethiopia, 1995.

125 Proclamation 414/2004 Criminal Code of the Federal Democratic Republic of Ethiopia, 9 May 2005.

126 Penal Code of the Empire of Ethiopia of 1957, Proclamation 158 of 1957 (repealed).

127 Criminal Code of Ethiopia, 2005: Title II, Chapter I Crimes in violation of International Law, art 269 (genocide), arts 270-273, 276, 277, 279-283, (war crimes).

128 On the trial of Mengistu, see Y Haile-Mariam 'The quest for justice and reconciliation: The International Criminal Tribunal for Rwanda and the Ethiopian High Court' (1999) 22 *Hastings International and Comparative Law Review* 675-679.

interpreted article 4 thereof (which is in *pari materia* with the 2005 law) to outlaw the immunity of state officials as raised by Mengistu. The High Court and Federal Supreme Court sentenced Mengistu to death for genocide.[129] In the judgment, the High Court interpreted the Genocide Convention and stated that the courts in Ethiopia were authorised to prosecute Mengistu for the crime of genocide[130] despite the fact that acts of genocide found in article 281 of the Penal Code of Ethiopia, 1957, had exceeded and contravened the requirements under the Genocide Convention.[131]

The Democratic Republic of the Congo (DRC), a state party to the Rome Statute since 2002, is currently considering the enactment of a law implementing the Rome Statute. A Bill to that effect is yet to be passed by Senate. The DRC has had two draft Bills on the implementation of the Rome Statute: the first drafted in 2001 and the second drafted in 2002. In this section, both draft Bills are considered.

In 2001, the DRC prepared the Implementation of the Statute of the International Criminal Court Draft, aimed at integrating the norms of the Rome Statute into the Congolese law following the ratification of the Rome Statute on 30 March 2002. It also required judicial cooperation between the ICC and Congolese institutions. The prosecution and punishment of international crimes recognised under the Rome Statute were aspects that the draft law was meant to address.

Article 9 of the 2001 Draft Legislation provides that it 'applies to all in like manner, with no distinctions made based on official capacity'. It expressly states that the 'immunities or rules of special procedures associated with persons of official capacity, by virtue of internal or international law, do not prevent the judge from exercising his or her competence with regards to the person in question'.[132] In October 2002, the DRC drafted a bill to replace the draft Bill of 2001, called Draft Law Implementing the Rome Statute of the International Criminal Court, Draft 2 of October 2002.[133] The 2000 Draft Bill has not yet been promulgated into law. Its purpose is to prosecute and punish those crimes addressed by the Rome Statute, and to regulate judicial cooperation with the ICC.

129 On the analysis of Mengistu trial, see FK Tiba 'The Mengistu genocide trial in Ethiopia' (2007) 5 *Journal of International Criminal Justice* 513-528.

130 ILDC 555(ET 1995), 77.

131 *Special Prosecutor v Col Haile-Mariam and 173 Others* Preliminary Objections, Criminal File 1/87, Decision of Meskerem 29, 1988 EC (GC).

132 Art 9 Implementation of the Statute of the International Criminal Court Draft 1 of 2001. The draft law is annexed in GM Musila *Between rhetoric and action: The politics, processes and practice of the ICC's work in the DRC* (2009) 91-113.

133 Draft Law Implementing the Rome Statute of the International Criminal Court 2 of October 2002, modified by the convocation organised by the Ministry of Justice of the Democratic Republic of the Congo on 21 to 23 October 2002 in Kinshasa and on 24 and 25 October 2002 in Lubumbashi. The Draft Law is also annexed in Musila (as above).

Article 10 of the 2002 Draft Bill states that the law shall apply equally to all persons with no distinction based on their official position. In particular, official capacity as the head of state or government, a member of a government or parliament, an elected representative or official of a state shall in no case exempt a person from criminal responsibility in the eyes of this law, nor shall it constitute in of itself a ground for reduction of sentence. The provision provides further that those 'immunities or those special procedural rules that may attach to the official capacity of a person, pursuant to the law or under international law shall not bar the jurisdictions from exercising their competent jurisdiction over that person'.[134]

6 Conclusion

This chapter has discussed the immunity of state officials – from the persective of customary international law, conventional international law and national law – with a particular focus on selected African national jurisdictions. Although a few African states have outlawed the immunity of state officials, others still recognise it. South Africa, Uganda, Senegal, Burkina Faso, Niger, Kenya, Congo, Burundi, Rwanda and Ethiopia are models for Africa on this.

International and national courts which have prosecuted state officials have faced challenges. Such challenges include jurisdictional matters and the enforcement of warrants of arrest and subpoenas against sitting state officials. Despite these challenges there is hope for the future because the statutes of international courts and international conventions prove clarity on the prosecution and punishment of international crimes. International law and courts have long held that the immunity of state officials is not a defence from holding state officials criminally responsible for international crimes. Neither is it a ground for mitigation of punishment for such officials convicted of international crimes.

However, state officials may still escape prosecution before foreign national courts, even for international crimes, as decided by the ICJ in the *Arrest Warrant* case in 2002. Nevertheless, the precedent from Ethiopia indicates that Ethiopia's national courts were able to prosecute former state official of Ethiopia, Mengistu Haile Mariam. They sentenced him to death, albeit *in absentia*. National jurisprudence on the immunity of state officials is still developing and would have a future impact as Africa is moving towards adopting a treaty to enable the African Court of Justice and Human Rights to establish a Chamber with jurisdiction over persons who commit international crimes in Africa, including state officials.

134 Art 10.

International courts have held differently regarding the immunity of state officials in respect of *subpoenas duces tecum* and *subpoenas ad testificandum* – where international crimes are at the core of discussion. This may be observed in the judgments of the Appeals Chamber of the ICTY in the *Blaškić* case in 1997 and the Trial and Appeals Chambers of the SCSL in the *Norman, Fofana* and *Kondewa* case. The correct authority is that which is stated in the *Sesay* case by the Trial Chamber of SCSL in 2008, the *Krštić* case by the Appeals Chamber of the ICTY in 2003, the Trial Chamber of the ICTR in the *Bagosora* cases, and the Trial Chamber of the ICTY in the *Blaškić* case in 1997. These precedents should assist the ICC in interpreting article 64(6)(b) of the Rome Statute. We may therefore conclude that state officials are not free from prosecution and the issuance of subpoenas. They have a duty, like private individuals, to cooperate and assist international courts. Subpoenas against sitting state officials may ensure the rights of accused persons and assist in the preparation and conduct of trials before international courts. As long as there is no immunity for state officials from prosecution or punishment for international crimes, there is equally no immunity from subpoenas being issued against state officials.

PART II: INTERNATIONAL COURTS AND PROSECUTION OF INTERNATIONAL CRIMES IN AFRICA

CHAPTER 3

THE CONTRIBUTION OF THE INTERNATIONAL CRIMINAL TRIBUNAL FOR RWANDA TO THE DEVELOPMENT OF INTERNATIONAL CRIMINAL LAW

*George William Mugwanya**

1 Introduction

This chapter explores the development of the international criminal law corpus through the International Criminal Tribunal for Rwanda (ICTR or Tribunal) since its inception in 1994. Established soon after the International Criminal Tribunal for the former Yugoslavia (ICTY), the ICTR has adjudicated many cases of genocide and crimes against humanity since its creation. It has also handled a number of cases dealing with violations of laws relating to internal armed conflict – article 3 Common to the Geneva Conventions, 1949, and Protocol II Additional to the Geneva Conventions, 1977. In adjudicating serious international crimes, the ICTR, like its sister tribunal, the ICTY, confronted multiple novel legal issues never before elaborated in international law, and without or with limited precedents to draw from. From its first cases, notably *Prosecutor v Akayesu*[1] and *Prosecutor v Kambanda*,[2] the Tribunal has implemented a process of interpreting and giving content to substantive, evidentiary and procedural aspects of international criminal law. It has engendered a jurisprudence the scope and legacy of which were unimaginable at the time of its creation.

Since its inception, overall, the Tribunal has confronted and addressed complex legal questions with prudence and creativity, engendering an impressive jurisprudence enriching the corpus of international criminal law. This chapter addresses only a few substantive, procedural and

* LL.B (Makerere); Postgraduate Diploma in Legal Practice, School of Post-graduate Studies, Law Development Centre (Uganda); LL.M (Pretoria); LL.M (Birmingham); LL.D (Notre Dame). Senior Appeals Counsel, UN International Criminal Tribunal for Rwanda; Advocate of Uganda's Courts of Judicature; formerly Senior Lecturer, Faculty of Law, Makerere University. The views expressed here are the author's personal views.

1 *Prosecutor v Akayesu* (Case ICTR-96-4-T) Judgment 2 September 1998.

2 *Prosecutor v Kambanda* (Case ICTR-97-23-S) Judgment and sentence 4 September 1998.

evidentiary areas of international criminal justice, with particular focus on those where the ICTR has pioneered the development of international law, breaking new grounds and moving the law forward. Further, the chapter addresses instances where the ICTR has offered important clarification or elaboration of existing jurisprudence, or applied it to novel or challenging factual circumstances.

2 Genocide: Group victims, physical and mental elements

Since the adoption of the ground-breaking and first binding United Nation's (UN) international human rights and penal treaty, the Convention on the Prevention and Punishment of the Crime of Genocide (Genocide Convention) of 1948,[3] no international tribunal envisaged by the Genocide Convention was established. The crime of genocide and other acts of genocide which the Convention proscribes were neither interpreted nor applied until the ICTR in 1998 adjudicated and issued judgments in the *Akayesu* and *Kambanda* cases. As generally predicted in academic and other efforts, for instance in the 1989 proceedings of renowned experts in international law,[4] multiple difficulties would confront the interpretation and application of the Genocide Convention.

In pioneering the adjudication, and being the first international tribunal to find an accused guilty of genocide, the ICTR confronted and addressed multiple issues relating to the group-victims of genocide (groups protected by the Genocide Convention) and the physical and mental elements of the crime of genocide.

Under article 2 of the ICTR's Statute, which is a verbatim reproduction of article 2 of the Genocide Convention (and is also similar to the provisions of articles 4 and 6 and of the Statutes of the ICTY and the International Criminal Court (ICC) respectively), certain enumerated acts (*actus reus*)[5] constitute genocide if committed with the intent to destroy in whole or in part a *racial, national, ethnical or religious group* as such. The identified groups are the groups that the prevention, prosecution and punishment of the crime of genocide are intended to protect – also called the 'group victims of genocide'. The ICTR Statute, like the Genocide Convention, and Statutes of the ICTY and ICC, does not identify criteria

3 Convention on the Prevention and Punishment of the Crime of Genocide, 9 December 1948 and entered into force on 12 January 1951.

4 C Bassiouni 'Genocide: The convention, domestic laws and state responsibility, prospects for implementation of the Genocide Convention under state laws' (1989) 83 *Proceedings of the American Society of International Law* 314.

5 Namely: killing members of the group; causing serious bodily or mental harm to members of the group; deliberately inflicting on the group conditions of life calculated to bring about the group's destruction; imposing measures intended to prevent births within the group; and forcibly transferring children of the group to another group.

for defining these protected groups. Beginning with the *Akayesu* judgment – the first judgment on genocide by an international criminal tribunal – the ICTR pioneered the elaboration of the group victims of genocide.

While some aspects of the jurisprudence engendered by the ICTR are contentious, the ICTR's jurisprudence constitutes a foundational attempt at elucidating a complex notion in the absence of existing precedents or extensive scholarly literature. The *Akayesu* case found that the group notion refers to stable groups constituted in a permanent fashion and whose membership is determined by birth in a continuous and irremediable manner.[6] Moreover, the groups which are protected are not limited to the enumerated four, but extend to any stable and permanent group.[7] Arguably, these positions raise controversy. With the possible exception of a racial group, the other three enumerated groups are all neither permanent nor stable.[8] Indeed, international law recognises that persons can always change their membership of those groups.[9] In light of the terms of the Genocide Convention, protection extends only to the four groups, and not to every stable and permanent group.

It is worth noting that the ICTR's judgments subsequent to *Akayesu* appear to have hedged *Akayesu's* position that the intention of the provisions of the Genocide Convention (which the statutes of the ICTR, ICTY and ICC mirror) was patently to protect only stable and permanent groups. Many of these judgments construe the tests of stability and permanence identified in *Akayesu* as mere presumptions which seem to suggest rather than stating something patently, while others seek to rely on objective and subjective perspectives to the definition of the notion.[10] Arguably, the positions taken by subsequent judgments created room for the clarification of the legal position taken in *Akayesu* and the further development of the jurisprudence.

The ICTR, notably in *Akayesu*, may also be credited for elaborating some objective criteria defining each of the four groups protected by the proscription of the crime of genocide. Its contribution also reflects a

6 *Prosecutor v Akayesu* para 511.

7 *Prosecutor v Akayesu* para 516

8 WA Schabas *Genocide in international law: The crime of crimes* (2001) 132-133; GW Mugwanya *The crime of genocide in international law: Appraising the contribution of the UN Tribunal for Rwanda* (2007) 70.

9 See eg Arts 15(a) and 18 Universal Declaration of Human Rights, 1948 GA Res 217A(III) UN Doc A/810; art 9(1) European Convention for the Protection of Human Rights and Fundamental Freedoms; art 20(3) American Convention of Human Rights. On controversies regarding the right to change one's religion, see P Taylor *Freedom of religion, UN and European human rights law and practice* (2006).

10 *Prosecutor v Rutaganda* (Case ICTR-96-3) Judgment and Sentence 6 December 1999 paras 57-58; *Prosecutor v Musema* (Case ICTR-96-13-T) Judgment and Sentence 27 January 2000 para 162; W Schabas 'The crime of genocide in the jurisprudence of the International Criminal Tribunals for the Former Yugoslavia and Rwanda' in F Horst *et al* (eds) *International and national prosecutions of crimes under international law: Current developments* (2001) 451; Mugwanya (n 8 above) 67-107.

pioneering effort in an area without or with very limited existing precedents. According to the ICTR, an ethnic group is a group 'whose membership shares a common language or culture'.[11] A racial group is based on hereditary physical traits often identified with a geographical region, irrespective of linguistic, cultural, national or religious factors.[12] A national group is 'a collection of people who are perceived to share a legal bond based on a common citizenship, coupled with reciprocity of rights and duties'.[13] With respect to a religious group, the ICTR took the position that it is 'one whose members share the same religion, denomination or mode of worship'.[14]

The ICTR's positions have generated controvercy. For instance, it has been argued that all the four groups are interrelated and that the drafters of the provisions of the Genocide Convention, which the ICTR Statute mirrors, did not seek to assign individual meanings to each of the four groups.[15] Nevertheless, the ICTR's jurisprudence constitutes an important effort underscoring the idea that group victims of genocide are not abstract, but must have a real existence. Although not offering definitions of the elements of each of the four groups, the International Criminal Court, invoking *inter alia* the *Akayesu* precedent, has recently stressed that:[16]

> [The] targeted group must have particular positive characteristics (national, ethnic, racial or religious), and not a lack thereof. In this regard it is important to highlight that, the drafters of the 1948 Genocide Convention gave close attention to the positive identification of groups with specific distinguishing well established, some said immutable, characteristics. It is therefore, a matter of who the targeted people are, and not who they are not. As a result, the majority considers that negative definitions of the targeted group do not suffice for the purpose of article 6 of the Statute.

Furthermore, in an apparent endorsement of the *Akayesu* and other ICTR precedents on the importance of identifying positive criteria defining each of the groups, the ICC observed that while the three target groups (the Far, Masalit and Zaghawa) shared Sudanese nationality and Islamic religion, each of them possessed its language, tribal customs and its own traditional links to its lands, and each thus constituted a distinct ethnic group.[17] From the ICTR's jurisprudence, which appears to inspire the ICC, it is clear that the proscription of the crime of genocide protects groups with real

11 *Prosecutor v Akayesu* para 513; *Prosecutor v Kayishema and Ruzindana* (Case ICTR-95-1-T) Judgment and Sentence, 21 May 1999 para 98.
12 *Prosecutor v Akayesu* para 514; *Prosecutor v Kayishema and Ruzindana* (as above).
13 *Prosecutor v Akayesu* para 512; *Prosecutor v Kayishema and Ruzindana.*
14 *Prosecutor v Akayesu* para 515.
15 Schabas (n 8 above) 113; Mugwanya (n 8 above) 73-85.
16 *Prosecutor v Al Bashir* (Case ICC-02/05-01/09) Decision on the Prosecution's Application for a Warrant of Arrest against Omar Hassan Ahmad Al Bashir, 3 April 2009 para 135. For a critique of the ICC's statement that 'negative' definitions cannot suffice for purposes of delineating protected groups, see generally Mugwanya (n 8 above) 72-77 & 92-101.
17 *Prosecutor v Al Bashir* para 137.

existence by their possession of a particular group identity, and not abstract groups, or groups entirely defined by subjective criteria.[18] Subjective criteria include, for instance, a situation where a group is entirely defined or identified by the perceptions of the perpetrator of the crime of genocide.

The ICTR also elucidated the definitions and scope of the physical and mental elements of the crime of genocide. Its jurisprudence is particularly noteworthy with respect to the physical elements (*actus reus*) of the crime that are generally worded. These include causing serious bodily or mental harm to members of the group, deliberately inflicting on the group conditions of life calculated to bring about the group's destruction and imposing measures intended to prevent births within the group. The ICTR has taken the position that several criminal acts are encompassed in these physical elements of genocide, one of which is rape.[19] The Tribunal's elucidation of rape and sexual violence as acts of rape are discussed below.

Finally, the ICTR may be credited for its elaboration of the psychological element of the crime of genocide in international law. The ICTR's jurisprudence establishes that to be guilty of the crime, any of the enumerated physical acts (*actus reus*, eg killing members of the group) must be perpetrated with specific intent to destroy a group in whole or in part. In other words, in addition to intending that the *actus reus* occurs, the accused must also intend to destroy the group in whole or in part. As explained by *Akayesu,* special or specific intent are required for the crime of genocide,[20]

> [i]s the specific intention, required as a constitutive element of the crime, which demands that the perpetrator clearly seeks to produce the acts charged. Thus, the special intent in the crime of genocide lies in the intent to destroy, in whole or in part, a national, ethnical, racial or religious group as such.

Proof of the specific intent of genocide is a complex task, given that perpetrators will rarely plead guilty to the crime and explain their mental orientation to the court. Through its jurisprudence, the ICTR has explained that establishing specific intent of genocide requires the examination of a totality of factors and circumstances. These include the general context, the general political doctrine which gave rise to the acts, the methodical way of planning, the perpetration of other culpable acts systematically directed against the same group, the scale of the atrocities perpetrated or the number of victims affected, the systematic manner of the killings or targeting of victims on account of their membership of a

18 *Prosecutor v Stakić* (Case IT-97-24-A) Judgment paras 20-28.
19 Mugwanya (n 8 above) 115-121.
20 *Prosecutor v Akayesu* para 498.

particular group, the repetition of destructive or discriminatory acts, and the use of derogatory language towards the targeted group.[21]

3 Rape and sexual violence as genocide

In the *Akayesu* judgment, for the first time in international law, an international court construed and applied the crimes of rape and sexual violence in an international context, finding that rape and sexual violence can constitute acts of genocide. Therefore, when committed with specific intent to destroy a group in whole or in part, rape and sexual violence constitute genocide.[22] The initial indictment against Akayesu had not charged rape and sexual violence, but during the early stages of the trial many witnesses recounted acts of rape and sexual violence. The Judges permitted an amendment to the indictment to add a count of a crime against humanity (rape). The amendment alleged that Tutsi women, who had sought refuge at the *Bureau Communal*, were repeatedly subjected to sexual violence, and that Akayesu knew and encouraged these acts of sexual violence. The evidence adduced in support of these allegations was overwhelming.

In addition to finding Akayesu culpable for rape as a crime against humanity, the Trial Chamber, of its own accord, made an important pronouncement, namely, that the same acts of rape and sexual violence underpinning crimes against humanity also constituted genocide. Article 2 of the ICTR Statute, like the Genocide Convention, does not expressly identify rape and sexual violence as acts of genocide, but includes two important *actus reuses*, namely, 'imposing measures intended to prevent births within a group' and 'deliberately inflicting on the group conditions of life calculated to bring about its physical destruction'.

In the Chamber's view, rape and sexual violence met the above two requirements or forms of *actus reus* of genocide. With respect to 'deliberately inflicting on the group measures intended to bring about its physical destruction', the Chamber observed as follows:[23]

21 *Prosecutor v Akayesu* para 523; *Prosecutor v Kayishema and Ruzindana* para 93; *Prosecutor v Musema* para 166; *Prosecutor v Kayishema and Ruzindana* (Case ICTR-95-1-A) Judgment (Reasons) 1 June 2001 para 159; *Prosecutor v Rutaganda* Case (ICTR-96-3-A) Judgment, 26 May 2003 para 525. For the ICTY see *Prosecutor v Kristić* (Case IT-98-33-A) Appeals Judgment, 19 April 2004 para 34; *Prosecutor v Jelišić* (Case IT-95-10-A) Judgment 5 July 2001 para 47. For a critique of the ICTR's position to specific intent (which has been described as the 'purpose-based approach to individual genocidal intent) see generally C Kress 'The Darfur Report and genocidal intent' (2005) *Journal of International Criminal Justice* 562-570; Greewalt, 'Rethinking genocidal intent: The case of a knowledge-based interpretation' (1999) *Columbia Law Review* 2259, 2288 (advocating for a knowledge-based approach); Mugwanya (n 8 above) 158-159.

22 *Prosecutor v Akayesu* para 731.

23 *Prosecutor v Akeyesu* para 731.

> Rape and sexual violence [...] constitute genocide in the same way as any other act as long as they were committed with the specific intent to destroy, in whole or in part, a particular group, targeted as such. Indeed rape and sexual violence certainly constitutes *(sic)* infliction of serious bodily and mental harm on the victims and are even [...] one of the worst ways of inflict (*sic*) harm on the victims as he or she suffers both bodily and mental harm. In light of all the evidence before it, the Chamber is satisfied that the acts of rape and sexual violence described above, were committed solely against Tutsi women, many of whom were subjected to the worst public humiliation, mutilated, and raped several times, often in the public, in the Bureau Communal premises or in other public places, and often by more than one assailant. These rapes resulted in physical and psychological destruction of Tutsi women, their families and their communities. Sexual violence was an integral part of the process of destruction, specifically targeting Tutsi women and specifically contributing to their destruction and to the destruction of the Tutsi group as a whole.

In relation to the second *actus reus* of 'imposing measures intended to prevent births within a group', the Chamber held that rape met its requirements. The Chamber held that rape can lead to the destruction of a group, in whole or in part, pronouncing that[24]

> measures intended to prevent births within the group may be physical, but can also be mental. For instance, rape can be a measure intended to prevent births when the person raped refuses subsequently to procreate, in the same way a group can be led, through threats or trauma, not to procreate.

Moreover, the Chamber considered the specific cultural and other circumstances obtaining in many African societies, including Rwanda, underlining that indeed in those contexts, rape can be used to destroy a group. The Chamber held that[25]

> [i]n patriarchal societies, where membership of a group is determined by the identity of the father, an example of a measure intended to prevent births within a group is the case where, during rape, a woman of the said group is deliberately impregnated by a man of another group, with the intent to have her give birth to a child who will consequently not belong to its mother's group.

In making the above pronouncements, overall, the ICTR provides limited sources to support its positions, or relies on secondary sources of international law, other than underscoring the terms of its Statute construed according to their natural meaning and their context as generally required under international law.[26]

24 *Prosecutor v Akeyesu* para 508.
25 *Prosecutor v Akayesu* para 507.
26 Art 31 Vienna Convention on the Law of Treaties (1969) UN Doc A/Conf39/27 289.

Indisputably, the absence of detailed prior judicial precedents underlines the difficulties the ICTR had to surmount. Nevertheless, its approaches appear to properly construe the provisions of the Statute,[27] which are a verbatim reproduction of the provisions of the Genocide Convention. The two actus reuses of genocide applied by the Chamber, ie of 'deliberately inflicting on the group conditions of life calculated to bring about its physical destruction,' and 'imposing measures intended to prevent births within the group', appear to encompass a wide range of criminal conduct.

Rape and sexual violence fall under conduct envisaged by the provisions. The Chamber's overall definitions of the two *actus reuses* demonstrate its conviction that the criminal acts encompassed in the two *actus reuses* are broad. In defining the first one, the ICTR underscored that it encompasses 'methods of destruction by which the perpetrator does not immediately kill the members of the group, but which, ultimately, seek their physical destruction',[28] or, as the subsequent ICTR judgment explained, 'all circumstances which will lead to slow death'.[29] With respect to the second one, the Chamber held that it encompasses a multiplicity of acts, including rape, sexual mutilation, sterilization, forced birth control, separation of the sexes, prohibition of marriages and deliberate impregnation with intent that a child of the perpetrator's group is born.[30]

The ICTR's jurisprudence will likely inspire approaches at the International Criminal Court, whose applicable law does not define the conduct encompassed in the two *actus reuses* as closed. With respect to the first one, the ICC's Elements of Crimes provides that 'conditions of life' may include, but is not necessarily restricted to deliberate deprivations of resources indispensable for survival, such as food and medical services, or systematic expulsions. In drafting the ICC Statute, delegates rejected a proposal by the United States that to be culpable, results must occur (ie that the group or part of it must be destroyed).[31] In rejecting the proposal, the French commentary relied on the *Akayesu* judgment. With respect to 'preventing births', the ICC's Elements of Crimes does not enumerate the acts covered, but broadly provides that the perpetrator must have imposed certain measures upon one or more persons, with the intent to prevent births within the group. The ICC delegates also rejected a proposal by the United States that to be culpable, the intended results must occur.[32]

27 For a critique of the ICTR's approach, see eg Schabas (n 10 above) 466 ('Such views may be seem exaggerated, because it is unrealistic and perhaps absurd to believe that a group can be destroyed in whole or in part by rape and similar crimes. In any case, this is not what the [Genocide] Convention provisions demands').

28 *Prosecutor v Akayesu* para 505; *Prosecutor v Kayishema and Ruzindana* para 115.

29 *Prosecutor v Kayishema and Ruzindana*, as above.

30 *Prosecutor v Akayesu* paras 507-508; Mugwanya (n 8 above) 118-119.

31 K Kittichaisaree *International criminal law* (2001) 79.

32 Kittichaisaree, as above, 81.

The ICTR's legacy may be demonstrated in the first ICC genocide case, brought against President Omar Al Bashir of Sudan.[33] The ICC Prosecutor, in differing from the conclusion of the UN International Commission of Inquiry on Darfur[34] that there was insufficient evidence to conclude the existence of a state policy to commit genocide, is indicting Omar Al Bashir with genocide, among other crimes. In establishing that there is reasonable ground to believe that the defendant acted with genocidal intent, the Prosecutor presented evidence attesting, *inter alia*, to the scale and manner in which the attacks have been perpetrated, and the staggering proof of sexual violence against the targeted group.[35] The Appeals Chamber of the ICC overturned a Pre-Trial Chamber's decision[36] that the Prosecutor had not established reasonable grounds to believe that Omar Al Bashir committed genocide as required under article 58 of the ICC Statute.[37] The effect of this judgment is that the Pre-Trial Chamber of the ICC had to reconsider the Prosecutor's application on the issue of genocide. As a result, on 12 July 2010, Pre-Trial Chamber I rendered a decision authorising a charge of genocide and the issuance of an arrest warrant for Omar Al Bashir in respect of genocide, in addition to crimes against humanity and war crimes.[38]

4 The elements of the crime of rape in international law

The ICTR has elucidated the elements defining rape in international law. Its approach enriches the understanding of the crime of rape in international law and is pivotal in the fight against rape and sexual violence. Compared with the approach to defining rape pursued in many national legal systems, which over-emphasises somewhat mechanist and restrictive details (for instance, that the non-consensual sexual intercourse must involve only a specific private body part of the perpetrator which must physically penetrate the victim's private organ) the ICTR's approach advances international jurisprudence which may also inform national legal systems.

33 *Situation in Darfur, The Sudan* (Case ICC-02/05) Summary of Prosecutor's Application Under Article 58, July 14, 2008 (Prosecutor's Darfur Application).

34 *Report of the International Commission of Inquiry into Darfur to the United Nations Secretary-General*, 25 January 2005, http://www.un.org/news/dh/sudan/com_inq_darfur.pdf (accessed on 15 June 2010).

35 Prosecutor's Darfur Application (n 34 above) paras 21-23 & 45-60.

36 *Prosecutor v Al Bashir* Warrant of Arrest for Omar Hassan Ahmed Al Bashir, 4 March 2009.

37 *The Prosecutor v Al Bashir* (Case ICC-02/05-01/09-OA) Judgment on the Appeal of the Prosecutor Against the Decision on the Prosecutor's Application for a Warrant of Arrest Against Omar Hassan Ahmad Al Bashir, 3 February 2010.

38 *Prosecutor v Al Bashir* (Case ICC-02/05-01/09) Second Decision on the Prosecution's Application for a Warrant of Arrest (Public) 12 July 2010 paras 1- 44.

The *Akayesu* judgment, in a pioneering elucidation of the law, underscored that, 'rape is a form of aggression and [...] the central elements of the crime of rape cannot be captured in a mechanical description of objects and body parts'.[39] This judgment thus elaborated an important principle in international law that rape is committed not only where there is non-consensual penetration of the victim's vagina or anus by the perpetrator's private organ, but also non-consensual insertion of objects and/or use of bodily orifices not considered to be intrinsically sexual. This approach is critical in achieving the effective protection of the sexual integrity of people by punishing multiple forms of its invasion. In further elaboration of this principle, *Akayesu* defines rape as '[a] physical invasion of a sexual nature, committed on a person under circumstances which are coercive. Sexual violence, which includes rape, is considered to be any act of a sexual nature which is committed on a person under circumstances which are coercive'.[40]

The above pioneering precedent has been endorsed in subsequent judgments, including those at the ICTY.[41] The ICTR's approach to the 'non-consent' requirement of the crime of rape is also ground-breaking. Where sexual intercourse occurs with the consent of the victim, there is no rape. In determining whether there was consent or not, the ICTR elucidated an approach that rejects a mechanistic construction of the element. The absence of consent, according to the ICTR, need not take physical force – i.e. the perpetrator need not use physical force, but a court must closely examine all surrounding circumstances to determine whether the victim consented or voluntarily submitted to the sexual act. The ICTR has underscored that, even if no physical force is used, the presence of coercive circumstances negates consent. It has held that:[42]

> Threats, intimidation, extortion and other forms of duress which prey on fear or desperation may constitute coercion and coercion may be inherent in certain circumstances, such as armed conflict or the military presence of *Interahamwe*[43] among refugee Tutsi women at the Bureau Communal.

The ICTR's approach above gives the element of 'non-consent' its proper content. The approach transcends mechanistic constructions and application of the law, advances the law's purposes, and enhances the protection of victims. The approach has been endorsed in subsequent judgments, including those at the ICTY. In *Kunarać*, the Appeals Chamber

39 *Prosecutor v Akayesu* para 597.
40 *Prosecutor v Akayesu* para 598.
41 *Prosecutor v Kunarać* (Case IT-96-23 & IT-96-23/I-A) Judgment 12 June 2002 para 127. For subsequent ICTR cases, see *Gacumbitsi v Prosecutor* (Case ICTR-2001-64-A) Judgment 7 July 2006 paras 147-157; *Prosecutor v Muhimana* Case (ICTR-95-1B-T) Judgment 28 April 2005 paras 550-551.
42 *Prosecutor v Akayesu* para 688.
43 The *Interahamwe* (in the Kinyarwanda language, literally means 'those who fight or work together') was a militia or paramilitary group that perpetrated many killings and other acts of violence during Rwanda's 1994 genocide.

held that, '[c]onsent [*in the perspective of the crime of rape*] must be given voluntarily, as a result of the victim's free will, assessed in the context of the surrounding circumstances'.[44]

5 Direct and public incitement to commit genocide: Protecting freedoms and punishing genocidal speeches

The ICTR may be credited for elucidating the elements of the crime of direct and public incitement to commit genocide in international law, and delineating its boundaries *vis-à-vis* freedom of expression. The ICTR is the first international criminal tribunal to adjudicate the crime, and to provide the first direct precedent for the construction of this crime in international law.

According to the ICTR, this crime is consummated by conduct which aims at directly coercing, persuading, inducing or arousing others to commit genocide.[45] The crime may be perpetrated through a wide range of means not limited to a defendant's own physical oral utterances, but also through the dissemination of written or printed material, the public display of placard or any other form of audio-visual communication and the mass media.[46] Even artistic expressions, such as songs or lyrics, are covered.[47] To be culpable of the crime, an accused must have 'directly and publicly incited the commission of genocide' (the material element or *actus reus*) and had the intent directly and publicly to incite others to commit genocide (the intentional element or *mens rea*). Such intent in itself presupposes a genocidal intent'.[48]

According to the ICTR, the notion 'direct' requires that the speech is a direct appeal to commit acts of genocide;[49] the speech has to be more than mere vague or indirect suggestions.[50] The ICTR has clarified that the notion of 'direct' must be examined on a case-by-case basis, taking into account the language and culture of the people. Such an approach is also critical in addressing speeches that are open to multiple interpretations,

44 *Prosecutor v Kunarać et al* (Case IT-96-23 and IT-96-23/1-T) Judgment 22 February 2001 para 460, and upheld by the Appeals Chamber *Prosecutor v Kunarac* paras 127-129 (emphasis added).

45 *Prosecutor v Akayesu* para 559; *Prosecutor v Kajelijeli* (Case ICTR-98-44A-T) Judgment and Sentence 1 December 2003 para 850; *Prosecutor v Nahimana et al* (Case ICTR-99-52-T) Judgment and Sentence 3 December 2003 para 1011.

46 *Prosecutor v Nahimana et al* (as above) paras 1011-1014; *Prosecutor v Akayesu* (n 1 above) para 559.

47 *Prosecutor v Simon Bikindi* (Case ICTR-01-72-T) Judgment 2 December 2008 (TC) para 384.

48 *Nahimana et al v Prosecutor* (Case ICTR-99-52-A) Judgment 28 November 2007 (AC) para 677.

49 *Nahimana et al v Prosecutor* para 692.

50 *Nahimana et al v Prosecutor* para 692.

particularly in light of differing cultural or linguistic contexts. Thus, in adjudicating incitement perpetrated in Rwanda's context, the ICTR has confirmed that,[51]

> the culture, including the nuances of the Kinyarwanda language should be considered in determining what constitutes direct and public incitement to commit genocide in Rwanda. For this reason, it may be helpful to examine how a speech was understood by its intended audience in order to determine its true message.

Therefore,[52]

> [T]he principle consideration is (...) the meaning of the words used in the specific context: it does not matter that the message may appear ambiguous to another audience or in another context. On the other hand, if the discourse is still ambiguous even when considered in its context, it cannot be found beyond reasonable doubt to constitute direct and public incitement to commit genocide.

The ICTR thus effectively prosecuted the crime by closely examining perpetrators' use of coded languages, or use of euphemisms in inciting the killing of members of the Tutsi group. For instance, instead of using the word *'kwica'* which directly means 'to kill', many perpetrators used the term *'ogukora'* ('to work') which was understood by the audiences in Rwanda during the 1994 events to mean 'killing' of the Tutsi. The perpetrators also widely referred to the 'Tutsi' as *'Inyenzi,'* 'enemy,' or 'accomplices of the enemy' or 'infiltrators'.[53]

With respect to the 'public' notion of the crime of direct and public incitement, the ICTR has explained that 'private' incitements fall outside the scope of the crime.[54] The ICTR has elucidated the factors delineating 'public' from 'private' incitements. In determining whether the incitement is 'public' and not private, the ICTR has identified two principle factors, namely, the place where it is perpetrated,[55] and whether assistance was selective or limited.[56] While use of the mass media, such as radios and televisions, may be non-contentious, incitements at other locations may. The criteria identified provide guidance, but in some cases the ICTR's approach raises some questions, which calls for further revisiting in the future. For instance, the Appeals Chamber recently overturned a conviction of an accused for incitement committed at roadblocks. According to the Chamber[57]

51 *Nahimana et al v Prosecutor* para 700.
52 *Nahimana et al v Prosecutor* para 701.
53 *Prosecutor v Niyitegeka* (Case ICTR-96-14-T) Judgment and sentence 16 May 2003 paras 432-437; *Prosecutor v Akayesu* paras 673-674.
54 *Prosecutor v Akayesu* paras 480 & 556.
55 According to the ICTR, words would be regarded as public where they are spoken aloud in a place that was public by definition *Prosecutor v Akayesu* 556.
56 *Prosecutor v Akayesu* para 556; *Prosecutor v Nahimana et al* para 1011.
57 *Nahimana et al v Prosecutor* para 862.

> the supervision of roadblocks cannot form the basis for the Appellant's conviction for direct and public incitement to commit genocide; while such supervision could be regarded as instigation to commit genocide, it cannot constitute public incitement since only individuals manning the roadblocks would have been the recipients of the message and not the general public. Therefore, the Appeals Chamber sets aside the Appellant's conviction under Article 6(1) of the Statute for direct and public incitement to commit genocide.

The Appeals Chamber provides no elaboration explaining why at roadblocks that were established in public places, and which were accessible by the public, only those manning them were necessarily the ones who received the incitements. Like the notion of 'direct', in dealing with the 'public' notion, there is need for judges to take into account the specific realities and contexts under which the incitement is alleged to have occurred. Probably unlike normal situations and unlike some countries where 'roadblocks' may be overly restrictive in terms of those accessing them, during Rwanda's genocide of 1994, overall, roadblocks were accessible to the general public. Moreover, given that for the most part, roadblocks had been established to intercept members of the general public, and indeed members of the public were intercepted, the Appeal Chamber's conclusion that only individuals manning the roadblocks would have been the recipients of the incitements is contentious.

The ICTR's contribution in delineating the crime of direct and public incitement from protected freedom of expression is also noteworthy. Overall, its jurisprudence has identified boundaries defining permissible free speech and the crime. Similarly, the jurisprudence clarifies the distinction between hate speech and the crime of direct and public incitement to commit genocide in international law. In a nutshell, the ICTR's jurisprudence underscores that the crime constitutes non-protected expression in the nature of criminal advocacy for the commission of genocide.

It is clear from the jurisprudence that not all expressions or criticisms with ethnic or other perspectives amount to the crime. For instance, individuals or the media may carry out historical or other forms of research and disseminate news and information highlighting problems existing in a given society, such as pervasive or widespread racial, ethnic or religious discrimination.[58] Moreover, individuals or the media may play a role in discourses on how to deal with inequities in society, such as discrimination on ethnic, religious, national, ethical or other grounds, and may mobilise the people or the civil defence in support of the government efforts to deal with rebellion or conflict.[59] In so doing, however, individuals or the media must act responsibly, and under no circumstances must they directly call

58 *Prosecutor v Nahimana et al* para 1008.
59 *Prosecutor v Nahimana et al* para 1025.

for the destruction of any racial, ethnic, religious or national group in whole or in part.

The ICTR has identified some factors that may be considered in distinguishing genocidal incitement from freedom of expression (or mere hate speech). Overall, the ICTR jurisprudence suggests a careful and objective approach that examines an expression or statement as a whole and in the light of the totality of the circumstances, and evaluating the intent or purpose of the speech; the actual language or tone, the content and accuracy of the statement and the totality of the surrounding context in which it is made. For instance, the ICTR has found the following statements as such (or when certain coded language embedded in some of them, such as *'Inkotanyi'* is construed against a context of widespread violence against Tutsis between 6 April and July 1994 in Rwanda) to constitute direct and public incitement to commit genocide targeting the Tutsi group:[60]

> In the 13 May 1994 RTLM broadcast, Kentano Habimana spoke of exterminating the *Inkotanyi* so as 'to wipe them from human memory', and exterminating the Tutsi 'from the surface of the earth ... to make them disappear for good'. In the 4 June 1994 RTLM broadcast, Habimana again talked of exterminating the *Inkotanyi*, adding 'the reason we will exterminate them is that they belong to one ethnic group'. In the 5 June 1994 RTLM broadcast, Ananie Nkurunziza acknowledged that this extermination was underway and expressed the hope that 'we continue exterminating them at the same pace'. On the basis of all the programming he listened to after 6 April 1994, Witness GO testified that RTLM was constantly asking people to kill others, that no distinction was made between the Inyenzi and the Tutsi, and that listeners were encouraged to continue killing them so that future generations would have to ask what Inyenzi or Tutsi looked like.

In the context surrounding the incitement, such terms as *Inkotanyi* meant members of the Tutsi group, and not members of the Rwandan Patriotic Front (RPF) that was fighting with the government. With respect to incitement perpetrated through *Kangura* newspaper in 1994 in Rwanda, the ICTR also carefully examined them holistically and in the context of the surrounding circumstances. The Tribunal concluded, *inter alia*, that calls for the population to eliminate the *Inyenzi*, or *accomplices*, of the RPF constituted, in the surrounding context, calls for the extermination of the Tutsi group.[61]

The mere fact that there was an ongoing conflict does not justify incitement to eliminate a protected group, nor does it impact on the court's approach in construing statements calling for the extermination of a group. The Appeals Chamber of the ICTR has put it clearly as follows:[62]

60 *Nahimana et al v Prosecutor* para 756.
61 *Nahimana et al v Prosecutor* paras 771-773.
62 *Nahimana et al v Prosecutor* para 757.

> Regarding the assertion by Appellant Barayagwiza that 'the country was under attack, and it could therefore be expected that the virulence of the broadcasts would increase in response to fear of what the consequences would be if the RPF invasion were successful', this has no impact on the finding that the RTLM broadcasts in fact targeted the Tutsi population. As the Trial Chamber noted, RTLM broadcasts exploited 'the fear of armed insurrection, to mobilize the population, whipping them into a frenzy of hatred and violence that was directed largely against the Tutsi ethnic group'.

Moreover, the political or community affiliation of the author may not change the approach taken in construing a statement to determine whether it constitutes a call for the commission of genocide.[63] Finally, the ICTR has contributed to the development of international criminal law by elucidating distinctions between the crime of direct and public incitement to commit genocide from hate speech as understood under international human rights law.

While hate speech (incitement to discrimination or violence) is non-protected speech under international human rights law, the ICTR has explained that hate speech *per se* is not equivalent to direct and public incitement to commit genocide. The ICTR recognises that direct and public incitement to commit genocide may be characterised or accompanied by hate speech, but only hate speech publicly and directly inciting the destruction of an ethnic, religious, national or racial group, in whole or in part, amounts to the crime of direct and public incitement to commit genocide.[64]

The distinction between hate speech that transcends mere calls for hatred to advocate violence against an ethnic, racial, religious or national group, *vis-à-vis* the crime of direct and public incitement to commit genocide, appears minimal. It follows that careful attention needs to be taken in construing such hate speech to ensure that only speech falling short of incitement to eliminate protected groups is excluded from the scope of the crime of direct and public incitement to commit genocide.

6 War crimes in non-international armed conflicts

In addition to the crime of genocide and crimes against humanity, the ICTR is empowered to prosecute war crimes committed in the 1994 non-international armed conflict in Rwanda. Under article 4 of its Statute, the ICTR is mandated to prosecute serious violations of article 3 Common to the Geneva Conventions of 12 August 1949 for the Protection of War Victims, and of Additional Protocol II thereto of 8 June 1977. The violations include: violence to life, health and physical or mental well-

63 *Nahimana et al v Prosecutor* paras 712-714.
64 *Nahimana et al v Prosecutor* paras 692-703.

being of persons, in particular murder and cruel treatment, such as torture, mutilation or form of corporal punishment; collective punishments; taking of hostages; acts of terrorism; outrages upon personal dignity, in particular rape, enforced prostitution, degrading treatment or any form of indecent assault; pillage; the passing of sentences and their execution without previous judgments by regularly constituted courts affording all judicial guarantees; and threats to commit any of the foregoing.

The ICTR Statute for the first time in international law specifically mandates an international criminal tribunal to prosecute violations committed in non-international armed conflicts as enshrined in Common article 3 and Protocol II Additional to the Geneva Conventions. In prosecuting these violations,[65] the ICTR has made a notable contribution to the elucidation of international law.

Firstly, the ICTR has made it clear that criminal responsibility for war crimes is not limited to any particular class of persons, such as soldiers or governmental agents or representatives, but extends to any person, including civilians not linked to government. Therefore, as a matter of law, the 'public agent or government representative' test is not applicable in determining culpability for war crimes. This was so in the case of *Akayesu* by the Appeals Chamber. The Trial Chamber had acquitted Akayesu on war crime charges. In its opinion,[66]

> For Akayesu to be held criminally responsible under Article 4 of the Statute, it is incumbent on the Prosecutor to prove beyond reasonable doubt that Akayesu acted for either the Government or the RPF in the execution of their respective conflict objectives. As stipulated earlier in this judgment, this implies that Akayesu would incur individual responsibility for his acts if it were proved that by virtue of his authority, he is either responsible for the outbreak of, or is otherwise directly engaged in the conduct of hostilities. He, the Prosecutor will have to demonstrate to the Chamber and prove that Akayesu was a member of the armed forces under the military command of either of the belligerent parties, or that he was legitimately mandated and expected, as a public agent or person otherwise holding public authority or *de facto* representing the Government, to support or fulfil the war efforts. Indeed, the Chamber recalls that Article 4 of the Statute also applies to civilians.

The Prosecutor appealed the Trial Chamber's approach. Upholding the appeal,[67] the Appeals Chamber found that the approach was not consistent with the provisions of the ICTR Statute and international

65 *Prosecutor v Akayesu* where the accused was charged with genocide, crime against humanity serious violations of art 3 common to the Geneva Conventions of 12 August 1949 for the Protection of War Victims, and of Additional Protocol II thereto of 8 June 1977 ('war crimes'). He was acquitted on war crimes. As shown below, the Prosecutor appealed this acquittal, and the Appeals Chamber allowed the appeal.

66 *Prosecutor v Akayesu* para 640. In the ICTY's *Prosecutor v Kunarać* para 407, a Trial Chamber had also held that common article 3 may require some relationship to exist between the perpetrator and a party to the armed conflict.

67 *Prosecutor v Akayesu* (Case ICTR-96-4-A) Judgment 1 June 2001 paras 430-445.

humanitarian law. The Appeal Chamber's approach carefully examined the provisions of the Statute as a starting point in line with the requirements of the Vienna Convention on the Law of Treaties, 1969. It found that the provisions of article 4, as well as those on individual criminal responsibility (article 1) as articulated by the Nuremberg Tribunal and on the ICTR's personal jurisdiction (article 5), did not explicitly provide that individual criminal responsibility was restricted to any particular class of individuals.[68]

The Appeals Chamber also examined the objects and purposes of article 3 of the Geneva Conventions, which called for a broader application of the law without distinction. It held that the objects and purposes of Common article 3 were 'to broaden the application of international humanitarian law by defining what constitutes minimum humane treatment and the rules applicable under all circumstances'.[69] Furthermore, in the view of the International Committee of the Red Cross[70]

> the purpose of common Article 3 [is] to ensure respect for the few essential rules of humanity which all civilized nations consider valid everywhere and under all circumstances and as being above and outside war itself. These rules may thus be considered as the quintessence of humanitarian rules found in the Geneva Conventions as a whole.

In the view of the Appeals Chamber, the effective punishment of persons culpable for serious violations above demands that 'punishment must be applicable to everyone without discrimination, as required by principles governing individual criminal responsibility as laid down by the Nuremberg Tribunal in particular'.[71] The Appeals Chamber's purposive approach ensures the effective punishment of all serious violations with a nexus to an armed conflict, regardless of the class of the perpetrator. This also ensures the effective protection of victims. As the Appeals Chamber has explained, 'international humanitarian law would be lessened and called into question if it were to be admitted that certain persons be exonerated from individual criminal responsibility for violations of Common Article 3 under the pretext that they did not belong to a specific category'.[72]

Additionally, the ICTR may be credited for its clarification of the 'war nexus' requirement, the proof of which is a mandatory element of war crimes. For any violation to constitute a war crime, whether committed in an international or non-international armed conflict, the Prosecutor must prove that such a violation was committed in conjunction with the armed

68 *Prosecutor v Akayesu* paras 434-439.
69 *Prosecutor v Akayesu* para 442.
70 *Prosecutor v Akayesu* para 442.
71 *Prosecutor v Akayesu* para 443.
72 As above.

conflict – the 'war nexus'. This is a principal element that distinguishes war crimes from crimes against humanity and genocide. The ICTR, in the *Rutaganda* appeal judgment,[73] may be credited for providing further elaboration to earlier jurisprudence, particularly from the ICTY, on the 'war nexus' requirement. According to earlier jurisprudence, notably *Tadic*,[74] *Kunarać*[75] and indeed from ICTR Chambers,[76] the 'war nexus' generally requires proof that the offence or violation in question was 'closely related' to the armed conflict.

Apart from the ICTY's *Kunarać* appeal judgment, which preceded the *Rutaganda* appeal judgment, and to a limited extent, the *Akayesu* appeal judgment,[77] overall, earlier jurisprudence did not provide detailed elucidation of the standard 'closely related' to the armed conflict. In other words, the jurisprudence did not detail the nature of the required relation between the violation and the armed conflict. *Kunarać* laid a vital foundation in this effort. In that case, the Appeals Chamber held that:[78]

> What ultimately distinguishes a war crime from a purely domestic offence is that a war crime is shaped by or dependent upon the environment – the armed conflict – in which it is committed. It need not have been planned or supported by some form of policy. The armed conflict need not have been causal to the commission of the crime, but the existence of an armed conflict must, at a minimum, have played a substantial part in the perpetrator's ability to commit it, his decision to commit it, the manner in which it was committed or the purpose for which it was committed. Hence, if it can be established, as in the present case, that the perpetrator acted in furtherance of or under the guise of the armed conflict, it would be sufficient to conclude that his acts were closely related to the armed conflict. The Trial Chamber's finding on that point is unimpeachable.
>
> In determining whether or not the act in question is sufficiently related to the armed conflict, the Trial Chamber may take into account, *inter alia*, the following factors: the fact that the perpetrator is a combatant; the fact that the victim is a non-combatant; the fact that the victim is a member of the opposing party; the fact that the act may be said to serve the ultimate goal of a military campaign; and the fact that the crime is committed as part of or in the context of the perpetrator's official duties.

73 *Rutaganda v Prosecutor* (Case ICTR-96-3-A) Judgment 26 May 2003 (AC).

74 *Prosecutor v Tadić* (Case IT-94 1 A-R72) Decision on the Defence Motion for Interlocutory Appeal on Jurisdiction, 2 October 1995 para 70.

75 *Prosecutor v Kunarac* paras 58-59.

76 *Prosecutor v Akeyesu* para 444; *Prosecutor v Akayesu* para 643; *Prosecutor v Musema* para 260.

77 *Prosecutor v Akayesu* para 444 (holding generally, that culpability for violations of common article 3 requires proof of a close nexus between the violation and the armed conflict. The Chamber also stressed that this nexus implies that, in most cases, the perpetrator will probably have a special relationship with one party to the conflict, but that such special relationship is not a condition precedent to the application of common art 3 and hence art 4 of the Statute). See also *Prosecutor v Akayesu* para 643; *Prosecutor v. Musema* para 260.

78 *Prosecutor v Kunarac* paras 58-59.

The ICTR's *Rutaganda* appeal judgment provided vital elaboration of some aspects of the 'war nexus' as elucidated in the *Kunarać* judgment, and also applied the notion to a complex factual situation. Firstly, *Rutaganda* clarified the meaning of the expression 'under the guise of the armed conflict'. Its approach suggests that the expression may not be construed restrictively, but must also be carefully approached:[79]

> It does not mean simply 'at the same time as an armed conflict' and/or 'in any circumstances created in part by the armed conflict'. For example, if a non-combatant takes advantage of the lessened effectiveness of the police in conditions of disorder created by an armed conflict to murder a neighbour he has hated for years, that would not, without more, constitute a war crime under Article 4 of the Statute. By contrast, the accused in *Kunarać*, for example, were combatants who took advantage of their positions of military authority to rape individuals whose displacement was an express goal of the military campaign in which they took part.

Secondly, and related to the approach explained above, *Rutaganda* underscores that proof of the 'war nexus' element is case-by-case, and like *Kunarać*, stated that proof of the element will usually require a holistic consideration of several factors.[80] It however cautioned that particular care is needed when the accused is a non-combatant.[81]

The Appeals Chamber's application of the 'war nexus' to the facts of the case, including the fact that Rutaganda was in a strict sense neither a member of the Rwandan Army (RAF) nor a combatant directly engaged in combat against the RPF, is also instructive. Rutaganda was a vice-chairman of the *Interahamwe* militias and he participated in the killings in which the *Interahamwe* alongside Rwanda Armed Forces perpetrated killings of non-combatants at the ETO school and Nyanza. The Trial Chamber had acquitted the accused of war crimes, and the Prosecutor appealed.

In overturning the acquittals and entering a guilty verdict, the Appeals Chamber closely examined the totality of the evidence adduced and accepted by the Trial Chamber. Noting that the Trial Chamber had itself found that the Prosecutor had established a nexus between killings at the ETO school and the armed conflict, coupled with several other factors also accepted by the Trial Chamber, the Appeals Chamber held that the Trial Chamber had erred in acquitting the Accused of war crimes.[82] In the Appeals Chamber's view, on the basis, *inter alia*, of the following factors, no reasonable trier of fact could have failed to find that a nexus between the armed conflict and Rutaganda's participation in the killings at ETO school had been established beyond reasonable doubt: Firstly, the Trial

79 *Rutaganda v Prosecutor* para 570.
80 As above.
81 As above.
82 *Rutaganda v Prosecutor* para 577.

Chamber had itself found in paragraph 440 of its judgment that, considering the position of authority of the accused over the *Interahamwe*, and the role that the *Interahamwe* served in supporting the RAF against the RPF, there was nexus between the crimes committed and the armed conflict. Moreover, the Chamber accepted the Prosecutor's submissions that the *Interahamwe* were the instrument of the military in extending the scope of the massacres. Furthermore, the *Interahamwe*, alongside soldiers of the Presidential Guard, attacked and massacred non-combatants at ETO school, namely internally displaced persons. Rutaganda personally participated in the ETO school attack with the *Interahamwe* over whom he exercised *de facto* influence and authority. The victims were persons protected under common article 3 of the Geneva Conventions and Additional Protocol II.[83]

With respect to forced diversion of refugees to *Nyanza* and their murder there, in overturning Rutaganda's acquittal by the Trial Chamber, the Appeals Chamber considered more or less the same factors as above, notably: the Trial Chamber's finding of a nexus between the crimes and the armed conflict; how the Rwanda Armed Forces and *Interahamwe* threatened and killed the refugees on their way to *Nyanza*; how Rutaganda personally participated in ordering and directing the attacks, besides transporting the *Interahamwe* as reinforcements; and how Rwandan Armed Forces participated in the massacres alongside the *Interahamwe*. Further, the Chamber considered that the Rwandan Armed Forces also told the *Interahamwe* to murder and look for those who were not dead and finish them off. It also considered that the victims were persons protected under common article 3 of the Geneva Conventions and Additional Protocol II.[84] The Tribunal's approach reflects an endeavour to closely construe and give content to novel elements of crimes, and to apply them in respect of complex factual scenarios. Its approaches give meaning and practicality to theoretical notions and further the development of international law.

7 Scope of 'commission' as a mode of criminal participation

The ICTR's Statute incorporates genocide, crimes against humanity, war crimes and the different modes of criminal participation, that is to say, the methods by which such crimes may be perpetrated. Commission is one of these methods. Earlier cases, particularly by the Appeals Chamber of the ICTY (which also serves the ICTR) notably the case of *Tadić*, defined 'commission' as covering 'first and foremost the physical perpetration of a crime by the offender himself, or the culpable omission of an act that was

83 *Rutaganda v Prosecutor* paras 577 & 580.
84 *Rutaganda v Prosecutor* paras 578-580.

mandated by a rule of criminal law'.[85] *Tadić* also recognised that 'commission' encompassed participation in the realisation of a common design, or purpose – or what subsequent jurisprudence, including from the ICTR, refers to a 'joint criminal enterprise' liability (JCE).[86]

Overall, the concept of 'commission' was understood to be limited to direct and physical perpetration of the crime by the accused using his own hands, or the accused's participation in a joint criminal enterprise.[87] The ICTR, in the *Gacumbitsi* and the *Seromba* appeal judgments, however, provided an important elucidation of the scope of the concept. They held that a person may be held criminally liable for commission in circumstances beyond the two just mentioned, and where other modes of criminal participation enshrined in article 6(1) of the ICTR's Statute, such as aiding and abetting or ordering, do not fully capture the accused's criminal conduct.

In the *Gacumbitsi* case, evidence established that the accused – a *bourgmestre* who exercised effective control as a superior over different categories of persons – physically killed only one victim (Mr Murefu) at the Nyarubuye Church. Tens of thousands of other Tutsi victims were, however, physically murdered by assailants who included many that Gacumbitsi had brought to the church. These murders were immediately carried out following Gacumbitsi's murder of Murefu. In the Trial Chamber's view, Gacumbitsi's murder of Murefu 'gave a signal for the massacres to commence'.[88] On appeal, Gacumbitsi challenged his conviction for genocide based on the Trial Chamber's finding that he murdered Murefu. He argued that the incident had not been pleaded in the indictment, and as such should not have formed the basis for his conviction.

The Appeals Chamber dismissed his appeal, finding that the alleged defect in the pleadings had been cured by post-indictment communication of timely, clear and consistent information.[89] In fact, in the view of Judge Shahabuddeen in his separate opinion,[90] the majority had imposed too formulaic pleading requirements on the Prosecutor and should not have

85 *Prosecutor v Tadić* (Case IT-94-1-A) Appeal judgment 15 July 1999 para 188.
86 *Prosecutor v Tadić* para 188.
87 Joint criminal enterprise, which is equivalent to the notions of acting in concert with others, or common purpose, arises when a group or a plurality of persons having a common criminal purpose (eg the perpetration of genocide) embark on a criminal activity that is then implemented either jointly or by some members of the group or persons outside the group. Criminal culpability of the members of the JCE also arises when a member of the JCE engages persons outside the JCE to implement the criminal activity. See *Prosecutor v Gacumbitsi* (Case ICTR-2001-64-A) Judgment 7 July 2006 para 158; *Prosecutor v Vaslajević* (Case IT-98-32-A) Appeal judgment 25 February 2004 para 100.
88 *Prosecutor v Gacumbitsi* (Case ICTR-2001-64-T) Judgment 19 June 2004 para 168.
89 *Prosecutor v Gacumbitsi* (n 87 above) paras 49-58.
90 *Prosecutor v Gacumbitsi* (n 87 above) Separate Opinion of Judge Shahabuddeen, paras 6-10.

found in the first place that the indictment was defective with respect to Gacumbitsi's murder of Murefu as far as the crime of genocide is concerned. He argued that the crime of genocide, as distinguished from murder (as a crime against humanity) does not require the pleading of every individual killing. Murder as a crime against humanity consists of the killing of individuals, and therefore, the deaths of individual victims are elements of the crime and must be referred to in the indictment.[91]

In contrast, the crime of genocide is different. It requires proof of specific intent to destroy a protected group. Like in the case of mass killing, where each individual murder need not be specifically pleaded, for the crime of genocide it is not required that each individual murder be specifically pleaded.[92]

Furthermore, the *Gacumbitsi* appeals judgment by the majority (Judge Guney dissenting), took the position that even if Murefu's killing were to be set aside, Gacumbitsi would nevertheless be culpable for the tens of thousands of deaths at the church, not merely for ordering or instigating them, but for 'committing' them. The majority explained that, in the totality of the circumstances, even though Gacumbitsi did not personally kill the victims, the totality of his criminal acts were much an integral part of the genocide as were the massacres which they enabled. In reaching the conclusion that Gacumbitsi was guilty of 'committing' genocide, the majority held as follows:[93]

> [In] the context of genocide, […], 'direct and physical perpetration' need not mean physical killing; other acts can constitute direct participation in the *actus reus* of the crime. Here, the accused was physically present at the scene of the Nyarubuye Parish massacre, which he 'directed' and 'played a leading role in conducting and, especially supervising. It was he who personally directed the Tutsi and Hutu refugees to separate – and that action, which is not adequately described by any other mode of Article 6(1) liability, was as much an integral part of the genocide as were the killings which it enabled. Moreover, these findings of fact were based on allegations that were without question clearly pleaded in the Indictment.

91 *Prosecutor v Gacumbitsi* (n 87 above) Separate Opinion of Judge Shahabuddeen, para 7.

92 Judge Shahabuddeen argued as follows: 'The essence of the crime of genocide is an intent to destroy a protected group. The persons in the group may be legion. It is settled jurisprudence that, in the case of a mass killing, individual victims do not have to be specifically referred to in the indictment. If the indictment does refer to them, it is only by way of illustration of the crime; there may be hundreds of illustrations […] What must be born in mind is the distinction between the material facts necessary to establish an offence and the evidence adduced to prove those material facts. The material facts must be pleaded. The material facts must be pleaded, the evidence need not. When an indictment alleged genocide, proof of any one killing is not a *material fact* as it would be in the case of murder; it is *evidence* of a material fact, namely, that the intent of the accused was the destruction of a group, as a group. Each individual killing does not have to be specifically referred to in the indictment'.

93 *Prosecutor v Gacumbitsi* (n 87 above) paras 60-61.

> The Appeals Chamber is persuaded that in the circumstances of this case, the modes of liability used by the Trial Chamber to categorize this conduct – 'ordering' and 'instigation,' – do not, taken alone, fully capture the Appellant's criminal responsibility. The Appellant did not simply 'order' or 'plan' genocide from a distance and leave it to others to ensure that his orders and plans were carried out; nor did he merely 'instigate' the killings. Rather, he was present at the crime scene to supervise and direct the massacre, and participating in it actively by separating the Tutsi refugees so that they could be killed. The Appeals Chamber finds by majority, Judge Guney dissenting, that this constitutes 'committing' genocide'.

In a subsequent judgment, *Seromba*,[94] the Appeals Chamber (Judge Liu dissenting) applied the *Gacumbitsi* precedent to find that Seromba was guilty not merely of aiding and abetting genocide as the Trial Chamber had found, but of 'committing' the crime. Like Gacumbitsi, Seromba did not personally, by his own hands, perpetrate the massacres at Nyange church in which approximately 1500 victims were murdered. In finding that Seromba was guilty of 'committing' genocide, the Appeals Chamber considered that given Seromba's several acts and other relevant factors, he became a principal perpetrator of the crime by approving and embracing as his own act, the decision to commit the massacres at the church. These included the following: when the other authorities realised that it was impossible to destroy the church by using bullets and grenades in order to massacre the Tutsis, they decided to use bulldozers. They turned to Seromba, who sanctioned their use of bulldozers. Seromba was the acting Priest at the Nyange Church. He was well known and respected in the Catholic community. When the bulldozer driver arrived, the authorities ordered him to destroy the church. He did not immediately destroy it, but turned to Seromba to receive instructions from him. The driver asked Seromba three times, and in all instances, Seromba sanctioned the destruction. Having received Seromba's agreement with the decision of the authorities to destroy the Church, the bulldozer driver immediately destroyed it, killing approximately 1500 victims. Seromba was present at the scene of the massacre. He pointed to the bulldozer driver to the most fragile part of the Church where he should start. In the view of the Appeals Chamber, Judge Liu dissenting, on the basis of these factual findings,[95]

> Athanase Seromba approved and embraced as his own the decision of Kayishema, Ndahimana, Kanyarukiga, Habarugira and other persons to destroy the church in order to kill Tutsi refugees. It is irrelevant that Athanase Seromba did not personally drive the bulldozer that destroyed the church. What is important is that Athanase Seromba fully exercised influence over the bulldozer driver who, as the Trial Chamber's findings demonstrate, accepted Athanase Seromba as the only authority, and whose directions he followed. The Appeals Chamber finds [...] that Athanase Seromba's acts, which cannot be adequately described by any other mode of liability pursuant to Article 6(1)

94 *Seromba v Prosecutor* (Case ICTR-2001-66-A) Appeal judgment 12 March 2008.
95 *Seromba v Prosecutor* para 171.

of the Statute than 'committing,' indeed were as much an integral part of the crime of genocide as the killing of the Tutsi refugees. Athanase Seromba was not merely an aider and abetter but became a principal perpetrator in the crime itself.

The *Seromba* Appeal judgment additionly illustrates that, notwithstanding the fact that Gacumbitsi's dictum was confined to genocide, the reasoning equally applies to the crime of extermination. This is because 'the key question raised by the Gacumbitsi dictum is what other acts constitute direct participation in the *actus reus* of the crime'.[96]

Judges Guney and Liu raised reservations to the approach of the majority in the *Gacumbitsi* and *Seromba* judgments.[97] For instance, in *Gacumbitsi*, Judge Guney criticised the majority for not providing reasons or authorities for the new form of commission that departs from existing jurisprudence.[98] While conceding that various municipal legal systems may recognise forms of commission other than the two identified here, Judge Guney argued that the majority offered no discussion to show that any of those other forms of commission are recognised under customary international law.[99] Moreover, contrary to the majority's view that Gacumbitsi's action of directing the Tutsi and Hutu to separate is not adequately described by any other mode of Article 6(1) liability, this action 'certainly constitute[d] a contribution to the commission of acts of genocide by others, in other words, participating in a joint criminal enterprise'.[100]

While the approach pursued by the majority enriches international jurisprudence, the views of the dissenting judges also create room for further development and clarification of the law. Arguably, the concerns raised by Judges Guney and Liu could be addressed in different ways. There is a need to expand the inquiry beyond the limited case-law cited by the majority,[101] to examine the practices of various municipal legal systems and establish the status of customary law. As noted above, Judge Guney argues that many legal systems may define 'commission' more broadly. Nevertheless, the ICTR needs to pursue the inquiry further to articulate more clearly and concretely the status of customary international law. For his part, Judge Shahabuddeen, one of the members of the majority in *Gacumbitsi* supporting the construction of 'commission'

96 *Seromba v Prosecutor* para 190.
97 See also FZ Guistiniani 'Stretching the boundaries of commission liability' (2008) 6 *Journal of International Criminal Justice* 783-799.
98 *Prosecutor v Gacumbitsi* (n 87 above) Partially dissenting opinion of J Guney para 5.
99 *Prosecutor v Gacumbitsi* (n 87 above) Partially dissenting opinion of J Guney para 6.
100 *Prosecutor v Gacumbitsi* (n 87 above) Partially dissenting opinion of J Guney para 7.
101 For instance, the majority in Gacumbitsi drew on the Nuremberg precedent, noting that the selection of prisoners for extermination played an integral role in the Nazi genocide (Judgment of the International Military Tribunal for the Trial of German Major War Criminals, Nuremberg, 30 September and 1 October, 1946, 63); *Prosecutor v Gacumbitsi* (n 87 above) fn 145.

beyond the two forms of commission discussed earlier, appears to also identify ways to address some of the concerns. The judge argues that critical criteria for 'commission,' are 'direct and physical perpetration' and the 'immediacy of the relationship between the accused and the results of his actions'.[102] Based on these, he takes the position that there should be no contestation why a person is not guilty of 'commission' where he perpetrates his crime through the instrumentality of another. In such situation, the proper charge cannot be ordering, or anthing else than 'commission'.[103]

Furthermore, in order to avoid blurring the distinction among the different article 6(1) modes of liability (ie commission, ordering, instigating, aiding and abetting) or 'subsuming' some into 'commission', in situations such as those in *Seromba* and *Gacumbitsi*, every Chamber needs to examine closely every case on its own merits so as to ensure that the majority's approach is only applied in exceptional cases where clearly characterising an accused's conduct as aiding and abetting does not realistically capture the accused's criminal conduct. Faced with situations such as those in *Gacumbitsi* and *Seromba*, judges need to closely examine whether or not the disputed acts constitute direct participation in the perpetration of the crimes, as opposed to mere aiding and abetting or ordering and instigation.

102 *Prosecutor v Gacumbitsi* (n 87 above) Separate opinion of J Shahabuddeen para 24.

103 J Shahabuddeen argues as follows: 'Questions have been raised on the Trial Chamber's observation that 'committing' refers generally to the direct and physical perpetration of the crime by the offender himself. Two glosses may be put on the Trial Chamber's observation. First, attention is invited to the word 'generally' in the Trial Chamber's statement. It is accepted that the statement does not deny that there can be 'committing' where the accused acts through a joint criminal enterprise. However, there are no two rules, but one; it is not the position that non-JCE cases are governed by the 'direct and physical perpetration' rule and JCE cases by another rule which, mysteriously, exempts them from the application of the 'direct and physical perpetration' rule. The matter always turns on whether there is 'direct and physical perpetration'. What happens is that, in the circumstances of a case of JCE, there is a 'direct and physical perpetration' even though the accused is not in personal contact with the victims: the JCE is his instrument. But I see no reason why the rationale of that view has to be limited to that situation. Why, for example, can there not be 'direct and physical perpetration' where the accused perpetrates his crime through the instrumentality of another, even though no JCE is involved and even though there is no personal contact between the accused and the victim? To say that in such a case the proper charge is one of 'ordering' and not of 'committing' imposes too great a strain on the legal apparatus. That may be defensible in some circumstances but not in all; it depends on the immediacy of the relationship between the accused and the result of his action. In any event, it is to be observed that in this case the Trial Chamber found that the applicant 'personally took part' in the attacks and in other ways directly participated in them. Why that should give difficulty in finding that he engaged in the 'direct and physical perpetration:' of the crime of genocide resulting in the attacks is not clear to me. Second, I agree with the Appeals Chamber that proof of personal killing is not required to show 'the direct and physical perpetration of the crime by the offender himself'. To hold the contrary will be too narrow. Even in relation to the charge of genocide by 'killing members of the group,' the 'direct and physical perpetration' test can be fulfilled even if it is not proved that the appellant himself killed anyone.' See *Prosecutor v Gacumbitsi* (n 87 above) Separate opinion of J Shahabuddeen paras 24-25.

The majority's approach not only ensures the appropriate characterisation of the accused's participation in certain circumstances where other modes of liability do not fully capture his/her participation, but also effectively punishes the criminality of persons who seek to hide behind and use others as their instruments in the perpetration of crimes.

The ICTR's jurisprudence effectively ensures the punishment as 'principal perpetrators', other than 'secondary perpetrators', of those who implement crimes through the instrumentality of others. As underscored by Judge Shahabuddeen in his separate (and concurring) opinion in the *Gacumbitsi* appeal judgment, a characterisation of the following acts of the accused in any other way than 'commission' would not serve the interests of justice: the accused was not at any time removed from the crime scene; he was physically present at the action; he gave the signal for the massacres to commence, and he ordered Hutu refugees to separate themselves from the Tutsi – a step indicating an intention to commit genocide which immediately followed. Gacumbitsi directed the attacks. He personally took part in them. He led the attacks against Tutsi civilians by example. He played a leading role in conducting and, especially, supervising the attacks.[104] A different characterisation of this conduct would be 'a misunderstanding and misapplication of the law'.[105] Therefore, notwithstanding the concerns raised above, the ICTR's elucidation of 'commission' as a mode of criminal responsibility provides vital inspiration and moves international law forward.

8 Superior responsibility is not mere negligence and extends to non-military superiors

Article 6(3) of the ICTR's Statute governs command or superior responsibility by which superiors are held culpable for failing to prevent or punish their subordinates' crimes, despite knowing that or having reason to know that their subordinates were about to commit or had committed these crimes, and failing to take measures to prevent or punish the subordinates.

The principle of command or superior responsibility has received extensive elaboration in the jurisprudence of the ICTR. It has also been developed in the ICTY's jurisprudence. However, the ICTR may be credited for its elaboration and application of some of the elements of superior responsibility. To be convicted under command or superior responsibility the following must be proven, namely: (a) a superior-subordinate relationship – i.e. that the accused was the superior of subordinates sufficiently identified over whom he had effective control.

104 *Prosecutor v Gacumbitsi* (n 87 above) Separate opinion of J Shahabuddeen para 21.
105 *Prosecutor v Gacumbitsi* (n 87 above) Separate opinion of J Shahabuddeen para 22.

Effective control requires a demonstration that the accused (superior) had the material ability to prevent or punish the subordinate's crimes (and the crimes for which the accused (superior) is alleged to be responsible); (b) the accused (superior) must have possessed knowledge or must have had reason to know that the subordinates were about to commit or had committed the crimes; and (c) the accused (superior) must have failed to take the necessary and reasonable measures to prevent or punish the crimes.[106]

Prior to the jurisprudence of the ICTR and the ICTY there was very limited elaboration of the content of the above elements underpinning superior responsibility. The ICTR's contribution to the elucidation of the law may be seen in the following: firstly, the ICTR has construed and applied the concept of command or superior responsibility beyond military circles to include civilian authorities or superiors. It has held that, given the terms of its statute (its use of 'superior' as opposed to 'commander') superior responsibility also covers non-military superiors.[107] The ICTR has underscored a case-by-case approach, underlining the criteria for determining superior-subordinate relationship as being one of effective control, which also turns on one's material ability to prevent or punish the commission of crimes by subordinates.[108]

Secondly, while command or superior responsibility arises from 'omissions,' (as opposed to 'direct' personal participation), the ICTR has clarified the essence of such responsibility as not being equivalent to mere criminal negligence. In the *Bagilishema* case,[109] the Appeals Chamber emphasised that a construction and application of superior responsibility must not be approached from the premises of criminal negligence. According to the Chamber, as opposed to liability based on mere negligence, a superior or commander is held criminally culpable in relation to his subordinates' crimes for deliberately failing to perform his duties as a superior or commander, or for culpably or willfully disregarding them, despite him or her having knowledge of the subordinates' crimes.[110] In the words of the Chamber:[111]

> References to 'negligence' in the context of superior responsibility are likely to lead to confusion of thought, as the Judgment of the Trial Chamber in the present case illustrates. The law imposes upon a superior a duty to prevent crimes which he knows or has reason to know had been committed, but subordinates over whom he has effective control. A military commander, or a civilian superior, may therefore be held responsible if he fails to discharge his

106 *Nahimana et al v Prosecutor* para 484; *Prosecutor v Gacumbitsi* (n 87 above) para 143.
107 *Prosecutor v Musema*; *Prosecutor v Kajelijeli* (Case ICTR-98-44A-T) Judgment and sentence 1 December 2003 para 85.
108 *Nahimana et al v Prosecutor* paras 484 & 788; *Prosecutor v Ntagerura et al* (Case ICTR-99-46-A) (AC) para 341.
109 *Prosecutor v Bagilishema* (Case ICTR-95-1A-A) Judgment 3 July 2002.
110 *Prosecutor v Bagilishema* para 35.
111 As above.

duties as a superior either by deliberately failing to perform them or by culpably or willfully disregarding them.

In discouraging reference to 'negligence'[112] when dealing with command or superior responsibility, the Appeals Chamber also pointed to the fact that before an accused is convicted under superior or command responsibility, it must be established that he knew or had reason to know that his subordinates were about to commit or had committed the crimes, and took no action. According to the Chamber, 'the test for criminal negligence (...) cannot be the same as the 'had reason to know' test in terms of Article 6(3) of the Statute'.[113]

It follows from the above that a superior's failing to discharge his obligations is a very serious failing that must attract serious penal consequences. In subsequent ICTR and ICTY cases, the Tribunals stressed that the fact that an accused is convicted for crimes pursuant to superior responsibility does not mean that he must get a light sentence. An ICTY judgment expressed this strongly '[i]t would constitute a travesty of justice and an abuse of the concept of command authority to allow the calculated dereliction of duty to operate as a factor in mitigation of criminal responsibility'.[114]

The jurisprudence has also accentuated that while an accused may not be convicted under both articles 6(1) and 6(3) for 'superior responsibility,' and that conviction may only be entered under article 6(1), the accused's article 6(3) responsibility is to be taken into account as an aggravating factor in sentencing.[115]

9 Other issues

In addition to the issues discussed thus far, the Tribunal has addressed several other issues related to the substantive, procedural and evidentiary aspects of international criminal law. However, only a brief commentary is possible. Firstly, the ICTR has dealt with immunity attaching to state officials. The ICTR was the first international criminal tribunal to prosecute and convict a former state official, Jean Kambanda, for genocide and other violations of international humanitarian law. The judgment sent a clear message that immunities, such as those enjoyed state officials, cannot be invoked as defences to international crimes, or as barring international criminal tribunals from exercising jurisdiction over state

112 The Appeals Chamber did not detail the distinction between 'negligence' and acting 'deliberately', but see *Prosecutor v Strugar* (Case IT-01-42-A) Judgment 17 July 2008 fn 670.

113 *Prosecutor v Bagilishema* para 37.

114 *Prosecutor v Celebici* (Case IT-96-21) Judgment 16 November 1998 para 125.

115 *Prosecutor v Kajelijeli* (Case ICTR-98-44A-A) 23 May 2005 para 317. For the ICTY, see *Prosecutor v Celebici* (Case IT-96-21-A) 20 February 2001 para 745.

officials. Based, *inter alia*, on the *Kambanda* precedent the attempt by the former President of Liberia (Charles Taylor) to invoke immunity before the Special Court for Sierra Leone, was dismissed. The ICTR has also highlighted that by participating in crimes, those in positions of authority abuse their power and trust and that is an aggravating factor in sentencing,[116] as was the case with Kambanda who was Prime Minister and head of government.

Moreover, the ICTR's approach to fair trial guarantees and related matters are noteworthy. Very early in its life, the Tribunal emphasised that, regardless of the unthinkable nature of the crimes such as those over which it exercises jurisdiction, defendants must enjoy fair trial guarantees. In the *Barayagwiza* case, the ICTR ordered the release of Barayagwiza, citing 'egregious' delays in indicting and bringing him to justice upon his arrest and detention. This showed that:[117]

> The Tribunal – an institution whose primary purpose is to ensure that justice is done – must not place its imprimatur on such violations. To allow the appellant to be tried on the charges for which he was belatedly indicted would be a travesty of justice. Nothing less than the integrity of the Tribunal is at stake in this case. Loss of public confidence in the Tribunal, as a court valuing human rights of all individuals – including those charged with unthinkable crimes – would be among the most serious consequences of allowing the appellant to stand trial in the face of such violations of his rights. As difficult as this conclusion may be for some to accept, it is the proper role of an independent judiciary to halt this prosecution, so that no further injustice occurs.

In addition to the redress of release, which appears to be available only in exceptional circumstances, the ICTR's jurisprudence holds that other forms of effective redress are also available to accused victims of rights violations, such as financial compensation[118] or a reduction of sentence.[119]

In other cases, the ICTR has provided clarifications on the scope of guarantees and rights. According to the Tribunal, an accused's right to be tried in his presence (as enshrined in its Statute and various international human rights instruments) means that he has the right to be physically

116 *Prosecutor v Kambanda* paras 42-44 & 61; *Kambanda v Prosecutor* (Case ICTR 97-23-A) Judgment 19 October 2000 paras 118-126.

117 *Barayagwiza v Prosecutor* (Case ICTR-97-19) Judgment 3 November 1999. The Appeals Chamber subsequently vacated the decision, because newly-discovered facts presented by the Prosecutor in a motion for review showed that the violations suffered by the Appellant and the omissions of the Prosecutor were not the same as those that underpinned the decision to release him. *Prosecutor v Barayagwiza* Decision (Prosecutor's Request for Review or Reconsideration) 31 March 2000.

118 *Rwamakuba v Prosecutor* (Case ICTR-98-44C-A) Decision on Appeal against Decision on Appropriate Remedy 13 September 2007.

119 *Prosecutor v Barayagwiza* Decision (Prosecutor's request for review or reconsideration) para 75.

present at the trial,[120] unless he waives the right, for instance by refusing to attend court.[121] Moreover, indigent accused persons have a right to competent assigned attorneys. However, in principle, the right to free legal assistance does not confer the right to retain the counsel of one's choosing. It only applies to those accused persons who can finically bear the costs.[122]

The Tribunal's Statute and Rules of Procedure and Evidence as further elucidated in its jurisprudence endeavor to ensure that the rights of accused are properly balanced with those of victims and witnesses. For instance, in order to guard against reprisals against victims and witnesses, the ICTR is mandated to protect them by ordering and implementing appropriate measures of protection, such as *in camera* proceedings, the non-disclosure of their identity to the public, testimony by video-link, and such, while at the same time ensuring that rights of the accused are respected.[123] The absence in the ICTR's Statute of a mandate to offer compensation and other forms of redress to victims of international crimes underlines the strides made by the International Criminal Court in incorporating such rights. Notwithstanding limitations in the Statute, the ICTR's effort of trying to reach out to victims in Rwanda in its outreach and other programmes is salutary.

The ICTR has enriched the existing jurisprudence on the criteria for determining an accused's fitness to stand trial. While the ICTY faced challenges regarding an accused's fitness to stand trial and the need to identify the applicable criteria, it appears that the ICTR, in the Ngeze case, made a notable contribution in identifying such criteria in some detail.[124]

120 *Prosecutor v Karemera* (Case ICTR-98-44-AR73.10) Decision on Nzirorera's interlocutory appeal concerning his right to be present during trial 5 October 2007 para 11.

121 *Nahimana et al v Prosecutor* paras 93-116.

122 *Prosecutor v Akayesu* paras 60-64 & 76.

123 Arts 19 and 21 Tribunal's Statute; Rules 69 and 75 Tribunal's Rules of procedure and evidence; *Prosecutor v Nahimana et al* Decision on the Prosecutor's application to add witness X to its list of witnesses and for protective measures 14 September 2001.

124 Arguably, the then existing ICTY cases did not provide detail on the applicable criteria, apart from evaluating the relevant expert reports and the accused's behavior during the proceedings. See *Prosecutor v Delalić* (Case IT-96-21-T) Order on the Prosecution's request for a formal finding of the Trial Chamber that the Accused Landzo is fit to stand trial 23 June 1997; *Prosecutor v Talic* (Case IT-99-36/1-T) Decision regarding fitness of the accused to stand trial 29 April 2003 (confidential, but cited in *Prosecutor v Strugar* (Case IT-01-42-A) para 45 and fn 120). In the *Goering* judgment, the IMT identified the following criteria: (a) whether the accused is sane or insane; (b) whether the accused is fit to appear before the IMT and present his defence; (b) whether the accused is able to plead to the indictment; (c) whether the accused is of sufficient intellect to comprehend the course of the proceedings of the trial so as to make a proper defence, to challenge a witness and to understand the details of the evidence. *The United States of America, the French Republic, the United Kingdom of Great Britain and Northern Ireland, and the Union of Soviet Socialist Republics v Hermann Wilhelm Goring et al* Order of the Tribunal granting postponement of proceedings against Gustav Krupp Von Bohlen 15 November 1945 I Trial of the major war criminals 143. Arguably, the IMT established a stricter threshold – particularly in its requirement that the accused needs

In the Ngeze case,[125] the accused's fitness to stand trial was the subject of evaluation. In ordering the evaluation of his fitness, the Chamber contributed to the development of international law by identifying the factors which are relevant, namely: (a) his ability to stand trial and his capacity to participate meaningfully in the said trial; (b) his mental capacity to communicate with his defence counsel in a comprehensive manner and his ability to instruct counsel with regard to his defence; and (c) the prognosis and proposed treatment, if any. Subsequent judgments, including that of Strugar by the ICTY's Appeals Chamber, have endorsed the above criteria, and applied it to complex situations.[126]

10 Concluding remarks

Since its inception, the ICTR has made a remarkable contribution to the evolution of international law relating to genocide, crimes against humanity and war crimes. In particular, during the early part of its life, the ICTR confronted and addressed vast areas of legal doctrine that had not been explored before. Overall, the ICTR has proceeded prudently and innovatively. The rate of innovation is slowing down as the tribunal is nearing the end of its work.

Many of its latest judgments are characterised by the application of established jurisprudence to differing and sometimes novel and complex factual situations. Nevertheless, even during the current stage of its life, the ICTR continues to address interesting and significant issues. Moreover, in order to solidify the gains realised since its inception, the ICTR needs to be pragmatic in its application of the jurisprudence to differing and complex factual situations.

It may be argued that in recent cases the ICTR has not drawn on and applied some of its innovations to effectively prosecute and punish

to be capable of making a proper defence, to challenge witnesses and to understand the details of the evidence. As shown below, the ICTR and ICTY, set a somewhat flexible threshold (closely similar to that set by the ECHR), underscoring that the accused need not be capable of understanding every point of law or evidential detail – the standard is that of meaningful participation which allows the exercise of his fair trial rights; capacity to testify and capacity to instruct counsel. According to the ECHR, fitness to stand trial presupposes the accused (a) has a broad understanding of the nature of the trial process and of what is at stake for him or her, including the significance of any penalty which may be imposed; (b) is able to understand the general thrust of what is said in court; (c) is able to follow what is said by the prosecution witnesses and, if represented, to explain to his own lawyer his version of events, point out any statements with which he disagrees and make them aware of any facts which should be put forward in his defence. *SC v The United Kingdom* 60958/00 para 29 ECHR 2004-IV; see generally *Prosecutor v Strugar* paras 46-49.

125 *Prosecutor v Nahimana et al* (Case ICTR-99-52-T) Decision on Motion by the Defence in Accordance with Rule 74 *bis* 20 February 2001 (confidential, but cited in *Prosecutor v Strugar* para 45 and fn 120 thereof).

126 *Prosecutor v Strugar* para 45.

international crimes. For instance, in *Muhimana*[127] the Appeals Chamber could have drawn, *inter alia*, on the *Gacumbitsi* jurisprudence to uphold the Trial Chamber's finding that Muhimana was guilty of committing rape as a crime against humanity. Even if it was not clear that Muhimana (other than other persons who were with him in the house at the time of the rapes) had personally with his own private parts raped the Tutsi victims, the following facts (all of which had been pleaded in the indictment and proven at trial) sufficiently established that Muhimana was a direct participant in the rapes: it was Muhimana who brought the victims to his house where they were raped; Muhimana was present throughout the rapes; after their rape, it was Muhimana who drove the victims out of the house stark naked and walking with their legs apart; he invited the militias and other civilians to come and see what naked Tutsi women looked like; and he directed the militias to part the victims' legs to provide onlookers with a clear view of their private parts. In the totality of the circumstances, Muhimana was responsible for committing the rapes.

The ICTR's jurisprudence, like that of the ICTY, has emphasised that in charging international crimes indictments must spell out the material facts underpinning the charges, as well as the specific modes of criminal responsibility by which the accused perpetrated the crimes (ie commission, ordering, instigation, aiding and abetting or command responsibility).[128] The Tribunal's jurisprudence that defects may be cured by post-indictment communication of clear, timely and consistent information promotes substantive justice.

Nevertheless, more needs to be done. In the *Muhimana* case mentioned above, even if the indictment had only pleaded the accused's 'commission' of the rapes, arguably the Appeals Chamber could have entered, at the very least, a conviction for aiding and abetting the rapes based on the facts summarised above that were specifically alleged in the indictment. Clearly the accused would not have suffered any prejudice in the preparation of his defence because the material facts alleged in the indictment at least supported aiding and abetting. Based on those facts the accused was sufficiently placed to mount a defence, including by disputing the alleged facts.

The Appeals Chamber could have advanced the 'pleading' jurisprudence by taking the position that in circumstances as that in *Muhimana*, the emphasis would not be on the specific inclusion or mention of a given mode of criminal responsibility in the indictment. Instead, in the interests of substantive justice, emphasis would be on the holistic reading of the material facts alleged in the indictment to determine whether the

127 *Muhimana v Prosecutor* (Case ICTR-95-1B-A) Judgment 21 May 2007 (AC).

128 *Prosecutor v Ntakirutimana and Gerard Ntakirutimana* (Case ICTR-96-10-A and ICTR-96-17-A) 13 December 2004 paras 25; 469-476. For the ICTY see *Prosecutor v Kupreškić et al* (Case IT-95-16) 14 January 2000 (AC) para 88.

accused was sufficiently informed of the charges to prepare his defence. By so doing, the Tribunal would buttress international jurisprudence by transcending 'technicalities' (for instance, the overemphasis on the mention of certain modes of criminal responsibility in the indictment)[129] to examining substantive questions that should underpin inquiries into alleged failing to respect the right of an accused to be informed of the charges, namely, whether in the totality of the circumstances, the accused's right to prepare his defence was materially impaired and whether the trial was rendered unfair by the failure to specifically mention the mode of participation in question.

The Appeals Chamber's recent clarification in the *Seromba* judgment that the *Gacumbitsi dictum* on the scope of commission transcends the crime of genocide, among other instances, is a welcome development. In applying the jurisprudence elucidated in its earlier cases, such approaches as that developed in *Seromba* are critical in the progression and maturation of jurisprudence. Arguably, even during the current stage characterised by the application of jurisprudence developed in its earlier cases, the approach just mentioned would enable the Tribunal to contribute to the further solidification of international jurisprudence.

In other instances, the ICTR needs to revisit certain aspects of its jurisprudence that appear controversial or unconvincing. This chapter has identified some of these. They include the Tribunal's approach to the crime of conspiracy to commit genocide. Undisputedly, proof of this crime (which is consummated by an agreement to commit genocide) will in most instances turn on circumstantial evidence, as finding a written agreement or other forms of direct evidence is basically impossible.

While the finding of guilt will in such a situation require that an agreement to commit genocide be the only reasonable inference, the ICTR's approach, including in the *Nahimana* Appeal judgment and subsequent cases such as *Bagosora*, will raise serious contestations. In particular, in light of the totality of the evidence accepted by the Trial Chamber in the *Nahimana* case, the Appeals Chamber's vacation of the conviction does not adequately explain why conspiracy to commit genocide was not the only reasonable inference, or why the alleged other alternative inferences were reasonable in the totality of the circumstances of the case. A detailed elaboration by the Appeals Chamber was particularly warranted given that the Chamber had no doubt that a genocidal purpose was compatible with a joint agenda of the appellants. Moreover, it was insufficient for the Chamber to hold, without detail, that the genocidal purpose was not the only inference to be drawn from the totality of the circumstances in a situation where the defendants neither

129 In a number of national jurisdictions, once it is proven that an accused is responsible for a crime, there is no requirement for a detailed account of the manner in which the accused participated in the crimes; see A Ashworth *Principles of criminal law* (1999) 421.

advanced nor argued any other alternative purpose underpinning their joint agenda.[130]

It is worth noting that, in relation to a number of the contentious areas of the ICTR's jurisprudence, the decisions were not unanimous. Instead, they generated important dissents, thus pointing to conflicting signals from the Tribunal. Nevertheless, the existence of dissent also has its advantages as it identifies potential alternative approaches and opens some room for the possibility of future revisiting and improvement of some of the questionable or controversial positions adopted by the ICTR.

130 *Nahimana et al v Prosecutor* paras 893-912; J Shahabuddeen's Partly dissenting opinion para 910.

CHAPTER 4

PROSECUTION AND PUNISHMENT OF INTERNATIONAL CRIMES BY THE SPECIAL COURT FOR SIERRA LEONE

*Chacha Murungu**

1 Introduction

Crimes against humanity and war crimes were committed during a non-international armed conflict between rebel forces and the armed forces of the government of Sierra Leone from 1991 to 2002. Rebel factions and government forces that participated in the conflict included the Revolutionary United Front (RUF), the Armed Forces Revolutionary Council (AFRC), the AFRC/RUF, and the Civil Defence Forces (CDF).[1]

Following the crimes committed during the war, the government of Sierra Leone requested the United Nations (UN) to assist in establishing a court that would prosecute and punish persons responsible for international crimes. By Resolution 1315 of 14 August 2000, the UN Security Council decided to establish the Special Court for Sierra Leone (SCSL) on the basis of an agreement between the UN and the government of Sierra Leone.[2] The Secretary-General of the UN negotiated and concluded an agreement with the government of Sierra Leone to establish the SCSL.[3] The Statute of the SCSL was annexed to that agreement.[4] Sierra Leone later enacted domestic legislation to give effect to the agreement with the United Nations on the establishment of the SCSL.[5] The basis for establishment of the SCSL is its Statute and the agreement concluded between the UN and the government of Sierra Leone.

* LL.B (Hons) (Dar es Salaam); LL.M; LL.D Candidate (Pretoria) ; Advocate of the High Court of Tanzania.

1 See Government of Sierra Leone *Truth and Reconciliation Commission Report* (2004) ch entitled 'Causes of Conflict' para 10 and 'Primary Findings' paras 12-19.

2 UNSC Res 1315(2000) of 14 August 2000 (UN Doc S/RES/1315).

3 Agreement between the United Nations and the government of Sierra Leone on the Establishment of the Special Court for Sierra Leone, 16 January 2002 UNSC Res 246 (UN Doc S/2002/246).

4 Statute of the SCSL UN Doc S/2000/915.

5 The Special Court Agreement (Ratification) Act 9 of 2002 *Supplement to the Sierra Leone Gazette*, CXXXIII (22) 25 April 2002.

Unlike the International Criminal Tribunal for the former Yugoslavia (ICTY) and the International Criminal Tribunal for Rwanda (ICTR) which are purely international tribunals established under Chapter VII of the Charter of the UN, the SCSL was established under Chapter VI of the Charter of the UN. The SCSL is a hybrid criminal court,[6] even though it has characteristics that may classify it as an international criminal tribunal. It is composed of international and national judges, lawyers, and other appointed staff. It applies international law and domestic law.[7] It is neither a national court of Sierra Leone nor part of the judicial system of Sierra Leone, nor is it governed by the Constitution of Sierra Leone.[8] The Trial Chamber and Appeals Chamber of the SCSL have, however, held that the SCSL is 'truly an international tribunal.'[9] It has characteristics like those of the International Criminal Court (ICC), the ICTY and ICTR in terms of personal and subject matter jurisdictions, its legal personality and its capacity to conclude agreements with states.[10] Thus, one cannot rule out the fact that the court is truly an international tribunal as the Appeals Chamber of the SCSL has found.[11]

The SCSL has power 'to prosecute persons who bear the greatest responsibility for serious violations of international humanitarian law and Sierra Leonean law committed in the territory of Sierra Leone since 30 November 1996'.[12] It has inherent jurisdiction over persons who commit war crimes and crimes against humanity,[13] particularly those 'persons who bear the greatest responsibility' for international crimes committed in

6 See generally, C Bhoke 'The trial of Charles Taylor: Conflict prevention, international law and an impunity-free Africa' in AV Menon (ed) *War crimes and law* (2008) 174-215.

7 Art 14(1) and (2) Statute of the SCSL.

8 *Prosecutor v Kondewa* (Case SCSL-03-12-PT) Decision on the urgent defence application for release from provisional detention, 21 November 2003 para 27; *Prosecutor v Norman, Kallon and Kamara* (Case SCSL-2004-14-AR 72(E), SCSL-2004-15-AR 72(E0 and SCSL-2004-16-AR 72(E)) Decision on constitutionality and lack of jurisdiction, 13 March 2004 paras 81-82; *Prosecutor v Kallon and Kamara* (Case SCSL-2004-15-AR 72(E) and SCSL-2004-16-AR 72(E)) Decision on challenge to jurisdiction: Lomé accord amnesty, 13 March 2003; *Prosecutor v Norman* (Case SCSL-04-14-AR 72) Decision on preliminary motion based on Lack of jurisdiction (child recruitment) 13 May 2004 paras 25, 53-55.

9 *Prosecutor v Taylor* (Case SCSL-2003-01-I) Decision on immunity from jurisdiction, 31 May 2004 paras 40-42; *Prosecutor v Kallon* (Case SCSL-04-15-AR 72) *Norman* (Case SCSL-04-16-72AR) *Kamara* (Case SCSL-04-16-AR72) Decision on constitutionality and lack of jurisdiction 13 March 2004 para 55.

10 *Prosecutor v Taylor* para 40.

11 *Prosecutor v Taylor* paras 37-38; *Prosecutor v Kanu* (Case SCSL-04-16-AR 72) Decision on motion challenging jurisdiction and raising objections based on abuse of process 25 May 2004 paras 2-5.

12 Art 1(1) Statute of the SCSL.

13 *Prosecutor v Kanu* (Case SCSL-04-16-PT) Written reasons for the Trial Chamber's oral decision on the defence motion on abuse of process due to infringement of principles of *nullum crimen sine lege* and Non-retroactivity as to several counts, 31 March 2004 para 33; *Prosecutor v Brima* (Case SCSL-04-16-PT) Decision on applicant's motion against denial by the acting principal defender to enter a legal service contract for the assignment of counsel, 6 May 2004 paras 39, 55-62. But see decisions of the Appeals Chamber of the SCSL: *Prosecutor v Norman, Fofana and Kondewa* (Case SCSL-04-14A) Decision on prosecution appeal against the Trial Chamber's decision of 2 August 2004

Sierra Leone.[14] The SCSL has competence to render justice to the 'victims and persons found guilty of serious violations of humanitarian law and Sierra Leonean law'.[15]

The SCSL commenced its operations on 1 July 2002. The first thirteen indictments were approved by the court on 7 March 2003.[16] Of the thirteen indictees, only twelve persons were arrested. John Paul Koroma still remains at large, but may have died in Liberia. Before the commencement of trials, Sam Bockarie and Foday Sankoh died. Samuel Hinga Norman died in detention whilst his trial was still proceeding. The court was left with nine persons who were prosecuted. These are Moinina Fofana, Allieu Kondewa, Issa Hassan Sesay, Morris Kallon, Augustine Gbao, Alex Tamba Brima, Brima Bazzy Kamara, Santigie Borbor Kanu and Charles Taylor. Of these nine persons, eight have been convicted of war crimes and crimes against humanity. The case against Charles Taylor is still on trial before the Trial Chamber of the SCSL –sitting in The Hague, The Netherlands.

On 27 January 2004, the Prosecutor of the SCSL joined the cases of nine accused persons under the *CDF Trial,*[17] the *RUF Trial*[18]and the *AFRC Trial.*[19] Charles Taylor is tried separately.[20] The three joinder cases involving nine accused persons have all been completed and the accuse have been sentenced to different terms of imprisonment. Moinina Fofana was sentenced by the Appeals Chamber of the SCSL to a total of fifteen

Refusing leave to file an interlocutory appeal, 17 January 2005 paras 31-32; *Prosecutor v Brima, Kamara and Kanu* (Case SCSL-04-16-AR 73) Decision on Brima-Kamara defence appeal motion against Trial Chamber II Majority decision on extremely urgent confidential joint motion for the re-appointment of Kevin Metzger and Wilbert Harris as lead counsel for Alex Temba Brima and Brima Bazzy Kamara, 8 December 2005 paras 72-78; 135-139.

14 *Prosecutor v Fofana* (Case SCSL-04-14-PT) Decision on the Preliminary Defence Motion on the Lack of Personal Jurisdiction Filed on behalf of the Accused Fofana, 3 March 2004 paras 21-27, especially para 24; *Prosecutor v Kallon, Norman and Kamara* Decision on constitutionality and lack of jurisdiction, 13 March 2004 paras 75, 78-79.

15 *Prosecutor v Norman, Fofana and Kondewa* (Case SCSL-04-14-T) Majority decision on the prosecution's application for leave to file an interlocutory appeal against the decision on the prosecution's request for leave to amend the indictment against Samuel Hinga Norman, Moinina Fofana and Allieu Kondewa, 2 August 2004 para 31.

16 See *Prosecutor v Koroma* (Case SCSL-03-03); *Prosecutor v Bockarie* (Case SCSL-03-04); *Prosecutor v Sankoh* (Case SCSL-03-02); *Prosecutor v Norman* (Case SCSL-03-08); *Prosecutor v Fofana* (Case SCSL-03-11); *Prosecutor v Kondewa* (Case SCSL-03-12); *Prosecutor v Sesay* (Case SCSL-03-05); *Prosecutor v Kallon* (Case SCSL-03-07); *Prosecutor v Gbao* Case (SCSL-03-09); *Prosecutor v Brima* (Case SCSL-03-06); *Prosecutor v Kamara* (Case SCSL-03-10); *Prosecutor v Kanu* (Case SCSL-03-13); *Prosecutor v Taylor* (Case SCSL-03-01).

17 *Prosecutor v Norman, Fofana and Kondewa Civil Defence Forces (CDF) Trial* (Case SCSL-04-14-I) 5 February 2004 (Indictment).

18 *Prosecutor v Sesay, Kallon and Gbao, Revolutionary United Front (RUF) Trial* (Case SCSL-04-15-PT) 13 May 2004 (Indictment).

19 *Prosecutor v Brima, Kamara and Kanu* (Case SCSL-2004-16-PT) 18 February 2005 (Indictment).

20 *Prosecutor v Taylor* (Case SCSL-2003-01-I) (Indictment) 3 March 2003; but see amended indictment in the case against Charles Taylor of 16 March 2006 reducing counts in the charges of war crimes and crimes against humanity from 17 to 11.

years imprisonment while Allieu Kondewa was sentenced to twenty years. They were all convicted for crimes against humanity and war crimes.[21] The Appeals Chamber sentenced Issa Sesay to 52 years imprisonment for crimes against humanity and war crimes, Morris Kallon to 40 years and Augustine Gbao to 25 years.[22]

On 19 July 2009, the Trial Chamber of the SCSL delivered a single sentence of 50 years for Tamba Brima, 45 years for Bazzy Kamara and 50 years for Borbor Kanu.[23] On 31 October 2009, all eight persons convicted and sentenced by the SCSL (the prisoners) were transferred to Rwanda to serve their sentences.[24] They are currently incarcerated in Mpanga Prison in Rwanda under an agreement signed between the SCSL and Rwanda in March 2009. That done, on 16 November 2009 the SCSL handed over the detention facility to Sierra Leone. Charles Taylor is the only one still on trial before the SCSL sitting in The Hague. The SCSL will be phased out once the trial of Charles Taylor is completed.

This chapter examines the contribution and legacy of the Court to the development of international law in Africa. The legacy of the SCSL is examined only in relation to the cases it prosecuted. Further, the principles of international criminal law and jurisprudence of the court are examined in such cases. Although the court has made a significant contribution to international law, including decisions on immunity of state officials,[25] enlisting or conscription of children under the age of 15 years into armed forces,[26] sexual violence,[27] forced marriage,[28] judicial impartiality, indictments and joinder of accused persons, this chapter does not cover such areas because they are beyond its scope of dealing only with selected principles and other new developments.

21 *Prosecutor v Fofana and Kondewa* (Case SCSL-04-14-A) Appeal judgment 28 May 2008 paras 1-10.

22 *Prosecutor v Sesay, Kallon and Gbao* (Case SCSL-04-15-1-A) Judgment 25 October 2009.

23 *Prosecutor v Brima, Kamara and Kanu* (Case SCSL-04-16-T) Sentencing judgment 19 July 2007.

24 'Special Court Prisoners Transferred to Rwanda to serve their sentences' Press Release, SCSL, 31 October 2009.

25 *Prosecutor v Taylor* paras 45-53, especially para 53.

26 *Prosecutor v Fofana and Kondewa* Judgment, Trial Chamber, 2 August 2007 paras 182-199; *Prosecutor v Norman, Fofana and Kondewa* Decision on motions for judgment of acquittal pursuant to rule 98, 21 October 2005 paras 123-124; *Prosecutor v Norman* Decision on preliminary motion based on lack of jurisdiction (child recruitment) 31 May 2004 paras 26-51.

27 Art 2(g) and (i) Statute of the SCSL; *Prosecutor v Norman, Fofana and Kondewa* (Case SCSL-04-14-T) Reasoned majority decision on prosecution motion for a ruling on the admissibility of evidence, 24 May 2005 para 19.

28 Art 2(g) Statute of the SCSL; *Prosecutor v Sesay, Kallon and Gbao* (Case SCSL-04-15-PT) Decision on prosecution request for leave to amend the indictment, 6 May 2004 paras 36, 50-51, 57; *Prosecutor v Brima, Kamara and Kanu* Case SCSL-04-16-PT Decision on prosecution request for leave to amend the indictment, 6 May 2004 paras 36, 51-52, 57-58; *Prosecutor v Brima, Kamara and Kanu* Case SCSL-04-16-T Decision on prosecution request for leave to call an additional witness (Zainab Hawa Bangura) pursuant to rule 73*bis* (E) and on joint defence notice to inform the Trial Chamber of its position *vis-à-vis* the proposed expert witness (Mrs Bangura) pursuant to rule 94*bis*, 5 August 2005 para 29.

2 Principles and jurisprudence developed by the Special Court for Sierra Leone

It is not possible to discuss everything decided by the Court. The selection of principles here is based on those which are key and novel in the field of international criminal law.[29] The jurisprudence of the SCSL on war crimes and crimes against humanity is examined. My purpose is to uncover the legacy of the SCSL in the prosecution and punishment of international crimes committed in Sierra Leone, and to examine the role it has played in the development of international law principles in Africa. The jurisprudence of the ICTY, ICTR and the ICC is generally omitted, unless it is specifically relevant.

2.1 Persons who bear the greatest responsibility for international crimes

A reading of the Statute of the SCSL reveals that the Court was established and given the 'power to prosecute persons who bear the greatest responsibility for serious violations of international humanitarian law and Sierra Leonean law committed in the territory of Sierra Leone since 30 November 1996, including those leaders who, in committing such crimes, have threatened the establishment of and implementation of the peace process in Sierra Leone'.[30] The Court is the first of its kind to use the phrase quoted above. None of its predecessors has such a mandate in their statutes.

Unfortunately, nowhere in the Statute of the SCSL is the phrase 'persons who bear the greatest responsibility for serious international humanitarian law and Sierra Leonean law' defined. An attempt is made to examine what the court has developed as its own jurisprudence regarding this concept as well as the interpretation given by the first Prosecutor of the SCSL. According to the Prosecutor of the SCSL, 'the people who caused and sustained the war are the persons bearing the greatest responsibility'.[31] The Prosecutor further maintains that such people include 'the planners and instigators of the terrible violence or those who instigated or caused and sustained the serious violations of international humanitarian law in the territory of Sierra Leone'.[32]

29 For a comprehensive digest of the jurisprudence of the court, see generally C Laucci *Digest of Jurisprudence of the Special Court for Sierra Leone 2003-2005* (2007) 1-787.
30 Art 1(1) Statute of the SCSL.
31 Interview with Desmond de Silva, former Prosecutor of the SCSL (Deputy Prosecutor at the time of interview) Monday 25 April 2005, Conference Room – Office of the Prosecutor (OTP).
32 Interview with David Crane, first Prosecutor of the SCSL Monday 25 April 2005, OTP.

The Prosecutor's definition of the persons who bear the greatest responsibility is informed by article 6(1) of the Statute of the SCSL.[33] Article 6(1) creates individual criminal responsibility for persons who committed international crimes in Sierra Leone. However, it has been correctly argued that the definition adopted by the Prosecutor is too narrow[34] and targets only a few culprits. It only targets those who 'caused' or 'instigated' the war in Sierra Leone, at least in the Prosecution's view. It leaves out the possibility of other persons equally responsible for fuelling the war, or all those that took part in the actual commission of international crimes in Sierra Leone even after the armed conflict had started. For instance, one wonders whether peacekeepers[35] and other foot soldiers under the command of rebel forces would not qualify as those who bear equal responsibility for international crimes. Arguably, the approach taken by the Prosecutor leaves too much discretion on whom to and not to indict, despite some people's clear role in the commission or participation in international crimes.

Despite the lack of a definition of 'persons who bear the greatest responsibility' in the Statute, the Court has been able to develop its own jurisprudence on this question. It did so for the first time in *Prosecutor v Fofana.*[36] The Trial Chamber of the SCSL traced the origin of the concept and noted that 'the issue of competence of the Special Court received significant attention during discussions on the establishment of the Special Court and drafting of its Statute, as discussed by the Parties'.[37] It further stated that the ICTY and ICTR have the 'power to prosecute persons responsible for serious violations of international humanitarian law'[38] while the SCSL has 'power to prosecute persons who bear the greatest responsibility for serious violations of international humanitarian law and Sierra Leonean law'.[39] It appears that the SCSL employs a higher and stricter threshold than that of the ICTY and ICTR. The Trial Chamber considered whether such a concept is a 'juridical requirement or merely an articulation of prosecutorial discretion'.[40] In this regard, it had to examine the drafting history of the provision of article 1 of the Statute. It concluded that the phrase was discussed between the Secretary-General of the UN and the Security Council. In the Report of the Secretary-General on the establishment of the SCSL, paragraph 30 states that:[41]

33 Bhoke (n 6 above) 179.
34 As above.
35 But see art 1(2) Statute of the SCSL.
36 *Prosecutor v Fofana* (n 14 above) Decision on the preliminary defence motion on the lack of personal jurisdiction filed on behalf of the accused, 3 March 2004 paras 21- 27.
37 As above, para 21.
38 Art 1 Statute of ICTY; art 1 Statute of ICTR.
39 *Prosecutor v Fofana* (n 36 above).
40 As above.
41 *Prosecutor v Fofana* (n 36 above) para 22 (quoting para 30 of the Report of the Secretary - General on the establishment of the SCSL).

> While those 'most responsible' obviously include the political or military leadership, others in command authority down the chain of command may also be regarded 'most responsible' judging by the severity of the crime or its massive scale. 'Most responsible', therefore, denotes both a leadership and authority position of the accused, and a sense of the gravity, seriousness or massive scale of the crime. It must be seen, however, not as a test criterion or a distinct jurisdictional threshold, but as [...] guidance to the Prosecutor in the adoption of a prosecution strategy and in making decisions to prosecute in individual cases.

The Trial Chamber then examined the letter exchanged between the President of the Security Council and the Secretary-General on 22 December 2000, 12 January 2001 and 31 January 2001 and noted that throughout the Security Council held the view that personal jurisdiction over persons who bear the greatest responsibility limited the 'focus of the Special Court to those who played a leadership role', and that, despite such wording, it 'does not mean that the personal jurisdiction is limited to the political and military leaders only'. Therefore, 'the determination of the meaning of the term "persons who bear the greatest responsibility" in any given case falls initially to the prosecutor and ultimately to the Special Court itself'.[42] The Trial Chamber noted the interpretation given by the Secretary-General to the President of the Security Council who said:[43]

> It is my understanding that, [...] the words 'those leaders who ... threaten the establishment of and implementation of the peace process' do not describe an element of the crime but rather provide guidance to the prosecutorial strategy. Consequently, the commission of any of the statutory crimes without necessarily threatening the establishment and implementation of the peace process would not detract from the international criminal responsibility otherwise entailed for the accused.

Based upon the above, the Chamber found that 'the issue of personal jurisdiction is a jurisdictional requirement, and that, while it does of course guide the prosecutorial strategy, it does not exclusively articulate the prosecutorial discretion'.[44] It is the judge who ultimately decides, based on sufficient evidence, to believe that a person bears the greatest responsibility.[45] The emphasis is that the phrase 'persons who bear the greatest responsibility' refers to the leaders both political and military who threatened the establishment of the court and of peace process in Sierra Leone.

42 See S/2000/1234 and S/2001/40 as quoted in *Prosecutor v Fofana* (n 36 above) paras 23-24.

43 S/2001/40 para 3, as quoted in *Prosecutor v Fofana* (n 36 above) para 24.

44 *Prosecutor v Fofana* (n 36 above) para 27.

45 *Prosecutor v Fofana and Kondewa* (Case SCSL-04-14-T (TC)) Judgment 2 August 2007 para 91.

2.3 SCSL and the Truth and Reconciliation Commission of Sierra Leone

The relationship between the Truth and Reconciliation Commission of Sierra Leone (TRC) and the SCSL reinvigorates the debate on prosecution and transitional justice mechanisms. The two are competing in international criminal law. One is the widely accepted principle that perpetrators of serious international crimes should be punished for their crimes after due process of law, and the other is the institutional role in developing and establishing historical records of truth for past conflicts in societies – an equally valid and legitimate societal interest. This is a widely recognised debate for international lawyers. It even touches on whether, by telling the truth, an individual should not be prosecuted on that basis, or whether prosecution should prevail over the truth telling. The SCSL has had to deal with this question in some of its cases. It will be noted that due to the delicate nature of the question of transitional justice mechanisms and retributive justice, the Trial Chamber and Appeals Chamber of the SCSL have given different positions. These are examined below.

When the TRC requested the SCSL to conduct public hearings in the trials of *Norman*[46] and *Gbao,*[47] the Trial Chamber (Justice Bankole Thompson) raised concerns regarding the likelihood of infringing the rights of the accused persons, especially the presumption of their innocence. The TRC had wanted Norman to testify before it in order to know the role he played in the armed conflict in Sierra Leone. The TRC's request was premised on two grounds: 'the first is that the accused did play a central role in the conflict in Sierra Leone; the second is that the Commission perceive[d] that the accused played a central role in the conflict as a "victim" or [was] invited to testify as an interested party.'[48] From this, the Chamber concluded that *Norman* was invited 'to testify as a perpetrator of abuses and violations'.[49]

The Trial Chamber cautioned itself not to draw any conclusions about the role of the accused person in the conflict as entertained by the TRC in its request. It emphasised that the jurisdiction to try the accused person fell exclusively within its competence and not any other institution and that the court could not delegate its jurisdiction to any other institution in that any attempt to delegate its exclusive jurisdiction would compromise its autonomy and the integrity of the trial of the accused person. The Chamber noted that the request by the TRC to conduct a public hearing

46 *Prosecutor v Norman* (Case SCSL-03-08-PT) Decision on the request by the Truth and Reconciliation Commission of Sierra Leone to conduct a public hearing with Samuel Hinga Norman 29 October 2003.
47 *Prosecutor v Gbao* (Case SCSL-03-09-PT) Decision on the Request by the TRC of Sierra Leone to conduct a Public Hearing with the Accused 2 November 2003.
48 *Prosecutor v Norman* Preamble paras 10 and 12.
49 *Prosecutor v Norman* (n 46 above) para 12.

with the accused on his role in the conflict clashed fundamentally with, and would have grave ramifications on the accused's presumption of innocence protected under article 11(1) of the Universal Declaration of Human Rights and article 17(3) of the Statute of the SCSL.[50] The Trial Chamber found that to agree to the request by the TRC would 'jeopardise the accused's right to a fair and public hearing and would constitute an unprincipled departure from a well-established and widely accepted judicial practice'.[51] In other words, the Chamber reasoned that to allow an accused to testify before the TRC would mean 'to incriminate himself elsewhere'[52] and therefore denied the request by the TRC to conduct a public hearing in *Norman*. The Trial Chamber's decision in *Norman* is the same as in *Gbao*.[53]

The position stated by the Trial Chamber suggests that prosecution is the preferred way to satisfying the interests of the victims rather than telling the truth about the past. In other words, the TRC may not prevail over international courts with a mandate to prosecute international crimes. However, it remains debatable whether this is the only solution for post–conflict reconciliation in societies emerging from armed conflicts. One is tempted to consider the position stated by the Appeals Chamber in the *Norman* case regarding the request by the TRC to conduct a public hearing with him.

On appeal by the TRC,[54] the Appeals Chamber differed with the decision of the Trial Chamber. The Appeals Chamber viewed the work of the TRC and the SCSL as complementary to each other, and that the two institutions 'must accommodate the existence of the other'. The Appeals Chamber held that the TRC is not in a position to suspend its work once trials begin. It emphasised that 'the Special Court respects the TRC's work and will assist it so far as is possible and proper, subject to [...] the overriding duty to serve the interests of justice without which there may not be the whole truth and there is unlikely to be reconciliation'.[55] The authoritative position is that given by the Appeals Chamber – it is also the correct approach because it harmonises the two competing and conflicting norms of prosecution and reconciliation. Basically, the Appeals Chamber's decision echoes that 'Truth Commissions and International Courts are both instruments for effectuating the promises made by states that victims of human rights violations shall have an effective remedy – a trial, followed by punishment of those found guilty, in this case of those

50 *Prosecutor v Norman* para 10.
51 *Prosecutor v Norman* para 14.
52 *Prosecutor v Norman* para 14.
53 *Prosecutor v Gbao* (n 47 above) paras 11-16, 18.
54 *Prosecutor v Norman* Decision on appeal by the Truth and Reconciliation Commission for Sierra Leone and Chief Samuel Hinga Norman JP against the decision of His Lordship, Mr Justice Bankole Thompson delivered on 30 October 2003 to deny the TRC's request to hold a public hearing with Chief Samuel Hinga Norman JP, 28 November 2003.
55 *Prosecutor v Norman* (as above) para 44.

who bear the greatest responsibility'.[56] The Appeals Chamber held that *Norman* was entitled to testify before the TRC. However, it cautioned that Norman should be advised of the dangers of testifying before the TRC, and that his testimony should be provided in a manner that does not endanger or 'influence witnesses or affect the integrity of court proceedings or unreasonably affect co-defendants and other indictees'.[57]

The TRC processes can help societies move forward from the past trauma of conflicts. In this regard, TRC reports can assist societies to forget about the past hatred that may have caused the war. Generally, TRCs offer two prospects for victims of armed conflicts: truth and reconciliation. Truth involves learning how and why the war occurred; reconciliation entails an understanding for and forgiveness of the perpetrators who genuinely confess in public and regret their wrongs. It is generally accepted that TRCs can succeed in some societies – for example in South Africa against the past injustices of apartheid. In fact, in most post-conflict societies, transitional justice mechanisms have become a way of recovering from the past. TRCs have always been accompanied by amnesties. For example, transitional justice mechanisms were used in South American countries: Bolivia, Argentina, Brazil, Chile, El Salvador, Guatemala and Haiti. To some extent, transitional justice mechanisms have had a good effect on these societies. In Africa, transitional justice mechanisms have been used in many countries: Ghana, Democratic Republic of Congo, Kenya, Liberia, Sierra Leone, Rwanda, Burundi, Mozambique and Angola. So far, however, the most successful transitional justice mechanisms were South Africa's TRC and amnesty.

2.4 Amnesty for international crimes

Is amnesty suitable where persons have been charged with international crimes? The question of amnesty[58] for international crimes is contentious. Scholarly views are sharply divided on the issue: there are those who support amnesty for purposes of transitional justice,[59] while others hold the view that amnesty is not a valid defence to the prosecution of perpetrators of international crimes.[60] The latter category holds greater

56 *Prosecutor v Norman* para 33.

57 *Prosecutor v Norman* para 41.

58 On amnesty, see G Robertson *Crimes against humanity: The struggle for global justice* (2003) 260-302; A O'Shea *Amnesty for crime in international law and practice* (2002) 1-325.

59 P Lenta 'In defence of Azapo and restorative justice' in W Le Roux and K Van Marle (eds) *Law, memory and the legacy of Apartheid: Ten years after AZAPO v President of South Africa* (2007) 149-182.

60 J Dugard 'Restorative justice: International law and the South African model' in AJ McAdams (ed) *Transitional justice and the rule of law in New Democracies* (1997) 269; N Roht-Arriaza and L Gibson 'The developing jurisprudence on amnesty' (1998) 20 *Human Rights Quarterly* 843; D Moellendorf 'Amnesty, truth and justice: AZAPO' (1997) 13 *South African Journal on Human Rights* 283; R Wilson *The politics of truth and reconciliation in South Africa: Legitimizing the post-Apartheid state* (2001); N Mogale 'Ten

sway in international criminal law and is followed here.

Amnesty for serious international crimes is contrary to international law.[61] This reasoning is premised on the fact that humanity requires that those who commit international crimes are held responsible for their acts. This is based on the duty to prosecute and punish persons who commit international crimes. While some may argue that there is yet no universal acceptance that amnesties are unlawful under international law,[62] one may point to several international law treaties requiring the prosecution of perpetrators of international crimes. These treaties include the Convention on the Prevention and Punishment of the Crime of Genocide,[63] the Convention against Torture and Other Cruel, Inhuman or Degrading Treatment or Punishment,[64] and the Geneva Conventions (I-IV).[65]

The conflict between amnesty and punishment is based on the idea that amnesty constitutes 'immunity' in law from criminal or civil responsibility for past crimes committed in a political context.[66] According to Geoffrey Robertson, 'pardons and amnesties have been used from time immemorial, benevolently (as a measure of forgiveness to those who have already suffered some punishment for their crimes), politically (to bring to an end civil wars and insurrections) and legally (to absolve convicts who later appear innocent)'.[67] Treaties conferring blanket amnesties are contrary to international obligations to bring perpetrators of international crimes to justice. Arguably, 'the real purpose of an amnesty statute is not always to promote national reconciliation as such, or to diminish in a new democratic society the debilitating desire for revenge, but rather, it is to enable government officials, and military and police officers, to escape

years of democracy in South Africa: Revisiting the AZAPO decision' in Le Roux and Van Marle (59 above)127-148; O'Shea (n 58 above); Y Naqvi 'Amnesty for war crimes: Defining the limits of international recognition' (2003) 85 *International Review of the Red Cross* 583; A Cassese 'The Special Court and international law: The decision concerning the Lome Agreement Amnesty' (2004) *Journal of International Criminal Justice* 1130; LN Sadat 'Exile, amnesty and international law' (2006) *Notre Dame Law Review* 955.

61 CB Murungu 'Judgment in the first case before the African Court on Human and Peoples' Rights: A missed opportunity or a mockery of international law in Africa?' (2010) 3 *Journal of African and International Law* 187-229.

62 A Cassese *International criminal law* (2003) 315.

63 Convention on the Prevention and Punishment of the Crime of Genocide, adopted by UN General Assembly, 9 December 1948.

64 Convention against Torture and Other Cruel, Inhuman or Degrading Treatment or Punishment, 1984.

65 Convention for the Amelioration of the Condition of the Wounded and Sick in Armed Forces in the Field; Convention for the Amelioration of the Condition of Wounded, Sick and Shipwrecked Members of Armed Forces at Sea; Convention Relative to the Treatment of Prisoners of War; Convention Relative to the Protection of Civilians in Time of War, Geneva, 12 August 1949.

66 B Brandon and M Du Plessis (eds) *The prosecution of international crimes: A practical guide to prosecuting ICC crimes in Commonwealth states* (2005) 118 119.

67 Robertson (n 60 above) 273.

responsibility for international crimes which they ordered or committed'.[68]

Amnesty functions as a transitional justice mechanism, especially in post- conflict societies. As such it is in constant conflict with the demands for justice for the victims of armed conflicts. The SCSL has approached the question of amnesty carefully. The Statute of the SCSL does not recognise amnesty granted to perpetrators who commit international crimes,[69] and amnesty therefore is not a bar to prosecution. However, the Lomé Accord signed between the rebel forces, particularly the RUF and the government of Sierra Leone, contained a provision in article IX which granted amnesty to all members of the rebel forces. It essentially barred prosecution of perpetrators of international crimes committed in Sierra Leone.[70]

However, it must be pointed out that the moral guarantors of the agreement were non-contracting signatories of the Lomé Agreement. The UN representative appended, in anticipatory avoidance of doubt, an understanding of the extent of the agreement to be implemented as not applicable to certain international crimes –particularly war crimes and crimes against humanity. When members of the RUF were indicted, they raised jurisdictional challenges on, among other things, the amnesty granted to them by the Lomé Peace Agreement. They argued that the SCSL was not supposed to prosecute them because of the amnesty provisions under article IX of the Lomé Accord. This is not withstanding the provisions of article 10 of the Statute of the SCSL.

The Appeals Chamber considered the question of amnesty.[71] Before dealing with the validity of amnesty for international crimes, the Chamber had to determine the status of the Lomé Agreement which was signed between members of the RUF and the Government of Sierra Leone. It concluded that the RUF did not have the status of a state; it was a mere rebel faction in Sierra Leone. The Chamber considered whether the agreement signed qualified as an international treaty and found that the Lomé Agreement cannot be characterised as such. The Chamber stated emphatically that 'the Lomé Agreement is neither a treaty nor an agreement in the nature of a treaty.'[72] Regarding the relevancy of amnesty to international crimes, the Chamber concluded that[73]

> the amnesty granted by Sierra Leone cannot cover crimes under international law that are the subject of universal jurisdiction ... It is clear that the question

68 As above.
69 Art 10 Statute of the SCSL.
70 O'Shea (n 58 above) 1-2.
71 *Prosecutor v Kallon, Kamara* paras 67-73, 80, 84 and 88.
72 As above, paras 39-49; *Prosecutor v Gbao* Case SCSL-04-14-AR72, Decision on Preliminary Motion on the Invalidity of the Agreement between the United Nations and the Government of Sierra Leone on the Establishment of the Special Court, 25 May 2004 (Appeals Chamber).
73 *Prosecutor v Kallon, Kamara* paras 71-72.

> whether amnesty is unlawful under international law becomes relevant only in considering the question whether article IX of the Lomé Agreement can constitute a legal bar to prosecution of the defendants by another State or by an international tribunal.

The Appeals Chamber concluded that amnesty is not a bar to prosecution. It found that article 10 of the Statute of the SCSL does not recognise amnesty granted to accused persons. It restated the position that there was no bad faith in article 10 of the Statute of the SCSL, and that there was a clear statement in the preamble to Resolution 1315 (2000) of the Security Council that: [74]

> The Special Representative of the Secretary-General appended to his signature of the Lomé Agreement a statement that the United Nations holds the understanding that the amnesty provisions of the Agreement shall not apply to international crimes of genocide, crimes against humanity, war crimes and other serious violations of international humanitarian law.

Further, the Chamber noted that amnesty was only intended to apply to national courts and not the SCSL. It decided that,[75]

> [w]hatever effect the amnesty granted in the Lomé Agreement may have on a prosecution for such crimes as are contained in Articles 2 to 4 in the national courts of Sierra Leone, it is ineffective in removing the universal jurisdiction to prosecute persons accused of such crimes that other states have by reason of the nature of the crimes. It is also ineffective in depriving an international court such as the Special Court of jurisdiction.

Hence, the Appeals Chamber confirmed the international law position that amnesty cannot bar the prosecution of perpetrators of international crimes before international courts.

2.5 Crimes against humanity and war crimes: A general interpretation

The SCSL defined elements of 'crimes against humanity' and 'war crimes'. In this section the court's definition and interpretation of such crimes are highlighted. In light of article 2 of the Statute of the SCSL, the court held that elements of crimes against humanity are that: 'there must be an attack; acts of the accused person must be part of the attack; the attack must be directed against any civilian population; the attack must be widespread or systematic; and the accused must know that his acts constitute part of a pattern of widespread or systematic crimes directed against a civilian

74 Para 81.
75 *Prosecutor v Kallon, Kamara* para 88.

population'.[76] The court stressed that for purposes of crimes against humanity, 'an attack constitutes "a course of conduct involving the commission of acts", which need not constitute a military attack'.[77] An attack may precede, outlast, or continue during the armed conflict. The SCSL has found that the term 'widespread' refers to the scale of the acts perpetrated and to the number of victims and that the adjective 'systematic' implies 'the organised nature of the acts of violence and the improbability of their random occurrence'.[78] Widespread refers to the large-scale nature of the attack and the number of victims involved. The *mens rea* of crimes against humanity is 'the knowledge that there is an attack on the civilian population and that the acts of the accused person are part thereof'. The prosecutor has to 'show that the accused either knew or had reason to know that his acts comprised part of the attack'.[79]

The requirement for an attack to be directed against any civilian population requires that 'the civilian population be the primary rather than an incidental target of the attack'.[80] Hence, the civilian population must be the primary object of the attack and must be predominantly civilians. In order to determine whether the attacks are systematically targeted against a civilian population, the test used by the SCSL (as taken from the ICTY) consists of the following aspects: the means and method used in the attack; the status and number of victims; the discriminatory nature of attack; the nature of the crimes; resistance against the attacks and assailants and the extent of force used in the attack.[81] For purposes of crimes against humanity, the term 'civilian population' has been interpreted to mean not only civilians, but also 'those who were members of a resistance movement and former combatants – regardless of whether they wear uniforms or not – but who were not longer taking part in hostilities when the crimes were perpetrated because they had either left the army or were no longer bearing arms or, ultimately, had been placed *hors de combat*, in particular, due to their wounds or their being detained'.[82]

From the above, the emphasis is on the 'specific situation of the victim' at the time the crimes were committed. Hence, 'the targeted population must essentially be predominantly civilian in nature, although the presence of a number of non-civilians in their midst does not change the character of that population as civilian'.[83] The SCSL also defined 'torture' as a crime against humanity and considered treatment that qualifies as 'degrading

76 *Prosecutor v Norman, Fofana and Kondewa* Decision on Motions for Judgment of acquittal pursuant to Rule 98, 21 October 2005 para 55; *Prosecutor v Fofana and Kondewa* paras 110-121.
77 *Prosecutor v Norman, Fofana and Kondewa* para 56.
78 As above, para 56.
79 *Prosecutor v Fofana and Kondewa* para 121.
80 *Prosecutor v Norman, Fofana and Kondewa* para 56.
81 *Prosecutor v Norman, Fofana and Kondewa* para 56 (citing *Prosecutor v Kunarac* Judgment of the Appeals Chamber ICTY, 12 June 2002 para 90).
82 *Prosecutor v Norman, Fofana and Kondewa* para 58.
83 *Prosecutor v Norman, Fofana and Kondewa* para 59.

treatment' may not necessarily amount to the elements of torture, but that 'torture, could encompass those acts that individually or collectively, constitute what is considered as being inhuman and degrading'.[84] The court found that 'other inhuman acts' – inhuman and degrading treatment – falls within crimes against humanity.[85]

With regards to war crimes, relying on article 3 of the Statute of the SCSL, the court elaborated on the elements of war crimes[86] as those similar to the provision of article 3 common to the Geneva Conventions and of Additional Protocol II. The Trial Chamber held that article 3 of the Statute requires that 'acts of the accused be committed in the course of an armed conflict'[87] regardless of whether it is an international or non-international armed conflict. Hence, the court only needs to be satisfied that an armed conflict existed and the acts were committed during that armed conflict.[88] Normally, 'an armed conflict exists whenever there is a resort to armed force between states or protracted armed violence between governmental authorities and organised armed groups or between such groups within a state'.[89] Generally, for war crimes to be found, there must be a nexus between the alleged violation against victims and the armed conflict. Also, the crime must be committed against a victim who is not taking direct part in the armed conflict. The accused must know or must have had a reason to know that the victim was not taking part in the armed conflict at the time of commission of the crime.[90]

After the preceding general interpretation of war crimes and crimes against humanity, the next section deals with selected specific crimes – which fall under crimes against humanity and war crimes. Although the SCSL has contributed immensely in developing jurisprudence on war crimes and crimes against humanity, its peculiarity lies in the new crimes it has dealt with. These crimes include rape; enforced prostitution; forced pregnancy; sexual slavery and forced marriage; the conscription of children into armed forces; acts of terrorism; attacks against peacekeepers; and pillage. These crimes are novel in international law. Sexual violence and forced marriage crimes are not discussed here.

84 *Prosecutor v Sankoh* (Case SCSL-03-02-PT) Ruling on the motion for a stay of proceedings filed by the applicant, 22 July 2003 9.

85 *Prosecutor v Sankoh* (as above) 9-11.

86 *Prosecutor v Fofana and Kondewa* para 122-137.

87 *Prosecutor v Norman, Fofana and Kondewa* paras 68-70. But see also paras 72-73 (murder); paras 93-95 (cruel treatment); paras 116-118 (collective punishment); paras 109-112 (acts of terror); and para 102 (pillage).

88 *Prosecutor v Fofana* Decision on preliminary motion on lack of jurisdiction *materiae*: Nature of the armed conflict, Appeals Chamber of the SCSL, 25 May 2004 para 25.

89 *Prosecutor v Norman, Fofana and Kondewa* para 69 (citing *Prosecutor v Tadic* Decision on defence motion for interlocutory appeal on jurisdiction, Appeals Chamber of the ICTY, 2 October 1995, para 70).

90 *Prosecutor v Fofana and Kondewa* para 122.

2.5.1 Acts of terrorism – war crimes

The Trial Chamber has dealt with acts of terror as war crimes.[91] The Chamber concluded that this kind of crime is comprised of elements constitutive of article 3 common to the Geneva Conventions as well as the following specific elements: 'acts or threats of violence directed against protected persons or their property; the offender wilfully made protected persons or their property the object of those acts and threats of violence; and, the acts or threats of violence were committed with the primary purpose of spreading terror among protected persons'.[92] The Chamber's reasoning was influenced by the jurisprudence of the Trial Chamber of the ICTY.[93] Consequently, the Chamber concluded that acts of terrorism are included in article 4(d) of Additional Protocol II to the Geneva Conventions – although not defined by Additional Protocol II. It defined acts of terrorism to mean specific type of violence or threat, directed towards terrorising the civilian population. The interpretation was sought from article 13(d) of Additional Protocol II. Relying on the commentary by the International Committee of the Red Cross,[94] the Chamber held that articles 4(d) and 13(d) of Additional Protocol II talk about the same thing, and that the ambit of Additional Protocol II in respect of 'acts of terrorism' extends 'beyond acts of threats of violence committed against protected persons to "acts directed against installations which would cause victims terror as a side-effect"'.[95]

2.5.2 Pillage – a war crime

Pillage as included in article 3(f) of the Statute of the SCSL has been defined by the SCSL to include the following constitutive elements: 'the perpetrator appropriated private or public property; the perpetrator intended to deprive the owner of the property and to appropriate it for private or personal use'; and, 'the appropriation was without the consent of the owner'.[96] The court reached that position because of the seemingly conflicting views on what constitutes 'pillage'. For example, it noted that there are various terms, such as 'pillage', 'plunder' and spoliation', used to describe the unlawful appropriation of private or public property during armed conflicts. This position was informed by the jurisprudence of the ICTY which says that '"plunder" should be understood as encompassing acts traditionally described as "pillage" and that pillage extends to cases of "organised" and "systematic" seizure of property from protected persons

91 *Prosecutor v Fofana and Kondewa* paras 167-175.
92 *Prosecutor v Norman, Fofana and Kondewa* para 112.
93 *Prosecutor v Galic* Judgment 5 December 2003 para 133.
94 ICRC *Commentary on Additional Protocols* 1375.
95 *Prosecutor v Norman, Fofana and Kondewa* para 111.
96 *Prosecutor v Norman, Fofana and Kondewa* para 102.

as well as to "acts of looting committed by individual soldiers for their private gain"'.[97]

2.5.3 Attacks on peacekeepers

The SCSL has developed law on crimes against humanity and war crimes by prosecuting individuals who attacked peacekeepers in Sierra Leone. Article 4(b) of the Statute of the SCSL makes it a crime to attack peacekeepers and a serious violation of international humanitarian law. The RUF Trial signifies the court's strong position on attacks against peacekeepers – as crimes against humanity and war crimes. The Prosecutor of the SCSL charged Sesay, Kallon and Gbao with counts of murder as a crime against humanity and a war crime for the killing of United Nations Mission in Sierra Leone (UNAMSIL) peacekeepers as part of the widespread attack against civilian population. Further, the accused were charged with serious violations of international humanitarian law for 'intentionally directing attacks against personnel involved in a peacekeeping mission, specifically the UNAMSIL peacekeeping personnel'.[98] The SCSL found the accused guilty of crimes against humanity and war crimes for directing attacks against peacekeepers.[99]

2.6 Application of international humanitarian law to non-international armed conflicts

In order to apply international humanitarian law to the conflict in Sierra Leone, the Appeals Chamber had first to determine the nature of the armed conflict that existed in Sierra Leone. Having noted that article 3 of the Statute of the SCSL does not define internal armed conflict, it concluded that – 'whether the conflict in Sierra Leone was of an internal or international character and at which point, if any, it became internationalised, does not have any bearing on the applicability of Articles 3 and 4 of the Statute and therefore need not be considered by the Appeals Chamber'.[100] The Chamber took judicial notice on the matter. There was a non-international armed conflict in Sierra Leone.

The Appeals Chamber considered the application of article 3 common to the Geneva Conventions and Additional Protocol II and noted that article 3 of the Statute of the SCSL is taken from the Geneva Conventions

97 See *Prosecutor v Delalic et al* Judgment, Trial Chamber of the ICTY, 16 November 1998 para 590.

98 *Prosecutor v Sesay, Kallon and Gbao* (Case SCSL-04-15-T) Judgment Summary 25 February 2009 paras 4-6.

99 *Prosecutor v Sesay, Kallon and Gbao* paras 57-72.

100 *Prosecutor v Fofana* Decision on preliminary motion on lack of jurisdiction *materiae*: Nature of the armed conflict 25 May 2004 paras 31-32.

and Additional Protocol II, both of which apply to internal armed conflicts. Given its *pari materia* nature with article 3 of the Geneva Conventions and Additional Protocol II, the Chamber concluded that article 3 of the Statute of the SCSL applies to internal armed conflicts.[101] Article 3 common to the Geneva Conventions and Additional Protocol II forms part of customary international law applicable to both international and non-international armed conflicts.[102]

The Chamber held that all parties to the armed conflict - whether state or non-state actors – are bound by international humanitarian law.[103] Regardless of the unanimity of international law theorists and lawyers on the duty of insurgents to observe the provisions of article 3 common to the Geneva Conventions, 'there is now no doubt that this article is binding on states and insurgents alike and that insurgents are subject to international law'.[104] Hence, even armed groups have to respect international humanitarian law. Taken in this way, all parties to the armed conflict in Sierra Leone were bound to respect international humanitarian law.

2.7 Criminal responsibility for international crimes

The SCSL issued decisions that contribute to the principle of criminal responsibility. Three types of criminal responsibility for international crimes are examined here: individual criminal responsibility, superior responsibility and command responsibility.

2.7.1 Individual criminal responsibility

The Appeals Chamber provided a test to determine whether a violation of international humanitarian law is subject to criminal responsibility. With regards to individual criminal responsibility, the Chamber set specific requirements for a crime to attract individual criminal responsibility under article 6(1) of the Statute of the SCSL. The following are the requirements: 'the violation must constitute an infringement of a rule of international humanitarian law'; 'the rule must be customary in nature or, if it belongs to treaty law, the required conditions must be met'; 'the violation must be "serious", that is to say, it must constitute a breach of a rule protecting important values, and the breach must involve grave consequences for the victim [...]' and; 'the violation of the rule must entail, under customary or conventional law, the individual criminal responsibility of the person

101 *Prosecutor v Fofana* para 20.
102 *Prosecutor v Fofana* paras 21-27; see also paras 18-20.
103 *Prosecutor v Norman* Decision on preliminary motion based on lack of jurisdiction (child recruitment) 31 May 2004 paras 22-23.
104 *Prosecutor v Kallon and Kamara* para 45.

breaching the rule'.[105] From this, a violation of a fundamental rule of international law attracts individual criminal responsibility. Taylor was charged with crimes against humanity and war crimes under individual criminal responsibility.[106]

Article 6(1) of the Statute of the SCSL sets parameters of personal responsibility for crimes.[107] The SCSL held that article 6(1) does not limit criminal responsibility 'to only those persons who plan, instigate, order, physically commit a crime or otherwise, aid and abet in its planning, preparation or execution'. It 'extends beyond that to prohibit the commission of offences through a joint criminal enterprise, in pursuit of the common plan to commit crimes punishable under the Statute.'[108] This introduces a new development on joint criminal enterprise[109] in international criminal law.

2.7.2 *Joint criminal enterprise*

Joint criminal enterprise is a form of criminal responsibility which is sometimes referred to as 'common plan', 'common purpose', or 'common plan liability'.[110] It is a theory of criminal responsibility which requires the prosecutor to prove several elements.[111] Basically, under joint criminal enterprise the prosecutor must prove that 'a group of people had a common plan, design, or purpose to commit a certain crime', the accused 'participated in some fashion' in the joint common plan to commit a crime and, that the accused 'intended the object of the common plan'.[112]

105 *Prosecutor v Norman* para 26, but see paras 27-51 (the SCSL referred to ICTY in *Prosecutor v Tadic* Case IT-94-1-A, Judgment of the Appeals Chamber, Jurisdiction, 15 July 1999 para 94).

106 *Prosecutor v Taylor* Case summary accompanying the amended indictment paras 1-6, 22, 31-34 and 59.

107 *Prosecutor v Kondewa* Decision and order on defence preliminary motion for defects in the form of the indictment, 27 November 2003 para 9; *Prosecutor v Sesay* (Case SCSL-2003-05-PT); *Brima* (Case SCSL-2003-07-PT), *Gbao* (Case SCSL-2003-09-PT), *Kamara* (Case SCSL-2003-10-PT), *Kanu* (Case SCSL-2003-13-PT), Decision and order on prosecution motions for joinder, 27 January 2004 paras 22-24; *Prosecutor v Norman* (Case SCSL-2003-08-PT), *Fofana* (Case SCSL-2003-11-PT), *Kondewa* (Case SCSL-2003-12-PT) Decision and order on prosecution motions for joinder 27 January 2004 para 11.

108 *Prosecutor v Norman, Fofana and Kondewa* para 130.

109 On joint criminal enterprise, see Bhoke (n 6 above) 179-180; AM Danner 'Joint criminal enterprise and contemporary international law' (2004) 98 *American Society of International Law Proceedings* 186; N Piacente 'Importance of the joint criminal enterprise doctrine for the ICTY prosecutorial policy' (2004) 2 *Journal of International Criminal Justice* 446; AM Danner and JS Martinez 'Guilty associations: Joint criminal enterprise, command responsibility, and the development of international criminal law' (2005) 93 *California Law Review* 75-169.

110 The ICTY first used these terms in *Prosecutor v Tadic* (Case IT-94-1-A) Judgment 15 July 1999 paras 175, 177, 186, 193, 196, 219-222, 224 and 227.

111 *Prosecutor v Fofana and Kondewa* paras 206-219 (indicating three categories of joint criminal enterprise).

112 Danner (n 109 above) 187.

Essentially, there must be a plurality of persons and the accused must voluntarily participate in one aspect of the common design, for example, by formulating a plan together with co-perpetrators to commit a crime in effecting the common plan. The accused must also have intended the final result of his participation in the crime, regardless of his or her non-commission of the crime personally. There must be a common plan between accused persons; an intention to participate in a joint criminal enterprise and to further that desire either individually and jointly; a common criminal plan within the criminal enterprise or group; and a purpose of a criminal plan. Further, crimes committed must constitute the purpose of the common plan; the intent of the accused must be to participate in the criminal enterprise; and finally, crimes committed must have been intended and included in the criminal enterprise by accused persons.[113] This form of criminal responsibility is a form of commission but not a form of accomplice. This form of liability is reflected in the indictment against Charles Taylor.[114]

2.7.3 Superior criminal responsibility

Superior criminal responsibility is addressed in article 6(3) of the Statute of the SCSL. Superiors are held responsible for acts of their subordinates, 'where a superior has knowledge or reason to know that subordinates are about to or have committed an offence and that superior fails to take the necessary and reasonable measures to prevent or to punish the perpetrators thereof'.[115] The SCSL has set legal requirements for superior responsibility.[116] In general, the prosecutor must prove the following conditions: the accused held a superior position in relation to subordinates sufficiently identified; and had effective control over the said subordinates. The accused must bear responsibility for their criminal acts and knew or had reason to know that the crimes were about to be or had been committed by his subordinates. There must be a related conduct of those subordinates for whom the accused is alleged to be responsible. Finally, 'the accused failed to take the necessary and reasonable means to prevent such crimes or to punish the persons who committed them'.[117] Superior responsibility may arise for military and civilian leaders alike provided that such leaders have and exercise effective control over their subordinates.

113 Bhoke (n 6 above) 180; Piacente (109 above) 449.
114 *Prosecutor v Taylor* paras 1-6, 22, 31-34 and 59
115 *Prosecutor v Norman, Fofana and Kondewa* (as above).
116 *Prosecutor v Fofana and Kondewa* (n 45 above) paras 232-251.
117 *Prosecutor v Sesay* (Case SCSL-03-5-PT) Decision and order on defence preliminary motion for defects in the form of the indictment 13 October paras 7, 12-14.

2.7.4 Command responsibility

Command responsibility is the third form of liability under article 6(3) of the Statute of the SCSL. This form of responsibility has been used by the SCSL in many cases,[118] and the court has applied settled jurisprudence of the ICTY and ICTR on command responsibility.[119] Command responsibility is customary international law, and applies to both international and non-international armed conflicts. In this theory of liability, there must be a direct or indirect commander and subordinate relationship (hierarchy or chain of command), the commander must exercise effective *de facto* or *de jure* control over the subordinates, and it is applicable only to military commanders and all persons exercising command control over their subordinates. The *mens rea* in command responsibility is the knowledge and reason to know that subordinates were about to or had committed crimes, and the commander failed to take the necessary measures to punish or prevent the crimes committed. This applies to both civilian and military leaders.[120]

3 Conclusion

This chapter has covered the contribution of the SCSL to the development of new principles of international law. Although the court has contributed significantly in many aspects, the chapter dealt with specific aspects only. In this regard, other important aspects - such as the right to bail for accused persons charged with international crimes; joinder of accused persons; requirement and contents of indictments; and the question of impartiality of judges of international courts - have been left out in this chapter. The main contributions of the court covered in this chapter include clarification of international law concepts and principles mostly found in the Statute of the SCSL, new developments on war crimes and crimes against humanity.

The court has developed law on persons who bear the greatest responsibility for international crimes, joint criminal enterprise, and the immunity of state officials charged with international crimes. It has also dealt with the relationship between transitional justice mechanisms such as amnesty and Truth and Reconciliation Commissions and international courts established to prosecute international crimes. It has echoed that the two mechanisms are complementary to each other in post-conflict societies. However, the court has emphasised that amnesty cannot bar the prosecution of persons for international crimes. Further, the court has contributed to international law in the areas of acts of terrorism, rape and other forms of sexual violence, enforced pregnancy and forced marriage,

118 *Prosecutor v Fofana and Kondewa* paras 42-44.
119 *Prosecutor v Norman* para 20.
120 *Prosecutor v Blagojević and Jokić* ICTY Trial Chamber Judgment of 17 January 2005 para 791; *Prosecutor v Blaškić* ICTY Trial Chamber Judgment of 3 March 2000 paras 300-301.

conscription of children under the age of 15 years into armed forces, pillage, and attacks on peace keepers. These fall within crimes against humanity and war crimes in which the court has developed its peculiar jurisprudence.

Furthermore, the court has developed the law on the criminal responsibility of individuals who commit international crimes: individual criminal responsibility; command responsibility and superior responsibility. All persons convicted by the court were charged under these forms of criminal responsibility. It is in the above and other aspects that the SCSL will be remembered as well as the role it played in rendering justice to the victims of the brutal armed conflict in Sierra Leone. The jurisprudence of the SCSL will certainly be helpful to international courts dealing with international crimes in Africa and other parts of the world.

CHAPTER 5

SENTENCING PRACTICE OF THE SPECIAL COURT FOR SIERRA LEONE

*Bonolo Dinokopila**

1 Introduction

Sierra Leone was plagued by a bloody and shocking war for slightly more than a decade. As described by the Sierra Leone Truth and Reconciliation Commission (TRC), it was the 'most shameful years of Sierra Leone's history' and a period which 'reflects an extraordinary failure of leadership on the part of all those involved in government, public life and civil society'.[1]

During the war many terrible atrocities were committed by the Revolutionary United Front (RUF), the Armed Forces Revolutionary Council (AFRC), the Sierra Leone Army (SLA) and the Civil Defence Forces (CDF).[2] The war was characterised by indiscriminate violence and was waged largely by Sierra Leoneans against Sierra Leoneans and all factions specifically targeted civilians.[3] More than half of the people of Sierra Leone were displaced during the civil war. Between 100 000 and 200 000 people were killed with more than 40 000 maimed during the conflict.[4] In short, gross human rights abuses were rampant during this decade-long war. The leadership of the various parties to the conflict were responsible for either authorising or instigating human rights violations against civilians or alternatively for failing to stop such practices.[5]

* LL.B (Botswana), LLM, Doctoral Candidate (Pretoria); Lecturer, University of Botswana, Gaborone, Botswana.

1 Report of the Truth and Reconciliation Commission of Sierra Leone (2004) 27.

2 The award-winning documentary film by Sorious Samura, *Cry Freetown*, shows the shocking nature of the atrocities committed, shown to the author on a visit to the SCSL in Sierra Leone. I visited the SCSL from 3 - 10 June 2008.

3 TRC Report (n 1 above) 27.

4 T Negash 'Accomplishments, shortcomings and challenges: Evaluation of the Special Court for Sierra Leone' Unpublished LLM dissertation, University of Pretoria (2000) 7.

5 MC Nicol-Wilson 'The realisation of the right to bail in the Special Court for Sierra Leone: Problems and prospects' (2007) 7 *African Human Rights Law Journal* 506-509.

The United Nations Security Council (Security Council) pursuant to its Resolution 315 of August 2000[6] established the Special Court for Sierra Leone (SCSL/ the Court) through an agreement with the government of Sierra Leone. The SCSL was set up with the mandate to punish those responsible for crimes committed during the war in Sierra Leone. Its mandate is set out in the Statute of the SCSL. Crimes within the ambit of the Court include crimes against humanity, violations of common article 3 to the Geneva Conventions and additional protocol II, other serious violations of international law and certain crimes under national law.[7]

There was a lot of scepticism surrounding the mandate and objectives of the SCSL and there is a plethora of scholarly work on the effectiveness or lack thereof of this Court. The SCSL was dismissed by some as yet another charade of victor's justice. The rationale behind the establishment of the SCSL remains that those who bore the greatest responsibility for the crimes committed during the war should not go unpunished.

That international crimes shall not go unpunished is beyond doubt. International law requires that perpetrators of crimes against humanity, war crimes and genocide are punished under international law.[8] In fact, paragraph 4 of the Preamble to the Rome Statute of the International Criminal Court (ICC) categorically states that grave crimes that threaten international peace and security are of concern to the international community as a whole and must not go unpunished. Much rhetoric about ending impunity surrounds the creation of international criminal tribunals aimed at meting out punishment for past atrocities. From Nuremberg to Rome, to the creation of the International Criminal Tribunal for Rwanda (ICTR) and the SCSL - all established with the sole aim of punishing perpetrators of international crimes. Through these mechanisms, the international community has witnessed the prosecution of persons accused of committing some of the most heinous crimes against mankind. These post- World War II trials have established many important principles. They have defined crimes against humanity, slowly dismantled the principle of sovereignty, rejected amnesties and immunity as a defence to international criminal charges, and established notions of criminal participation through the principle of command responsibility.[9]

The growth in popularity of these institutions and their quest for legitimacy have not been without challenges. For example, the SCSL has had to convince ordinary Sierra Leoneans, through its outreach programmes, of the importance of its work and, at the implementation level, the rights of the accused and detained persons in the international

6 UNSC Res 1315 UN Doc S/Res /1315 (Aug. 14 2000).
7 Art 1 Statute of the SCSL.
8 J Dugard *International law: A South African perspective* (2005) 195.
9 WA Schabas 'Sentencing by international tribunals: A human rights approach' (1997) 7 *Duke Journal of Comparative and International Law* 461.

criminal justice system.[10] This was a necessary exercise considering that persons charged with international crimes are in the eyes of the general public guilty of the crimes levelled against them and in the opinion of the public deserve to be punished swiftly. The question now arises, what is the purpose of punishment at the international level? Is it purely retributive, or does it serve deterrence or rehabilitative purposes? Does it serve all the functions as propounded by the different theories of punishment? Further, do judges at the international level actually take into account such issues as the rehabilitation of prisoners, protection of the society, deterrence as well as punishment of offenders during the sentencing stage?

This chapter revisits the debate as to the purpose and function of punishment at the international level as evidenced by the decisions of the SCSL. It looks at various theories of punishment and how they have been interpreted at national level and it then considers whether such theories are indeed applicable at the international level. It presents a discussion on sentencing principles as expounded by the SCSL as well as how they have been informed by national principles as discernible from the sentencing practice of the Court. It addresses some of the issues raised in sentencing offenders by the SCSL and ascertains whether the Court takes into account the purpose and function of punishment during the sentencing process. Finally, it examines whether the jurisprudence of the SCSL has added value to the already-existing jurisprudence on the subject.

2 Theories and objectives of punishment

The primary function of criminal law is to announce certain standards of behaviour and by so doing attaches penalties for deviation from it, making it less eligible, and then leaving individuals to choose.[11] The state has a duty to punish those who deviate from this set of rules.[12] For years, 'philosophers, criminologists and lawyers have attempted to explain the link between wrongdoing and punishment'.[13] However, there is no consensus yet as to the rationale behind punishment and as a result any attempt to unequivocally explain this will be a mammoth task. However, classical criminal law theory identifies several functions of punishment such as retribution, deterrence, incapacitation and rehabilitation.[14]

10 SCSL 'Fourth Annual Report of the President of the Special Court for Sierra Leone' (January 2006 – May 2007) 42.

11 AK Kumari 'Roles of theories of punishment in the policy of sentencing' (10 January 2007) 1 http://ssrn.com/abstract=95623 (accessed 1 December 2010).

12 As above.

13 M Bagaric 'Scientific proof that human enjoy punishing wrongdoers: The implications for punishment and sentencing' (2005) 1 *International Journal of Punishment and Sentencing* 98.

14 See FP King and A La Rosa 'Penalties under the ICC Statute' in F Lattanzi and W Schabas (eds) *Essays on the Rome Statute of the International Criminal Court* (1999) 311, 316-319, 329.

There are two main theories of punishment developed over time, namely, utilitarianism and retributivism (or just desserts).[15] These theories are largely used as a means of justifying sentencing or the punishment of offenders. It has been argued by some commentators that these theories of punishment do not explain fully the reasoning behind punishment but rather are mere aspects of punishment.[16] They argue that deterrence and retribution may be aims of possible *justifications for punishment* and that specifying the end(s) is merely one aspect of a theory.[17] Public attitudes on sentencing have also shown that people support multiple sentencing goals. Thus, expressions of retribution co-exist with support for rehabilitation as well as other sentencing options.[18] To that extent, as rightly pointed out by Chirwa, 'choosing penal objectives and allocating their relative weight are therefore critical in any criminal justice system'.[19] People are generally not wedded to a particular philosophy of punishment; they just want something done which changes offenders' behaviour.[20] That notwithstanding, theories and philosophical underpinnings of punishment have been crafted to assist in understanding the role of punishment – and by necessary implication – the end means of punishment in society.

Of all the theories of punishment, retributive theory is perhaps the most famous and probably the oldest justification for punishment. Essentially the retribution school of thought is to the effect that punishment should be based on just desserts, in other words, that offenders ought to be punished or sentenced not for any other reason but for breaking the law.[21]

Retributivism adopts a backward-looking perspective focusing on the moral duty to punish past wrongdoing.[22] The proponents of this theory are of the view that '*lex talions*' is right and a killer must be killed, an eye for an eye.[23] As a result, retentionists of the death penalty, for example, argue that someone who has intentionally killed another person should be subjected to the death penalty. This theory has been criticised as not taking into account factors otherwise relevant, such as error of judgment or resource constraints.[24] In essence – the argument goes – this theory does not offer any guidance as to the more general issues of implementation in a system bound by resource constraints, imperfect information and other

15 Bagaric (n 13 above) 102.
16 K Huigens 'On commonplace punishment theory' (2005) *University of Chicago Legal Forum* 437.
17 As above.
18 R Matthews 'The myth of punitiveness' (2005) *Theoretical criminology* 191.
19 DM Chirwa 'The implications of the emerging jurisprudence in international criminal law for penal regimes in post-independent Africa' (2004) 17 *South African Journal of Criminal Justice* 193, 195.
20 R Morgan 'Privileging public attitudes to sentencing' in J Roberts & M Hough (eds) *Changing public attitudes to punishment* 215-28, quoted in R Matthews (n 18 above) 1.
21 As above.
22 MT Cahill 'Retributive justice in the real world' (2007) 85 *Washington Law Review* 818.
23 As above.
24 Cahill (n 22 above).

limitations.[25] This is notwithstanding that the operation of retribution in the ancient world resulted in harsh and indiscriminate punishment without regard to the particularities of the offender and his crime.[26]

By contrast, utilitarians hold the view that any punishment should achieve some purpose and that punishment is generally a bad thing because it causes unhappiness to the offender.[27] The originators of utilitarian penology were Cesare Beccaria, Jeremy Bentham and John Stuart Mill, who derived their conception of utilitarianism from Baron Helvetius.[28] Utilitarian penology has been identified as a system based on utility.[29] This means that it gauges the appropriateness of the sentence by reference to social costs of wrongful conduct and the social costs necessary to prevent it.[30] According to the utilitarian theory, if there are several forms of punishment which produce the same good consequences, society must opt for the one which is the least pleasant to the offender[31] or one that will maximise utility.[32] Utilitarians appreciate that it is not possible to have a crime-free society but they endeavour to inflict only as much punishment as is required to prevent future crimes.[33] Accordingly, laws that spell out punishment for criminal conduct should be designed to deter future criminal conduct by a particular individual or society in general by way of putting them on notice that future criminal conduct will not go unpunished.[34]

Another utilitarian rationale for punishment is rehabilitation.[35] The aim of rehabilitation is to prevent people from committing future crimes by giving them the opportunity and ability to succeed within the confines of the law.[36] Rehabilitation is another utilitarian rationale for the incarceration of offenders. From this perspective, some of the actions of the criminal are as a result of a general breakdown in the social norms and laws and to that end proper punishment can address some of those criminal tendencies.[37] Many penal reforms are geared towards the rehabilitation of offenders as there is a general belief that some criminal tendencies can be easily corrected through proper punishment. The main

25 Cahill (n 22 above).
26 M Sigler 'The story of justice: Retribution, mercy, and the role of emotions in the capital sentencing process' (2000) 19 *Law and Philosophy* 339.
27 Bagaric (n 13 above) 102.
28 G Binder 'Punishment theory: Moral or political?' (2002) 5 *Buffalo Criminal Law Review* 333.
29 As above.
30 Binder (n 28 above).
31 Bagaric (n 13 above) 103.
32 Binder (n 28 above) 323.
33 http://law.jrank.org/pages/9576/Punishment-THEORIES-PUNISHMENT.html (accessed 14 April 2010).
34 As above.
35 Kumari (n 11 above) 1.
36 http://law.jrank.org/pages/9576/Punishment-THEORIES-PUNISHMENT.html (accessed 14 April 2010).
37 As above.

goal of rehabilitation is to curb crime by giving criminals the tools to survive without resorting to criminal activities. Through the use of educational programmes, the creation of diversion programmes, probation and paroles, rehabilitation oriented systems strive to reduce crime by ensuring that those who once resorted to crime no longer have any reason for doing so. It is perhaps worth mentioning here that over time rehabilitation has emerged as a theory of punishment independent from the utilitarian conception of the role of punishment. Rehabilitation as a theory demands that any penal system should be guided by a desire to ensure that offenders are reformed for eventual re-integration into society through various programmes and skills-sharing or acquisition detention programmes.

As much as the retributive theories of punishment have been challenged as flawed, so are the utilitarian rationales for punishment.[38] One major criticism of utilitarianism being that the weakness of the utilitarian theory is that it is conceivable that an innocent person might be punished as a way of ensuring that pain is inflicted to achieve a greater social 'pleasure' which will be in the in the form of promoting deterrence in the community.[39]

Issues relating to punishment are sometimes described as complex; however, they are rather more ambiguous than complex. As a result, sentencing at the domestic level is largely dependent on the rules of sentencing in a particular country and at most, it is largely dependent on the criminal codes as they prescribe the sentences to be imposed for a particular offence. To a larger extent the purpose and function of sentencing are similar in most criminal jurisdictions. Thus, the theories of punishment seem to apply in most domestic jurisdictions as evidenced by decisions of national courts.[40]

3 Purpose of sentencing at the international level

Experts on criminal law have 'debated over justifications for imposing punishment, the proper limitations on who may be punished, and the appropriate extent of punishment for any particular person'.[41] This section focuses on the first question and provides a discussion on whether the justification of sentencing and/or punishment by *ad hoc* international criminal tribunals amounts to a veneer to the real reason behind their justifications for punishment. It will thus be a discussion on the theories of punishment as regards the approach taken by the SCSL.

38 As above.
39 JT McHugh 'Utilitarianism, punishment, and ideal proportionality in penal law: Punishment as an intrinsic evil' (2008) 10 *Journal of Bentham Studies* 1.
40 *Maphorisa & Others v State* [1996] BLR 133 141; *S v Shilubane* 2008 (1) SACR 295 (T).
41 AM Danner 'Constructing a hierarchy of crimes in international criminal law sentencing' (2001) 87 *Virginia Law Review* 419.

Like any other system of criminal justice, international law is informed by certain rules crafted to ensure that there is at least a set criterion for imposing sentences.[42] In a bid to come up with such a criterion, *ad hoc* international criminal tribunals have made attempts to set out these rules and apply them to cases before them. These attempts have yielded some results. However, despite such efforts the objectives of sentencing at international level remain – murky as they are – relatively similar as in the domestic sphere.

The approaches taken by the ICTY and the ICTR have been adequately discussed elsewhere.[43] In the *Erdemović* decision, the ICTY came to the conclusion that the 'international tribunal's objectives as seen by the United Nations Security Council are generally prevention or deterrence, reprobation, retribution, as well as collective reconciliation'.[44] Henceforth, it should provide guidance in determining the punishment for a crime against humanity.[45] Put forward in that sense, the conclusion by the ICTY creates hope that at the international level there is indeed room for an acceptance of the role of other sentencing objectives. The fact that international criminal tribunals are notorious for convictions has caused some commentators to question whether the international criminal law system is purely retributory and whether it leaves room for rehabilitation.

The above question should perhaps be answered within the context of the ever-controversial notions of peace and justice and, to a certain extent, reconciliation at the international level. As Gonno and O'Brien point out, 'clearly peace and justice are complementary in that justice can deter abuses and can help make peace sustainable by addressing grievances non-violently'.[46] But then, how do you put across such ideals in a situation – such as in Sierra Leone in the case of Charles Taylor and the Lord's Resistance Army (LRA) in Uganda – where the retributive sentiments of the victims and their families and of the international community in general seem to be very strong? Is it possible to preach rehabilitation as an objective of sentencing at the international level?

The ICTY in *Prosecutor v Tadić* has taken the position that deterrence and retribution serve as the primary purpose of sentencing at the international level. The Trial Chamber took cognisance of the purposes of sentencing as one of the relevant factors in the determination of an appropriate sentence. The Trial Chamber pointed out that

> [i]t is the mandate and duty of the international Tribunal, in contributing to reconciliation, to deter such crimes and to combat impunity. It is only right

42 Danner (n 41 above) 418.
43 Danner (n 41 above) 419; Chirwa (n 19 above).
44 *Prosecutor v Erdemović* (Case IT-96-22-S) Sentencing judgment 5 March 1998 para 58.
45 As above.
46 N Grono and A O'Brien 'Justice in conflict? The ICC and peace processes' in N Waddel and P Clark (eds) *Courting conflict? Justice, peace and the ICC in Africa* (2008) 13.

> that *punitur quia peccatur* (the individual must be punished because he broke the law) but also *punitur ne peccatur* (he must be punished so that he and others will no longer break the law). The trial chamber accepts that two important functions of the punishment are retribution and deterrence.[47]

The above quotation from the decision of the ICTY highlights the importance that *ad hoc* international criminal tribunals attach to the purpose and functions of sentencing. Whether they adequately elaborate on them in their sentencing judgments is now a matter of debate[48] and has been described as inadequate. However, the attention paid by *ad hoc* international criminal tribunals may be the result of the unique mandate of international tribunals to put an end to widespread violations of international humanitarian law and to maintenain peace.[49]

The ICTY Appeals Chamber endorsed the principle of retribution as the purpose of international sentencing and highlighted that retribution in that context should not be equated with revenge but should be viewed as 'duly expressing the outrage of the international community at these crimes'.[50] The ICTY in *Prosecutor v Tordorović*[51] pointed out that if the principle of retribution is to be applied in the context of sentencing, it must be understood as reflecting a fair and balanced approach to the imposition of punishment.

Likewise, the trial chambers of the ICTR have consistently been upheld in the light of the object and purpose of the establishment of the ICTR that the sentences imposed must be directed mainly at retribution and deterrence.[52] In *Kambanda*, the ICTR trial chamber stated that the penalties imposed on accused persons found guilty by the tribunal must be directed at retribution and that the accused persons must witness their crimes punished.[53] This is not at all surprising considering that crimes that fall within the jurisdiction of these tribunals usually attract public outrage and demands for justice. Further, 'the primacy of the retributive dynamic

47 *Prosecutor v Tadić* (Case IT-94-1-A) 26 January 2000 para 9.

48 See Danner (n 41 above) 418 arguing that the 'judgments from the Nuremberg and Tokyo Tribunals span thousands of pages, but their sentences were given in terse one-line declarations, with little or no explanation of the bases for the distinctions between the various sentences imposed on the defendants. The brevity of the sentencing decisions from the Tokyo and Nuremberg judgments may spring from a source more profound than judicial fatigue'. See further RD Sloane 'The evolving "Common Law" of sentencing of the international Criminal Tribunal for Rwanda' (2007) 5 *Journal of international Criminal Justice* 713-734, 719 arguing that the ICTR has done a far much better job than its predecessors.

49 *Prosecutor v Tadić* para 7.

50 *Prosecutor* v *Aleksovski* (Case IT-95-14/1-A) Judgment 24 March 2000.

51 (IT-95-9/1-S) Sentencing judgment 31 July 2001.

52 *The Prosecutor v Kayishema and Ruzindana* (Case ICTR-95-1-T) Sentence 21 May 1999 para 2; *The Prosecutor v Serushago* (Case ICTR-98-39-S) Sentence 5 February 1999 para 20; *The Prosecutor v Akayesu* (Case ICTR-96-4-T) Sentence 2 October 1998 para 19; *The Prosecutor v Kambanda* (Case ICTR-97-23-S) Judgment and sentence 4 September 1998 para 28.

53 *Kambanda* (n 52 above) para 28.

in international sentencing is evidenced by the fact that a culture of conviction rather than a culture of acquittal now predominates'.[54] The ICTR in the *Kambanda* case highlighted that deterrence is largely aimed at dissuading those who will attempt in future to perpetrate those atrocities and also showing them that the international community will not let those who commit such serious crimes go unpunished.[55]

The statutes of the ICTY, ICTR and the SCSL contain provisions dealing with sentencing. According to these provisions, sentences should be limited to imprisonment – the death penalty as well as corporal punishment, imprisonment with hard labour and fines are excluded.[56] In addition to these sentencing rules, judges of the international tribunals are supposed to have 'recourse to the general practice regarding prison sentences of the ICTY or the ICTR as the case may be'.[57] Further, when imposing sentences the Trial Chamber is supposed to 'take into account such factors as the gravity of the offence and the individual circumstances of the convicted person'.[58] The ICTY and the ICTR have identified retribution, deterrence, incapacitation, rehabilitation and reconciliation as the main objectives of international sentencing.[59]

However, the sentencing judgments of the tribunals do not yet provide entirely persuasive explanations on why particular sentences are imposed on particular offenders.[60] The law and practices of the tribunals are also noted for incorporating human rights in their sentencing regime, such as excluding the death penalty and corporal punishment.[61]

4 The sentencing practice of the Special Court for Sierra Leone

Sentencing in the SCSL is regulated by the provisions of article 19 of the Statute of the SCSL and Rule 101 of the Rules of Procedure and Evidence. Article 19 of the Statute provides that in determining the terms of imprisonment, the trial chamber shall, as appropriate, take into account aggravating and mitigating factors and the general practice regarding prison sentences in the ICTR and the domestic courts of Sierra Leone.[62] Further, during the sentencing process the Trial Chamber should take into account such factors as the gravity of the offence and the individual

54 King and La Rosa (n 14 above) 331.
55 As above.
56 King and La Rosa (n 14 above) 462.
57 Art 24(1) Statute of ICTY; art 23(1) Statute of ICTR; Schabas (n 5 above) 468.
58 Art 19(2) Statute of SCSL.
59 Chirwa (n 19 above) 195.
60 Sentencing Observer 'Sentencing and the International Criminal Court' (2002) 2.
61 GW Mugwanya 'Criminal justice through international criminal tribunals: Reflections on some lessons for national criminal justice systems' (2006) 6 *African Human Rights Law Journal* 59.
62 As above.

circumstances of the convicted person.[63] In addition to imprisonment, the Trial Chamber may order the forfeiture of property, proceeds or any assets that were unlawfully procured and may order their return to their rightful owners.[64] Rule 101 of the Rules of Procedure and Evidence provides that a person convicted by the Special Court, other than a juvenile offender, may be sentenced to imprisonment for a certain number of years.[65] Rule 101(B) provides that '[i]n determining a sentence, the Trial Chamber shall take into account the factors mentioned in article 19(2) of the Statute as well as factors such as any aggravating circumstances, any mitigating circumstances as well as the extent to which any penalty that may have been imposed by a court of a state for the same offence has already been served'. Citing the ICTR Appeals Chamber decision in *Prosecutor v Kambanda,*[66] the SCSL pointed out that these requirements are not exhaustive. The Trial Chamber has the discretion to determine an appropriate sentence.[67] The Trial Chamber also pointed out that the final sentence should reflect the totality of culpable conduct or it should reflect the gravity of the offences, so that it is both just and appropriate.[68]

Rule 100 provides that where the Trial Chamber finds an accused person guilty or that person enters a guilty plea, the prosecutor and the accused person shall submit information that may assist the Chamber in determining the appropriate sentence after such a conviction or guilty plea. The parties must then make submissions as regards the sentencing of the accused person at the sentencing hearing following which the sentence is pronounced in a judgment in public and in the presence of the convicted person. Submissions made at the sentencing hearing, it appears, are meant to give each side the opportunity to respond to the arguments raised by the other side.

This approach has raised questions as to whether the Prosecutor could submit new factual statements from alleged victims who were not called to give evidence during its case in chief. During the AFRC sentencing hearing the defence objected to the documents annexed to the prosecution sentencing brief on the basis that such evidence was tantamount to introducing new evidence through said documents.[69] It was argued that the introduction of new evidence amounted to an abuse of process and must be rejected by the court.[70] On the contrary, the Prosecutor argued that since there were two distinct procedures it was inappropriate to submit evidence relevant to sentencing at the trial stage.[71] The Chamber upheld

63 *Prosecutor v Brima, Kamara and Kanu* (Case SCSL-2004-16-T) Sentencing judgment 19 July 2007 para 11 (AFRC Sentencing Judgment).
64 Art 19(3) Statute of SCSL.
65 Rule 101(A).
66 *Prosecutor v Kambanda* Appeals judgment para 13.
67 AFRC Sentencing judgment para12.
68 As above.
69 AFRC Sentencing judgment para 6.
70 As above, para. 6.
71 AFRC Sentencing judgment (n 63 above) para 7.

the defence's objections and stated that it did not take into account the documents submitted together with the prosecution brief.[72] The Chamber did not state reasons behind its decision to uphold the defence's arguments. Considering the importance of the question raised, that is, whether it was fair that evidence relevant to sentencing should only be adduced during the case in chief, one would have expected that the Chamber would state reasons behind its decision. An opportunity was therefore missed by the Court to fully support the bifurcated nature of its trials.[73]

Unlike the ICTY and the ICTR, the SCSL holds sentencing hearings following a conviction or a guilty plea. That the SCSL holds sentencing hearings has been held as indicative of the importance the Court attaches to the sentencing stage of the trial process. Conversely, that the ICTR abandoned its distinct sentencing hearings and instead announced sentences along with judgments has been said to be evident of the lack of attention by the ICTR to sentencing.[74] This inadequacy has been described by Sloane as treating sentencing as a mere afterthought which in turn 'inhibits the common law evolution of a mature penal jurisprudence that can contribute to the long-term normative goals of international justice'.[75]

The attitude of international criminal tribunals towards sentencing has been noted by Sloane in the following words:[76]

> In general, they [international criminal tribunals] recite the crimes of conviction; emphasize their gravity; list, without elaboration, the conventional goals of punishment; set out the relevant portions of the Statute and Rules; reference Rwandan law to confirm that it has been 'duly considered'; note the duty to individualize sentences, taking account of aggravating and mitigating circumstances; list those circumstances; and then pronounce the sentence, often offering no more by way of analysis (particularly where, as is frequently the case, the sentence is life imprisonment) than a variant of this conclu[ding] statement: 'Having reviewed both mitigating and aggravating circumstances, the Chamber finds that the aggravating circumstances outweigh the mitigating circumstances in the Accused's case.

The SCSL has not departed – except for the bifurcated nature of its trials – from the approach adopted by other international criminal tribunals. Its sentencing judgments follow more or less the same style as highlighted by Sloane in the above quotation. In its discussion of the objectives of sentencing, which are generally not exhaustive of issues relevant to the objectives of sentencing, the SCSL duly endorsed the position that

72 As above, para 8.
73 King and La Rosa (n 14 above) 316-331.
74 Sloane (n 48 above) 713.
75 As above.
76 Sloane (n 48 above) 716.

retribution, deterrence and rehabilitation are the main sentencing objectives in international criminal justice.[77]

4.1 Objectives of punishment and the Special Court for Sierra Leone

4.1.1 Retribution

The Trial Chamber in the *Brima* sentencing judgment cited with approval the Preamble of the United Nations (UN) Security Council Resolution 1315 (2000),[78] according to which,[79]

> [...] in the particular circumstances of Sierra Leone, a credible system of justice and accountability for the very serious crimes committed there would end impunity and would contribute to the process of national reconciliation and to the restoration and maintenance of peace.

It then endorsed the position that retribution, deterrence and rehabilitation are the main sentencing purposes in international criminal justice. In relation to retribution, the Trial Chamber pointed out that other international criminal tribunals have held that retribution should not be 'understood as fulfilling the desire for revenge but rather as duly expressing the outrage of the national and international community at these crimes, and that it is to reflect a fair and balanced approach to punishment for wrongdoing'.[80] The Trial Chamber emphasised that punishment must fit the crime and the penalty must be proportionate to the crime.[81] In *Prosecutor v Fofana and Kondewa*,[82] the Trial Chamber adopted the definition of retribution provided by Lamer J of the Supreme Court of Canada in the case of *R v M*[83] who held that retribution in a criminal context, by contrast to vengeance, represents a measured and seasoned determination of an appropriate punishment and furthermore, unlike vengeance, retribution requires the imposition of a just and appropriate sentence and nothing more.[84] The Trial Chamber in the *Sesay* case[85] also highlighted the same principles as adopted in the other cases and essentially highlighted that the main objectives of punishment at the international level are retribution, deterrence and rehabilitation.

77 AFRC Sentencing judgment para 14.
78 UN Sec Res 1315 (2000) 14 August 2000.
79 Para 7.
80 AFRC Sentencing judgment para 16.
81 As above.
82 (Case SCSL-04-14-T) (CDF Sentencing judgment).
83 [1996] 1 SCR 500.
84 As above, para 86.
85 *Prosecutor v Sesay, Kallon and Gbao* (Case SCSL-04-15) para 13 (RUF Sentencing judgment).

4.1.2 Deterrence

If it was previously unclear as to whether deterrence has been a penal objective at international level, then an observation across all international tribunals over the years has shown that this is no longer the case. According to the Trial Chamber of the SCSL, the penalties imposed must be sufficient to deter others from committing similar crimes and that 'sentencing is intended to convey the message that globally accepted laws and rules have to be obeyed by everybody'.[86] This is particularly important in so far as it goes to show that the international community is not ready to tolerate serious and heinous human rights violations.[87] In the same vein, the SCSL has pointed out, as mentioned before, that the aim of punishment at the international level is 'to influence the legal awareness of the accused, surviving victims, their relatives, the witness and the general public in order to assure them that the legal system is implemented and enforced'.[88]

Like the ICTY and ICTR, the jurisprudence of the SCSL has highlighted the importance of deterrence as a penal objective.[89] It has however not put forward deterrence as an overriding penal objective of punishment. Deterrence in that respect alludes to the notion that a person punished for committing international crimes may be an example to others.[90] This is in clear contrast to the approach taken by the ICTY and the ICTR which have identified deterrence as an overriding penal objective.[91] This is a welcome development considering that deterrence is not only problematic in relation to international criminal justice[92] but it is also substantially susceptible to immense criticism.[93] Chirwa asserts that a deterrence-based approach to international sentencing is questionable because, among others, it assumes that people take note of sentences imposed on others or that they generally take note of the earlier sentences passed by courts.[94] Further, a deterrence-based approach is predicated upon 'unproven assumptions about a perpetrator's rationality'[95] in the context of international crimes. Chirwa further asserts that factors such as the ones highlighted above render a penal policy based on deterrence as the overriding objective inappropriate.[96]

86 AFRC Sentencing judgment para 16; Chirwa (n 19 above) 199.
87 AFRC Sentencing judgment para 16.
88 As above.
89 AFRC *Sentencing* judgment para 14.
90 As above.
91 Chirwa (n 19 above) 199.
92 R Henham 'Developing contextualized rationales for sentencing in international criminal trials: A plea for empirical research' (2007) 5 *Journal of International Criminal Justice* 757.
93 Chirwa (n 19 above) 201.
94 Chirwa (n 19 above) 200.
95 As above; Henham (n 95 above) 385.
96 Chirwa (n 19 above) 200.

Another argument in this respect is that which is raised by Ohlin when he argues that those who are convicted by the ICTY are housed in countries where there are excellent prison conditions, including access to television.[97] He argues that such conditions are a far cry from the conditions in military service and as such will are a welcome change, assumedly to convicts, and not something to be feared. During my visit to the SCSL in 2008, it emerged that members of the public were of the view that the establishment of the court was a waste of resources as the accused persons were rapists and killers who deserved to be punished as swiftly as possible. To some, the treatment that the detainees were afforded was a mockery of justice as they were living comfortably despite the atrocities they committed.[98]

It is submitted that this argument is flawed in that it is based upon an assumption that prison conditions must be so harsh that a convicted person is seen to be and equally feels punished. The argument loses sight of the fact that when prisoners or detainees are incarcerated they only lose their right of mobility and right of association but do not necessarily lose the other important rights which are not relevant to the attainment of the objectives of punishment. As such, the rights of incarcerated convicts at the international level are sacrosanct and must comply with regional and international rules of detention such as the UN Standard Minimum Rules for the Treatment of Prisoners (UNSMR).[99] The argument is further flawed in that it assumes that once incarcerated, the comfort that may be found in detention facilities is comparable to the comfort an individual may derive from their home and association with their families.

Some of the reasons highlighted above are valid reasons which perhaps go to show that international criminal justice revolves around retribution.[100] Deterrence as a rationale for punishment, generally or in respect of the SCSL, does leave certain issues unresolved.

4.1.3 Rehabilitation

Rehabilitation as a penal objective has received less attention from international tribunals. The ICTY and the ICTR have accorded rehabilitation a lesser role than other penal objectives.[101] This is contrary to what international instruments have pointed out in relation to

97 JD Ohlin 'Towards a unique theory of international criminal sentencing' in G Sluiter and S Vasiliev (eds) *International criminal procedure: Towards a coherent body of law* (2009) 384.

98 Discussion held on Wednesday 4 June 2008 at SCSL with Mrs Claire Castins, the then Deputy Principal Defender at the SCSL.

99 R Igweta 'The African Commission on Human and Peoples' Rights and the promotion and protection of prisoners' rights' Unpublished LLM thesis, University of Pretoria (2008) 13.

100 Henham (n 95 above) 757.

101 Chirwa (n 19 above) 202

rehabilitation, especially in the context of criminal law and human rights.[102] The ICTY has declared that the nature of the crimes within the jurisdiction of *ad hoc* international criminal tribunals rules out considerations based on rehabilitation.[103] Even though *ad hoc* international criminal tribunals have afforded less attention to rehabilitation as a penal objective, they have shown support for rehabilitative programmes for young offenders.[104] It has been argued as a result that rehabilitation is well justified as a penal objective especially in the context of reconciliation and social reconstruction[105] aimed at reintegrating back into the society those who played a minor role in the commission of heinous crimes. Those will include low-ranking soldiers or civilians who were acting under orders at the time of the commission of the crimes.[106]

The SCSL Trial Chamber has noted that rehabilitation cannot be considered as a predominant consideration in determining a sentence, as the sentencing aims of national jurisdictions are different from the aims of international criminal tribunals.[107] The Trial Chamber in the *Sesay* case pointed out that '[r]ehabilitation as a goal of punishment means restoration of the convicted person to a state of physical, mental and moral health through treatment and education, so that he can become a useful and productive member of society'.[108] In the CDF and RUF sentencing judgments the Trial Chamber pointed out that even though rehabilitation 'is considered as an important element in sentencing, it is of greater importance in domestic jurisdictions than in International Criminal Tribunals'.[109]

Unfortunately, the Trial Chamber did not offer any insight as to how it came to its conclusion that rehabilitation is more suited to domestic jurisdictions than international ones. It has been rightly pointed out in the context of Sierra Leone that the 'punishment of juvenile soldiers challenges both rehabilitative assumptions of the TRC and the propriety of informal, non-punitive, and relatively short-term social control'.[110] The approach taken by the Sierra Leone TRC that confessions by children who committed some of the atrocities were enough punishment has been rejected by some commentators as casting a shadow on the objective of criminal law, the attainment of justice and the accountability of such

102 Chirwa 202; King and La Rosa (n 18 above) 332; art 14 ICCPR.
103 *Prosecutor v Furundžija* (Case IT-95-17/1-T) Trial Chamber 10 December 1998 paras 290 - 291.
104 King and La Rosa (n 14 above) 332; *Prosecutor v Erdomvić* (n 44 above) paras 64-65.
105 Chirwa (n 19 above) 202.
106 King and La Rosa (n 14 above) 332.
107 AFRC Sentencing judgment para 17.
108 RUF Sentencing judgment para 16.
109 CDF Sentencing judgment para 28; RUF Sentencing judgment para 16.
110 JA Romero 'The Special Court for Sierra Leone and the juvenile soldier dilemma' (2004) 2 *North-Western University Journal of International Human Rights* 8, 9.

children.[111] Those opposing such an approach are of the following view:[112]

> The most effective solution is to treat juvenile soldiers (at least fifteen years old) similar to their adult counterparts upon a finding that they voluntarily joined a warring faction and voluntarily committed heinous crimes. The gravamen of the two-prong requirement is that the soldier possessed the requisite *mens rea* to join a warring faction and the *mens rea* to commit the crime.

Romero is of the view that the rehabilitation of juvenile offenders would be important if their role in the commission of crimes was minimal. Otherwise, he asserts, they should be accordingly punished for whatever crimes they have committed with the necessary *mens rea.* Such argument notwithstanding, it is submitted that article 7 of the SCSL Statute which provides for the rehabilitation and reintegration of any child who comes before the court, is laudable. According to article 7, the SCSL does not have jurisdiction over children below the age of 15 at the time of the commission of the offence. If children between the ages of 15 to 18 at the time of the commission of the offence were brought before the court, the court could[113]

> ... order any of the following: care guidance and supervision orders, community service orders, counselling, foster care, correctional, education and vocational training programmes, approved schools and as appropriate, any programmes of disarmament, demobilization and reintegration or programmes of child protection agencies.

The 'central objectives of the trial processes at the international level are vague and capable of reformulation for different audiences. For some, the central objectives will be retribution and/or deterrence, for others pedagogical performance, national reconciliation or exculpation'.[114] This uncertainty impacts on ascertaining the objective/purpose of sentencing at this level which normally appears to be revenge packaged as retribution. It is submitted that attractive as it is, to put forward rehabilitation as a central penal objective of international sentencing will be inappropriate. This is in light of the fact that it is those who bear the greatest responsibility that are brought before these international tribunals. To this end, rehabilitation as a penal objective at the international level remains an ideal. This is particularly so because if rehabilitation was to be the overriding objective of international sentencing, international criminal tribunals are likely to be faced with the challenge of assessing 'sincerity and genuine rehabilitative potential'.[115]

111 Romero (n 110 above) 11.
112 Romero (n 110 above) 16.
113 Art 7(2) Statute of SCSL.
114 R Henham 'Conceptualising access to justice and victims' rights in international sentencing' (2004) 13 *Social Legal Studies* 29.
115 Sloane (n 49 above) 730.

However, it should be noted that international criminal law is part of the larger framework of international human rights protection and international criminal tribunals should be sensitive to this. The manner in which the SCSL Statute treats juvenile offenders is an example of this and is testimony that rehabilitation has and may play an important role in the international criminal justice arena.

For international sentencing, striking a balance between delivering retribution for the community, deterring would-be criminals from breaking the law, protecting the community from anti-social behaviour and rehabilitating the offender, is rather problematic and will for some time remain contentious. It has been argued that this balance may be achieved through restorative and responsive regulation within competent states, rather than by selective criminal enforcement which encourages setting up scapegoats instead of compliance with the law.[116]

The objectives of sentencing as espoused by the SCSL are no different from that of other tribunals. They are however markedly different to that of national jurisdictions, especially in light of its approach to rehabilitation as its penal objective. The sentencing and punishment practice of international criminal tribunals will forever be tainted by sentiments of revenge as complimented or fuelled by public sentiments about such trials. Even though international tribunals have pointed out that such is retribution and wholly different from revenge,[117] the perception in some quarters that international criminal tribunals may be a true example of victor's justice cannot be ignored. This perception is perhaps caused by the thin line between revenge and retribution as measured against the gravity of the crimes involved as well as the ensuing sentences and by the high rate of convictions before such tribunals.

4.1.4 Sentencing factors

In determining appropriate sentences, the SCSL has taken into account several factors likely to contribute to achieving the penal objectives discussed above.[118] These include the gravity of the offence, aggravating circumstances, mitigating circumstances, and where appropriate, the general sentencing practices of the ICTR and national courts of Sierra Leone as provided for by article 19 of the Statute of the SCSL and Rule 101(B) of the Rules of Procedure and Evidence.

The SCSL Trial Chamber has thus held, '[i]n determining an appropriate sentence, the gravity of the crime is the primary consideration or "litmus test" with the gravity of the crime having to be individually

116 Henham (n 95 above) 34.
117 *Prosecutor v Popović et al* ICTY (Trial Chamber) (Case IT-05-88-T) 10 June 2010 para 2128.
118 AFRC Sentencing judgment para 18.

assessed'.[119] In making an assessment of the gravity of the offence, the Chamber may examine among other things,[120]

> the general nature of the underlying criminal conduct, the form and degree of participation of the accused or the specific role played by the accused in the commission of the offence, the degree of suffering, impact or consequences of the crime for the immediate victim in terms of physical, emotional and psychological effects, the effects of the crime on relatives of the immediate victims and/or the broader targeted group, the vulnerability of the victims, and the number of victims.

The approach adopted by the SCSL Trial Chamber in the *Brima* case has been repeated almost verbatim in other cases concluded by the court.[121] In relation to the gravity of the offence the SCSL Trial Chamber has pointed out that it is the 'litmus test for the appropriate sentence'.[122] For example, the Prosecution highlighted Sessay and Kallon's positions within the RUF and the Junta alliance, especially within the Supreme Council, Sessay's role in planning and organising forced mining activities as well as his endorsement of instructions to kill civilians as well as to burn civilian houses.[123] Having fully considered the submissions of the parties during the sentencing hearing, the Chamber came to the conclusion that the inherent gravity of the crimes in question, which included sexual offences, was exceptionally high and increased the gravity of the underlying offence.[124] The Trial Chamber has also found that the killing of civilians ordered by Kamara showed that he was a violent and active participant in the crimes and in that case amounted to an aggravating factor.[125]

The court in the *Sessay* sentencing judgment pointed out that, based on established jurisprudence, factors considered aggravating in other international criminal jurisdictions include the leadership role of the accused, premeditation and motive, the length and time during which time the offence was committed, the location of the attacks, sadism and desire for revenge as well as total disregard for the sanctity of human life and dignity.[126] The approach taken by international criminal tribunals, to use the gravity of the offence as a litmus test, has been dismissed by some as fiction or as a ploy to set a high baseline for most of the crimes under the jurisdiction of international tribunals.[127]

119 As above.
120 AFRC Sentencing judgment para 19.
121 RUF Sentencing judgment para 18; CDF Sentencing judgment para 32.
122 As above.
123 RUF Sentencing judgment para 43.
124 RUF Sentencing judgment para 116.
125 AFRC Sentencing judgment para 86.
126 RUF Sentencing judgment para 25; AFRC Sentencing judgment para 21; CDF Sentencing judgment para 37.
127 Sloane (n 49 above) 724.

Like the ICTY and the ICTR, the SCSL Trial Chamber has held that aggravating factors must be established by the Prosecution beyond reasonable doubt and that only circumstances directly related to the commission of the offence the accused person is charged with and for which they are subsequently convicted, could be considered to be aggravating.[128] The Trial Chamber has also held that if a particular circumstance is an element of the underlying offence, it cannot be considered to be an aggravating factor.[129] To that end, if an accused person has been found guilty under article 6(3) of the Statute of the SCSL, his leadership position cannot be taken as an aggravating circumstance as it is in itself a constitute element of the offence.[130]

The aggravating and mitigating circumstances to be taken into account by the trial chamber are not exhaustively set out in the Rules of Procedure and Evidence and accordingly, the Trial Chamber is reminded to weigh up the individual circumstances of each case.[131] The Trial Chamber has taken into account mitigating factors in its sentencing decisions such as remorse, lack of formal education or training, individual circumstances, subsequent conduct and lack of prior convictions.[132] The Chamber has held that mitigating factors must be established by the defence on a balance of probabilities,[133] placing a much lower burden of proof on the defence as required of the prosecution in its establishment of aggravating circumstances.

The prosecution in the *Brima* case submitted that no mitigating circumstances existed as he did not cooperate with the prosecution or expressed any remorse[134] and further that there was no evidence that he acted under duress. On the contrary, the Brima defence submitted that he was of good character with a history of philanthropy as well as no prior criminal record.[135] In its final determination, the Court outrightly rejected the Brima defence's argument that Brima's service in the Army was a mitigating factor.[136] The Chamber also came to the conclusion that the statements made by Brima at the sentencing hearing could not be accepted as genuine remorse and were accordingly disregarded as a mitigating factor.[137] In respect of Kamara, the Trial Chamber came to the conclusion

128 CDF Sentencing judgment para 36.
129 As above.
130 CDF Sentencing judgment para 38. Art 6(3) provides that '[t]he fact that any of the acts referred to in articles 2 to 4 of the present Statute was committed by a subordinate does not relieve his or her superior of criminal responsibility if he or she knew or had reason to know that the subordinate was about to commit such acts or had done so and the superior had failed to take the necessary and reasonable measures to prevent such acts or to punish the perpetrators thereof'.
131 AFRC Sentencing judgment para 21.
132 CDF Sentencing judgment para 40.
133 As above.
134 AFRC Sentencing judgment para 58.
135 AFRC Sentencing judgment para 61.
136 Para 64.
137 Para 67.

that there were no mitigating circumstances as he failed to express any genuine remorse whatsoever for his crimes. Arguably, the practice by the SCSL is similar to the approach taken by the ICTR and the ICTY in so far as mitigating and aggravating factors are concerned. The Trial Chamber, however, has offered limited insight into reasons behind their decisions to accept and or reject the defence's submissions both in the *Brima* and *Kamara* cases on mitigating circumstances.

As said before, the SCSL is also mandated by article 19(3), where appropriate, to take into account the sentencing practice by the Sierra Leone national courts and other *ad hoc* tribunals. In the *Brim*a case, the prosecution submitted that the comparisons with sentences imposed by the ICTR were of limited value because most ICTR cases were concerned with genocide a crime outside the jurisdiction of the SCSL. Further that, in many cases the penalty for genocide has been life imprisonment which the SCSL cannot impose.[138] The Chamber, rejecting this submission, held that it will consider the sentencing practice of the ICTR in determining the terms of imprisonment,[139] And that it would take into account the sentencing practice of the ICTY since its statutory provisions were analogous to those of the SCSL and the ICTR.[140]

The Prosecution further argued that there was no specific guidance discernible from the national courts of Sierra Leone because the crimes under the jurisdiction of the court were not specifically addressed under Sierra Leonean law.[141] The Chamber pointed out that even though it is authorised to take into account the practice regarding prison sentences in the national courts of Sierra Leone as and when it is appropriate, this does not oblige the Chamber to conform to that practice.[142] To that end, the Chamber held that it was not appropriate to adopt the practice in the case as none of the accused persons was charged with or convicted of crimes under Sierra Leonean law as provided for under article 5 of the Statute of SCSL.[143] This pronouncement seems to espouse the position that the sentencing practice of the Sierra Leonean national courts only become relevant if the offence is one provided for under article 5 of the Statute of the SCSL, that is, offences relating to the abuse of girls under the Prevention of Cruelty to Children Act (1926) and offences relating to the wanton destruction of property under the Malicious Damage Act (1861). As highlighted by the decisions of the SCSL Trial Chamber, most of the crimes falling within the jurisdiction of the SCSL find no corresponding offence within the penal laws of Sierra Leone. The application of the

138 Para 26.
139 Para 32.
140 Para 33.
141 Para 27.
142 Para 32.
143 Para 33; the said offences are offences relating to abuse of girls under the Prevention of Cruelty to Children Act of 1996 (Cap 31) as well as offences relating to the wanton destruction of property under the Malicious Damage Act, 1861.

sentencing practice of the Sierra Leonean courts are therefore of little relevance in determining an appropriate sentence, save in relation to the offences under article 5 of the Statute of the SCSL.

What is also discernible from the sentencing judgments of the SCSL is that the Trial Chambers did not go to great lengths to adequately explain the reasons behind their reliance on the sentencing factors so employed. For example, during the sentencing hearing, Kondewa addressed the court and the public in the following terms, 'Sierra Leoneans, those of you who lost your relations within [sic] the war, I plead for mercy today, and remorse, and even for yourselves'.[144] In conclusion, the Chamber held that even though Kondewa did not recognise his own participation in the crimes for which he was found guilty, the empathy he showed was real and sincere. It is submitted that the SCSL took a superficial approach to remorse as a mitigating factor which approach makes the conclusions arrived at by the Chamber in this particular case inadequate and unconvincing. Such an important sentencing factor should be approached with a critical mind and deserves to be properly interrogated before a determination is made by the court that the remorse shown was a genuine factor in the case.[145] Even though the Chambers in certain instances rejected the submission of remorse as a mitigating factor by the defence, their discussion on the issue of remorse did not reflect the Trial Chamber's awareness of the subjective nature of remorse.[146]

In the end, the Trial Chamber of the SCSL has tried and convicted a total of eight people indicted for the heinous crimes committed during the Sierra Leonean conflict. In the RUF case, Issa Sessay was convicted on seventeen counts, each carrying a sentence of a minimum of twenty years with the count carrying the highest sentence being a prison sentence of 51 years to run and be served concurrently. Morris Kallon was convicted on seventeen counts, each carrying a minimum sentence of fifteen years, the highest being a prison sentence of 40 years to run and be served concurrently. Augustine Gbao was convicted of fourteen counts, each carrying a sentence ranging from a six-year prison sentence to 25 years.

In the AFRC case, Alex Tamba Brima was sentenced to a single term of imprisonment of 50 years for all the counts he was found guilty of by the Trial Chamber. Ibrahim Bazzy Kamara was sentenced to a single term of imprisonment of 40 years for all the counts he was found guilty of and

144 CDF Sentencing judgment para 65.

145 A Teiger 'Remorse and mitigation in the International Criminal Tribunal for the Former Yugoslavia' (2003) 16 *Leiden Journal of International Law* 777, 780.

146 The ICTY on the contrary has been identified as being fully aware of the subjective nature of remorse as a mitigating factor. In the *Jelisić´* case the Court took into account the accused's alleged expressions of remorse to a court-appointed psychiatrist. In the *Erdmović* case the Chamber cited the testimony of an investigator from the Office of the Prosecutor of the ICTY who at one point worked closely with the accused and was of the strong opinion '... that the accused's remorse was genuine and sincere'; see Teiger (n 145 above) 780.

Santigie Borbor Kanu was sentenced to a single term of imprisonment of 50 years for all the counts he was found guilty of by the Trial Chamber.

In the CDF case, Moinina Fofana was convicted on four counts each carrying a prison term. The minimum prison sentence imposed in respect of each count was three years with the maximum being six years. The Chamber then ordered that Fofana serve a total term in prison of six years with the term calculated as from the 29 May 2003. Allieu Kondewa was convicted on five counts, each carrying a term of imprisonment. The minimum sentence imposed in respect of each count was five years with the highest sentence being eight years. The total term of imprisonment for Kondewa was eight years and calculated as from 29 May 2003.

The sentences passed by the SCSL Trial Chambers are certainly based upon the factors that are employed by the Statute of the SCSL and the Rules of Procedure and Evidence. The practices of other *ad hoc* international criminal tribunals have also played a role in the sentencing practice of the SCSL. What is not clear, though, is whether the sentences passed by the SCSL were at all informed by those of the ICTY and the ICTR. This is evidenced by the Chambers' limited discussion on the sentences passed by other *ad hoc* tribunals, perhaps fortifying the Brima defence's argument that those sentences passed by the ICTR were of limited value to the SCSL in its determination of appropriate sentences.

5 The contribution of the Appeals Chamber in the sentencing practice of the SCSL

The Appeals Chamber's role in the sentencing practice of the SCSL has been somehow limited, understandably so, because of the nature of the rules of appellate review that guide the court. On appeal, pursuant to article 20 of the Statute and Rule 106 of the Rules of Procedure and Evidence (Rules),[147] only arguments relating to errors in law that invalidate the decision of the Trial Chamber would merit consideration.[148] As regards errors of fact, the Appeals Chamber will only overturn the decision of the Trial Chamber where no reasonable trier of fact could have reached the same finding or where the finding is wholly erroneous.[149] With regard to procedural errors, although not expressly provided for in article 20 of the Statute, not all procedural errors can render the proceedings a nullity.[150]

147 Rule 106 Rules of Procedure and Evidence, Special Court for Sierra Leone, 12 April 2002 (as amended 19 November 2007); *Fofana* Appeal judgment para 32.

148 As above.

149 *Prosecutor v Kupreškić* (Case IT-95-16-A), Appeal judgment para 30; *Prosecutor v Ntakirutimana* (ICTR-96-10-A & ICTR-96-17-A), ICTR Appeals Chamber judgment 13 December 2004 para 12 (*Ntakirutimana* Appeal judgment).

150 CDF Appeal judgment paras 34-36.

Notwithstanding its limited appellate review, the Appeals Chamber has in some instances set aside convictions by the Trial Chamber and at times substituted a verdict of not guilty with a verdict of guilty in respect of certain counts. For example, the Appeals Chamber set aside verdicts of guilty for Sesay for planning enslavement in the form of mining and the killing of a Limba man in Tongo Field.[151] After assessing the considerations that influenced the exercise of the Trial Chamber's discretion, the Appeals Chamber came to the conclusion that the Trial Chamber proceeded on an erroneous basis and therefore it had to review the sentences.[152] The Trial Chamber had stated that the fact that Fofana and Kondewa 'stepped forward in the efforts to restore democracy to Sierra Leone, and, for the main part, they acted from a sense of civic duty ... significantly impacted the influence to the reduction of the sentences to be imposed for each count'.[153] Interestingly, the Appeals Chamber emphasised that the SCSL was an international tribunal which punishes international crimes '... and not political crimes, in which consideration of national interest may be a relevant issue'.[154] According to the Appeals Chamber what was paramount were international interests in protecting humanity, hence in assessing an appropriate sentence it was obligated to impose a sentence that reflected the revulsion of the international community about the crimes for which the accused persons have been convicted.[155] The Appeals Chamber accordingly revised the sentences imposed by the Trial Chamber in respect of the charges and imposed slightly heavier sentences.[156]

The Appeals Chamber will only interfere with the decision of the Trial Chamber as regards the sentence passed if the latter has committed a discernible error in exercising its discretion or has failed to follow the applicable law.[157] That is why in the *Brima* case, the Appeals Chamber dismissed the defence's appeal against the sentence imposed by the Trial Chamber and held that the Trial Chamber had exercised its discretion properly within the provision of the Statute of the Court.[158] The Appeals

151 RUF Appeal judgment para 477.
152 CDF Appeal judgment paras 554 - 555.
153 CDF Sentencing judgment para 94.
154 CDF Appeal judgment para 563.
155 CDF Appeal judgment paras 562- 566.
156 That is in respect of Moinina Fofana the sentences of 6 years each imposed by the Trial Chamber on Counts 2 and 4 were increased to 15 years imprisonment, and the sentence of 3 years imposed on Count 5 was increased to five 5 years imprisonment. In respect of Allieu Kondewa, the sentences of 8 years each imposed by the Trial Chamber on Counts 2 and 4 were increased to 20 years imprisonment. The sentence of 5 years imposed on Count 5 was increased to 7 years imprisonment. In respect of Counts 1 and 3, the Appeals Chamber imposed sentences of 15 years imprisonment on Fofana on each of the Counts, and sentences of 20 years imprisonment on Kondewa on each of the Counts, with all the sentences to run concurrently.
157 CDF Appeal judgment para 309.
158 CDF Appeal judgment para 326.

Chamber found no reason to interfere with the exercise by the Trial Chamber of its discretion in sentencing the Appellants.[159]

In the RUF Appeal, the Appeals Chamber came to the conclusion that Issa Hassan Sesay was to serve a total term of imprisonment of 52 years; Morris Kallon and Augustine Gbao were both to serve a total term of imprisonment of 25 years with sentences to run concurrently.[160] The Appeals Chamber highlighted that the Trial Chamber was correct in declining to mitigate the sentences of the accused in light of the finding that they are likely to serve their sentences outside Sierra Leone. It further endorsed the position adopted by the ICTY Appeals Chamber that sentences of similarly situated individuals should be comparable, more particularly, that the determination of sentence involves the individualisation of the sentence so as to appropriately reflect the particular circumstances of the convicted person.[161] In the end, the Appeals Chamber came to the conclusion that previous sentencing practice is one among a host of factors which must be considered when determining an appropriate sentence.[162]

Arguably, the Appeals Chamber did not add much to the sentencing practice of the SCSL, except to emphasise that the punishment meted out to those brought before the court should display the disdain with which the international community views their actions. It is also reasonable to conclude that by necessary implication, the Appeals Chamber confirmed the Trial Chamber's approach in so far as the issue of sentencing or the penal objectives are concerned.

6 Relevance of the jurisprudence of the SCSL

The importance of the jurisprudence of the SCSL cannot be disputed. It is the relevance of the principles enunciated in the several judgments handed down by the court that perhaps will influence the decision of tribunals and national courts alike saddled with a similar mandate.[163] Most importantly, it will be of persuasive value to future *ad hoc* international criminal tribunals.

In terms of sentencing, are there any vital lessons that Sierra Leone national courts could learn from the SCSL? This aspect is particularly relevant when one considers that one of the reasons for situating the SCSL in Sierra Leone, rather than outside Sierra Leone as is the case with the ICTY and ICTR, was to have a 'trickle down effect' in the sense that the

159 CDF Appeal judgment para 329.
160 RUF Appeal judgment para 480.
161 RUF Appeal judgment para 1317.
162 RUF Appeal judgment para 1318.
163 CC Jalloh 'The contribution of the Special Court for Sierra Leone' (2007) 15 *African Journal of International & Comparative Law* 173.

SCSL would contribute *inter alia* to rebuilding the criminal justice system in Sierra Leone.[164] In this regard and as has been indicated, the application of the sentencing practice of the Sierra Leone national courts has been of little relevance in determining and influencing the sentencing practice of the SCSL. This is particularly so because of the nature of the crimes that fell within the jurisdiction of the SCSL. The converse is likely to be true for crimes under article 5 of the Statute of the court. Unfortunately, offences defined as such and punishable under Sierra Leonean law have not been invoked by the Prosecutor before the court, notwithstanding that the court has mixed jurisdiction *ratione materiae*.[165] Perhaps the sentencing jurisprudence of the SCSL will be able to influence the future work of the national courts of Sierra Leone in their administration of justice if it happens that they choose to exercise universal jurisdiction over certain international crimes.

7 Conclusion

The sentencing practice of the SCSL has not been subjected to enough scrutiny. Perhaps this is largely due to the fact that the ICTY and the ICTR have been subjected to scrutiny and have covered most of the issues that eventually came before the SCSL. The fact that the decisions of the ICTY and the ICTR have discussed some of the issues relating to sentencing is likely to explain the manner in which the SCSL approached its decisions, in that it has been brief in its determination of the appropriate sentences. The objectives of sentencing as espoused by the SCSL are no different from those of the other tribunals. The main purpose of sentencing at the international level largely remains deterrence and retribution.

A popular argument is that international criminal tribunals should not put forward retribution as the chief objective of punishment at the international level.[166] It is submitted that such an argument is appealing, admittedly for the sole reason that 'it is theoretically unacceptable for ... any tribunal created to respond to human rights violations to found its operations chiefly on retribution'.[167] It is however imperative to note that an argument that international criminal justice is not about victor's justice and retribution is divorced from reality. The international community is out to punish perpetrators of international crimes and the wording of international instruments, particularly the wording of the Rome Statute,

164 In terms its legacy, the Court acknowledged that 'in operating in a context such as Sierra Leone, the prosecution of individuals must be pursued along with other transitional justice strategies in order to achieve the desired objectives: the restoration of the rule of law and the development of the national legal system, which are necessary conditions for the prevention of future conflict'; see VO Nmehielle and CC Jalloh 'The legacy of the Special Court for Sierra Leone' (2006) 30 *The Fletcher Forum of World Affairs* 109.

165 Jalloh (n 163 above) 173.

166 Chirwa (n 19 above) 195.

167 As above.

has adopted a tone that reflects public sentiments. Accordingly, serious international crimes should not go unpunished. Sentencing before the SCSL has not escaped this anomaly as it has endorsed principles of sentencing as espoused by the decisions of the ICTY and the ICTR. To that end, and as evidenced by the preceding discussion, principles of national law have played a limited role in the sentencing of offenders by the SCSL.

CHAPTER 6

POLITICS OF INTERNATIONAL CRIMINAL JUSTICE: THE ICC'S ARREST WARRANT FOR AL BASHIR AND THE AFRICAN UNION'S NEO-COLONIAL CONSPIRATOR THESIS

*Steve Odero**

1 Introduction

International criminal justice has for long been the jealous preserve of lawyers who in practice have always been reluctant to acknowledge that, more often than not, they operate in an environment that is profoundly imbued with politics. Likewise, political scientists have traditionally either seemed oblivious to the potentially challenging qualities of international criminal justice or have turned a blind eye to such possibility.[1] They have frequently reduced the entire legal enterprise to a more or less arbitrary exercise of power, and in so doing pledging allegiance to the realist school of international relations theory. These two professional trajectories can be explained as follows. For the lawyer, whereas legal phenomena and reality often mix, he has been preoccupied with the use of legal phenomena to influence the factual or political reality. In the lawyer's world, law is sacrosanct and the reality on the ground ought to conform to it. In contrast, for the political scientist, legal phenomena are born of social science and ought to be reflective of it. Social patterns are attributable to calculated and overt human actions, seldom finding expression in law, aimed at influencing various behavioural patterns. Hence, political scientists are preoccupied with the political reality and what actions can influence it, sometimes to the extent of belittling the relevance of the law in this respect. With regards to international criminal justice in particular, political scientists have mostly been disparaging, considering it ornamental at best and relegated to some discrete sub-discipline, for example under the catch-all expression 'transitional justice', somewhere in between public policy, history and ethical theory.

* LL.B (Nairobi); LL.M (Pretoria); PhD (Luiss, Italy). Lecturer in Law and Political Science, Africa Nazarene University, Kenya.

1 F Megret 'The politics of international criminal justice' (2002) 13 *European Journal of International Law* 1262.

However, with the advent of the International Criminal Tribunal for the Former Yugoslavia (ICTY), the indictment and transfer of Slobodan Milosevic and Radovan Karadzic to the ICTY, and most recently the indictment and issuance of an arrest warrant for Sudan's President Al Bashir, lawyers and political scientists alike have had to re-examine their traditional conceptions about each other's role and place in international relations. Indeed, somewhere on the fault-lines of law and politics a number of publications are already sprouting, seeking to tackle the idea that there is more to international criminal justice than law and that there is more to international political relations than the power pragmatics of everyday reality. This chapter is one such publication, seeking to urge both lawyers and political scientists to face up to the political reality of international criminal justice and, vice versa, the legal reality of international politics. Through an examination of the ICC's experience with the Sudanese President, in particular the African Union's (AU) dissatisfaction with his indictment, what has been considered as the politics of the indictment, this chapter emphasises the need for lawyers and political scientists to attempt to synchronise their work. The analysis is hybrid in nature, drawing from the disciplines of law and political science, and is therefore a challenge to lawyers, calling on them to unpack controversial factual issues and in so doing, add to their understanding of the complex non-legal factors that are at play in international criminal justice. Likewise, it is a challenge to political scientists to pay more attention to legal phenomena that are often at play and likely to influence political processes. It is only through a meeting of minds by scholars, practitioners and policy makers from these two fields that sound judgments grounded in law and political reality may be reached and successfully implemented.

2 Background

In July 2008, the prosecutor of the International Criminal Court (ICC), Luis Moreno-Ocampo, accused Sudanese President Hassan Omar Al Bashir of genocide, crimes against humanity and war crimes in Darfur and requested the issuing of an arrest warrant against the sitting head of state. The AU together with Organization of the Islamic Conference sought to block this action by requesting the United Nations Security Council to defer ICC proceedings for twelve months in accordance with article 16 of the Rome Statute, a request which has to date remained unanswered.[2] The Court issued an arrest warrant for Al Bashir on 4 March 2009 for the commission of war crimes and crimes against humanity but ruled that

2 C Gosnell 'The request for an arrest warrant in Al Bashir' (2008) 6 *Journal of International Criminal Justice* 841-851 and A Ciampi 'The proceedings against president Al Bashir and the prospects of their suspension under article 16 ICC Statute' (2008) 6 *Journal of International Criminal Justice* 885-897.

there was insufficient evidence at the time to prosecute him for genocide.[3] In its decision approving the arrest warrant, the ICC Pre-Trial Chamber found that the information supplied by the ICC Prosecutor did not show reasonable grounds to believe that the Sudanese government acted with specific intent to destroy, in whole or in part, the Fur, Masalit and Zaghawa groups. Charges of genocide were therefore not included for the arrest warrant.

Nonetheless, the Chamber left a window open for an amendment or modification in light of any information submitted subsequently under article 58(6). Indeed, later on and in accordance with the said article of the Rome Statute, on 3 February 2010, the Appeals Chamber of the ICC reversed the earlier decision of the Pre-Trial Chamber rejecting the genocide charge, ruling that the Chamber had applied too stringent a standard of proof. The consequence of this is that the prosecutor is at liberty to add genocide to the list of charges against the President of Sudan. Unlike the three other African countries under ICC investigation, namely Uganda, Central African Republic (CAR) and Democratic Republic of Congo (DRC), Sudan is not a party to the Statute of the ICC (Rome Statute). The Court derives its jurisdiction over Sudan's case of Darfur through a Security Council Resolution of March 2005. As a rejoinder, in July 2009 at the 13th AU Summit, the AU voted by a large majority not to cooperate with the ICC over its indictment of Sudanese President Omar Hassan Al Bashir.[4] From among the concerns that were raised by AU leaders over the actions of the prosecutor, this chapter addresses two, namely:

(a) The issuance of an arrest warrant for Sudanese President Al Bashir was prejudicial to ongoing peace processes.[5]

(b) The action has been taken without due regard to sustainable peace in Sudan, and is therefore a toothless stooge of ex-colonial powers.[6]

Before examining the plausibility or otherwise of these arguments, a brief historical account of the relationship between Africa and the ICC as foundation for the ensuing analysis is in order.

3 AT Cayley 'The prosecutor's strategy in seeking the arrest of Sudanese President Al Bashir on charges of genocide' (2008) 6 *Journal of International Criminal Justice* 829-840 and De Waal 'Darfur, the Court and Khartoum: The politics of state non-cooperation' in N Waddell and P Clark (eds) *Courting conflict? Justice, peace and the ICC in Africa* (2008) 125.

4 Assembly of the African Union 2009 'Decisions and declarations' Assembly/AU/Dec 243-267 (XIII).

5 African Union Communique 2008 'Communique of the 142nd meeting of the Peace and Security Council'.

6 'AU justice Ministers protest abuse of universal jurisdiction' *New York Times* 5 November 2008 available at http://allafrica.com/stories/200811050742.html (accessed 1 June 2010).

2. 1 Africa-ICC relationship

From the onset of discussions about a permanent international criminal court, Africa had a very positive attitude towards the ICC. Indeed, an African country, Senegal, was the first in the world to ratify the Rome Statute on 2 February 1999.[7] This is an illustration of Africa's early support for the idea of a permanent international criminal court with jurisdiction over the 'most serious crimes of concern to the international community as a whole'. This support also finds expression in the remarks of the then Organization of African Unity's (OAU) representative during the final five weeks of the Rome negotiations. According to OAU's representative, the continent of Africa had a special interest in the establishment of the ICC because its people had for centuries endured human rights atrocities such as slavery, colonial wars and other horrific acts of war and violence which continue today despite the continent's post-colonial phase.[8] In view of the lack of strong institutional structures, a court of this nature was expected to supplement the course of justice in regional and domestic jurisdictions. Further, vivid memories of the Rwandan genocide of 1994, in which the international community was forewarned but failed to act, strengthened Africa's resolve to support the idea of an independent and effective international penal court that would punish, and hopefully deter, perpetrators of such heinous crimes in the future.[9]

Naturally, Africa went on to play a significant and constructive role in the Rome negotiations, ultimately leading to the creation of the Court.[10] The continent's strong backing for the Court has not been limited to state governments. With many African non- governmental organisations (NGOs) and civil society working under regimes that are not accountable or are outright dictatorships that pay little or no heed to basic human rights principles, these two entities made a significant contribution to the promulgation process. Their contribution was made principally through domestic advocacy and an international organization born of such advocacy, the NGO Coalition for the Establishment of an International Criminal Court (the Coalition),[11] that comprised activists from Africa and

7 UN Doc A/CONF 183.9.

8 T Maluwa, Legal Adviser OAU Secretariat Statement at the 6th Plenary, 17 June 1998; Official records of the United Nations Diplomatic Conference of Plenipotentiaries on the Establishment of an International Criminal Court, UN Doc A/CONF 183/13 (Vol II) 104, 115-118 para 116.

9 Maluwa (as above).

10 H Jallow and F Bensouda 'International criminal law in an African Context' in M Du Plessis (ed) *African guide to international criminal justice* (2008) 41; P Mochochoko 'Africa and the International Criminal Court' in E Ankumah and E Kwakwa (eds) *African perspectives on international criminal justice* (2005) 15 and S Maqungo 'The establishment of the International Criminal Court: SADC's participation in the negotiations' (2000) 9 *African Security Review* 42.

11 R Pace and M Thieroff 'Participation of non-governmental organizations' in S Lee (ed) *The International Criminal Court: The marking of the Rome Statute – issues, negotiations, results* (1999) 395.

their counterparts in other parts of the world. Their objective was to stir the conscience of world governments towards agreement on contentious issues and so paving the way for the Court's establishment.[12] While the stated preferences of the individual advocacy groups were not met to the letter, the end product of the negotiations was a more robust instrument than even the ICC's strongest supporters could sensibly have hoped for.[13] With the adoption of the Rome Statute, the Coalition quickly transformed itself into an effective global campaign for swift achievement of the 60 ratifications required for it to enter into force. Their efforts enabled the entry into force of the Statute in July 2002, much sooner and more dramatically than could have been reasonably anticipated.[14] Even after its entry into force, the Coalition continued to support the work of the Preparatory Commission to assist in developing important ancillary legal instruments, for example, the Court's Rules of Procedure and Evidence and the elements of crimes.[15]

Today, African civil society appears to have entered a third phase of advocacy whereby it leverages prior contacts within governments to not only lobby for the remaining ratifications, but also adopt the necessary legislation and domestic programmes to give effect to their Rome Statute obligations.[16] On the whole, given the serious governance deficit on the continent, local and international human rights NGOs played an important role in sensitising political leaders to the potential benefits of a strong court for Africa. Until last year, over a decade after the Rome Statute was adopted, African countries, many of which are either embroiled in conflicts of one sort or another or newly emergent from them, had continued to invest their yearnings for peace and stability in the hope that the ICC would become a success story and of benefit to them.

To illustrate this point, Africa is on record for having generated the largest support base for the Court with at least 30 ratifying states, over half of the continent's 53 countries with another thirteen countries having signalled their support for the treaty through their signatures.[17] Indeed, of the five cases presently before the Court, three of them are from Africa by way of self referral, an indication of what was until recently the continent's wide embrace of the Court.[18] However, following the indictment of Sudanese President Al Bashir for crimes against humanity and faced with the possibility of a genocide case at a time when Sudan was on the eve of

12 As above.

13 Note by the UN Secretary-General 'Non-governmental organizations accredited to participate in the conference' UN Doc A/CONF 183/INF/3 5 June 1998.

14 WA Schabas *An Introduction to the International Criminal Court* (2004) 19

15 Pace and Thieroff (n 11 above).

16 C Jalloh 'Regionalising international criminal law' (2009) 9 *International Criminal Law Review* 445.

17 As above.

18 C Kress 'Self-referrals' and 'waivers of complementarity' (2004) 2 *Journal of International Criminal Justice* 944 and P Gaeta 'Is the practice of "self-referrals" a sound start for the ICC?' (2004) 2 *Journal of International Criminal Justice* 951.

national elections, coupled with a looming referendum to decide the fate of the country as a whole, the relationship between the ICC and Africa seems to be on the rocks.

3. AU's bones of contention regarding the ICC

3.1 Al Bashir's arrest warrant as prejudicial to Sudan's peace processes

One of the AU's most persistent criticisms of the ICC's actions in Africa has been that, by prosecuting active participants in ongoing or recently settled conflicts, the Court risks prolonging the violence or endangering fragile peace processes currently in place in Sudan.[19] The plausibility or otherwise of these sentiments inevitably takes us into the political reality of Sudan's conflicts, where an even-handed appreciation of the facts is paramount. Any analysis or criticism devoid of such an appreciation is bound to be baseless and out of touch with the reality on the ground. Therefore, in investigating the soundness of this argument, the following questions are of vital importance. What is the nature or typology of the Sudanese conflicts? Who are the key actors or players in these conflicts? What efforts have been put in place in the past or are currently in place to deal with these conflicts? What does conflict resolution theory and practice provide as elements of a successful conflict-resolution exercise? In what way, if any, do Luis Moreno's actions impede successful conflict resolution in Sudan?

3.1.1 Typology of Sudan's conflicts

Sudan has been the scene of Africa's longest civil war – the one between the Northern Khartoum government and the South's Sudan Peoples Liberation Movement. The war was brought to an end following a protracted peace process culminating in a Comprehensive Peace Agreement (CPA) and an Interim National Constitution with both documents embracing an intricate design of two conflict management mechanisms, namely, power sharing and autonomy. In the case of the North-South conflict, there are two main actors, each led by a dominant elite in the personalities of Al Bashir and Salva Kirr who command overwhelming support of their followers.

Another conflict in the Darfur region is more complex and has more than two actors: the Northern Khartoum government, *Janjaweed* militia, two rebel movements, the Justice and Equality Movement (JEM) and the

19 'Communique of the 142nd meeting of the Peace and Security Council' African Union (2008).

Sudanese Liberation Army/Movement (SLA) comprising of the Masalit, Fur and Zaghawa ethnic groups. A recent push towards a peaceful resolution of this conflict has seen the brokerage of a deal between the Khartoum government and Darfur's largest rebel group, JEM. This truce and power-sharing agreement was signed on 23 February 2010 in Doha, Qatar, by Sudan's President Al Bashir and JEM representation. From the foregoing it is apparent that Al Bashir is not only part of the problem in Sudan's seemingly intractable conflicts, but an integral part of the promulgated solutions that have so far facilitated some semblance of stability.

3.1.2 Conflict resolution theory and practice

Conflict resolution theory has it that conflicts tend to escalate. The logical stages of their progression are often indicated as follows: a discussion dialogue stage, where the parties may disagree but work together; polarisation, where parties distance themselves from each other; segregation, where parties move away from each other completely; and destruction, where there is all-out antagonism, including violence and war, among the parties.[20] An escalation of conflict may occur at any stage of this exercise when actions are taken either by the parties or by an external party that has the effect of fatally altering one or more of the three pillars of conflict resolution as outlined by Wallensteen. According to Wallensteen, the basic elements of a conflict resolution exercise are:[21]

(a) An agreement, that is, a formal understanding among the parties where a signed document is produced.

(b) The continued existence of the opposing parties, not a situation of defeat and win or capitulation, but the fighting parties accept each other also as parties in future dealings with one another.

(c) The termination of violent actions against each other where war ends fear and insecurity of persons including former belligerents.

A post-conflict situation follows the aforementioned stages and that is the situation in which Sudan finds itself since the enactment of the CPA and the Darfur Agreement. This is a very uncertain stage where a relapse into violent conflict or war is a real possibility. During this phase, events known as conflict triggers may cause intergroup relations to move away from relative accommodation to hostility and violence.[22] Conflict triggers can include provocative acts by political leaders, international institutions, failed elections or violent upsurges such as riots.[23] This scheme of conflict

[20] P Harris and B Reilly (eds) *Democracy and deep-rooted conflict: Options for negotiators* (1998) 3.

[21] P Wallensteen *Understanding conflict resolution* (2002) 16

[22] T Northrup 'The dynamic of identity in personal and social conflict' in L Kriesburg *et al* (eds) *Intractable conflicts and their resolution* (1989) 52.

[23] Northrup (as above).

resolution may be illustrated by three examples, namely, Rwanda's Arusha Accords, the Dayton Accords of Bosnia and former Yugoslavia, and the more recent Kenyan power-sharing deal.

In the case of Rwanda, the Arusha Accords (also referred to as the Arusha Peace Agreement) were negotiated and signed in Arusha, Tanzania on 4 August 1993 by the government of Rwanda and the rebel movement, the Rwandan Patriotic Front (RPF), to end a three-year-long Rwandan Civil War. The Arusha Peace Agreement established a Broad-Based Transitional Government (BBTG) which included the insurgent Rwandese Patriotic Front (predominantly composed of Tutsi minority) and the five political parties of the time that had been part of a temporary government since April 1992. The Agreement also included various points considered necessary for lasting peace such as the rule of law, repatriation of refugees both from fighting, power sharing agreements, and the merging of government and rebel armies. Before the Agreement could even be implemented, the death of the Rwandan President who was an integral part of the process triggered a bloody genocide with both sides blaming each other for the assassination.

In Kenya, following a disputed election in late 2007, ethnic clashes engulfed Kenya in January and February 2008. Under an accord brokered by former UN Secretary-General Kofi Annan, Kenya's two main political parties agreed to a power-sharing arrangement as a way to end the violence. The accord called for the creation of a Grand Coalition government in which the two parties would be equal partners. The agreement has so far proven effective in restoring peace in Kenya; yet there remains significant potential for future conflict, and the success of the agreement in coming years will largely depend on how Kenya's political leaders negotiate a number of divisive issues. The importance of the two leaders to the peace process was stressed by chief negotiator Kofi Anan throughout the negotiations and has been underscored during the tenure of the Agreement, particularly during moments of disagreement.

The Dayton Agreement is a pact entered into by the Republic of Bosnia and Herzegovina, the Republic of Croatia and the Federal Republic of Yugoslavia which put an end to the three-and-a-half-year-long war in Bosnia and one of the armed conflicts in the former Socialist Federative Republic of Yugoslavia. The main participants from the region were Serbian President Slobodan Milošević (representing the Bosnian Serb interests in the absence of Radovan Karadžić), Croatian President Franjo Tuđman, and Bosnian President Alija Izetbegović with Bosnian Foreign Minister Muhamed Sacirbey. It is noteworthy of the Dayton case that Slobodan Milosevic was later indicted by the ICTY and transferred to The Hague where he passed away in custody long after the peace process in the Balkans had been secured.

3.1.3 ICC arrest warrant for Al Bashir is ill-timed and a 'provocative act' in conflict resolution theory and practice

From a conflict resolution perspective and going by the various ongoing political processes in Sudan, the issuing of an arrest warrant by the ICC for Al Bashir can rightfully be construed as a provocative act and a potential conflict trigger, thereby explaining the AU's sentiments. The warrant is ill-timed and seeks to tamper with an essential element of the Sudan's peace processes - the continued existence of both parties. As outlined above, according to Wallensteen's theory of conflict resolution, operationalised by the examples discussed above, one of the central elements to a resolution exercise is the continued existence of the opposing parties and not a situation of defeat and win or capitulation. The fighting parties must accept each other also as parties in future dealings with one another. In this case, Al Bashir, President and part of a dominant elite representing the Northern government, is a key element to the success of the North-South accord and the recently-promulgated North-Darfur Accord. In so far as the actions of the ICC have the potential of terminating or fatally jeopardising the existence of one of the parties to these conflicts – Al Bashir – they ought to be construed as provocative and carried out in disregard to the objective of sustainable peace in Sudan. As alluded to earlier, not only is Al Bashir part of the problem in these conflicts but he is also an integral part of the solution. Therefore, any application of international criminal justice/law devoid of a careful consideration of his position and role in the conflict and the peace process attendant thereto, can only be self-defeating. On the issue of timing, having emphasised the critical role of Al Bashir in the peace processes and with a looming Southern Sudan referendum on their future as part of Sudan, the arrest warrant could not have come at a more inappropriate occasion.

This point seems of little relevance to the OTP, following the position of the ICC Prosecutor on the need to take into consideration the interests of justice when discharging his duties. His interpretation excludes matters of peace and security. In September 2007, the OTP published a Policy Paper on the Interests of Justice.[24] In this document, the ICC prosecutor states, amongst other things, that the criteria for the exercise of article 53 of the Rome Statute 'will naturally be guided by the objects and purposes of the Statute, namely the prevention of serious crimes of concern to the international community through ending impunity'. He also notes that 'there is a difference between the concepts of the interests of justice and the interests of peace and that the latter falls within the mandate of institutions such as the UN Security Council other than the Office of the Prosecutor'.[25]

24 'Policy paper on the 'interests of justice' Office of the Prosecutor ICC September 2004 www.icc-cpi.int/NR/rdonlyres/.../ICCOTPInterestsOfJustice.pdf (accessed 1 June 2010).

25 As above, 1.

He has added that his office will 'pursue its own judicial mandate independently' and will not submit to the political pressure of those trying to mislead the ICC in the face of other conflicting questions.[26]

If the law – and by extension, international criminal law – is a social science just as much as political science (and international conflict resolution) then the Prosecutor's narrow conception of the interests of justice as applying only to legal practice is at best preposterous. In fact, it is the kind of attitude that has worked to entrench the recent AU's distrust and resistance towards the Court. International criminal justice cannot operate outside the purview of political reality and neither can political scientists engaged in conflict resolution mediate and promulgate peace arrangements without due consideration of international criminal justice. International criminal justice operates in a political environment and is more often than not called into action following a political process. In more cases than not the negotiation of a peace agreement is what opens the door for the effective operation of international criminal justice. Without a successful peace process, international criminal justice remains but an illusion - an objective that international lawyers aspire to. Therefore, the interests of justice cannot be restricted to the legal realm as advanced by the ICC Prosecutor, but must reasonably include political realities.

3.2 ICC's actions as a neo-colonial conspiracy

Having illustrated that the AU's position that Bashir's arrest warrant is prejudicial to ongoing Sudanese peace processes is plausable, the examination turns to the neo-colonial nature of this action. Neo-colonialism is a term used to describe certain operations at the international level which alledgedly have similarities to traditional colonialism of the 16th to the 19th centuries. The contention is that governments aim to control other nations through indirect means; that in lieu of direct military-political control, neo-colonialist powers employ various economic, financial and legal policies to dominate less powerful countries.[27] The effect is *de facto* control over targeted nations. While the first point discussed above is clearer and has a robust foundation in theory and practice, the neo-colonial argument can easily be relegated to the realm of conspiracy theories if not well-posited by its proponents. Hence, the following section endeavours to provide that explanation under two different headings: (a) Africa's colonial legacy; and (b) American exceptionalism or the 'double standard'-problem.

26 Policy paper (n 25 above) 8.
27 I Gasssama 'Africa and the politics of destruction: A critical re-examination of neo-colonialism and its consequences' (2008) 10 *Oregon Review of International Law* 338.

3.2.1 Africa's colonial legacy

Africa's bitter experience with colonialism has proven to be a challenge to the ICC's work on the continent. The reality is that African countries are scarred by the depredations of colonialism. The situation is not helped by the fact that, during Africa's encounter with colonialism, international law was used to further the civilising mission by offering intellectual justifications thereof. Third World Approaches to International Law (TWAIL) scholars like Anghie and Chimni argue that it was 'principally through colonial expansion that international law achieved one of its defining characteristics of universality'.[28] TWAIL scholars have conducted research on how international law was used to justify and legitimise the suppression of Third World peoples and was therefore instrumental in the shaping of the power and subordination presently inherent in the colonial order. According to them, it is expected of former colonies to be apprehensive of the use of international law, including international criminal law, by powerful states. Mohamed Mamdani suggested that the language of law is often subverted by powerful states with the effect of establishing a 'new humanitarian order' in which the principle of state sovereignty obtains in the larger parts of the world but is suspended or virtually non-existent in many countries in Africa and the Middle East.[29] He represents views that capture the sentiments of contemporary African leadership; that it is a mockery for the big powers who were at the time of colonialism the greatest perpetrators of abuses against Africans to style themselves as the custodians of human rights internationally.[30] Even if one does not subscribe to the aforementioned views, one cannot help but appreciate the legitimacy challenges that international criminal law is bound to face in such a historical reality.

3.2.2 Africa's colonial scars and the ICC's work

The ICC's investigations in sub-Saharan Africa have already stirred concerns over African sovereignty and the long history of foreign intervention on the continent. Rwandan President Paul Kagame has portrayed the ICC as a new form of 'imperialism' that seeks to 'undermine people from poor African countries, and other powerless countries in terms of economic development and politics'.[31] Other pundits have used the cases before the Court as an illustration of the prosecutor's selective focus on Africa. The view expressed in this respect is that the prosecutor has limited his investigations to Africa because of geopolitical pressures, either

28 A Anghie and B Chimni 'Third world approaches to international law and individual responsibility in conflicts' (2003) 2 *Chinese Journal of International Law* 88.

29 M Mamdani 'Darfur, ICC and the new humanitarian order: How the ICC's "responsibility to protect" is being turned into an assertion of neo-colonial domination' *Pambazuka News* 396 http://www.pambazuka.org (accessed 1 June 2010).

30 As above.

31 AFP 'Rwanda's Kagame says ICC Targeting Poor, African Countries' 31 July 2008.

out of a desire to avoid confrontation with major powers or as a tool of Western foreign policy. Critics of this view have referred to the fact that the cases before the Court have not been initiated by the Prosecutor but have come by way of self referrals by the states in question. Further; that the Prosecutor is at present analysing other situations in countries outside of Africa. In addition, observers have pointed out that national legal systems in Africa are particularly weak, a fact which has allowed the ICC to assert its jurisdiction under the principle of complementarity.[32]

3.2.3 American exceptionalism: The double standard problem

Perhaps the biggest political challenge for the Court at this juncture, especially in relation to its legitimacy in Africa, is what scholars like Jalloh has referred to as the 'double standard' problem.[33] Domestic legal systems are founded on – amongst other core principles – the notion of equality before the law. The principle is not different under international law applicable between states (at least in theory) and is enshrined in the Preamble and in article 2(1) of the UN Charter. Article 2(1) affirms the 'equal rights of men and women and of nations large and small' and the 'principle of sovereign equality of all' states. This principle prohibits arbitrary distinctions in respect of its application based on states' or individuals' social, wealth, moral or other status. American exceptionalism, the antithesis of the equality principle, in the ICC-US relationship, has only served to fortify Africa's sense of the ICC being a neo-colonial conspirator rather than an impartial arbiter.[34] American exceptionalism is the theory that the US occupies a special niche among the nations of the world in terms of its national credo, historical evolution, political and religious institutions and unique origins.[35] This concept is used to justify or excuse the actions of the US in various instances when they would conventionally be considered to be acting contrary to expected norms. That American exceptionalism has been a feature of the ICC relationship may be illustrated in the following aspects of this superpower policy.[36]

(a) ICC conduct in the aftermath of the US 'War on Terror'

It is now widely accepted by both political and legal analysts that the incursion by the US into Iraq under the banner of the 'War on Terror' was

32 Jalloh (n 16 above).
33 Jalloh (n 16 above).
34 W Schabas 'United States hostility to the International Criminal Court: It's all about the Security Council' (2004) 15 *European Journal of International Law* 705.
35 J Thimm 'American exceptionalism: Conceptual thoughts and empirical evidence' available at http://www.politikwissenschaft.tu-darmstadt.de/fileadmin/pg/Sektion stagung_IB/Thimm-American_exceptionalism.pdf (accessed 1 June 2010).
36 Schabas (n 34 above).

fundamentally baseless.[37] To aggravate the situation, in addition to the complete breakdown of political and social order that followed the invasion, were allegations of serious human rights violations committed against Iraqi prisoners of war by US military personnel.[38] The cases that emerged from the Abu Ghraib prison in Iraq were shattering to the conscience of humanity and the impunity or façade of justice that followed only served to add insult to injury. If there was any time the ICC was required to act against the US military and political leaders involved, it was then. Of course, from a realistic perspective the prospect of such a course of action is ludicrous, given the fact that the US is not party to the Rome Statute, nor is it a member of the UN Security Council, the only body with the mandate to subject a non-party state to the ICC's jurisdiction. The veto power held by the US and her allies, France and Britain, made it even more impossible for the prospects of any action. To the already skeptical AU, this state of affairs is a strong affirmation of the skewed nature of global politics and has adverse implications for the authenticity international criminal law. Issues of justice, international criminal justice included, have become mired in – some might even say held hostage by – big power politics.

Moreover, the response of the ICC Prosecutor, upon being notified and receiving numerous complaints about the Iraq situation requiring him to investigate possible international crimes, casts his office and the Court in a bad light. Indeed, in the month of February 2006, he publicly acknowledged that he had received many complaints regarding the Iraq situation but that he had no competence to prosecute the crime of aggression (which had yet to be defined).[39] Oddly, relying on information partly furnished by British authorities, a party to the war on terror, he concluded that there were no reasonable indicia of elements of genocide, crimes against humanity and war crimes and, importantly, that the requisite gravity threshold had not been achieved.[40] The question then truly begs how this threshold was achieved in the CAR situation, despite the low number of reported victims over a two-year period. Not only has this explanation been unsatisfactory in Africa, but also in other parts of the world with various commentators contributing to the debate.[41]

37 Cuba Centre for Constitutional Rights *Report on Torture and Cruel, Inhuman, and Degrading Treatment of Prisoners at Guantanamo Bay* (2006) New York.

38 'Army Private is convicted in Abu Ghraib abuse case' Associated Press 26 September (2005); 'Private gets 3 years for Iraq prison abuse' 28 September (2005) *New York Times*; 'England convicted of Abu Ghraib abuse, *Washington Street Journal Online* 26 September (2005); 'The reach of war: The verdict; US soldier found guilty in Iraq prison abuse case 15 January' (2005).

39 'Statement on communication concerning the situation in Iraq' Office of the Prosecutor ICC, 9 February 2006.

40 K Chitiyo and L Devlin 'The International Criminal Court and Africa' (2008) 28 *The Royal United Services Institute Newsbrief* 69.

41 As above.

(b) US legislation to prevent a Hague invasion

The systematic adoption by the US of domestic legislation precluding cooperation with the ICC is another illustration of American exceptionalism in the US-ICC relationship. These pieces of legislation include the American Service Members Protection Act (2002), also known as the 'Hague Invasion Act' that provides for a mechanism of penalising any country that hands over a US national to the ICC, including the use of military force.[42] Despite the complete absurdity of this position clearly meant to undermine the universality of international criminal law and frustrate the work of the ICC, the Court has not publicly expressed a position condemning it. This loud silence may be interpreted as acquiescence and is deafening to Africa. Predictably, this state of affairs bolsters the AU's sentiments that the ICC is being used as a whip by former colonial masters to discipline weaker and poorer developing countries in impoverished continents such as Africa. Moreover, during the Bush Administration, the US used its powerful position in the global community to negotiate article 98 agreements with developing countries wherein promises were made not to hand over American nationals to the ICC without the US consent. As would be expected, a failure or refusal to enter into such agreements would have dire consequences, including the loss of financial, military and humanitarian aid. In fact, human rights activists coined the term 'bilateral impunity agreements' for these agreements.[43]

3. 3 Note on UN Security Council composition

The composition of the UN Security Council, the body meant to be the decider of what is in the interest of justice and peace, according to the Court Prosecutor comprises the US, China and Russia, neither of which is a party to the Rome Statute. This body was at the centre of the process that referred Sudan to the ICC. Of relevance here are the remarks already mentioned above of ICC Prosecutor who considers the Security Council to be the ultimate custodian of the political implications of any case that he may intend to prosecute through their powers as conferred in the Statute. These now seemingly imprudent remarks buffer the AU's view that the ICC is but a neo-colonial stooge, given the immense criticism the Security Council's has faced regarding its impartiality.[44] In the midst of these criticisms and in a bid to curb the impartiality of the Council, the AU has

42 'US Congress Passes Anti-ICC Hague Invasion Act' Coalition for the International Criminal Court, Press Release, 26 July 2002 http://www.iccnow.org/documents/07.26.02ASPAthruCongress.pdf (accessed 15 May 2009).

43 Coalition for the International Criminal Court 'USA and the ICC: Bilateral Immunity Agreements' http://www.iccnow.org/?mod=bia (accessed 15 May 2009) and Human Rights Watch 'Briefing Paper on Bilateral Immunity Agreements' New York, 20 June 2003.

44 S Odero 'A Liberal-realist conception of international relations: A pragmatic approach to understanding the United Nations' www.scribd.com/.../Steve-Odero-Ouma-PhD-International-Relations-Theory (accessed 9 April 2010).

called for the reservation of a permanent seat for the Africa coupled with veto power to protect and safeguard the continent from the perceived neo-colonialist and imperialistic tendencies of its present composition.

4 Conclusion

It is clear from the discussion above that, whereas some of AU's concerns regarding the actions of the ICC Prosecutor are legitimate, they do not find expression in law. This is the reason why some analysts have been quick to dismiss the arguments as an attempt by the AU to hoodwink the international community. This piece is a call for a considered re-examination of some of the original hard-line positions against the AU's actions in response to Al Bashir's indictment. Indeed, the AU has shown an increasing commitment to addressing serious human rights abuses perpetrated by non-state actors within its territories. Its regional peace and security architecture, equipped with a legal mandate to take concrete steps, including military action in the form of humanitarian intervention, is all but evidence of this commitment. Africa is the first continent in the world to legislate on the responsibility to protect, a subject that has mostly been restricted to theoretical discussion in other jurisdictions.

It is also evident that Africa has since day one had a significant interest in the establishment of a permanent international criminal court, largely because of its historical experience of untold atrocities and a postcolonial era characterised by weak or non-existing institutional structures. Moreover, three African countries have already taken the first crucial steps to refer situations to the ICC. It only follows that, rather than being an attempt to deceive the international community, the AU is genuinely concerned about how international criminal prosecutions fit into the AU's broader peacemaking and peace-building objectives. In fact, regarding Al Bashir's case, the AU has not opposed the intended prosecution as such, but has expressed disquiet about its timing. This concern is rightly based on conflict resolution concerns and the potential for such warrant to be a conflict trigger.

Another illustration of good faith on the part of African countries and the AU at large is their consistency in urging Sudanese authorities to take concrete steps to improve human rights conditions on the ground, all the while pressing for a comprehensive peace agreement between the warring sides. The CPA Agreement, brokered between the North and South under the auspices of the Intergovernmental Authority on Development (IGAD, a seven-country regional development organisation) is a clear example of such commitment. Further, in collaboration with the UN, African countries have contributed, over recent decades, to the thousands of peacekeepers in Sudan. Even if extreme action, such as a withdrawal of ratifications or referrals of one or more African states parties, has not so far been taken, the damaged relationship between the Court and the AU may encourage countries on the continent to drag their feet in domesticating the Rome Statute. This is important because, out of 30 states parties from the continent, only Burkina Faso, Kenya, Senegal, South Africa and Uganda have so far passed implementing legislation. Furthermore, other African state parties may withhold their planned referrals and their planned ratifications. Improved relations, which can be achieved through an appreciation of the issues raised here, will in the long run embolden some countries (for instance Rwanda and Angola) which have vowed never to become part of the ICC. At the same time, the Court as a legal institution, whose very essence is to help build an international rule of law, must jealously guard its mission to ensure that it is not subverted, or perceived to have been subverted, as an instrument for great powers to target weaker states or defeat adversaries in less influential regions of the world.

All in all, the controversy sparked by Bashir's case is a wake-up call. It ought to be clear that the practice of international criminal law cannot be conducted devoid of attention to the political environment that informs it. International criminal law does not operate in a vacuum and, in the case of Sudan it must function within the larger context of the country's history. Sudan has been the venue of one Africa's longest and bloodiest civil wars. The present-day Sudanese government is the result of a long period of international and regional negotiations and mediation between the two parties. Given the fragility of the transitional arrangements, the issuing of an arrest warrant for Al Bashir by the ICC is, arguably, badly-timed and capable of destabilising the already fragile peace processes in place. It may lead to the increased isolation of the Court by the community of nations.

PART III: NATIONAL COURTS AND THE PROSECUTION OF INTERNATIONAL CRIMES

CHAPTER 7

THE TRIAL OF MENGISTU AND OTHER DERG MEMBERS FOR GENOCIDE, TORTURE AND SUMMARY EXECUTIONS IN ETHIOPIA

*Firew Tiba**

1 Introduction

The Chief Special Prosecutor in his latest report to the House of Peoples Representatives (Federal Parliament) on 4 February 2010 indicated that the trials which started eighteen years ago against former Ethiopian government officials accused of committing various international crimes would come to an end in two months' time. In his report – which appears to be the last major report of such nature – he indicated that 384 criminal investigation files were opened in various regions of the country in Addis Ababa (Federal Court) and in the Oromia, Amhara, Tigray, Harari and South Regional states. The case of *Special Prosecutor v Colonel Mengistu Haile-Mariam & Others* is the most prominent of these. This essay examines these trials by the federal courts and their contributions to post-conflict justice in Ethiopia.

2 Brief history

The historical events the trials aim to address are the results of the political upheaval that followed the 1974 revolution which brought down the several thousand year-old monarchy. By historical accident, more than one hundred junior officers who were spontaneously sent to Addis Ababa from various divisions of the Army and Police to negotiate with the Emperor about various administrative matters, unexpectedly ended up

* LL.B (Addis Ababa); LL.M (Pretoria); LL.M (Kyushu); PhD (Hong Kong); Lecturer, University of Waikato, New Zealand. I would like to thank the editors, the anonymous referee and participants of the Workshop on Prosecuting International Crimes in Africa organised by the Centre for Human Rights, University of Pretoria, for their comments on the draft version of this chapter.

becoming collective heads of state. There was no plan to their rise to power, but they were aided by the deteriorating conditions and the popular anger against the ageing monarch's inability to solve various deep-rooted problems faced by the country. They called themselves the *Derg* (committee or council). Long before *Derg* members got proficient in the language of Marxist-Leninism and tried to ally themselves with or against various radical students and intellectuals-led groups of similar persuasion, they had started their killing spree by summarily executing sixty officials of the former regime and by carrying out purges within their own ranks. The sixty former officials that included the former long-time Prime Minister, Ministers, various army generals and feudal Lords, were killed by a decision of the *Derg* committee members. Emperor Haileselassie himself was killed in prison sometime later.

The *Derg*-led revolution started to claim more victims when an ideological battle between various factions started - drawing from Marxist interpretations.[1] Political parties started mushrooming. The Haileselassie I University, later renamed Addis Ababa University, was one of the main breeding grounds of student political movements. Some activists who were in exile saw an opportunity and returned home, forming their own political parties and even advising the junta. All sought to influence the direction of the revolution. Strategy wise, while some were directly opposed to the *Derg* from the start; others saw a short-cut to power, piggybacking the *Derg*. In the end, the junior officers, led by Mengistu Haile-Mariam, managed to destroy their opponents until it was their turn to be ousted from power seventeen years later.

The ideological battle of controlling the hearts and minds of the populace reached a new level when adversaries from both sides decided to physically eliminate each other's key figures. The lexicons of White Terror and Red Terror, copycats from the brutal Russian and other revolutions, became the staples of Ethiopian 'revolutionaries'. To this date, many Ethiopian political parties – including the governing party – carry the word 'revolutionary' as part of their official names.

At the height of this abuse of power the *Derg* empowered its security apparatus – urban and rural dweller associations of militias – to kill, torture and maim with impunity anybody they labeled 'subversives', 'anti-revolutionaries', 'counter-revolutionaries', or 'anti people'. At the end of the campaign, tens of thousands of people were either killed or had disappeared. Leaving other controversial figures aside, the charges filed by the Special Prosecutor, obviously a conservative figure, lists 12315

1 The history of the Red Terror is very contentious with regards as to who started it, how many people suffered and the respective roles of the various warring parties. See B Zewde 'The history of the Red Terror: Contexts and consequences' in K Tronvoll, C Schaefer & GA Aneme (eds) *The Ethiopian Red Terror trials: Transitional justice challenged* (2009)17-32.

individuals as killed and the courts thus far have found that 9546 of these were indeed victims of the crimes perpetrated during this period. Of these, 228 victims were females.[2] Furthermore, 1500 victims were confirmed by the courts as having suffered bodily injury.[3] The charges also included 2681 individuals as victims of torture, and the courts have confirmed 1687 of these cases. Of these, 172 were females.[4] These numbers do not necessarily represent the actual number of victims; as in addition to those directly killed, those whose lives were cut short due to misguided polices of the *Derg* could run into millions.

3 Post-conflict justice

The notion of post-conflict justice is sometimes used interchangeably with concepts such as 'transitional justice', 'strategies for combating impunity', 'peace building' and 'post conflict reconstruction.'[5] Post-conflict justice is a delicate matter. There is no formula that applies to all countries. An ideal model of post-conflict justice has to balance the demands of justice, peace and reconciliation in society. These three demands do not necessarily sit together in harmony. The Chicago Principles of Post-conflict Justice put together by eminent legal and transitional justice experts indicate that the following factors need to be taken into account: 'human suffering and demands for justice; grounding in international law; accountability, peace and democracy; victim centered approach; context-specific strategies; interdisciplinary nature and long term commitment.'[6] Undoubtedly, the legal process is but only one way of addressing the past. Thus:

> The Chicago Principles on Post-Conflict Justice present the search for accountability in the aftermath of conflict as a complex, multifaceted, interdisciplinary process that extends beyond a formal legalistic approach. Domestic and international prosecutions on their own rarely provide victims and a suffering society with a complete approach to justice for past atrocities. Relying solely on formal legal action generally fails to fully address victims'

2 Report of the SPO of 4 February 2010 to the House of Peoples' Representative. See the documentary produced by the state-run Ethiopian Television in Amharic which includes the SPO Report as well as MP comments on this video-sharing website http://www.ethiotube.net/video/8192/Documentary--findings-of-human-rights-abuses-during-Red-Terror-era--Part-1 (part I) and http://www.ethiotube.net/video/8194/Documentary--findings-of-human-rights-abuses-during-Red-Terror-era--Part-2 (Part II) (both accessed 1 June 2010). For an interview with the Special Prosecutor in Amharic (The Reporter Amharic News Paper, 7 February 2010), see http://www.ethiopianreporter.com/index.php?option=com_content&view=article&id=1159:q--q&catid=100:2009-11-13-13-45-06&Itemid=619 (accessed 1 June 2010). For an immediate reaction to the report in transitional justice context, see L Degu Report from Special Prosecutor Office of Ethiopia: Half-Way Transitional Justice, 11 February 2010 http://www.ictj.org/en/news/coverage/article/3447.html (accessed 1 June 2010).

3 Report (n 2 above).

4 As above.

5 Chicago Principles on Post-Conflict Justice (2007) 7 http://www.isisc.org/public/chicago%20principles%20-%20final%20-%20may%209%202007.pdf (accessed 1 June 2010).

6 As above, 15.

> needs and may reveal serious limitations within a transitional government that weakens society's faith in the legitimacy of judicial processes.

That is why several measures ought to be considered cumulatively in addressing legacies of past human rights violations. These consist of prosecution; truth telling and the investigation of past violations; consideration for victims' rights, remedies and reparations; vetting, sanctions and administrative measures; memorialisation, education and the preservation of historical memory; traditional, indigenous and religious approaches to justice and healing; institutional reform and effective governance.

As has been made abundantly clear, Ethiopia chose to deal with impunity by prosecuting those responsible. Prosecution alone, however, is not a solution for the post-conflict reconstruction. There are other associated measures one must take to bring about peace, justice and reconciliation. The following seven measures – including prosecution – will be addressed briefly within the framework of post-conflict justice.

3.1 Prosecution

As noted above, Ethiopia's response to the violence during the *Derg* has chiefly been engaging in a massive project of prosecuting suspects who planned the crimes and those who carried out those criminal plans. Ethiopia, among others, opted for this solution as a matter of political expediency.[7] For what it is worth, the Ethiopian trials represent one of the most known, yet under-reported, completely domestic initiatives that sought to hold perpetrators of gross human rights abuse accountable. It is true that no post conflict justice measure would be complete without at least prosecuting those individuals most responsible for the major human rights violations. All other initiatives will be discredited if major actors are sheltered from prosecution. On that account alone these trials deserve to be hailed. In the next section the various components of the prosecution project are examined.

3.1.1 Special Prosecutor's Office (SPO)

The Special Prosecutor's Office (SPO) was established in 1992 by a proclamation issued by the House of Representatives of the Transitional Government of Ethiopia (TGE).[8] The House of Representative was not a popularly elected body. It was a collection of individuals and political

7 See detailed discussion in K Tronvoll 'A quest for justice or the construction of political legitimacy? The political anatomy of the Red Terror trials' in Tronvoll *et al* (n 1 above) 84-97.

8 For detailed accounts of the SPO, see S Vaughan 'The role of the Special Prosecutor's Office' in Tronvoll *et al* (n 1 above) 51-67.

entities that formed the Transitional Government after the collapse of Mengistu's regime. The TGE lasted for two years. However, the collection is relatively more representative than the post-transition parliament which came to be fully controlled by the Ethiopian Peoples Revolutionary Democratic Front (EPRDF).

As its designation 'special' indicates, the prosecution's office was specifically constituted for this purpose and directly reports to the Prime Minister, bypassing the Minister of Justice to which other regular prosecutors report.[9] Furthermore, unlike regular prosecutors, the SPO enjoys powers to investigate the crimes it is empowered to prosecute.[10]

The SPO, in addition to investigating and prosecuting the crimes perpetrated, also has the mandate of producing a historic record of what had happened. Thus, its foundational proclamation states that 'it is in the interest of just historical obligation to record for posterity the brutal offences, the embezzlement of property perpetrated against the people of Ethiopia and to educate the people and make them aware of these offences in order to prevent the recurrence of such a system of government'.[11] This is a laudable objective, but critics blame the SPO for having used the forum to introduce too many witnesses to allow them to air their grievances, while he could have gotten the job done with fewer witnesses or even through the use of documentary evidence as the crimes perpetrated were meticulously recorded by the perpetrators themselves.

In terms of political persuasion, the only excluding factor for the appointment to Chief Special Prosecutor, is the fact of being a member of the Worker's Party of Ethiopia (WPE) or its security forces.[12] However, in light of the parties involved in conflict during the Red Terror, this should have excluded others who were members of any of the parties that took part in the conflict. In this regard, critics often point to the past membership of the Chief Prosecutor in Ethiopian Peoples Revolutionary Party (EPRP), a party which is accused of firing the first shot which started the Red Terror.[13] Although it is the members and supporters of this party who faced the full force of the *Derg*'s crackdown, the party, in the eyes of many observers, committed a strategic blunder by starting urban warfare and targeting leading members of the *Derg* for assassination. Thus, appointing as a prosecutor a person who had allegedly directly or indirectly suffered at the hands of the *Derg* is like appointing a holocaust survivor as a prosecutor for the Nuremberg Tribunal.

9 Art 2(2) Proclamation Establishing the Office of the Special Prosecutor, Proclamation 22/1992 (8 August 1992).
10 n 9 above, art 6.
11 n 9 above, Preamble.
12 n 9 above, art 5(4).
13 Parliamentary discussion (n 2 above).

Perhaps, it is not the mere fact of being a supporter or even a member of a party that played a part in the conflict that one should be concerned about. The Chief Special Prosecutor appears in public only on rare occasions, is known for using highly emotive language against suspects, and sometimes even against the bench, so putting his credibility and objectivity on the line.[14] This impression is strengthened by the fact that the Prosecutor was not given the mandate to investigate crimes allegedly committed by various non-state actors during the Red Terror, including a party he once belonged to or supported. It is a historical fact that crimes were committed by various parties to the conflict; however, singling out the *Derg*, which is responsible for the bulk of the crimes, does not do justice to the truth of what happened.

3.1.2 The charges

In his report of February 2010, the Special Prosecutor indicated that charges were filed against 5119 suspects for genocide, crimes against humanity, war crimes of murder and rape; the abuse of power and various other crimes.[15] These suspects were charged and later convicted for violations of various pre-existing provisions of the 1957 Penal Code. The Ethiopian Penal Code at the time was progressive in its inclusion of the prevailing international criminal law and international humanitarian law standards. In fact, in certain respects, it went beyond what was and still is customarily provided in genocide-related provisions in international treaties and various domestic laws.[16] In particular, one notes the expanded protection given to members of political groups against genocide. The controversy surrounding this unique provision has probably been the bane of the trials, especially in light of the political context.

The serious crimes committed during the seventeen-year-rule by the military are too many to be prosecuted in such a short period of time. The acts of killing and torture committed qualify as some of the most horrendous acts of savagery committed by men against men. The following lists demonstrate this savagery. The killings as revealed to Parliament by the Special Prosecutor are the following: executions; beatings with sticks; throwing people off cliffs; throwing people into rivers alive; strangling with a cord or nylon rope; injection of poison; electric shock; suffocation with an anesthetic agent and then strangulation (particularly used against the former Emperor Haileselassie). Forms of torture include: whipping with an electric cable or leather whip after

14 In his last report to Parliament this came to light when an MP pointed this out. He was once sentenced to a few months in prison for contempt of court when he alleged that one of the judges on the bench was a member of Mengistu's defunct Workers Party of Ethiopia (WPE).

15 Report (n 2 above).

16 See FK Tiba 'The Mengistu genocide trial in Ethiopia' (2007) 5 *Journal of International Criminal Justice* 513-28.

binding the victim's legs and hands and stuffing objects into their mouths; whipping while the victim is suspended; keeping a bound victim suspended for long time; torture by electric shock; applying a burning newspaper to the body; pulling out hair; mutilating the body; rubbing a dry body or bones with a wooden board; stretching nails and nipples with pincers; pulling out fingernails; killing or torturing others in the presence of the victim; frightening by setting dogs on a person; taking victim for a false execution; suspending heavy objects from men's genitals; inserting heavy objects into a woman's uterus; forcing a victim with wounded feet to walk on gravel; as well as other forms of torture not included here.

The accused persons were grouped into three categories. The first category included policy-makers, senior government, and military officials of the *Derg*. The two other groups were 'military and civilian field commanders who carried out orders as well as passed orders down, and the individuals who actually carried out many of the brutal and deadly orders'.[17] The cases of the accused persons in the first category were heard by the Federal High Court First Criminal Division. The trials of those in the second category were conducted in Addis Ababa in the Federal High Court Sixth Criminal Division and in the Regional Supreme Courts.

In *Special Prosecutor v Mengistu Haile-Mariam,* against top-tier accused persons, four charges were filed.[18] The first charge of public provocation and preparation to commit genocide in violation of articles 32(1)(a) and 286(a) of the 1957 Penal Code reads:[19]

> The defendants in violation of Articles 32 (1) (a) and 286(a) of the then 1957 Penal Code of Ethiopia beginning from 12 September 1974 by establishing the Provisional Military Administration Council, organising themselves as the general assembly, standing and sub-committees; while exclusively and collectively leading the country, agreed among themselves to commit and caused to be committed crimes of genocide against those whom they identified as members of anti-revolution political groups. In order to assist them carry out these, they recruited and armed various *kefitegna* and *kebele* [administrative units] leaders, revolutionary guards, cadres and revolutionary comrades whom as accomplices, they incited and emboldened in public meeting halls, over the media by calling out the names of members of political groups calling for their elimination using speeches, drawings and writings until 1983 in various months and dates thereby causing the death of thousands of members of political groups.

The second charge of the commission of genocide in violation of article 281 of the 1957 Penal Code reads:[20]

17 F Elegesem & GA Aneme 'The rights of the accused: A human rights appraisal' in Tronvoll *et al* (n 1 above) 37.
18 n 17 above, 37-41.
19 *Special Prosecutor v Colonel Mengistu Haile-Mariam & others* Federal Supreme Court, Criminal File 30181, 26 May 2008 17 (my translation).
20 n 19 above, 17 (my translation).

> The defendants in violation of Articles 32 (1)(a) and 281 of the 1957 Penal Code of Ethiopia, beginning from 12 September 1974 while exclusively and collectively leading the country by establishing the Provisional Military Administration Council or government, organising themselves as the general assembly, standing and sub-committees, planned, participated and ordered the destruction in whole or in part, members of politically organised socio-national groups thereby committed genocide. To accomplish this goal, they created various investigation, torturing and execution institutions, hit squads and *Nebelbal* army divisions; carried out campaign 'clearing fields', 'free measures' and 'red terror' to kill or cause the killings of members of political groups and cause injury to their physical and mental health or cause their total disappearance by banishing them in a manner calculated to cause them social harm or cause their death.

This second charge had four components (murder; bodily harm, serious injury to physical and mental health; placement under living conditions calculated to result in death or disappearance; and the alternative charges of aggravated homicide and grave and willful injury). As regards the second charge, the prosecutor alternatively filed charges of homicide and causing grievous bodily injury. The third charge was carrying out unlawful detention in violation of articles 32(1)(b) and 416 of the 1957 Penal Code; while the fourth charge was abuse of power by illegally confiscating private property worth millions of Birr in contravention of articles 32(1)(b) and 414 of the same Penal Code.

3.1.3 The trials

The Special Prosecutor filed charges against Colonel Mengistu Haile-Mariam and others in December 1994 while most of the accused were in detention since May 1991. The trials of some accused, including Colonel Mengistu Haile-Mariam, were conducted *in absentia*. The trials are currently being finalised after eighteen years. A number of death penalties have been imposed. At the time of writing, none of the imposed capital punishments has been carried out. Under Ethiopian law, the President must certify that such a punishment may be carried out.[21]

3.1.4 The verdicts

In this section, the verdicts of the Ethiopian courts in major Red Terror cases, notably those involving Colonel Mengistu and his co-accused, are briefly examined.[22] The first obstacles to the viability of the charges filed were overcome on 9 October 1995 with the Federal High Court First

21 Art 117(2) Criminal Code of the Federal Democratic Republic of Ethiopia, May 2005.

22 The decisions in *Special Prosecutor v Colonel Mengistu Haile-Mariam* have been covered elsewhere. See K Tronvoll, C Schaefer & GA Aneme 'Concluding the main Red Terror Trial: *Special Prosecutor v Colonel Mengistu Haile-Mariam et al*' in Tronvoll *et al* (n 1 above) 136-152; Tiba (n 16 above).

Criminal Division's rulings on the preliminary objections mounted by the defendants. The defendants' lawyers raised various objections, ranging from technical matters relating to the charges to that of the sustainability of the charge of the crime of genocide.

The objections raised by the defence were briefly as follows: the inclusion of political groups as protected groups against genocide under article 281 of the 1957 of the Ethiopian Penal Code is incompatible with international law; the victims' political groups allegedly targeted were not legally registered political parties; the charges did not distinguish between the crimes of genocide and crimes against humanity as article 281 of the 1957 Penal Code itself lumps the two crimes together; the accused persons should not concurrently be charged for crimes of provoking (inciting) the commission of the crimes of genocide and for actually committing them; it is improper to charge the accused both for genocide and alternatively for aggravated homicide due to the significant differences between the nature of both crimes, the number of victims and the consequences of conviction; that the accused enjoyed immunity from prosecution; that the accused should be tried by an international court as the national court established by a transitional government lacked legitimacy and the accused have the right to choose a court according to article VI of the Genocide Convention and article 10 of the Universal Declaration of Human Rights.[23] These objections were rejected one after another by the Federal High Court, paving the way for the continuation of the case to the merits phase. Similar objections were also rejected by the Federal Supreme Court of Appeal as will be shown later.

Many years later in 2006, in a landmark decision, the Federal High Court returned a verdict in the case of *Special Prosecutor v Colonel Mengistu Haile-Mariam & others*, convicting the accused.[24] In a majority judgment of two to one, the court convicted the accused of genocide while the dissenting judge found them guilty of aggravated homicide. The sentencing judgment was not unanimous, with the majority going for life while the dissenting judge favoured capital punishment. Both parties appealed. The Special Prosecutor thought that the imposition of a life sentence was too lenient, while the accused contested both the conviction and the sentence.

The Federal Supreme Court in 2008 upheld the conviction of the accused, reversed the life sentence and imposed the death penalty on the persons most responsible, including Mengistu Haile-Mariam (*in absentia*). The judgments and sentencing decisions have been covered elsewhere and

23 For a discussion of the rulings, see S Yeshanew on www.oxfordlawreports.com (subscription required) International Law in Domestic Courts (ILDC) on the Case of *Special Prosecutor v Colonel Mengitu Haile-Mariam & Others.*

24 Tiba (n 16 above).

will not be repeated here.[25] It is only necessary to pose critical remarks about the judgments as indicated below.

3.2 Critique of the trials[26]

As has been indicated before, the trials are not without their problems. Without denying their symbolic significance, it is prudent to highlight some of the most-often cited weaknesses. These critiques relate to the rights of the accused; the issue of victor's justice; their length; problems relating to defense legal counsel; and that some of the trials were held *in absentia.*

3.2.1 The rights of the accused

Some of the most trenchant critiques of the *Derg* trials as well as other Red Terror trials relate to protections offered to suspects. Commentators have roundly criticised the new regime for failing to accord full fair trial guarantees to those accused. Here, one considers among others, the right to an expeditious trial, access to and choice of counsel and the right to be present at one's trial and its corollary – the right to confront one's accusers and witnesses. Before considering these issues, the general accusation of victor's justice, which has a bearing on the broader question of justice and the role or impact of politics on criminal prosecutions, is addressed below.

3.2.2 Victor's justice and the role of politics

Like many trials conducted after a change in regimes in Africa at the end of an armed conflict, and like its historical antecedent – Nuremberg - the prosecution of the *Derg* era crimes has not been immune to accusations of 'victor's justice. These accusations mainly stem from the historical circumstances surrounding the beginning of the 'Red Terror' which the *Derg* portrayed as a reaction to the 'White Terror' initiated by the Ethiopian People's Revolutionary Party (EPRP) that targeted officials of the *Derg* in the cities. Although EPRP and its alleged members were met with unmatched brutality for their infractions in the cities, the *Derg* believed that it was defending itself and the revolution. Nevertheless, it bears noting that EPRP was not part of the coalition that overthrew the *Derg,* and it was in fact undermined and outmaneuvered by the TPLF (a core within the EPRDF coalition) early on. However, a previous split within the EPRP created a splinter group that later joined the EPRDF.

25 n 22 above.

26 This section is based on my yet unpublished work, 'Mengistu and Red Terror Trials' in G Musila *Domestic prosecution of international crimes and the role of regional organizations: Some African case studies* Institute of Security Studies, South Africa (forthcoming). I would like to thank Godfrey Musila for his comments on this section.

Most of the leaders of this coalition partnership were high-ranking officials of the TGE, including a Prime Minister. Some of these still wield significant power in the government. Although there has not been any public information about the individual culpability of these former members of the EPRP who became part of the TGE, it was thought unfair that the actions of those who belonged to the EPRP and other radical groups were not subjected to investigation and prosecution.

The other complaint relates to crimes committed in the context of the armed conflict. Accordingly, even if the *Derg* sought to stamp out the armed resistance in various parts of the country using brutal tactics in violation of the laws and customs of war, it could not be said for sure that the rebels themselves never resorted to such tactics. Thus, an honest and objective prosecutor could not have proceeded against only one side of the conflict. In short, the selective prosecution of members of the *Derg*, while there are also other people who could have been made to bear responsibility for the ultra-radicalisation of a generation and their victimisation, is an example of victor's justice in operation. Although it was legally imperative and the right thing to prosecute *Derg* officials, one could argue that the process was not designed to get to the bottom of the country's past problems. The idea that the trials were aimed at bringing about internal reformation of the system by punishing perpetrators loses some credibility due to the perceived partiality of the process.

3.2.3 Problems related to delay, pre-trial detention and the right to expeditious trial

International human rights and international criminal law guarantee the accused's right to a free, fair, and expeditious trial. The International Covenant on Civil and Political Rights as well as the African Charter on Human and Peoples' Rights to which Ethiopia is a party, unequivocally affirm these guarantees.[27] These rights also have an equivalent protection in the statutes of the various international criminal tribunals.[28] The Constitution of the Federal Government of Ethiopia that came into effect in 1995 contains similar rights.[29]

27 Art 14 (3) International Covenant on Civil and Political Rights UN Doc A/6316 (1966), entered into force 23 March 1976,; art 7(1)(d) African Charter on Human and Peoples Rights, OAU Doc CAB/LEG/67/ 3 Rev 5 (1981) (entered in to force 21 October 1986); see also art 6(1) European Convention for the Protection of Human Rights and Fundamental Freedoms 213 UNTS 222, entered into force 3 September 1953.

28 The Statutes of the ICTY and ICTR require the Tribunals to ensure that a trial is 'fair and expeditious'. See art 20(1) Statute of the International Criminal Tribunal for the Former Yugoslavia, UN Doc S/Res/827/Annex (1993); art 19(1) Statute of the International Criminal Tribunal For Rwanda, UN Doc S/Res/955/Annex (1994); art 67(1)(c) Rome Statute of the International Criminal Court, A/Conf. 138/9, 1998.

29 Art 20(1) Constitution of the Federal Democratic Republic of Ethiopia.

The *Derg* trials as well as the other Red Terror trials were criticised for delays in their completion.[30] The *Derg*-WPE trial alone took 13 years to complete, excluding two to three years of pre-trial detention for suspects arrested when EPRDF took over in 1991. The majority of suspects were arrested by triumphant EPRDF forces without warrants and did not appear in court for three years after their arrest. They had been incarcerated for more than 10 years before judgment was rendered. Some were also kept in detention without being charged for a lengthy period of time during the early phases of the prosecution.[31] That is a long time by any standard, and far removed from the test of a 'reasonable period of time' demanded by all human rights standards and treaties. However, one misses the point by simply focusing on numbers alone. Trials of such magnitude are not easy to prosecute. Even the International Criminal Tribunals for the former Yugoslavia and Rwanda are still in business, despite the large number of resources they enjoy and the limited number of suspects they have been able to try. As will be shown below, the usual suspects – lack of resources and the complexity of the cases – are present in Ethiopia's case too. The question would then be whether there was anything the SPO or courts could have done to speed up the process within the bounds of the resources and goodwill they had at the beginning.

At the beginning, suspects were not arrested through the usual process by means of court-issued arrest warrants.[32] The prosecution's decision to seek the mass arrest of all those implicated meant that the Prosecutor himself was bound to be overwhelmed by the number of cases he had to investigate. There was a risk of flight of suspects. In fact, many who feared arrest did flee at the beginning. Apart from clogging the system and dividing the attention of the SPO, the mass detention of suspects increased the risk of prolonged detention of individuals against whom there was no sufficient evidence. There have been cases where individuals were in detention for 10 years, but received only a six-year jail sentence. Neither the SPO, nor the Ethiopian courts had any remedy for those unduly detained for a long time. The unusual decision to prosecute both high ranking and low ranking members of the *Derg* in part created the situation such that there were far too many to be tried. The lesson here is that the SPO should first have focused on the most serious cases.

Apart from the number of perpetrators, the prosecutorial strategy was in general problematic. Once the trial started in 1994, the strategy devised by the SPO in presenting its evidence, mainly witness testimony, ensured that the trial would take longer than was necessary. The SPO introduced far too many witnesses to prove certain issues. For instance, the SPO has

30 For possible causes that contributed to the delay, see Vaughan (n 8 above) 52-53.

31 See J Mayfield 'The prosecution of war crimes and respect for human rights: Ethiopia's balancing act' (1995) 9 *Emory International Law Review* 553.

32 Human Rights Watch/Africa (1994) 11 *Ethiopia: Reckoning under the law* 19 http://www.unhcr.org/refworld/pdfid/45cc5ece2.pdf (accessed 15 March 2009).

been criticised for calling many witnesses who testified about 'the commission of the alleged acts without an identification of who the actors were'.[33] Haile-Mariam records that by 1998, the Prosecutor had called more than 500 witnesses and was promising to call another 500, in addition to physical evidence.[34] Kidane has pointed to the limited utility of the many witnesses being called noting the following:[35]

> Of the 581 prosecution witnesses, about 90% of them testified about isolated incidents that happened over an extended period of time. For example, more than 300 witnesses testified that they saw, one or more of the victims listed in any of the 211 counts in prison, and either heard the killing on the radio, read in the newspaper, or saw the corpses at one or another place. Many of them were relatives of the victims who witnessed the taking of their loved ones from their homes and their death or disappearance. And others told the Court about the prison conditions and the severity of the torture.

Given that the accused were top policy and decision-makers and in consideration for the need for a speedy trial, the preferable strategy for the SPO would have been to present evidence that showed the existence of a common plan among the co-accused to commit the alleged acts.[36] It was also imperative to prove that the accused was not only implicated in his leadership capacity but also personally had committed or ordered the commission of such acts or had participated in the commission in a certain capacity. However, very few prosecutor witnesses were able to point to the direct participation of most of the accused in the act.[37] In other words, the witnesses probably contributed little to the trial which the prosecutor might have proved with documentary and physical evidence, as well as records of the triumphant radio and television broadcasts that followed most executions of the so-called counter revolutionaries or enemies of the revolution.

It appears that the SPO, by choosing this strategy wanted to create a forum for witnesses, most of whom were affected in some way, to vent their sorrow and testify in public against leaders who were responsible for some of the most atrocious crimes. In a sense, it is like trying to 'kill two

33 WL Kidane 'The Ethiopian "Red Terror" trials' in MC Bassiouni (ed) *Post-conflict justice* (2002) 685.

34 Y Haile-Mariam 'The quest for justice and reconciliation: The International Criminal Tribunal for Rwanda and the Ethiopian High Court' (1998-99) 22 *Hastings International & Comparative Law Review* 679, citing 'Trial of former *Derg* officials once again adjourned' *Addis Tribune* 24 July 1998.

35 n 35 above, 685-686.

36 n 35 above, 685.

37 However, testimonies of the 3rd, 4th, 5th, 6th and 7th witnesses were found to be well organised. The 43rd witness had also testified to an event that directly implicated Capitain Legesse Asfaw and Major Berhanu Bayeh; the 183rd witness testified about the death of her very well known novelist husband (Behalu Girma); the 356th witness saw the execution of 13 detainees in an interrogation room; the 482nd who was Mengistu Haile-Mariam personal guard (himself in prison) who testified about the killing of the former *Derg* Chairman, General Teferi Benti and other *Derg* officials. See Kidane (n 33 above) 688-689.

birds with one stone' at the expense of a speedy trial. Views vary on whether these two goals may be achieved at once. The defence team objected to the prosecutor's strategy, arguing that the approach suited a truth commission, rather than an adversarial courtroom scenario. Expressing displeasure, one defence counsel noted that 'if what SPO is trying to do is record keeping, it could be done more effectively by a truth commission; it need not be done in a court room'.[38]

The SPO originally enjoyed a lot of goodwill and was able to attract donor's direct assistance to help it prosecute cases in line with international standards. The assistance consisted in direct financial support as well as technical assistance.[39] Although not significant in monetary terms, the continued support nonetheless waned due to the deterioration of the relationship between the SPO and international donors.[40] The deterioration in their relationship was chiefly attributed to factionalism and an internal power struggle within the SPO.[41] Eventually, donors either reduced or withdrew from the programme. One of the donors to withdraw its support was the Carter Center, which had in the past assisted the SPO by sponsoring forensic experts from Argentina.[42] Foreign consultants were also fired for suspicious activities.[43] Clearly, the SPO could have benefited from support from the donor community. As it turned out, the honeymoon did not last more than two years and the SPO had to continue on its own thereafter.

Ethiopian courts are generally plagued by backlogs and a lack of sufficient trained personnel. Although the trials in Addis Ababa were assigned to at least three divisions (1st, 2nd, and 6th) of the Federal High Court, the judges' task was not limited to trying such cases. They had to juggle these high profile cases with their other judicial commitments. On balance, however, the delay is rather because of the Prosecutor's strategy that led to his inability to wrap up the prosecution's case in time. In hindsight, however, talking about delays in relation to those convicted and sentenced to life in prison or death may seem academic. What about those acquitted after a lengthy detention? The truth is that it has been done for those people; no apology has been offered and there have been no instances of reparation for unjustified detention. In terms of international criminal law as currently codified by the Rome Statute, anyone who has been the victim of unlawful arrest, detention or miscarriage of justice has an enforceable right to compensation.[44] Failure to compensate suspects

38 Kidane (n 33 above) 688.

39 T Howland 'Learning to make proactive human rights interventions effective: The Carter Center and Ethiopia's Office of the Special Prosecutor' (2000) 18 *Wisconsin International Law Journal* 419-420.

40 As above, 419, for the committed support.

41 n 39 above, 422-423.

42 n 39 above.

43 n 39 above, 423 (fn 46).

44 Art 85 Rome Statute of the International Criminal Court.

who suffered a long period of detention or a miscarriage of justice is another significant way that the Ethiopian trials failed to meet international standards.

3.3.4 Right to adequate legal counsel

Adequate legal counsel is a right guaranteed to accused persons in criminal trials under domestic and international law.[45] This right entails that the accused person be allowed to be represented by a legal counsel of his/her choice, and be provided with one at the state's expense if he/she is unable afford one.

The court appointed thirty-six attorneys for some of the high-profile suspects from among private law practitioners, while a few others were retained by their clients.[46] The court-appointed lawyers were paid five thousand Ethiopian Birr (750USD at the then prevailing exchange rate) to defend an accused.[47] This was the only payment they received for a trial that took nearly thirteen years.[48] Furthermore, they were not reimbursed for the expenses they incurred in connection with the preparation of their cases.[49] This clearly shows the relative position of disadvantage in which the defence teams stood.

The government also established the Public Defenders Office (PDO) in January 1994 under the supervision of the Ethiopian Supreme Court. The PDO was to provide legal assistance to the indigent accused.[50] The PDO started its work with five Ethiopian lawyers early in 1994, only one of whom was an experienced trial attorney.[51] This pales in comparison to thirty lawyers and four hundred investigators put at the disposal of the SPO at the beginning of the trial.[52] The PDO was established mainly to defend low-level suspects.[53] At its early stages, it was reported that the PDO suffered from lack of resources.[54] The PDO was also staffed with newly graduated and inexperienced staff. Clearly, the quality of the services and the resource allocated to defend indigent accused were inadequate.[55]

45 Art 21(4) ICTY Statute; art 20(4)(d) ICTR Statute; art 67(1)(d) Rome Statute; art 20(5) Constitution of the Federal Democratic Republic of Ethiopia (1994).
46 Haile-Mariam (n 34 above) 723.
47 n 39 above.
48 H Tsadik *Prosecuting the Past … Affecting the Future?* A SIDA Minor Field Study of the Ethiopian Transitional Justice Trials, Department of Peace and Conflict Research, Uppsala University (2007) http://www.pcr.uu.se/pcr_doc/mfs/mfs_Tsadic.pdf (accessed 9 April 2010).
49 Haile-Mariam (n 34 above) 724.
50 Human Rights Watch/Africa (n 32 above) 49.
51 As above, 49-50.
52 Haile-Mariam (n 34 above) 723.
53 Human Rights Watch/Africa (n 34 above) 50
54 As above.
55 For prosecutorial resources and assignment of counsel at the Ethiopian Court, see Haile-Mariam (n 36 above) 722-724.

The work of the defence counsel was also made difficult because no right to discovery existed in criminal trials in Ethiopia.[56] This meant that the Prosecutor was under no obligation to share incriminatory or exculpatory evidence with the defence before the trial.

In general, although the defence was put at a relative disadvantage in terms of resources, there has always been the impression that they carried out their jobs with integrity and in the interest of their clients. There were, however, certain instances in which some of the accused dismissed their assigned lawyers to conduct their own defence. It is also worth mentioning that lawyers representing the accused are thought not to have been harassed by members of the public or by the government.

3.3.5 Trials in absentia

As noted already, a number of those suspected of *Derg* era crimes had fled the country by the time EPRDF took Addis Ababa or did so soon thereafter. Mengistu fled to Zimbabwe where he still lives. The SPO decided to charge those who fled anyway and they were subsequently tried *in absentia*. Trials in absentia are controversial under both international and domestic law. Most international instruments provide for the accused's right to be present at his or her trial, although they do not outrightly prohibit trials *in absentia*. Treaty rules on trial proceedings, such as the International Covenant on Civil and Political Rights (article 14(3)) and the European Convention on Human Rights (article 6(1)) have been interpreted by the relevant tribunals as not ruling out trials *in absentia.*[57] While article 12 of the Charter of the International Military Tribunal allowed trials *in absentia,* the Statute of the ICC in article 63(1) requires the accused to be present for the trials to commence. The Statutes of the ICTY (article 21(4) (d), and ICTR (article 20(4) (d)) also provide that the accused has the right 'to be tried in his presence.'

However, the position seems different under a number of domestic jurisdictions.[58] In terms of articles 160 and 161 of the Ethiopian Criminal Procedure Code, a trial *in absentia* is allowed if the accused fails to show up for his trial after being summoned and notified to do so, including publication of summons in a widely-circulated paper, provided the offence committed is punishable with rigorous imprisonment not less than twelve years.[59] This is a common feature of criminal trials in most civil law countries that follow the inquisitorial system of criminal litigation, unlike

56 See also Human Rights Watch/Africa (n 32 above) 50-51.

57 A Casesse *International criminal law* (2008) 390-391.

58 As above, 390.

59 In terms of art 162, where the court decides to hear the case in the absence of the accused, the judge must order the publication of the summons showing the date fixed for the hearing and a notification to the accused that he will be tried in his absence if he fails to appear.

the adversarial systems.[60] Antonio Cassese gives two reasons why trials *in absentia* are admissible in Romano-Germanic legal traditions.[61] Firstly, the investigating judge gathers evidence not only for the prosecution but also for the defence, which means that when the trial proceedings begin, the court has exculpatory evidence available, and is therefore in a position to evaluate both the evidence against and that in favour of the accused. Secondly, in most civil law systems (including those such as Italy where the accusatorial system has been adopted) it is considered that the interest of the community adjudicating alleged criminal offences should prevail over the right of the accused to be present in court, at least whenever the accused voluntarily tries to evade justice.

Although Ethiopia follows a predominantly civil law system with regards to its substantive law, its procedural law is mainly adopted from common law jurisdictions.[62] That means its Criminal Procedure Code does not include an investigative judge, a feature common to inquisitorial systems. In the same breath, it also has to be pointed out that the role of the judge in criminal trials in Ethiopia is not as limited as its adversarial counterpart. It incorporates features from both systems. But this mix does not make up for the lack of an investigative judge, who in other civil law systems is responsible for collecting both exculpatory and incriminatory evidence for the sake of seeking the truth. Furthermore, the Ethiopian prosecutor is not under any special legal duty to reveal any exculpatory evidence to the court, a matter that is critical in trials *in absentia*.

As we noted previously, certain accused persons have been found guilty *in absentia* and have been given the death penalty. There has so far been only one instance, which this author is aware of, where a convicted person was deported back to Ethiopia to serve a sentence imposed *in absentia*. The accused, Kelbesa Negewo, was found guilty and sentenced to life imprisonment by the Federal High Court on 20 May 2002. He was deported from the United States in October 2006, stripped of his US citizenship on the ground that he lied to immigration officers about the human rights violations he had committed. He was also found liable to his former victims under the Alien Tort Claims Act. He is currently serving life in prison.

Courts have also rejected the plea by another accused through his lawyer to have his in absentia decision set aside. This happened in the case of *General Embibel Ayele v Special Prosecutor*, where the Federal High Court refused to set aside the accused's in absentia conviction and life

60 Casesse (n 57 above) 360.
61 n 57 above, 360-361.
62 Its 1961 Criminal Procedure Code was drafted by Sir Charles Mathew was mainly based it on the Malayan Criminal Procedure Code, while its Civil Procedure Code, drafted by Ato Nerayo Isayas, was heavily inspired by its Indian counterpart.

sentence.[63] On appeal, the Federal Supreme Court ruled that in absentia decision can only be set aside when the accused appears before the court - either in person or accompanied by his lawyer according to article 127(1) of the Criminal Procedure Code.

3.3 Truth telling and investigation of past violations

Because of the trials, we now know more about what had happened. At least some of the relatives who did not know about the fate of their loved ones were for the first time made to face the truth of what had happened. Many bodies were exhumed and laid to rest. The remains of the Emperor Haileselassie I had to be exumed from underneath Mengistu Haile-Mariam Secretary's Office. Former government archives have been opened up to the prosecution and some of these documents have been submitted to the courts and have become part of the official account of who committed some of these crimes. It is hoped that these documents will be digitised and put in a museum, be it physically or electronically.

On the other hand, prosecution by its very nature does not reveal the entire truth. The adversarial nature of the process naturally prompts the parties to use or vie for winning strategies. Calls for the establishment of a truth and reconciliation commission (TRC) were never given serious thought by the EPRDF which formed and run the government since Derg lost power. There has not been any public consultation on the matter. Members of the transitional parliament who passed the SPO Proclamation were not elected by the public. It seems that the ruling party is dead-set against a TRC. The Federal High Court in its ruling of 9 October 1995 made the point that courts are not legally empowered to decide whether national reconciliation is the best option.[64] Prosecution and TRCs need not be mutually exclusive. In fact, some of those convicted had indicated a willingness to seek forgiveness from the public by telling the truth unconditionally. For unexplained reasons this has not been accepted by the government either. This leaves one with a question of why the government is afraid of the truth.

3.4 Consideration for victims' rights, remedies and reparations

Principle three of Chicago's Principles on Post-Conflict Justice requires that states shall acknowledge the special status of victims, ensure access to justice, and develop remedies and reparations. The Ethiopian trials have to

63 *General Embibel Ayele v Special Prosecutor* Criminal Appeal File 34459 Federal Supreme Court. The application to set aside could be made pursuant to arts 196 and 201(1) of the Criminal Procedure Code.

64 *Special Prosecutor v Col Mengistu Haile-Mariam & Others* Federal High Court, First Criminal Division, Ruling on Prelimenary Objections 9 October 1995 para 90.

a large extent allowed victims and victims' families access to the courts. At the beginning, the SPO's investigation was assisted by the victims' and their families who came forward and provided information about the crimes committed and those responsible. At a later stage, some have appeared before courts and provided their testimonies.

The participation of victims go only to the point of assisting the prosecution. So far there has not been any mention of remedies or reparation for the victims individually or collectively. Restitution of illegally confiscated property in the context of red terror is not known. The judgment of the courts do not provide for any reparation measures for the victims. The government has no plans to compensate the victims of these violations, nor has it apologised to the public although it is not responsible for these violations. Given the destitution of most of the suspects, there has not been any civil suit against them for compensation. For the same reason, it is unlikely that any future civil suits will be filed.

3.5 Vetting, sanctions and administrative measures

As an aspect of post-conflict justice, states should carry out vetting, sanctions and administrative measures against suspects of human rights violations during transition. The defeat of the *Derg* was total: among others, the government was dismantled; the constitution was suspended and courts reconstituted; the Workers Party of Ethiopia (WPE) was declared illegal; and its security, intelligence, police and military forces were disbanded. At the end, all key positions were filled by the members and loyalists of the rebels who ousted the *Derg*.

When it comes to the judiciary, most if not all experienced judges were dismissed from their jobs on the ground that they belonged to the Marxist Worker's Party of Ethiopia. This took its toll on the judiciary which was already understaffed. It is understandable that the judiciary has to be free of partisan politics. However, in those days, it was unlikely to find any key government official who was not a party member. Some care should have been exercised before depriving the judiciary of its most experienced personnel.

Overall, the vetting exercise has made it difficult for individuals with questionable human rights records in the past government to be involved in the transitional government and afterwards. However, it also created a situation whereby all key positions were given to partisans of the new regime.

3.6 Memorialisation, education and the preservation of historical memory

According to the Chicago Principles, states should support official programmes and popular initiatives to memorialise victims, educate society regarding political violence and preserve historical memory. These memorialisations may include:[65]

> built memorials such as monuments, statutes and museums; sites of memorialisation such as former prisons, battlefields or concentration camps; and, commemorative activities including official days of mourning, renaming streets, parks and other public sites and various forms of artistic, social and community engagement with past violations.

There is no question about the relevance of such programs. Post-conflict measures have to go beyond merely dealing with the past. The new generation has to be taught about the horrors of the past so as not to repeat them.

Memorialisation efforts regarding the victims of the Red Terror have usually been spearheaded by the victims' associations themselves. There is no doubt that they receive some government support to that effect. However, it needs to be pointed out that the government has so far taken a back-seat in regards to efforts of memorialisation and preserving the historical memory.

3.7 Traditional, indigenous and religious approaches to justice and healing

The justification for encouraging such forms of dispute settlement is their legitimacy. Thus, 'traditional, indigenous and religious approaches to justice have high levels of local legitimacy and are generally integrated into the daily lives of victims, their families, communities and the larger society'.[66] The majority of Ethiopians are deeply religious people and in touch with their diverse cultures. It is hardly possible to imagine that these religions and cultures have nothing to contribute to the healing and reconciliation process if they were allowed to play a role.[67] However, the purely legalistic approach adopted by the government made it impossible for this to happen. On the other hand, even organised religious groups rarely venture out of their comfort zone and engage in such meaningful national exercises. This, in part, could be explained by the past and

65 n 5 above, 34.
66 n 5 above, 36.
67 For an attempt to show the existence of restorative justice traditions in Ethiopia which the legalist approach sidelined, see C Schaeffer 'The Red Terror trials versus traditions of restorative justice in Ethiopia' in Tronvoll *et al* (n 1 above) 68-83.

continued association of these religious establishments with the ruling regime. In the current Ethiopia, this association pervades all aspects of civic life where it is rare to find an independent institution which dares to question the official line and proposes an alternative approach.

3.8 Institutional reform and effective governance

The last of these important Chicago Principles of Post-Conflict Justice urges states to engage in institutional reform to support the rule of law, restore public trust, promote fundamental rights and support good governance. Again, the importance of these is not hard to see.[68] The gains from well-planned and executed accountability mechanisms could easily be reversed if these efforts are not followed through by institutional reform and effective governance that can restore the public's trust in government. How has the Ethiopian government fared on these issues?

It would be irresponsible not to admit that there have been some fundamental structural changes towards a better future. Regardless of the political disagreement about the government structure, the 1994 Constitution of the Federal Democratic Republic of Ethiopia entrenched fundamental rights and freedoms, established key institutions and guaranteed their independence, at least on paper. However, the human rights practice of the incumbent regime has been subjected to severe criticism to the extent of prompting some to openly claim that the *Derg* had been better since it did not recognise human rights to begin with, let alone mowing down people who believed it was their right do so under the Constitution as has happened in post-*Derg* era. In other words, the rights in the Constitution are there only to enhance the democratic credentials of the incumbents in the eyes of western donors without whose support the regime could not survive and could not have become what it is today. This is a serious indictment of the regime's performance.

4 Concluding remarks

The human rights abuses committed by the *Derg* in Ethiopia from 1974 to 1980, including the Red Terror era, represent only a portion of the human rights violations that occurred during the *Derg*'s seventeen-year-rule. Ironically, the prosecution of the suspects took nearly eighteen years, longer than the *Derg*'s stay in power. The big fish, Colonel Mengistu Haile-Mariam, is still at large, sheltered by Zimbabwe. Given his key role in what had happened during his rule, one cannot underestimate the impact his capture and surrender will have on the Ethiopian justice system as well as on the victims.

68 For more see GA Aneme 'Beyond the Red Terror Trials: Analyzing guarantees of non-repetition' in Tronvoll *et al* (n 1 above) 116-135.

This brief essay examined the Ethiopian process in light of the Chicago Principles of Post–Conflict Justice which provide a holistic and interdisciplinary approach to the business of transitional justice. Seen in light of this framework, Ethiopia's endeavor is found wanting. In its favour it may be said, however, that the Ethiopian experience represents a home-made, albeit legalistic, response to a legacy of human rights abuses. Despite the trials' shortcomings, it is fitting to say 'better late than never'. Furthermore, no two wrongs make a right. Some have been tempted to delve into a comparison of the incumbent regime's bad human rights record with that of Mengistu's to downgrade the symbolic significance of the Red Terror trials both for Ethiopia and Africa.

Despite the fact that the Ethiopian judiciary had to deal with this novel issue, it wasted an ideal opportunity for dialogue with the burgeoning jurisprudence of international criminal courts. In fact, it could be said that the courts progressively lost touch with international and comparative materials as the trials progressed. While the Federal High Court in its first ruling on preliminary issues in 1995 engaged with substantive international law, albeit in favour of the prosecution's case, its decision on merit in 2006 as well as the decision of the Federal Supreme Court in 2008, are both found wanting with respect to their legal rigour and international comparative significance. Nevertheless, it is important to note that the Ethiopian courts have rendered an important contribution to the law on genocide, especially at the domestic level.

CHAPTER 8

THE TRIAL OF HISSÈNE HABRÉ IN SENEGAL AND ITS CONTRIBUTION TO INTERNATIONAL CRIMINAL LAW

*Kameldy Neldjingaye**

1 Introduction

Hissène Habré, former President of the Republic of Chad, ruled the country from 1982 until he was overthrown in 1990.[1] During his tenure as President of Chad, Hissène Habré instituted an autocratic rule characterised by a single party system and massive human rights violations. He ordered the collective arrests and mass murders of several Chadian ethnic groups when he believed that their leaders posed a threat to his regime. The Documentation and Security Directorate (DDS), a political police created by him and placed under his direct authority,[2] perpetrated cruelty of almost inconceivable magnitude against thousands of individuals suspected of not supporting his regime.

After being deposed, Hissène Habré fled to Senegal where he resides today. On 26 January 2000, a complaint was for the first time filed against him by seven Chadian victims and the Chadian Association of Victims of Political Repression and Crime (AVCRP)[3] before the Dakar *Tribunal*

* LL.B (Nd'jamena); LL.M (Pretoria); Legal Officer, Institute for Human Rights and Development in Africa, Banjul, The Gambia. I am grateful to Humphrey Sipalla for his comments on an earlier draft of this chapter.

1 The *Coup d'Etat* was led by one of his close commanders, Colonel Idriss Déby Itno, who since then became President of the Republic of Chad.

2 The Documentation and Security Directorate was created by the Decree 005/PR of 6 January 1983. Art 1 of the Decree provides that the DDS is 'directly responsible to the office of the President of the Republic because of the confidential nature of its activities'. A National Commission of Inquiry set up by the Chadian government after Habré's downfall from power underlined the dependence of the DDS on Hissène Habré by quoting one of his former closest collaborator who stated that '... everything concerning the DDS is reserved for the president and no person of that time, regardless of his rank or post, can interfere in the business of that office'; quoted from Amnesty International *Chad: The Habré legacy* (2001) 12.

3 The French version of the complaint is available at http://www.hrw.org/legacy/french/themes/habre-plainte.html (accessed 4 March 2010).

régional hors classe.[4] The complaint was anchored on the Convention against Torture and other Cruel, Inhuman or Degrading Treatment or Punishment (CAT)[5] and the general obligation on states, by virtue of customary international law, to prosecute international crimes.[6] The matter turned into the 'Hissène Habré case' when the investigating Judge Demba Kandji, indicted Hissène Habré on 3 February 2000 and placed him under house arrest. Later on, the *Chambre d'accusation* of the Dakar Court of Appeal[7] and the Court of *Cassation*,[8] one after another, asserted that Senegal lacked jurisdiction to prosecute Hissène Habré.[9]

The victims appealed to the Committee against Torture by virtue of the Committee's mandate to examine communications alleging violation of CAT.[10] In its decision on the merit of the communication, the Committee against Torture declared that Senegal had violated CAT by failing to prosecute or extradite Habré for many years.[11] Consequently, the Committee requested Senegal to submit the case to its competent jurisdictions for the purpose of prosecution or otherwise comply with the extradition request made by Belgium or, should the case arise, with any eventual extradition request made in accordance with CAT.[12]

In order to escape the political consequences of legal proceedings in its domestic courts, Senegal referred the case to the African Union (AU) for it to indicate a competent jurisdiction to prosecute Habré. At its January 2006 summit, the AU set up a Committee of Eminent African Jurists (CEAJ) to consider all the aspects and implications of the Habré case.[13]

4 The complainants submitted in support of their complaint, documents related to 97 alleged political killings, 142 alleged cases of torture, 100 alleged 'disappearances' and 736 alleged arbitrary arrests, mostly allegedly perpetrated by the DDS.

5 CAT was adopted by the United Nations General Assembly resolution 39/46 of 10 December 1984. It entered into force on 26 June 1987 and Senegal ratified the Convention on 21 August 1986.

6 Section V of the complaint, see n 3 above.

7 *Ministère public et Francois Diouf Contre Hissene Habré* Dakar Court of Appeal, Judgment 135 of 4 July 2000; the French version of the decision is available at http://www.hrw.org/legacy/french/themes/habre-decision.html (accessed 4 March 2010).

8 *Souleymane Guengueng et Autres Contre Hissene Habré* Court of *Cassation,* Judgment 14 of 20 March 2001; the French version of the decision can be accessed at http://www.hrw.org/legacy/french/themes/habre-cour_de_cass.html (accessed 4 March 2010).

9 The *Chambre d'accusation* of the Dakar Court of Appeal and the Court of *Cassation* anchored their decision in the fact that the alleged crimes were committed elsewhere and Senegal had not incorporated the provisions of CAT into its Code of Criminal Procedure.

10 *Souleymane Guengueng et Autres c. Senegal* submitted to the Committee Against Torture in compliance with art 22 of CAT. Senegal made the declaration under art 22 of CAT on 16 October 1996, accepting the competence of the Committee to examine individual complaints filed against it.

11 Communication 181/2001: Senegal, 19/05/2006 CAT/C/36/D/181/2001 (Jurisprudence) paras 9.5, 9.6 and 9.7.

12 As above, para 10.

13 Decision on the Hissène Habré Case and the African Union (Doc Assembly/AU/8 (VI)) Add 9 http://www.africa-union.org/root/au/Documents/Decisions/hog/AU6th_ord_KHARTOUM_Jan2006.pdf (accessed 4 March 2010).

The CEAJ consequently recommended that there should be preference given to an African solution to the matter and that Senegal was the most suitable country to hold the trial, although an *ad hoc* tribunal could also be established.[14] The AU accordingly called on Senegal to prosecute and ensure that Hissène Habré be tried 'on behalf of Africa', by a competent Senegalese court with guarantees for fair trial.[15] Following the AU decision, Senegal took legislative measures incorporating the provisions of CAT into is domestic legal order.

Although Senegal is yet to obtain the financial assistance it requested from the community of international donors for the organisation of the trial, the above mentioned development represents a sign of hope for the Habré victims who have been pressing for his trial. In fact, the trial of Hissène Habré in Senegal will be a trial of particular relevance in the evolution of international law and the fight against impunity for egregious human rights violations in that it will be the first time a former African head of state will be prosecuted by a foreign African domestic jurisdiction for serious human rights violations committed while in power.

Before analysing the particular relevance in international law of the trial of Hissène Habré in Senegal, this chapter in the first place provides the background of the Habré case by examining the Hissène Habré's human rights legacy and discusses the Belgium extradition request as well as the role played by CAT in the case.

2 Hissène Habré's human rights legacy

Hissène Habré was deposed in 1990 after an eight-year-rule. During the eight years of his presidency, the Chadian administration was notorious for its poor human rights record. After Hissène Habré's downfall in 1990, the Chadian government established a National Commission of Inquiry[16] tasked with the investigation of illegal detentions, assassinations, 'acts of barbarity' as well as any other human rights violations committed during Habré's tenure as president.[17]

Despite the enormous difficulties faced by the Commission of

14 Report of the Committee of Eminent African Jurists on the Case of Hissene Habré http://199.173.149.120/justice/habre/CEJA_Repor0506.pdf (accessed 4 March 2010).

15 Decision on the Hissene Habré case and the African Union, Assembly/AU/Dec 127 (VII).

16 Decree 014/P CE CJ/90 (29 December 1990) creating the '*Commission d'enquete sur les crimes et détournements commis par l'ex- president, ses co-auteurs et/ ou complices*'.

17 As above, art 2.

Inquiry,[18] the work it carried out remains the most extensive investigation ever carried out on the alleged human rights violations committed during the Habré era.[19]

2.1 Torture

Torture was committed systematically and at the highest levels of the Chadian state from 1982 to 1990, the period during which Hissène Habré was President. CAT defines torture as:[20]

> any act by which severe pain or suffering, whether physical or mental, is intentionally inflicted on a person for such purposes as obtaining from him or a third person information or a confession, punishing him for an act he or a third person has committed or is suspected of having committed, or intimidating or coercing him or a third person, or for any reason based on discrimination of any kind, when such pain or suffering is inflicted by or at the instigation of or with the consent or acquiescence of a public official or other person acting in an official capacity. It does not include pain or suffering arising only from, inherent in or incidental to lawful sanctions.

During the presidency of Habré, thousands of people suspected of not supporting his regime were taken to secret detention centres controlled by the DDS[21] and were subjected to torture and cruel, inhuman and degrading treatment. The UN Special Rapporteur on Torture draws a clear distinction between torture and cruel, inhuman or degrading treatment, by asserting that the decisive criteria for distinguishing the first from the second 'may best be understood to be the purpose of the conduct and the powerlessness of the victim, rather than the intensity of the pain or suffering inflicted.'[22] Torture was used by DDS agents to obtain confessions, punish or simply instill fear in the victims.

18 The National Commission of Inquiry did not receive any form of assistance from the international community and had even to fight to obtain a minimal budget. The Commission was obliged to use the former offices of the DDS since it had no headquarters and that discouraged some victims from coming and giving evidence. Furthermore, former members of the DDS who had been appointed in high positions within some governmental agencies such as the new *Centre de Recherches et de Coordination de Renseignements* (Centre for Research and Co-ordination of Intelligence), were accused of intimidating the victims and witnesses. See Amnesty international (n 2 above) 5 & 6.

19 The Commission of Inquiry was able to interview over 1 700 people, including 662 former detainees, 786 close relatives of victims who died in detention or were summarily executed, 236 prisoners of war, 30 former DDS agents and 12 of Habré's former senior officials. See Amnesty International (n 2 above) 6.

20 Art 1 CAT.

21 There were several DDS detention centres throughout N'djamena during the Habré rule. The most-cited is the headquarters of the *Brigade special d'intervention rapide* (BSIR) and the *piscine*, a swimming pool converted into a prison. Some prisoners that Hissène Habré wanted to have close at hand were detained within the presidential palace.

22 Report of the Special Rapporteur on torture and other cruel, inhuman or degrading treatment or punishment, Manfred Nowak, UN Doc E/CN 4/2006/6 (23 December 2005).

The torture methods used were so barbaric that the National Commission of Inquiry depicted the DDS as an 'institution which distinguished itself through its cruelty and its contempt for human life'. Due to the secrecy in which the DDS carried out its activities and also the fact that the majority of people who were tortured had not survived, the exact number of people who were subjected to torture under the Habré rule is unknown. Some of the few survivors alleged that Hissène Habré personally had given the order for certain people to be tortured and was even present during some torture sessions.[23]

3 The trial of Hissène Habré in Senegal

Following the AU decision urging Senegal to try Hissene Habré 'on behalf of Africa', Senegal adopted legislative measures which incorporated the provisions of CAT into its domestic legal order. Senegal also prepared a budget of 28 million Euro for the trial of Habré that it submitted to international donors for assistance. The European Union as well as some individual countries, including France and Switzerland, publicly committed themselves to assisting Senegal.

3.1 Argument of non-retroactivity of criminal law

An attempt to stop the proceedings against Hissène Habré surfaced before the African Court of Human and Peoples' Rights (African Court). In August 2008, the African Court received a communication against Senegal filed by Michelot Yogogombaye, a national from Chad.[24] The complainant contended in his communication among other things, that by amending its constitution to authorise a retroactive application of its criminal laws in order to prosecute Hissène Habré, Senegal had violated the principle of non retroactivity of criminal law enshrined in article 7(2) of the African Charter on Human and Peoples' Rights.[25] Consequently, he requested the African Court to order the end of proceedings against Habré in Senegal.[26]

However, the African Court did not examine the merit of the complaint since it was obvious that it lacked jurisdiction to entertain it.[27]

23 Amnesty International (n 2 above) 26; see also Benetech *Violations de droits de l'homme par l'Etat Tchadien sous le regime de Hissène Habré* (2010), for more details in the personal involvement of Habré in the human rights violations committed under his rule.

24 Communication 001/2008.

25 African Court on Human and Peoples' Rights *Michelot Yogogombaye v The Republic of Senegal*, Communication 001/2008 Judgment para 21.

26 As above, para 23.

27 Art 34(6) Protocol to the African Charter on Human and Peoples' Rights on the Establishment of an African Court on Human and Peoples' Rights provides that at the time of ratification of the Protocol or any time thereafter, the state shall make a

It should be noted that the argument of non-retroactivity of criminal law in relation to Habré was also raised before the Court of Justice of the Economic Community of West African States (ECOWAS Court).[28] The ECOWAS Court found Senegal in violation of the principle of non-rectroativity of laws and punishment under article 7(2) of the African Charter, article 8 of the Universal Declaration of Human Rights and article 3(4) of the ICCPR. The ECOWAS Court's decision has the effect that Senegal should not try Habré unless he can be tried before an international tribunal.

As far as the principle of non retroactivity is concerned, international law does not accept the application of the principle in circumstances where the crimes were prohibited by customary international law at the time of their commission. The *Eichmann* case, a well-known example of a domestic court exercising jurisdiction over international crimes, constitutes a very interesting jurisprudence on the legal obligation of states to prosecute international crimes suspects, no matter the fact that the crime is not punishable under the domestic legislation of the concerned state.[29]

Adolf Eichmann was abducted from Argentina by Israeli secret police in 1960 and taken to Israel to be prosecuted under Israeli and Nazi Collaborators Punishment Law of 1950, a law similar to the 1948 Convention on the Prevention and Punishment of the Crime of Genocide. Eichmann strongly objected to the retroactive application of the Punishment Law but his objection was dismissed by both the District Court of Jerusalem and the Supreme Court of Israel on the grounds that the crimes with which Eichmann was charged were prohibited under international law at the time they were committed.[30]

Contrary to the decision of the ECOWAS Court, Senegal may have not violated the principle of non-retroactivity of criminal law by amending its legislation in order to criminalise acts of torture even though the reasons for the amendment should be researched elsewhere than in the desire for creating the legal framework for the trial of Hissène Habré. In fact, as monist state where international treaties are directly part of the domestic legal order,[31] Senegal did not need to amend its legislation to incorporate acts of torture before prosecuting Hissène Habré. Furthermore, Senegalese

declaration accepting the competence of the Court to receive petitions filed by individuals or nongovernmental organisations (NGOs). The article further declares that the Court shall not examine communications filed by individuals or NGOs against a state that has not made such declaration. Senegal did not make the declaration at the time the communication was filed by Mr Yogogombaye.

28 The argument was raised in a communication filed at the time, by Habré himself.

29 Supreme Court of Israel, *Attorney General v Eichmann* [1961] 36 ILR277, 288-83 (1968).

30 As above.

31 Art 98 Senegalese Constitution: 'international treaties or agreements regularly ratified or approved have on their publication, an authority superior to that of the national laws.'

courts also had the possibility of using the passive personality principle[32] to exercise jurisdiction over Hissène Habré since two Senegalese nationals are among Habré's victims. Ultimately, the position of the Dakar Court of Appeal and the Senegalese Court of *Cassation* according to which Senegal lacked jurisdiction to prosecute Habré on the ground that it had not incorporated CAT into its domestic legislation was a mockery of international law.

3.2 The Belgian extradition request

A number of Habré's victims filed a case against him before a Belgian court of first instance, immediately when the Senegalese Court of Appeal declared that Senegal did not have competence to prosecute Habré.[33] The complaint was filed under a law on universal jurisdiction adopted by Belgium in 1993.[34] In its original form, the Belgian law on universal jurisdiction allowed Belgian courts to prosecute serious international crimes, such as genocide, crimes against humanity, or war crimes, regardless of the nationality of the victim and the place where the crimes were committed.[35]

After a four- year-long investigation, Judge Fransen from the Belgian Court of First Instance issued an international arrest warrant against Hissène Habré for crimes against humanity, war crimes, and acts of torture and serious violations of international humanitarian law.[36] On the same day, Belgium asked for Habré's extradition from Senegal.

Seized with the Belgian extradition request, the Indicting Chamber of the Court of Appeals of Dakar ruled that Hissène Habré enjoys immunity from jurisdiction pursuant to the *Arrest warrant* decision by the

32 The passive personality principle allows a state to exercise jurisdiction over a person suspected of having committed an offence abroad which harm one of more of its nationals.

33 There were 21 victims and three of them had Belgian nationality.

34 The Belgian law on universal jurisdiction was not yet amended at the time and the complaint was declared admissible. From 26 February to 7 March 2002, Fransen J conducted investigations in Chad during which he interviewed witnesses, Habré-era officials, toured former grave sites and visited five jails where the DDS had systematically tortured prisoners. See Amnesty International (n 2 above) 6.

35 The Belgian Act, named the Act Concerning the punishment of Grave Breaches of International Humanitarian Law (the law on universal jurisdiction), adopted on 16 June 1993, was repealed following the position adopted by the International Court of Justice in the *Arrest warrant* case and new legislation was promulgated in its place. Under the new legislation, Belgian courts have jurisdiction only for international crimes if the suspect is Belgian or has primary residence in Belgium; or if the victim is Belgian or has lived in Belgium for at least three years at the time the crimes were committed. Most cases filed under the original Belgian law on universal jurisdiction, including the case filed against Mr Yerodia, were dismissed. However, the *Habré* case was maintained as it complied with the criteria of a transitory clause contained in the new Belgian legislation which allows cases in which judicial investigations had already begun and plaintiffs are Belgian, to proceed.

36 The arrest warrant was issued on 19 September 2005.

International Court of Justice and, therefore, the matter is beyond its jurisdiction.[37] Even though having Habré tried in Belgium is not foreseeable at the current time,[38] the proceedings initiated by the Belgian court of first instance played the role of catalyst in the Habré case in that it added pressure on the Senegalese authorities. The mention 'on behalf of Africa' in the AU decision requesting Senegal to prosecute Habré could be interpreted as an expression of the AU's desire not to see Habré prosecuted by a western country. However, the fact that the AU mandated Senegal to prosecute Hissène Habré without providing the necessary funding and timeline for the trial, raises questions with regards to the AU's commitment for the organisation of the trial. To date, the majority of donors which pledged funding for the trial of Habré in Senegal are from the western world. This is troubling when one recalls the position unanimously taken by AU members to see Habré prosecuted by an African state for Africa.

4 Relevance of the Habré trial in international law

Instead of asserting that the trial of Habré in Senegal is a certainty, this section tries simply to examine the impact an eventual prosecution in Senegal would have on international law. If prosecuted by a Senegalese court, Hissène Habré would become the first former African head of state to be tried by a foreign domestic court. This section examines the role played by CAT in the *Habré* case and the precedent that would be set in international law should the trial of Habré take place in Senegal.

4.1 CAT and the case of Habré

International law allows states to exercise universal jurisdiction over international crimes, but it does not compel them to do so in the absence

37 See extract of the decision, http://www.hrw.org/legacy/french/docs/2005/11/26/chad12091.htm (accessed 4 April 2010). The decision of the Court of Appeals of Dakar was a voluntary misinterpretation of the *Arrest warrant* decision because, although the ICJ seized the opportunity given by the complaint filed by DRC on behalf Mr Yerodia, to make a pronouncement regarding the immunity of jurisdiction from prosecution that certain high ranking sitting officials enjoy before the courts of other states, it did not dwell on the issue of immunity of jurisdiction for former high ranking officials such as former head of states.

38 On 19 February 2009, Belgium filed a case against Senegal before the ICJ in compliance with art 30(1) of CAT. Belgium referred to a statement made by the President of Senegal, Mr Abdoulaye Wade, whereby the latter declared that 'Senegal could lift his house arrest if it fails to find the budget which it regards as necessary in order to hold the trial of Mr. Habré' and argued that in the event Senegal lifts the house arrest, it would be easy for Habré to leave Senegalese territory and escape prosecution. Belgium concluded that this would cause irreparable prejudice to the right conferred on it by international law to bring criminal proceedings against Habré. See ICJ *Case concerning questions relating to the obligation to prosecute or extradite (Belgium v Senegal)* Request for the indication of provisional measures 28 May 2009 para 13.

of a specific treaty. That trend was outlined in the *Lotus* case where the ICJ stated that:[39]

> The first and foremost restriction imposed by international law upon a State is that – failing the existence of a permissive rule to the contrary – it may not exercise its power in any form in the territory of another State. In this sense jurisdiction is certainly territorial; it cannot be exercised by a State outside its territory ...

In contrast to other international crimes, the prosecution of which depends on the good will of interested states, torture is one of the rare international crimes over which a number of states have decided to pass jurisdiction to each other, creating an obligation for themselves to prosecute or extradite individuals suspected of torture found in their territories. The adoption of the CAT in 1984 opened a new page in the evolution of international law, in that it was the first international human rights instrument to attempt a transformation of the universal jurisdiction principle from a non-binding principle to a binding norm.[40]

The *Habré* case has indeed provided a golden opportunity to test the principle of *aut dedere aut punire*, encapsulated under article 7 paragraph 1 of CAT. The article alluded to the very *raison d'être* of CAT: before the adoption of the Convention, torture was prohibited both by customary international law and domestic legislation yet torture suspects could escape justice by moving from one place to another. One of the main objectives of CAT was therefore to establish universal jurisdiction over acts of torture so that they could be prosecuted no matter where suspects found themselves. Despite the fact that acts of torture amounting to crimes against humanity[41] can today fall under the jurisdiction of the ICC,[42] CAT remains of particular importance in the fight against impunity for egregious human rights violations, specially when only a certain number of crimes fall under the competence of the ICC.

39 *SS Lotus* (*France v Turkey*) (1927) PCIJ Rep Ser A, 10.

40 Art 7 CAT obligates state parties to either prosecute suspects of torture found in their territories or extradite them to another state willing to prosecute them. CAT was preceded by international instruments which, notwithstanding their nonbinding character, serve as guiding principles to national and international bodies. These instruments are, among others, the Declaration on the Protection of All Persons from being subjected to Torture and Other Cruel, Inhuman and Degrading Treatment or Punishment; the Standard Minimum Rules for the Treatment of Prisoners (1977); and the Principles on the Protection of Persons under Detention or Imprisonment.

41 In the *Akayesu* case, for example, the International Tribunal for Rwanda established that torture can constitute a crime against humanity if is perpetrated as part of a widespread or systematic attack against the civilian population on discriminatory grounds; see *Prosecutor v Akayesu* (Case ICTR-1996-4-T) Judgment 2 September 1998 (ICTR Reports, 1998, 44-404).

42 Ideally, the International Criminal Court (ICC) would be the best organ to examine the Habré case. However, the ICC lacks the *temporis* jurisdiction to examine the case because the aledged crimes occurred before the entry into force of the Rome Statute.

CAT has played a crucial role in the *Habré* case through the fact that it was the legal instrument relied upon by Habré's victims to argue that the Senegalese courts were competent to hear their case even if Hissène Habré was suspected of having committed other international crimes. The Committee Against Torture ruled that by having failed to take the necessary steps within a reasonable time to confer universal jurisdiction on its courts over acts of torture, Senegal had violated CAT.[43] This statement sounds like a clear criticism of the views expressed by the Dakar Court of Appeal and the Senegalese Court of *Cassation*. It is also somewhat contrary to what the ECOWAS court held on retro-active application of the law in Senegal.

There is no doubt that CAT is not a self-executing treaty; however, article 5, paragraph 2 imposes an obligation on states parties to take the necessary legislative measures in a reasonable time to confer on their courts universal jurisdiction over acts of torture. Article 5(2) of CAT should be interpreted as obligating states parties to the Convention to take not only legislative measures but also practical measures aiming at ensuring the effective and timely prosecution of any suspect of torture found in its territory.

The critics of putting Habré on trial in Senegal argue that the case is directed solely against the former president of Chad because, if real justice had to be done, Habré should have been prosecuted along with all those who collaborated closely with him and participated in the alleged human rights violations. Although these critics raise the relevant question of the accountability of Habré accomplices, the trial of Habré in Senegal should be confused with the prosecution of his accomplices. The reason being that Senegal cannot exercise jurisdiction over senior officials of the Habré administration accused of participation in the human rights abuses because they are not in Senegalese territory at present. If article 7 of CAT obligates state parties to either extradite suspects of torture found on their territory or prosecutes them, it is mainly because jurisdiction is first and foremost a matter of sovereignty, meaning that a state cannot exercise jurisdiction over crime suspects living in another state.

4.2 Landmark case on universal jurisdiction

The term universal jurisdiction refers to jurisdiction established over a crime, regardless of the place it has been committed, the nationality of the suspect, or of the victim or any other connection between the crime and the prosecuting state.[44] Universal jurisdiction is limited to specific international crimes such as war crimes, crimes against humanity and torture. The idea that universal jurisdiction should be exercised over

43 Committee Against Torture Communication 181/2001, May 2006, paras 9.5 & 9.6.
44 R Cryer *et al An introduction to international criminal law and procedure* (2007) 44.

international crimes such as torture arose from the fact that torture violate the domestic legal order of a state as well as the international legal order as a whole.[45]

In practice, international law distinguishes two types of universal jurisdiction. On the one hand there is an absolute or pure universal jurisdiction which arises when a state wants to assert jurisdiction over an international crime although the suspect is not present on its territory. On the other hand, the conditional universal jurisdiction which is exercised when the suspect is already on the territory of the state asserting jurisdiction exists. Both pure universal jurisdiction and conditional jurisdiction are subject to controvercy. If pure universal jurisdiction is found in many cases to be a violation of the jurisdictional principle,[46] conditional jurisdiction have consistently raised controvercy when a state competent to have recourse to it fails to do so. As far as pure universal jurisdiction is concerned, its implementation is confronted with practical challenges namely, the fact that it does create an obligation on the side of the territory or nation to assist in the investigations, provide evidence or extradite the suspects.[47]

Today, with the emergence of human rights instruments such as CAT whereby states agree between themselves to pass jurisdiction onto one another, the problem with universal jurisdiction tends to be rather with the failure of states to exercise jurisdiction over suspects of international crimes found in their territories than with states seeking to exercise universal jurisdiction for crimes not committed in their territories.

The trial of Hissène Habré in Senegal would be a landmark case regarding universal jurisdiction in that it would be the first time an African state is compelled by virtue of international law to exercise jurisdiction over a person suspected of international crimes. If for some reason Hissène Habré fails to appear before a court for the human violations he is suspected of having committed, the fact that Senegal was compelled to confer jurisdiction upon its courts over the matter is already a situation that is a first of its kind in the history of international law.

Although the *Eichmann* case previously referred to is an interesting case in the international criminal law literature, care must be taken, however, to allude to it as a universal jurisdiction case. This is because the

45 R Higgins *Problems and processes: International law and how we use it* (1994) 56-63; H Jallow and F Bensouda 'International criminal law in an African context' in M du Plessis *African guide to international criminal justice* Institute for Security Studies (2008) 16.

46 J Dugard *International law: A South African perspective* (2005) 157; *Roitman Rosenmann v Spain* CAT Communication 176/2000, 30 April 2002, para 6.7.

47 B Broomhall *International justice and the International Criminal Court: Between state sovereignty and the rule of law* (2003) 119-23.

crimes allegedly committed by Eichmann occurred before the coming into existence of the state of Israel.

Before Habré, Augusto Pinochet was the first former head of state to be prosecuted in a domestic court for human rights violations allegedly committed while serving as head of state. Proceedings were instituted against Pinochet in the United Kingdom for the crimes he aledgedly committed while President of Chile from 1973 to 1990. These proceedings were terminated, based on the fact that Pinochet was deemed unfit to stand trial. The case was a landmark case on the immunity of former heads of state.[48] The Habré case has caused a state of confusion by different fora: the ICJ, Senegalese courts, UN Committee Against Torture, the ECOWAS Court, and Belgium courts. These institutions have given conflicting positions on retroatctivity and universal jurisdiction in respect of Habré.

5 Conclusion

Unpunished human rights violations in other parts of Africa permanently remind one that the trial of Hissène Habré in Senegal is not an end but rather a beginning and that it will contribute to the development of international law in Africa. Particularly, it will unveil the duty to prosecute or extradite suspects of international crimes under customary international law. It is also likely to echo the sentiment that no person, including a former state official, is above the law. Further, the trial is likely to explain that international crimes are punishable regardless of the defences regarding the non-retroactivity of law and punishment. Importantly, the trial will shed light on the principles of universal jurisdiction, territoriality and passive nationality, and will re-state the principle that the immunity of a state official is not a defence in international criminal justice.

The trial of Habré in Senegal has also helped the African Court on Human and Peoples' Rights to give its position on the admissibility of cases before that Court pursuant to articles 5(3) and 34(6) of the Protocol establishing the Court. Further, the case has enabled Senegal to enact laws that enforce the principles of international criminal law as found in the Constitution. Article 9 of the Constitution of Senegal provides for universal jurisdiction over genocide, war crimes and crimes against humanity committed in the past and outside the territory of Senegal.

48 The House of Lords which examined the issue of Pinochet's immunity as former head of state was of the opinion that 'a former head of state may only benefit from immunity for acts carried out in the exercise of legitimate state functions, which cannot include international crimes such as torture'.

CHAPTER

9 PROSECUTING INTERNATIONAL CRIMES COMMITTED BY THE LORD'S RESISTANCE ARMY IN UGANDA

*Christopher Mbazira**

1 Introduction

Many African countries have over the last four decades experienced economic, social and political upheavals characterised mainly by civil wars and resultant civil unrest.[1] Uganda stands out in the catalogue of countries with experiences of this nature. Uganda gained its independence from Britain on 9 October 1962; however, less than a decade into its independence the country was subjected to the dictatorship of Idi Amin (1971 to 1979). The Amin-period was characterised by massive human rights violations, economic breakdown and untold suffering of the masses. Although the overthrow of Idi Amin in 1979 came as a reprieve for Ugandans, the subsequent period, albeit on a moderate scale, could be described as putting old wine into a new bottle.

Rather than heralding democratic rule, the first multi-party elections held in 1980 ignited a civil war in which thousands of Ugandans lost their lives. The end of the civil war in 1986 when Museveni and his National Resistance Army (NRA) seized power was greeted with a sigh of relief. Overnight guns became silent and peace returned to the country. However, as had been the case after the overthrow of Idi Amin, Ugandans were mistaken; civil wars immediately erupted in several parts of the country. Although situations in some parts of the country, including the East and the West, were quickly contained, the civil war in Northern Uganda was

* LL.B(Makerere);LL.M(Pretoria); PhD(Western Cape); Lecturer and Deputy Dean (Postgraduate & Administration) Faculty of Law, Makerere University. I would like to thank the anonymous referee for the comments on an earlier draft of this chapter.

1 In 2000, the *Yearbook of World Armaments and Disarmaments* (Stockholm International Peace Research Institute) took note of the fact that Africa was the most war-ridden region of the world and one in which war was on the increase.

to endure for over two decades, unleashing untold suffering on the people in this region. This civil war was fought between the government forces, the Uganda Peoples Defence Forces (UPDF) and a group of rebels, the Lord Resistance Army (LRA) led by Joseph Kony.

Although calm has returned to Northern Uganda, the region is yet to get back on its feet in economic and social terms. In addition, there are a number of human rights, and transitional justice issues that need to be addressed. These include questions on how to address the many years of human rights violations; steps that need to be taken to end impunity in the region in particular and the country in general; and realising the economic and social rights of an entire generation that witnessed conflict for over two decades.

This chapter examines the genesis and causes of the LRA war, the different attempts to end the war and mechanisms that have been put in place to deliver justice and end impunity in the country. It is apparent from this exploration that the causes of the war are deeply rooted and could be traced as far back as to the colonial era. While the threat of the LRA in the region has diminished, it is important to understand and resolve the historical causes of the conflict in order to avoid similar conflicts in the future.

For over 20 years, Uganda unsuccessfully tried to end the conflict by military means. It was only after the issuing of warrants of arrest by the International Criminal Court (ICC) against some of the LRA leaders that the LRA was forced to take part in peace negotiations brokered by the government of Southern Sudan. Meanwhile, the warrants of arrest were at the same time viewed as obstacles to the peace process in Uganda. In effect, the warrants and peace talks illustrate what has been described as a classic dilemma of transitional justice arising from the question of whether and to what extent criminal justice may be compromised for the sake of peace.[2] Although the final peace accord was never signed, the process of the peace talks resulted in the enactment of the International Criminal Court Act (ICC Act), domesticating the Rome Statute. This chapter also reviews some of the important provisions of this historic law, enacted before the ICC Review Conference held in Kampala (31 May – 11 June 2010). Also reviewed is a constitutional petition which challenges the consistency of the ICC Act with the Constitution which is the supreme law in Uganda.

2 A Greenawalt 'Complementarity in crisis: Uganda, alternative justice, and the International Criminal Court' (2009) 50 *Virginia Journal of International Law* 108.

2 Genesis of the conflict

Traces of the causes of the conflict could be found in the period when Uganda was still under British colonial administration. Like in many parts of the world, the British colonial administration in Uganda used the divide and rule technique. In Uganda, the colonial administration, amongst others, created inter-ethnic competition for power, which, coupled with the regional income inequalities, resulted in a North-South divide.[3] Most economic activities, including crop production, were undertaken in the South, while the North was treated as a reservoir for cheap labour. In the last years of its rule, the colonial administration had also recruited large numbers of northerners into the armed forces, especially the Acholi, based on the myth that the Acholi were a 'martial tribe'.[4] The colonial administration's decision to select the military from the North was also based on a fear of the impact of arming members of consolidated kingdoms and chiefdoms in Southern Uganda. The administration thus found it safer to arm dispersed tribes in Northern Uganda.[5]

At independence the army was dominated by northerners. Hence, although the North remained economically inferior, it remained militarily superior to the economically superior South.[6] When it became necessary for politicians - like Apollo Milton Obote[7] - to resort to military force to satisfy political ends, the northerner-dominated army lent support. In 1966, Obote used the army to overrun the palace of Buganda, the most powerful kingdom in the country, forcing its King (the Kabaka) into exile.[8] These events were recorded by the Baganda, a dominant southern ethnic group, who extended the blame to all northerners, especially the Acholi.[9]

The period after 1966 and during the reign of Amin was dominated by ethnic politics and manoeuvres. During the Obote II government (1980 to 1985) ethnicity became part of the politics of the military, the Uganda National Liberation Army (UNLA), with Acholi and Langi (Obote's ethnic group) rivalling for control. In 1985, Acholi officers, in a bid to survive against the Langi, precipitated a *coup d'etat* that gave the Acholi

3 International Crisis Group (ICG) *Northern Uganda: Understanding and solving the conflict* Africa Report 77 (2004) www.up.ligi.ubc.ca/ICGreport.pdf (accessed 2 February 2010) 2.

4 S Lwanga-Lunyigo 'The colonial roots of internal conflict' in K Rupesinghe (ed) *Conflict resolution in Uganda* (1989) 24.

5 H Lunde *Night commuting in Gulu, Northern Uganda: From spontaneous strategy to new social institutions* Master's Thesis in Peace and Conflict Studies (2006) Fafo – Institute for Applied International Studies 31.

6 As above, 32.

7 First Prime Minister of Independent Uganda.

8 G Kanyeihamba *Constitutional and political history of Uganda: From 1894 to the present* (2002) 99.

9 Human Rights and Peace Centre (HURIPEC) and Liu Institute for Global Issues *The hidden war: The forgotten people, war in Acholi and its ramifications for peace and security in Uganda* (2003) 22.

officers full control of the army. The honeymoon was short-lived though. In 1986 the NRA staged a *coup*, overthrowing Tito Okello's Acholi-dominated government. Museveni's NRA rebellion had exploited the ethnic tension between the southerners and northerners to marshal support, and had gained access to power because of the Acholi Langi rift.[10] As a result, the war in the Luwero Triangle (the epicentre of the NRA rebellion) was seen as a war between southerners and northerners (the Acholi).[11]

When the NRA took control of the government, it ordered the subdued belligerent combatants to return to their barracks, which the Acholi soldiers refused to do. The soldiers saw this as a repeat of the 1971 Amin massacre of Acholi and Langi soldiers after they were ordered to return to the barracks.[12] They instead retreated to the north, determined not only to defend themselves, but to regain political power. Reports indicate that retaliation massacres were carried out against civilians in northern Uganda by the forces of the new government.[13] This is in addition to a witch hunt of UNLA soldiers by the NRA 35th Battalion, accompanied by ethnically-provoked looting of the Acholi people's properties.[14] To resist the new government, the UNLA soldiers re-organised and decided to use the north as their base. However, later several rebel groups sprang up. These included the Uganda Peoples Democratic Army (UPDA), the Holy Spirit Mobile Forces (HSMF) and the Uganda Christian Democratic Army (UCDA), later renamed the Lord's Resistance Army (LRA).[15]

In subsequent years other groups, including the UPDA and HSMF, either disappeared or joined the LRA, which endured for over two decades as the symbol of resistance in Northern Uganda. At the mantle of the LRA leadership is Joseph Kony who triples as a military, political and spiritual leader. Under his spiritual leadership Kony claimed to represent a new generation of Acholi on a mission to purify Acholi and implement a new moral order.[16] Although support for the LRA was built around Acholi nationalism, it does not have any identifiable political agenda.[17] Yet, paradoxically, the majority of violent attacks, involving massacres and abductions, were directed at Acholi people.

What over the years reduced LRA's vulnerability to attacks was the fact that it never established a base inside Uganda. It instead used Southern

10 As above, 25.
11 R Gersony *The anguish of Northern Uganda: Results of a field-based assessment of the civil conflicts in Northern Uganda* (1997).
12 ICG (n 3 above) 3.
13 As above.
14 HURIPEC and Liu (n 9 above) 35.
15 HURIPEC and Liu (n 9 above) 34.
16 Lunde (n 5 above) 32.
17 ICG (n 3 above) 5.

Sudan, with its polarised borders, as the base for its operations. This is one of the factors that explain Kony's ability to sustain the war for such a long time, coupled with direct logistical support from the government of Sudan. The Sudanese government supported the LRA as retaliation for Uganda's alleged support of the Sudanese Peoples Liberation Army (SPLA).[18] The war was described as two conflicts in one:[19]

> [A] multi-faceted northern rebellion against the NRM government whose root causes have never been fully resolved, and a war with an LRA that does not fit conventional models of political insurgency and is motivated by an Old Testament-style apocalyptic spiritualism.

2.1 LRA brutality and the impact of war

The tactics of the LRA were brutal and directed mainly against civilians. The attacks were characterised by killings and the cutting off of ears, lips, breasts and hands of civilians suspected of being sympathetic to the government. This is in addition to the abduction of civilians, including children, who were recruited either as combatants, porters or used as sex slaves for Kony and his commanders. This dire situation was summarised in a 2006 report by Civil Society Organisations for Peace in Northern Uganda (CSOPNU) in the following words:[20]

> [A]lmost 8 per cent of Uganda's population have been forced to live in extreme poverty and suffering, ravaged by war that targets civilians and children; in which 1.8 million people are forced to live in squalid and life-threatening conditions, displaced from their homes by violence and coercion; in which tens of thousands of children are unable to sleep in their beds for fear of abduction; in which violence, torture and abuse have become normal; in which livelihoods have been destroyed, cultural norms have collapsed, and where hope for the future of an entire generation has withered away.

At its beginning, the war in Northern Uganda involved only military objectives. The situation changed in 1994 when the LRA started systemically attacking and killing civilians.[21] The most horrific attacks include the 1995 Atiak massacre in which over 300 civilians were killed. It is reported that the Atiak massacre, which took place on 20 April 1995, occurred when the LRA rebels seized the Atiak trading centre from the government forces. The LRA then rounded up all people in the trading centre, marched them to a nearby river from where over 300 people were shot. Some of the survivors were abducted and forced to join the LRA.[22]

18 HURIPEC and Liu (n 9 above) 80.

19 Z Lomo and L Hovil *Behind the violence: Causes, consequences and the search for solutions to the war in Northern Uganda* Refugee Law Project Working Paper 11 (2004) Report summary.

20 CSOPNU *Counting the cost of twenty years of war in northern Uganda* (2006) 7.

21 As above, 9.

22 Liu Institute for Global Issues *Remembering the Atiak massacre, April 20th 1995* The Justice and Reconciliation Project, Field Notes 4 (April 2007).

The LRA used these killings as retaliation for the support the Acholi people had given the government in the war, especially during the government's 'Operation North' in which many Acholi fought alongside government forces as a 'Bow and Arrow' force. To Kony, this was a grave betrayal by his own kin.[23] The Atiak massacre was followed by the 1997 massacre of over 400 people in the Kitgum district.[24]

From this time on LRA abductions became routine. Estimates indicate that between 1986 and 2006, the LRA abducted a total of 75 000 people of whom approximately 38 000 were children.[25] Adduction was used by the LRA for several reasons, one of which being a means of replenishing its army. By 2004, it was estimated that over 80 per cent of LRA's ranks consisted of abducted children.[26] In addition, these abductions were used as a means of stopping the local population from supporting the government. This is because the local community would in effect be supporting the army to kill its own children.[27]

All efforts at using a military solution to end the war failed, some with a boomerang effect. An example of this is 'Operation Iron Fist', launched in May 2002, whereby government forces entered Southern Sudan and attacked the LRA camps in what the military had pre-determined to lead to a decisive victory against the LRA. The Operation did not achieve this result. The LRA rebels trekked back to Uganda, launching a number of attacks on civilians.[28] Fearing for their lives, tens of thousands of people abandoned their homes and moved into Internally Displaced Persons' camps (IDPs). By 2006, it was estimated that between 1.8 and 2 million people were living in IDP camps.[29]

A sizeable number of the population did not go into the camps but remained night commuters. They would remain in the villages during the day, of course at the risk of being abducted, and then trek to neighbouring towns like Gulu and Kitgum to spend the night. This practice was a spontaneous response to the LRA attacks that usually occurred in the dead of the night.[30] It is reported that at some point, over 40 000 people would escape to Gulu every night, especially in the period after Operation Iron Fist.[31] Female night commuters were exposed to the risk of sexual violence.[32]

23 Lunde (n 5 above) 33.
24 As above.
25 See Pham *et al Abducted: The Lord Resistance Army and forced conscription in Northern Uganda* (2007) Human Rights Center, University of California Barkley http://escholarship.org/uc/item/7963c61v (accessed 23 February 2010).
26 World Vision *Pawns of politics: Children, conflict and peace in Northern Uganda* (2004)18.
27 Lunde (n 5 above) 34.
28 CSOPNU (n 20 above) 10.
29 As above, 11.
30 Lunde (n 5 above) 34.
31 As above, 38.
32 World Vision (n 26 above) 19.

In 1996, the government announced that it would create 'protected villages'. Shortly, people were forcibly removed and taken to the villages. Some circles considered this to be a military strategy undertaken in the guise of protecting civilians. It is reported that artillery and mortar bombs were fired into villages to scare people away from their homes into the newly-established IDP camps.[33] In some cases people were given the ultimatum to leave the villages, and anyone found in a village after the ultimatum would be considered a rebel.[34]

The forced displacements created a humanitarian crisis; in a short time some camps received over 60 000 people.[35] The conditions in the camps were squalid, with very high mortality rates arising from violence and the health conditions in the camps. Between January and July 2005, it was estimated that the daily mortality rate was 1.54 per 10 000, compared to 0.46 obtaining in the rest of Uganda.[36] When the United Nations Under-Secretary-General for Humanitarian Affairs and Emergency Relief Co-ordinator, Jan Egeland visited Uganda, he described Northern Uganda as 'the world's biggest neglected humanitarian crisis'.

2.2 Attempts at a peaceful solution

There were several attempts to resolve the conflict through peaceful means, including negotiations. However, most of these efforts did not yield any fruits, mainly because of LRA's intransigence and the government's inconsistent approach in this regard.[37] The first serious attempt at peace negotiations was initiated by Betty Bigombe, then a government Minister hailing from the Acholi region.[38] Bigombe's initiative, which had started yielding results was frustrated when in the middle of negotiations the President announced that he was bent on using military force to end the conflict. The President ordered the rebels to surrender. Another round of negotiations (between 2004 and 2005) also failed when the government resorted to military force.

In 2000, the government decided to extend amnesty to rebels who could surrender and renounce violence. Pressure to adopt a law on amnesty came from the Acholi region, spearheaded by religious and cultural leaders, who thought that a military approach to the conflict was

33 Lunde (n 5 above) 35.
34 As above.
35 CSOPNU (n 20 above) 13.
36 CSOPNU 14.
37 T Dagne *Uganda: Current conditions and the crisis in Northern Uganda* Congressional Research Service Report to Congress (2010) 6.
38 Bigombe has recently been awarded the Dutch Geuzen Medal for 2010 for her efforts to end the war in Northern Uganda.

not a solution.[39] Amnesty was viewed by many in the region as formalising the traditional mechanisms of dispute resolution and reconciliation.[40] The Amnesty Act was adopted,[41] defining the parameters for amnesty and setting up an Amnesty Commission. The mandate of the Amnesty Commission included monitoring programmes of demobilisation, reintegration and resettlement of persons granted amnesty.[42] It is reported that long before the Amnesty Act was adopted, some military leaders had used amnesties alongside military solutions to diffuse conflicts. In this respect, the example is given of the West Nile Bank Front rebellion.[43] It is reported that by January 2008, 15 300 combatants and abductees had been granted amnesty.[44] In spite of making significant gains, the amnesty processes did not end the conflict. The processes suffered from a number of setbacks, the major one being the government's inconsistency in supporting the process.[45]

3 Referral of situation to the ICC and the process of peace talks

On 16 December 2003, the Government of Uganda formally invited the Prosecutor of the ICC to investigate the situation in Northern Uganda with a view of prosecuting members of the LRA. The Prosecutor formerly accepted the invitation in January 2004 and began investigations in August 2004. The Prosecutor determined that the referral required him to investigate not only the LRA but the whole situation in Northern Uganda, including crimes committed by government forces. Subsequently however, the Prosecutor reached the conclusion that crimes committed by the LRA were much more numerous and of higher gravity than those alleged to have been committed by government forces.[46] At the beginning of 2005, the ICC opened a field office in Kampala for the purposes of coordinating the investigations and giving support to local authorities.

On 8 July 2005, the ICC issued sealed arrest warrants against Joseph Kony and three of his top commanders: Vincent Otti (Vice Chairman and Second-in-Command); Okot Odhiambo (Brigade Commander); and

39 L Hovil and Z Lomo *Whose justice? Perceptions of Uganda's Amnesty Act 2000: The potential for conflict resolution and long-term reconciliation* Refugee Law Project Working Paper 15 (2005) 6.
40 As above, 10.
41 Chapter 294, Laws of Uganda 2000, amended in 2006.
42 Sec 8, Amnesty Act.
43 Hovil and Lomo (n 39 above) 7.
44 See Justice in Perspective *Uganda Amnesty Commission* http://www.justice inperspective.org.za/index.php?option=com_content&task=view&id=39&Itemid=79 (accessed 23 March 2010).
45 Hovil and Lomo (n 39 above) 18.
46 Statement by the Chief Prosecutor Luis Moreno-Ocampo, 14 October 2005 http://www.icc-cpi.int/NR/rdonlyres/2919856F-03E0-403F-A1A8-D61D4F350A20/277305/Uganda_LMO_Speech_141020091.pdf (accessed 23 March 2010).

Dominic Ongwen (Brigade Commander). The warrants were unsealed on 13 October 2005 and served on governments including that of Uganda, Democratic Republic of Congo and Sudan. The four were accused of having committed crimes against humanity and war crimes including murder, rape, enslavement, sexual enslavement, inhumane acts of inflicting serious bodily injury and suffering, cruel treatment of civilians, intentionally directing attacks at civilian populations, forced enlisting of children and pillaging. A total of 33 counts of crimes against humanity and war crimes were listed against LRA rebel leaders.[47]

3.1 Process of peace talks

A few months after the issuing of the warrants by the ICC, Kony indicated that he was prepared to engage in peace talks.[48] It is believed that the warrants had isolated the LRA and forced them to hold peace talks. Thus, in May 2006, the First Vice-President of Sudan and President of Southern Sudan, Salva Kiir, delivered a message from Joseph Kony to President Yoweri Museveni in which Kony asked for peace talks.[49] Museveni's response was positive, he promised that if they renounced violence, he would extend amnesty to all LRA rebels, including the top leadership and not surrender them to the ICC.[50] This marked the beginning of a process of peace talks brokered by the government of Southern Sudan.

It should be noted that the issuing of warrants gave rise to controversy among some people, including those in Northern Uganda, who argued that the ICC prosecution would be detrimental to ongoing attempts to end the conflict peacefully, which included the use of amnesties by the Amnesty Commission.[51] Indeed, some people looked at the ICC prosecutions as the greatest threat to peace in Northern Uganda.[52] Arguments made against the prosecution included the fact that the ICC was only complementary and in the circumstances it was better to try LRA members domestically.[53] Some went as far as arguing that the ICC process was a neo-liberal imposition of western values of justice in an African

47 See 'Situation in Uganda' www.icc-cpi.int (accessed 23 March 2010).

48 Uganda Law Society and Friedrich Ebert Stiftung *The international justice system & the international criminal court: Opportunities and challenges for Uganda* Synthesis Report of a Dialogue, February 2007 htt://www.fes-uganda.org/docs (accessed 24 March 2010).

49 Uganda Joint Christian Council *The quest for peace and justice in Northern Uganda: Dealing with conflicting philosophical, moral and ethical values* htt://www.ikvpaxchristi.nl/.../AF%20Uganda/statement%20UJCC%20060710.doc (accessed 24 March 2010).

50 As above.

51 B Chinedu 'Implementing the International Criminal Court treaty in Africa: The role of non-governmental organizations and government agencies in constitutional reform' in KM Clarke (ed) *Mirrors of justice: Law and power in the post-Cold War era* (2010) 114.

52 As above.

53 A Perkins *Justice for war criminals - or peace for northern Uganda?* http://www.guardian.co.uk/society/katineblog/2008/mar/20/justiceforwarcriminalsorp (accessed 24 March 2010).

context.[54] In some quarters the ICC was viewed as imposing justice on Uganda in what was comparable to imposed aid with all its negativities.[55]

A number of stakeholders, including religious and traditional leaders, were of the view that the rebels would not surrender because of the threat of prosecution by the ICC. The ICC was advised to suspend the warrants and postpone the investigations.[56] The rebels had throughout the negotiation process insisted on the lifting of warrants. From a more analytical standpoint, the ICC warrants were looked at as a double-edged sword:[57]

> When the ICC indicated that it was unwilling to lift the indictments before the indicted rebel leaders had their day in court, the warrants of arrest were transformed from a tool that had helped force the rebels to the negotiating table, to one that was hindering the peace process.

An insistence on prosecution was viewed as promoting 'negative peace' at the expense of 'positive peace'. Negative peace 'is (...) where there is no direct physical violence, but where the structures in place continue to oppress and exploit people'.[58] By contrast, positive peace 'is when, in addition to ensuring people's physical security, structural issues, or the underlying causes of war, are also addressed'.[59] From a victim's perspective, 'peace without justice may make decidedly more sense than justice without peace'.[60]

Looking at the situation, it philosophically represented a multifaceted tension characterised first by the tension between justice and peace and secondly by the tension between traditional justice and 'western' justice. It had been argued throughout the negotiations that the traditional mechanisms of justice were the most viable alternatives to what was considered to be obstructionist 'western-type' justice. To the Acholi people, justice is supposed to be restorative and not punitive.[61] The tension here between 'traditional' and 'western' arises from the varied objectives of the two, premised on the paradigm of retributive justice *vis-a-vis* the paradigm of restorative justice. While the former is primarily concerned

54 Perkins, as above.

55 C Dolan *Imposed justice and the need for sustainable peace in Uganda presentation to Beyond Juba* Project//AMANI Project Transitional Justice Training Programme for Parliamentarians (2008) http://www.beyondjuba.org/Conference_presentations/Imposed_Justice_and%20the_need_for_Sustainable_Peace_in_Uganda.pdf (accessed 4 April 2010) 1.

56 Statement by the Uganda Human Rights Commission to 61st Session of the UN Commission on Human Rights (April 2005) http://www.nhri.net/pdf/UG18b.pdf (accessed 4 April 2010).

57 Uganda Law Society and Friedrich Ebert Stiftung Synthesis Report (n 48 above).

58 Dolan (n 55 above) 2.

59 As above.

60 P Hoening 'The dilemma of peace and justice in Northern Uganda' (2008) *East African Journal of Peace and Human Rights* 338.

61 T Allen 'Ritual (ab)use? Problems with traditional justice in Northern Uganda' in N Waddell and P Clark (eds) *Courting conflict? Justice, peace and the ICC in Africa* (2008) 47.

with accountability and ensuring that perpetrators do not go unpunished, the latter is concerned with ensuring restorative justice involving active participation of the victim, the perpetrator and the community in a process that aims at the restoration of a harmonious relationship between victim and perpetrator.[62]

Some quarters supported a resort to traditional justice based on the fact that the majority of the LRA rebels had forcefully been recruited, some as children, and forced to commit terrible crimes against their own people.[63] Other weaknesses pointed out with retributive justice in the context of the ICC include the limited scope and reach of this form of justice since it focuses only on perpetrators of serious international crimes. Thus, justice of this nature will only 'scratch the surface of the suffering heaped upon the local population in a war that has lasted two decades'.[64]

3.2 Peace agreements

In spite of the above and several disagreements, negotiations continued. Although a final agreement was never signed, agreement was reached on several issues, including a ceasefire, demobilisation, reintegration and accountability and reconciliation. The most relevant of these agreements in the context of this chapter is the Agreement on Accountability and Reconciliation, reached on 29 June 2007. The Preamble to this agreement indicates consciousness of the parties to the immense pain, suffering, injury and adverse socio-economic and political impact of the war and the serious crimes and human rights violations committed. To this end, the parties commit to preventing impunity and promoting redress in accordance with the Constitution and international obligations. Express reference is made to the principle of complementarity, applicable in the context of the Rome Statute. Further, the Preamble indicates that the agreement was driven by the need to adopt appropriate justice mechanisms, including customary processes that would resolve the conflict while promoting reconciliation.

Substantively, the parties committed themselves to promoting national legal arrangements consisting of formal and informal institutions and measures of ensuring justice and reconciliation.[65] In this regard, the parties reckoned that they believed that a comprehensive, independent and impartial analysis of the history and manifestations of the conflict, especially the human rights violations and crimes committed during the course of the conflict, was an essential ingredient for attaining

62 M Maloney and B Harvey *Breaking eggs/re-building societies: Traditional justice as a tool for transitional Justice in Northern Uganda* (2006) 372 *Public Policy and Dispute Resolution* 4.
63 As above 6.
64 Hoening (n 60 above) 343.
65 Para 2.1 Agreement on Accountability and Reconciliation.

reconciliation at all levels.[66] In what appears to be an assertion of the relevance of the principle of complementarity, the parties expressly affirmed that:[67]

> Uganda has institutions and mechanisms, customs and usages as provided for and recognised under national laws, capable of addressing the crimes and human rights violations committed during the conflict. The parties also recognise that modifications may be required within the national legal system to ensure a more effective and integrated justice and accountability response.

Thus, in line with the agreement on informal measures of justice, the parties endorsed 'as a central part of the framework for accountability and reconciliation', traditional justice mechanisms such as Culo Kwor, Mato oput, Kayo Cuk, Ailuc and Tonu ci Koka as practised in the communities affected by the conflict.[68] The parties also agreed on the application of alternative justice mechanisms such as traditional justice processes, alternative sentences and reparations.[69] It was, however, agreed that the formal courts would exercise jurisdiction over individuals that bore particular responsibility for the most serious crimes, especially crimes amounting to international crimes.[70] This was in addition to gross human rights violations arising from the conflict.[71]

Legislative changes were to be made to introduce a regime of alternative penalties and sanctions which would apply and replace existing penalties with respect to serious crimes and human rights violations.[72] Such alternative penalties were to reflect the gravity of the crimes or violations; promote reconciliation; promote rehabilitation of offenders; and require perpetrators to make reparation to victims.[73] Other provisions dealt with the place and role of victims;[74] reparations;[75] the special position and needs of women, girls and children;[76] and the resources for implementation of the agreement.[77]

The Annexure to the Agreement, dated 19 February 2008, sets out a framework by which the provisions of the Principal Agreement are to be implemented. The Annexure makes provision for the establishment of a number of institutions, including a special division of the High Court to try

66 Para 2.3.
67 Para 5.1.
68 Para 3.1.
69 Para 5.3.
70 Para 6.1.
71 Para 6.2.
72 Para 6.3.
73 Para 6.4.
74 Para 8.
75 Para 9.
76 Paras 11 and 12.
77 Para 13.

individuals who are alleged to have committed serious crimes.[78] The Annexure also makes provision for the establishment of a special unit in the office of the Director of Public Prosecutions (DPP) for the purposes of carrying out investigations and supporting prosecution of crimes as agreed.[79]

Unfortunately, the final peace accord was not signed. Kony did not turn up on two of the occasions set for the act of signing. It is believed that Kony is now operating between the DRC and the Central African Republic. Calm has returned to Northern Uganda. Government, development partners and Civil Society Organisations are in the process of rehabilitating the region and re-settling IDPs.

As one would have expected, the Agreement on Accountability and Reconciliation stirred controversy. Some quarters criticised the Agreement and the Annexure as failing to decisively combat impunity. One of the leading critiques in this regard came from Amnesty International, which pointed to the fact that the Agreement and Annexure fell short of a comprehensive plan to end impunity.[80] In the first place, Amnesty International read the drafts as working toward ensuring that the LRA leaders charged before the ICC are not arrested and surrendered to the ICC.[81] It was argued that the proposed War Crimes Division of the High Court could not be used to render inadmissible the LRA case before the ICC.[82] According to Amnesty International, the viability of the War Crimes Division to effectively try the LRA would have to be examined against the background of the efficiency of the entire criminal justice system. Specific focus was put on the efficacy of the criminal justice system, quoting a report from the United Nations Office of the High Commissioner for Human Rights:[83]

> Administration of justice structures and institutions are weak and virtually nonexistent in the rural areas. They are often not perceived as impartial and their accessibility is limited, for both logistical and economic reasons. The process of taking cases to the formal justice system is cumbersome and expensive, not least because of the significant lack of judicial personnel in northern and north-east Uganda. Corrupt practices reportedly discourage victims from seeking a legal remedy. There is a general lack of confidence within the justice system due to delays in judicial proceedings, disregard of victims' rights, a high number of dismissals in court and a lack of free legal assistance.

78 Para 7.
79 Para 10.
80 Amnesty International *Uganda: Agreement and Annex on Accountability and Reconciliation falls short of a comprehensive plan to end impunity* (March 2008) AI Index: AFR 59/001/2008.
81 As above, 6.
82 As above, 9.
83 Report on the Work of the Office of the High Commissioner for Human Rights in Uganda, UN Doc A/HRC/4/49/Add2, 12 February 2007 para 31.

In the above respect, Amnesty International argued that the War Crimes Division would have very limited capacity to prosecute the large number of cases involving the commission of serious crimes in Northern Uganda. Yet, delays arising from this capacity problem could be enhanced by delays in the processes leading to the establishment of the special division, which include adopting special legislation; establishing procedures; recruiting staff; and finding facilities.[84]

The Agreement was also faulted for its definition of crimes and criminal responsibility: '[T]he threshold set out in the Annex is significantly higher than the definition of crime in Article 7 of the Rome Statute.'[85] Clause 13(a) of the Annex limited investigations to individuals who are alleged to have planned or carried out widespread, systemic, or serious attacks directed against civilians, or who are alleged to have committed grave breaches of the Geneva Conventions. In contrast, article 7 of the Rome Statute defines crimes against humanity as acts 'when committed as part of a widespread or systematic attack directed against any civilian population, with knowledge of the attack'. The difference is that article 7, unlike clause 13, is not limited to individuals who commit widespread or systematic attacks; it also covers those who commit crimes which are not themselves widespread or systematic but which form part of a widespread or systematic attack.[86]

Some people expressed support for the agreement on the use of the traditional justice mechanisms. The Refugee Law Project of the Faculty of Law, Makerere University for instance, while opposed to the 'twin-track system ... whereby LRA soldiers are supposed to go through the traditional justice while UPDF soldiers go to court martial', endorsed the inclusion of traditional justice mechanisms 'as an indicator of how alternative models do have resonance and should not be dismissed out of hand'.[87]

In addition to the above, the negotiations and Agreement stirred a lot of debate on the issue of the role that traditional processes of conflict resolution, especially *Mato Oput*, would play in ending the conflict. On the basis of this, it is imperative to understand the practice of *Mato Oput* and its potential to lead to reconciliation and healing.

3.3 Understanding *Mato Oput*

Although the *Mato Oput* may be belittled simply as a process where perpetrators of serious crime take a bitter drink extracted from tree roots and walk away scot-free, the process is much more complex than that. As

84 Amnesty International (n 80 above) 15 – 16.
85 As above, 16.
86 As above.
87 Dolan (n 55 above) 4.

will be seen below, the drinking of the bitter drink comes at the end of the processes, after protracted engagement between the victim's family or clan and the perpetrator's family or clan.

By description, *Mato Oput* is an Acholi ritual performed for the purposes of bringing reconciliation and justice after a conflict. It involves the perpetrator acknowledging responsibility, repenting, asking for forgiveness and paying compensation to the victim.[88] Traditionally, *Mato Oput* takes place after an accidental or intentional killing.[89] Although an offence may be committed by an individual perpetrator, Acholi culture dictates that his/her family, clan or tribe as a whole bears collective responsibility.[90] Procedurally, the whole of the perpetrator's family, clan or tribe would be expected to begin by accepting responsibility, being repentant and seeking forgiveness from the victim and his/her family, tribe or clan.[91] Compensation is conceived as an indicator of repentance. Some of the historical modalities of compensation in cases involving murder are summarised by John Baptist Odama:[92]

> Traditionally, the offender's community was required to pay 10 heads of cattle if the murder was not deliberately committed. However, if it was proved to have been a deliberate murder or crime, the offender's community was required to give one of their young daughters to the victim's community. The girl child given at the age of 6 to 10 years would become, by adoption, a daughter of the victim's community. Compensation was not a punitive imposition but it was deemed as a process of healing, affirmation of personhood and for the enhancement of life within the community. Compensation, therefore, opened the gateway of reconciliation so both sides can walk through each other (reconciled with one another).

It is only after compensation is agreed upon that the two parties are brought together. Prior to this, the family or clan of the victim and that of the perpetrator are not allowed to meet, which is intended to prevent revenge killings.[93] The initial processes, including acknowledging

88 P Bako 'Does traditional conflict resolution lead to justice? – The *Mato Oput* in Northern Uganda' (2009) 3 *Pretoria Student Law Review* 103.

89 Mato Oput Project *Community perspectives on the Mato Oput process: A research study by the Mato Oput Project* (October 2009) Collaborative Transitions Africa, The Institute for Global Leadership (Tufts University) and Institute for Peace and Strategic Studies (Gulu University) 10.

90 JB Odama 'Reconciliation process (Mato oput) among the Acholi tribe of Northern Uganda' Commemorative address made during the ceremony for 21st Niwano Peace Prize Award Japan www.npf.or.jp/peace_prize_f/21/speech_e.pdf (accessed 8 July 2010).

91 As above.

92 Odama (n 90 above). Odama argues that the willingness and readiness of the offender's community to sacrifice one of their daughters to the victim's community affirm the genuineness of their commitment to peace and co-existence following the reconciliation.

93 Mato Oput Project (n 89 above).

responsibility, repentance, forgiveness and compensation, are concluded at the behest of the clan elders who go back and forth between the parties.[94]

The actual reconciliation ceremony, *Mato Oput*, comes after responsibility has been acknowledged, repentance offered, forgiveness given and compensation agreed on. The major feature of the reconciliation ceremony is the drinking of a drink extracted from bitter roots. The accompanying ceremonies include slaughtering a sheep or goat, participating in a ritualising ceremony (such as a mock fight) and a ritual of exchanging the cooked meat in a celebratory manner.[95] The bitter drink is symbolic; the drink symbolises the sacred blood of the victim and the bitterness of the conflict which resulted in death.[96] The sharing of a meal has been interpreted as establishing a covenant of peace witnessed by the ancestral living dead and the creator.[97]

The above description is evidence of the importance of and the value that Acholi people attach to the traditional process of reconciliation. Thus, *Mato Oput* cannot simply be dismissed as an impunity-sustaining process. If honestly and genuinely carried out, the process can be a long-lasting healing process. Nonetheless, there are questions on how this traditional process can be integrated with modern justice challenges and the demands of human rights standards. The act of disposing of a child, for instance, and a girl in particular, raises human rights issues with gender-related implications. The biggest challenge therefore is refining *Mato Oput* and making it workable in a manner that integrates it with the modern justice system. Although no comprehensive legislative reforms have been undertaken, this is what the Agreement on Accountability and Reconciliation tried to achieve. Unfortunately, enforcement of the Agreement has not come to fruition, denying us the opportunity to test the proposed justice system. The question then is whether the recently-adopted ICC Act, domesticating the Rome Statute, is a panacea.

4 Punishing international crimes in Uganda

Before examining the process of domesticating the Rome Statute, it is important to understand the nature of Uganda's legal system, its criminal laws and the preparedness of the judiciary to prosecute serious international crimes. Being a former British colony, Uganda's legal system is based on the common law system with all its attendant legal and judicial traditions. The powers to institute criminal proceedings are constitutionally vested in the Director of Public Prosecutions (DPP).[98] The

94 As above.
95 Mato Oput Project (n 89 above).
96 Odama (n 90 above).
97 As above.
98 Art 123(3)(b) Constitution of Uganda, 1995.

Constitution gives the DPP the discretion to institute, take over or discontinue any criminal proceedings. In exercising his discretion, the DPP is required to have regard to the public interest, the interests of the administration of justice and the need to prevent abuse of the legal process.[99] International treaties, although ratified by the executive, have no legal force until they have been domesticated by Parliament.[100]

Judicial power in Uganda is constitutionally vested in courts of judicature which are established in a hierarchal manner from the Supreme Court, as the most superior court, followed by the Court of Appeal (which also doubles as the Constitutional Court), the High Court and other subordinate courts (including magistrates courts).[101] These courts exercise both criminal and civil jurisdiction. It is important to note that since independence, Uganda's judiciary has faced a number of challenges. The institution was almost annihilated during the era of Idi Amin, when the Chief Justice was abducted by security operatives from his office and has never been found. During this time, formal judicial institutions were replaced by ad hoc military tribunals which operated under military decrees in total disregard of due process rights. Although one may argue that the period since 1986 has witnessed stability and registered improvements in the judiciary, the institution still faces a number of challenges.

The biggest challenge which the institution has faced since then is assaults on its independence by the executive arm of government.[102] Events providing evidence of this are well-documented. For instance, in 2004 the President openly attacked judges of the Constitutional Court after a ruling which was favourable to the political opposition. The President accused the judiciary of being staffed by persons sympathetic to the opposition; he promised to sort them out.[103] Two years later, gun-wielding government security operatives invaded the High Court premises, assaulted legal practitioners and re-arrested treason suspects released on bail and had them arraigned before military courts.[104]

In addition to assaults on its independence, the judiciary has over the years faced numerous logistics-related problems and continues to be understaffed. The recently published National Development Plan (NDP) acknowledges inadequate financial and human resources as one of the

99 Art 120(5) Constitution of Uganda, 1995.

100 Sec 4 Ratification of Treaties Act, Ch 204, Laws of Uganda 2000.

101 Arts 129 – 138 Constitution of Uganda, 1995.

102 J Oloka-Onyango 'Judicial power and constitutionalism in Africa: A historical perspective' in M Mamdani and J Oloka-Onyango (eds) *Uganda: Studies in living conditions, popular movements and constitutionalism* (1994) 470.

103 C Mbazira 'Dream deferred? Democracy and good governance: An assessment of the findings of Uganda's Self-Assessment Report under the African Peer Review Mechanism' (2008) *Human Rights and Peace Centre Working Paper 19*, October 2008.

104 International Bar Association *Judicial independence undermined: A report on Uganda* (September 2007).

constraints in the Justice, Law and Order Sector.[105] The judicial system, with a case-disposal rate of only 41 per cent, is also clogged with a huge backlog in cases, which slows down the processes of the administration of justice.[106] This is in addition to overcrowding in prisons which are holding twice the number of persons they were originally designed to accommodate.[107] All these constraints have the potential of impacting negatively on the prosecution of international crimes.

4.1 Geneva Conventions as a source of international criminal justice

It may appear that domesticating the Rome Statute is the first attempt to punish international crimes under Uganda's laws. On the contrary, though not comprehensive, the domestic prosecution of international crimes has always been part of Uganda's laws. Domestic laws governing the conduct of armed conflicts can be used to prosecute leaders of the LRA in relation to the armed conflicts in Uganda. Although the law in Uganda applies essentially to members of the Armed Forces of Uganda, it can still be extended to cover rebels as well. This position is reflected in the 1964 Geneva Conventions Act,[108] domesticating the 1949 Geneva Conventions. This Act makes punishable grave breaches of the Geneva Conventions, when committed by '[a]ny person, whatever his or her nationality ... whether within or outside Uganda'.[109] The principle of universal jurisdiction is emphasised, and the relevant provision provides as follows:[110]

> (2) Where an offence under this section is committed [outside] Uganda, a person may be proceeded against, indicted, tried and punished for that offence in any place in Uganda as if the offence had been committed in that place, and the offence shall, for all purposes incidental to or consequential on the trial or punishment of that person be deemed to have been committed in that place.

The punishments range from imprisonment for a term not exceeding fourteen years and life imprisonment in the case of a grave breach involving the wilful killing of a protected person.[111] The Act makes legal representation mandatory for persons charged with grave breaches as described above.[112] It is important to note that although this Act was promulgated in 1964, not a single person has been prosecuted under its provisions and as a result no opportunity has arisen to test its provisions.

105 National Planning Authority *National Development Plan* (2010) 296.
106 As above, 292.
107 As above, 295.
108 Ch 363, Laws of Uganda, 2000.
109 Sec 2(1) Geneva Conventions Act.
110 Sec 2(2) Geneva Conventions Act.
111 Sec 2(1) Geneva Conventions Act.
112 Sec 4 Geneva Conventions Act.

One flaw with the Act is that it does not describe with sufficient clarity the court that has jurisdiction to try the offences defined. The definition of the word 'court' in the interpretation section is of no use. The word is defined to the effect that court does not include a court-martial. However, deductive interpretation, supported by other laws, particularly the Magistrates' Court Act (MCA),[113] gives Magistrates' Courts the jurisdiction to try offences under the Geneva Conventions Act. Section 161(1)(a) of the MCA allows a Chief Magistrate to try any offence other than those in respect of which the maximum penalty is death. Grade I Magistrates may try offences other than those in respect of which the maximum penalty is death or imprisonment for life.

The question which arises from the above is whether Magistrates' Courts have the capacity to handle offences of a complex nature as may arise from the Geneva Conventions. An international crime is complex and hard to prosecute, especially in cases where the offences are committed outside the country. Although Chief Magistrates and Grade I Magistrates are required as a minimum qualification to have a bachelor of laws degree, this may not be sufficient for them to try complex cases. Usually, Grade I Magistrates are graduates from law school without much experience. Apart from their qualifications and experience, they are not properly facilitated in logistical terms and may be described as the face of a logistically ill-equipped judiciary.

Another shortcoming with the application of the Geneva Conventions Act is its limited nature arising from the fact that grave breaches of the Geneva Conventions relate only to breaches committed in the course of conflicts with an international character. Although Uganda has been involved in what may be described as international wars (especially in the Democratic Republic of Congo), the bulk of its conflicts (and the most devastating such as the LRA one) are non-international armed conflicts.

4.2 International Criminal Court Act, 2010

On 10 March 2010 the Parliament of Uganda passed the International Criminal Court Bill, domesticating the Rome Statute after almost eight years since Uganda ratified the Rome Statute. It appears that the hasty passing of the overdue Bill was catalysed by Uganda's hosting of the ICC Review Conference from 31 May to 11 June 2010. The delay in passing the Bill could be explained by the events surrounding the Government/LRA peace negotiations described above. As indicated above, the peace agreements envisaged a number of legislative reforms, which appears to have motivated the government to halt the Rome Statute domestication process. With the failure of the LRA to sign the final peace accord and the

[113] Magistrates Court Act, Ch 16 Laws of Uganda, 2000.

hosting of the ICC Review Conference, the government hastily revived the domestication process.

The objectives of the Bill that originated in the International Criminal Court Act were set out in detail in its memorandum which, among others, include: (a) giving force of law in Uganda to the Rome Statute of the ICC; (b) the implementation of obligations assumed by Uganda under the Rome Statute; (c) making further provision in Uganda's law for the punishment of the international crimes of genocide, crimes against humanity and war crimes; (d) enabling Uganda to co-operate with the ICC in the performance of its functions; (e) providing for arrest and surrender to the ICC of persons alleged to have committed crimes referred to in the Rome Statute; (f) providing for various forms of requests for assistance to the ICC; (g) enabling Ugandan courts to try, convict and sentence persons who have committed crimes referred to in the Rome Statute; (h) enabling the ICC to conduct proceedings in Uganda; and (i) providing for the enforcement of penalties and other orders of the ICC in Uganda.

To fulfil the above objectives, the ICC Act makes the provisions of the Rome Statute applicable in Uganda. It defines and makes applicable the offences of genocide, crimes against humanity, and war crimes as defined by the Rome Statute. The Act adopts the same substantive elements of the crimes as described by the Rome Statute. Some variances are however noticeable with regard to some of the sentences. This is true in respect of offences against the administration of justice as defined in article 70 of the Rome Statute. Under the ICC Act, any judge of the ICC who, elsewhere or in Uganda, corruptly accepts or obtains a bribe in respect of acts in his or her judicial capacity, commits an offence and is liable on conviction to imprisonment of up to fourteen years.[114] Registrars and Deputy-Registrars of the ICC found guilty of similar charges are liable to imprisonment of up to seven years.[115] The same punishment is applicable to officials of the ICC found guilty of corruption.

In contrast, under the Rome Statute conviction in respect of offences against the administration of justice attracts a punishment of imprisonment not exceeding five years or a fine.[116] Variations are also noticeable with respect to other offences against the administration of justice, including giving false evidence, fabricating evidence, conspiracy to defeat the ends of justice before the ICC, and interference with witnesses or officials of the ICC. Under the ICC Act, all these offences attract a punishment of imprisonment of up to seven years, in contrast to the five years and a fine under the Rome Statute.

114 Sec 10(1) ICC Act.
115 Sec 10(2) ICC Act.
116 Art 70(3) Rome Statute.

In keeping with the principle of universal jurisdiction, the Act is explicit in respect of persons who may be prosecuted for the offences prescribed. Courts in Uganda can only exercise universal jurisdiction over the following persons responsible for crimes recognised both under the Rome Statute and the ICC Act: (a) a person who is a citizen or permanent resident of Uganda; (b) a person who is employed by the Uganda government in a civilian or military capacity; (c) a person who has committed the offence against a citizen or permanent resident of Uganda; and (d) a person who after the commission of the offence is present in Uganda.[117]

Other sections of the Act effect provisions of the Rome Statute that impose obligations on states to co-operate with the ICC on such matters as accessing evidence; arresting and surrendering persons to the ICC; the enforcement of penalties including orders for reparation of victims; and facilitating searches and seizures. Going by the provisions of the ICC Act, leaders of the LRA could be prosecuted in Uganda, thereby completing the processes initiated in the ICC regarding rebels. This can easily be achieved because the ICC Act has retrospective effect over the events in Uganda, which could be extended to the crimes committed by the LRA. It would be equally relevant to argue that the ICC Act should apply to both the responsible members of the armed forces and the rebel forces who are responsible for crimes against humanity and war crimes committed in Northern Uganda. Since section 25(1) of the ICC Act removes immunity for crimes under the Act, it means that the law can equally apply to government officials who may bear responsibility for the crimes committed in Northern Uganda.

4.2.1 Pending constitutional challenges

The Constitution of Uganda is the supreme law and any other law inconsistent with it is void to the extent of its inconsistency.[118] Article 137(3) of the Constitution allows any person who alleges that an Act of Parliament or any other law is inconsistent with the Constitution to petition the Constitutional Court for a declaration to that effect, and redress where appropriate.

Even before the ICC Act had been gazetted, someone filed a legal challenge in the Constitutional Court seeking declarations to the effect that several provisions of the ICC Act are inconsistent with the constitution.[119] In the petition, Jowad Kezaala (the petitioner), alleged that the ICC Act is inconsistent with the Constitution in a number of respects. First, the petitioner alleged that at times the ICC acts at the insistance of the Security

117 Sec 18 ICC Act.
118 Art 2.
119 *Jowad Kezaala v Attorney General* Constitutional Petition 24 of 2010.

Council of the United Nations, yet the Security Council comprises member states not party to the Rome Statute. According to the petitioner this erodes the partiality and independence of the ICC, violating the provisions of articles 126(2) and 128(1) of the Constitution. Article 126(2) requires courts in adjudicating cases to apply principles which include applying justice to all irrespective of their social or economic status; that justice shall not be delayed; that adequate compensation is to be awarded to victims; the promotion of reconciliation; and that justice be administered without undue regard to technicalities. Article 128(1) provides that in the exercise of judicial power, courts be independent and not subject to the control or direction of any authority.

The petitioner's second claim is that constitutionally the ICC is not part of the hierarchy of courts as envisaged by the Constitution. The petitioner also argues that sections 7(3), 8(3), 9(3), 15 and 16 of the ICC Act are discriminatory and unconstitutional for prescribing penalties that are less than those for the same crime punishable under sections 188 and 189 of the Penal Code Act. This is inconsistent with article 21(1), (2) and (3) of the Constitution. As already indicated above, section 189 of the Penal Code Act defines death as the maximum penalty. Article 21 of the Constitution relates to equality and freedom from discrimination. In effect, the petitioner is arguing that while a person charged with wilful killing under the Penal Code Act faces the possibility of death, a person charged with wilful killing under the ICC Act may only be imprisoned for life as the maximum penalty, which is discriminatory.

The petitioner also challenges section 19(v) of the ICC Act, which excludes persons under 18 years from being subjected to the Act. It is claimed that this is inconsistent with articles 2 and 34(6) of the Constitution, which subject children to the law. The petitioner argues that this is discriminatory. Article 34(6), which the petitioner refers to, provides that a child offender who is kept in lawful custody or detention shall be kept separately from adult offenders. The relevance of this provision is not clear and would probably be clarified at the hearing.

Furthermore, the petitioner also contests section 25 of the ICC Act which excludes immunity of state officials as a ground for not arresting and handing over an indicted person. The petitioner avers that this section is inconsistent with articles 98(4) and (5) and 128 of the Constitution. Article 98(4) provides that while holding office, the President shall not be subjected to proceedings in any court. Similarly, article 128(4) provides that a person exercising judicial power is not subject to any act or omission in the exercise of judicial power.

Also contested is section 31 of the ICC Act which makes provision for bail applications. The section requires a magistrate before whom an application is made to adjourn the hearing and notify the Minister of Justice, who shall in turn consult the Pre-Trial Chamber of the ICC. The petitioner argues that this section is inconsistent with articles 23(6)(a) and 128(1) of the Constitution. Article 23(6)(a) provides that where a person is arrested in respect of a criminal offence the person is entitled to apply to the court to be released on bail, and the court may grant that person bail on such conditions as the court considers reasonable.

Additionally, section 59 of the ICC Act which makes provision for freezing property at the request of the ICC is contested. The petitioner contends that this provision is inconsistent with article 26 of the Constitution which guarantees the right to property. Section 90 of the ICC Act, which allows the ICC prosecutor to conduct investigations on Ugandan territory is contested as inconsistent with articles 120(3) and 120(6) which vest powers of investigation and prosecution in the Director of Public Prosecutions. Lastly, the petitioner contests section 94 of the ICC Act, which prohibits judicial review of judgments or orders of the ICC by Uganda courts. The provision is contested as being inconsistent with article 139. This provision gives the High Court unlimited original jurisdiction and such appellate jurisdiction as is conferred by law.

Although the response of the state, among others, has been to dismiss the petition as misconceived, an objective assessment shows that the petition raises a number of fundamental questions. The most important of these relate to procedures and processes for the domestication of international treaties. As already mentioned, Uganda is a dualist state, hence, international treaties acquire domestic legal effect only after ratification by an Act of Parliament.[120] As a matter of fact, Uganda has signed and ratified a number of international treaties. In spite of this, only a few of these instruments have been translated into domestic policies or laws.[121]

Where the government has taken steps to ratify domestic treaties, as is the case with the Rome Statute, the process has not followed a comprehensive review of domestic legislation to avoid inconsistencies. Academically assessed, it is this flawed process that Kezaala's petition in effect sets out to challenge. Indeed, one needs not be a constitutional or international law expert to identify some of the inconsistencies between the ICC Act and the Constitution as pointed out in the petition. An example is the inconsistency relating to the presidential immunity clause. That the inconsistencies between the ICC Act and the Constitution were at all material times known to the government is evidenced by concessions made by senior government officials.[122] What is left to be seen is how the court responds to this interesting petition.

120 See Ratification of Treaties Act, Ch 204, Laws of Uganda.
121 African Peer Review Mechanism Country Review Report 7 (January 2009) 282.
122 See 'ICC conflicts with constitution' *The New Vision* 12 November 2009.

5 Conclusion

The situation in Northern Uganda and the attempts to bring to an end the two decade-old war raise a number of questions from which lessons may be learnt as the international campaign takes root to end impunity by punishing genocide, war crimes and crimes against humanity. The Ugandan experience illustrates how deep-rooted causes of tensions leading to armed conflicts may be, and the necessity to deal with them comprehensively. The situation in Uganda illustrates some of the challenges African countries could face in trying to punish international crimes, dealing with impunity and finding lasting peace in armed conflict situations. One of the challenges is balancing traditional mechanisms of dispute resolution based on restorative justice, on the one hand, and the formal retributive and punitive justice mechanisms, on the other. It is unfortunate that neither system has been put to test. The viability of each as a vehicle of peace has remained a matter of academic discussion. Nonetheless, it is apparent that traditional mechanisms of dispute resolution are an important mechanism of accountability and have a role to play in ending conflict and healing the wounds of those affected.

The Uganda experience also illustrates how perpetrators of international crimes can elude both international and domestic judicial processes. In spite of the ICC's warrants, the international community has failed to arrest and surrender Kony and his accomplices to the ICC. In the same way, the War Crimes Division of the High Court of Uganda, established in anticipation of signing peace agreements, in the absence of accused persons remains idle.

The adoption of the ICC Act is commendable, considering that Uganda has ratified a number of treaties but incorporated only a few. This is a clear indication that the days of impunity are over as perpetrators can be apprehended in any part of the world and prosecuted. In spite of this, the constitutional petition challenging the provisions of the ICC Act raises fundamental issues regarding the processes of ratification and domestication of international treaties. The petition unveils a fundamental flaw – the fact that processes of ratifying international treaties are neither followed up with nor preceded by a comprehensive process of reviewing domestic laws to ensure their consistency with international treaties. At the time of writing this chapter the petition had not been set down for hearing. It remains to be seen how the Constitutional Court deals with the petition.

CHAPTER 10

GENOCIDE AS PROSECUTED BY THE INTERNATIONAL CRIMINAL TRIBUNAL FOR RWANDA AND *GACACA* COURTS IN RWANDA

*Christian Garuka**

1 Introduction

In 1994, while the World was celebrating the beginning of a new era of a democratic and multiracial society in South Africa, Rwanda was experiencing one of the most serious human rights violation in which between 800 000 and 1 000 000 people were killed – mostly Tutsi and moderate Hutus. Indeed, many people were involved in the killings, including top government officials, the National Gendarmerie, the Rwanda Armed Forces (FAR), MRND-CDR militia (*Interahamwe*), local officials, and many *Hutu* in the general population.[1]

2 Definition of the crime of genocide

The definition of genocide under the Convention on the Prevention and Punishment of Genocide (Genocide Convention) is the oldest and has been referred to subsequently by International tribunals as well as domestic legislation. Article 2 of the Convention on the Prevention and Punishment of Genocide reads as follows:

> In the present Convention, genocide means any of the following acts committed with intent to destroy, in whole or in part, a national, ethnical, racial or religious group, as such:
>
> (a) Killing members of the group;
>
> (b) Causing serious bodily or mental harm to members of the group;
>
> (c) Deliberately inflicting on the group conditions of life calculated to bring about its physical destruction in whole or in part;
>
> (d) Imposing measures intended to prevent births within the group;
>
> (e) Forcibly transferring children of the group to another group.

* LL.B (National University of Rwanda); LL.M (Pretoria); Legal Researcher.

1 http://www.gov.rw/page.php?id_article=19 (accessed 7 April 2010).

The convention goes further by enumerating acts which shall be punishable under article 3:

(a) Genocide;
(b) Conspiracy to commit genocide;
(c) Direct and public incitement to commit genocide;
(d) Attempt to commit genocide;
(e) Complicity in genocide.

The definition of genocide under article 2 of the Statute of the International Criminal Tribunal for Rwanda (ICTR) is identical to the definition provided under the Genocide Convention. Though a legal basis exists to empower the *gacaca* courts to rule on cases related to genocide as it is discussed subsequently in this chapter, it is surprising that the *gacaca* law does not have any provision defining the crime of genocide.

3 Legal basis for the prosecution of genocide in ICTR and *gacaca* courts in Rwanda

Pursuant to Chapter VII of the United Nations (UN) Charter, the UN Security Council created the ICTR by Resolution 955 of 8 November 1994. The ICTR was created because the Security Council was of the view that the violation of international humanitarian law constituted a threat to international peace and security. Though Rwanda had ratified the Genocide Convention and the Geneva Conventions, it did not have any legislation to deal with genocide, war crimes and crimes against humanity. Rwanda therefore enacted the Organic Law 08/96 of 30 August, 1996, on the Organization of Prosecutions for Offences constituting the Crime of Genocide or Crimes against Humanity committed since 1 October 1990. Article 1 of the Organic Law provided:

> The purpose of this organic law is the organization of criminal proceedings against persons who are accused of having since 1 October 1990, committed acts set out and sanctioned under the Penal Code and which constitute:
>
> (a) either the crime of genocide or crimes against humanity as defined in the Convention on the Prevention and Punishment of the Crime of Genocide of 9 December 1948, in the Geneva Convention relative to the Protection of Civilian Persons in Time of War of 12 August 1949 and its additional protocols, as well as in the Convention on the Non-Applicability of Statutory Limitations to War Crimes and Crimes Against Humanity of 26 November 1968, the three of which were ratified by Rwanda; or
>
> (b) Offences set out in the Penal Code which the Public Prosecution Department alleges or the defendant admits were committed in connection with the events surrounding the genocide and crimes against humanity.

There should be no doubt that the law refers to the Genocide Convention in its preamble. However, the law assumes that persons accused of genocide as well as the prosecutor are aware of the definition of genocide as provided for under the Genocide Convention and also the definition of crimes against humanity as provided for under international law. It should be noted that in terms of this law, sentences for crimes depend on the individual's responsibility during the genocide. An in-depth analysis of the categorisation of criminal responsibility will be undertaken later in the chapter. Nevertheless, it is worth noting that Rwanda has enacted a new law on genocide and crimes against humanity which complies with the definition of these international crimes.[2] This law only applies to people transferred to Rwanda from either the ICTR or foreign countries.

With the large number of people awaiting trials related to genocide, Rwanda was not able to try all the genocide suspects. Indeed, conventional courts were overwhelmed with genocide cases and it was estimated that more than 120 000 individuals were detained on genocide allegations.[3] Rwanda decided to establish traditional courts known as *gacaca* to speed up genocide-related cases. *Gacaca* jurisdictions brought together modified elements of customary practices for resolving conflicts and aspects of a conventional state-run punitive justice system. *Gacaca* jurisdictions (courts) have been inspired by customary dispute settlement in Rwanda.[4] Judges of the *gacaca* courts are known as *inyangamugayo* and are elected at the community level by their peers. Their eligibility is based only on their moral integrity and most have no legal background.

Unlike conventional courts, no prosecution is represented in *gacaca* proceedings as such - the parties are the accused, victims, judges and the community (witnesses and observers). The first law to establish *gacaca* courts is known as Organic Law 40/2000 of 26 January 2001 (Establishing the Organization, Competence and Functioning of Gacaca Courts Charged with Prosecuting Establishing the Organization, Competence and Functioning of Gacaca Courts Charged with Prosecuting and Trying the Perpetrators of the Crime of Genocide and other Crimes Against Humanity, Committed between October 1, 1990 and December 31, 1994).

2 Law 33 bis/2003 of 6/09/2003 Repressing the crime of genocide, crimes against humanity and war crimes. One would assume that the English translation of this law is not accurate. The word 'repressing' would have been replaced by 'prosecuting'. Probably the translator tried to translate the French word 'reprimant'' with repressing.

3 Penal Reform International *La contribution des juridictions Gacaca au règlement du contentieux du genocide : Apports, limites et attentes apres Gacaca* http://www.penalreform.org/files/Gacaca_final_2010_fr.pdf (accessed 6 April 2010).

4 See Human Rights Watch *Law and Reality: Progress in Judicial Reform in Rwanda* (2008).

The law has been amended several times.[5]

One could argue that the Statute establishing the ICTR and the law on *gacaca* and its subsequent amendment relating to the prosecution of genocide in Rwanda are ex *post facto* aimed at indicting and then punishing the perpetrators of genocide and other international crimes[6] and therefore retroactive. However, it is worth mentioning that these laws do not violate the International Covenant on Civil and Political Rights (ICCPR)[7] which prohibits the retroactive prosecution of acts. The ICCPR provides as follows in article 15(2):

> Nothing in this article shall prejudice the trial and punishment of any person for any act or commission which, at time when it was committed according to the general principles of law recognized by the community of nations.

Nevertheless, as far as the right of the accused is concerned, it should regrettably be noted that the accused does not have a right to legal counsel. This has been criticised as a violation of the right to a fair trial as guaranteed by the ICCPR, the African Charter on Human and Peoples' Rights and, more interestingly, the Constitution of Rwanda.[8]

4 Relevance and aims of the prosecution of the crime of genocide

As far as customary international law is concerned, it should be borne in mind that genocide as well as war crimes and crimes against humanity belong to the category of *ius cogens,* and therefore constitute obligations which are *erga omnes*, creating non-derogable duties upon states to prosecute them.[9]

Both the ICTR Statute and the *Gacaca* law deals with the fight against impunity and reconciliation in Rwanda.[10] The fight against impunity is crucial because impunity leads to an acceptance of these crimes as

5 Organic Law 16 /2004 of 19/06/2004 Establishing the Organization, Competence and Functioning of Gacaca Courts Charged with Prosecuting and Trying the Perpetrators of the Crime of Genocide and other Crimes Against Humanity, Committed between October 1, 1990 and December 31, 1994, as amended by Organic Law 28/2006 of 27/06/2006 and amended by Organic Law 10/2007 of 01/03/2007 and (finally) Organic Law 13/2008 of 19/05/2008.

6 H Ball *Prosecuting war crimes and genocide: The 20th century experience* (1999) 49.

7 General Assembly Resolution 2200 A (XXI) of 16 December 1996.

8 Rwanda ratified the ICCPR in 1976 and the African Charter on Human and Peoples' Rights in 1983. The ICCPR provides in art 14(3)(d) for the right to an accused to have a legal counsel of his choice, the African Charter in art 7(c), and the Constitution of Rwanda in art 18(2).

9 C Than and E Shorts (eds) *International criminal law and human rights* (2003) 10.

10 Statute of the International Criminal Tribunal for Rwanda; read also FX Nsanzuwera *La Justice rwandaise et les juridictions Gacaca: Le pari du difficile équilibre entre châtiment et pardon* available at http://aircrigeweb.free.fr/ressources/rwanda/RwandaNsanzuwera.html (accessed 31 March 2010).

inevitable.[11] In addition, impunity might also lead to victims to seek revenge and therefore ultimately undermine peace.[12]

5 Jurisdiction

Since the ICTR and *gacaca* courts are *ad hoc* tribunals, their statutes and or laws set conditions related to the scope of prosecution namely, competence *ratione loci*, competence *ratione personae*, competence *ratione temporis*, and competence *ratione materiae*. Each is discussed below.

5.1 Comptence *ratione loci* (territorial limitation) and competence *ratione personae*

The ICTR has jurisdiction over crimes committed by Rwandans in the territory of Rwanda and in the territory of neighboring states, as well as crimes committed by non-Rwandan citizens in Rwanda.[13] It is worth noting that the ICTR statute has extended its jurisdiction to neigbouring countries because it was anticipated that genocide and other serious violations of international humanitarian law may have been committed by Rwandans in neighbouring countries. However, the ICTR has neither indicted not prosecuted any individual for committing these crimes in Rwanda's neighbouring countries.

Gacaca courts have jurisdiction over genocide and crimes against humanity committed on Rwandan soil by Rwandans and foreigners residing in Rwanda. An example is Father Guy Theunis, a foreigner indicted by the *gacaca* courts who later was transferred to Belgium. He was therefore never prosecuted in Rwanda.[14]

5.2 Competence *ratione temporis* (temporal jurisdiction)

Although the international community and Rwanda agree on the period covered in the case of genocide, there is disagreement on the period covered for war crimes and crimes against humanity. The ICTR Statute sets the period between January 1994 and December 1994. On 1 October 1990 a civil war broke out in Rwanda between government forces and the Rwanda Patriotic Front and a peace accord was signed only in 1993.

11 A Neier *War crimes: Brutality, genocide, terror, and the struggle for justice* (1998) 212.
12 BH Weston & SP Marks (eds) *The Future of international human rights* (1999) 281.
13 So far the ICTR has only tried one foreigner for genocide, George Ruggiu, a Belgian journalist who was working for RTLM (a privately-owned radio service notorious for hate speech which contributed to the genocide in Rwanda).
14 See '*Priest faces Rwanda genocide trial*' http://www.theage.com.au/news/world/priest-faces-rwanda-genocide-trial/2005/09/12/1126377255807.html (accessed 29 March 2010); 'Belgian courts urged to exonerate Guy Theunis' http://www.ifex.org/rwanda/2005/11/24/belgian_courts_urged_to_exonerate/ (accessed 29 March 2010).

However, later on in April 1994 hostilities resumed and genocide was committed. It remains a mystery why the ICTR Statute does not extend the Tribunal's jurisdiction to the period starting on 1 October 1990 because crimes against humanity and war crimes were committed during that time.

The *gacaca* law covers the period between 1 October 1990 and 31 December 1994. It should be borne in mind that the *gacaca* law covers both genocide and crimes against humanity. Since genocide was committed between April and July 1994, one would conclude that the period between 1 October 1990 until 31 December 1994 covers only crimes against humanity.

5.3 Competence *ratione materiae* (subject matter)

The competence *ratione materiae* of the ICTR and *gacaca* courts differs. Pursuant to the its Statute, the ICTR has jurisdiction over genocide, crimes against humanity and violations of article 3 common to the Geneva Conventions and Additional Protocol II. On the other hand, the *gacaca* courts have jurisdiction over genocide and 'other crimes against humanity'. The Rwandan lawmaker has not defined the concept 'other crimes against humanity'. In the way it is construed, one could ask whether the Rwandan lawmaker considered genocide as the only crime against humanity and then had to add 'other' crimes against humanity. If this was the case then he was mistaken because genocide and crimes against humanity are two different crimes. Although both are international crimes, they differ mostly on the intent (*mens rea*) of the individuals who commit them.

5.4 Concurrent jurisdiction

Since the ICTR and Gacaca courts have jurisdiction over the crime of genocide, it is worth mentioning that article 8 of the ICTR Statute reads as follows:

> (1) The International Tribunal for Rwanda and national courts shall have concurrent jurisdiction to prosecute persons for serious violations of international humanitarian law committed in the territory of Rwanda and Rwandan citizens for such violations committed in the territory of neighbouring States, between 1 January 1994 and 31 December 1994.
>
> (2) The International Tribunal for Rwanda shall have primacy over the national courts of all States. At any stage of the procedure, the International Tribunal for Rwanda may formally request national courts to defer to its competence in accordance with the present Statute and the Rules of Procedure and Evidence of the International Tribunal for Rwanda.

Despite the fact the statute gives the ICTR primacy over the national courts of all states, Rwanda included, the ICTR has never made use of this article and requested the government of Rwanda to transfer an individual accused before both the *gacaca* courts and conventional courts. It would have been difficult to get plausible reasons which might justify this reluctance from the Office of the Prosecutor of the ICTR due to the fact that this office has the discretionary power on deciding who to prosecute or not.

6 Prosecution of genocide in the ICTR and *gacaca* courts

As previously discussed, both the ICTR and *gacaca* courts have jurisdiction to try and prosecute genocide.

6.1 Mental element (*mens rea*) of the crime of genocide

Since the Gacaca Law does not define genocide, this section focuses only on case law-related elements of the crime of genocide as developed by the ICTR with regard to *mens rea*. In fact, the mental element is very important in determining whether an act constitutes genocide or not. Interestingly, the Trial Chamber held as follows in *Akayesu*:[15]

> Genocide is distinct from other crimes inasmuch as it embodies a special intent or *dolus specialis.* Special intent of a crime is the specific intention, required as a constitutive element of the crime, which demands that the perpetrator clearly seeks to produce the act charged. Thus, the special intent in the crime of genocide lies in 'the intent to destroy, in whole or in part, a national, ethnical, racial or religious group, as such.' [T]he offender is culpable only when he has committed one of the offences charged under Article 2(2) ... with the clear intent to destroy, in whole or in part, a particular group. The offender is culpable because he knew or should have known that the act committed would destroy, in whole or in part, a group.

In addition, it is worth noting that when confronted with the absence of direct evidence related to *mens rea*, the ICTR held in *Nshamihigo* that[16]

> [i]n the absence of direct evidence, the following circumstances have been found, among others, to be relevant for establishing intent: the overall context in which the crime occurred, the systematic targeting of the victims on account of their membership in a protected group, the fact that the perpetrator may have targeted the same group during the commission of other criminal acts, the scale and scope of the atrocities committed, the frequency of destructive and discriminatory acts, whether the perpetrator acted on the basis of the victim's membership in a protected group and the perpetration of acts which violate the very foundation of the group or considered as such by their perpetrators.

15 *Prosecutor v Jean Paul Akayesu* (Case ICTR-96-4-T) paras 498 -520.
16 *Prosecutor v Siméon Nchamihigo* (Case ICTR-01-63-T) para 331.

As well, the ICTR interestingly held in *Muhimana* that:[17]

> The perpetrator's specific genocidal intent may be inferred from ... the general context of the perpetration, in consideration of factors such as: the systematic manner of killing; the methodical way of planning; the general nature of the atrocities, including their scale and geographical location, weapons employed in an attack, and the extent of bodily injuries; the targeting of property belonging to members of the group; the use of derogatory language towards members of the group; and other culpable acts systematically directed against the same group, whether committed by the perpetrator or others.

6.2 Individual responsibility

In the case of genocide, obeying a superior's order cannot be used as an excuse; the emphasis falls on individual accountability.[18] Under article 6(1) of the ICTR Statute, individual criminal responsibility is attributable to one who plans, instigates orders, commits or otherwise aids and abets in the planning, preparation or execution of any of the crimes referred to in articles 2 to 4 of the ICTR Statute. In addition, article 6(2) of the ICTR Statute provides that the official position of any accused person, whether as head of state or government or as a responsible government official, does not relieve that person of criminal responsibility nor does it mititgate punishment.

Though gacaca law is silent on individual criminal responsibility, in practice this principle is applicable in the proceedings. It is worth noting that individuals are prosecuted under categories as far as cases in gacaca jurisdictions are concerned. Article 51 of Organic Law 13/2008 of 19 May 2008 outlines three categories of criminal responsibility.[19] In light of the above, an individual's sentences will vary according to the category in which he or she falls.

17 *Prosecutor v Micah Muhimana* (Case ICTR-95-1B-T) para 496.

18 See L Leibman 'From Nuremberg to Bosnia: Consistent application of international law' 42 *Cleveland State Law Review* (1994) 12 *Cleveland State Review* 705.

19 **First Category:**

(1) any person who committed or was an accomplice in the commission of an offence that puts him or her in the category of planners or organisers of the genocide or crimes against humanity.

(2) any person who was at a national leadership level and that of the prefecture level: public administration, political parties, army, gendarmerie, religious denominations or in militia group, and committed crimes of genocide or crimes against humanity or encouraged others to participate in such crimes, together with his or her accomplice;

(3) any person who committed or was an accomplice in the commission of an offence that puts him or her among the category of people who incited , supervised and ringleaders of the genocide or crimes against humanity;

(4) any person who was at the leadership level at the Sub-Prefecture and Commune: public administration, political parties, army, gendarmerie, communal police, religious denominations or in militia, who committed any crimes of genocide or other crimes against humanity or encouraged others to commit similar offences, together with his or her accomplice;

To conclude, individual criminal responsibility is crucial as far as reconciliation is concerned. This is because holding individuals criminally responsible avoids assigning guilt collectively, therefore enhancing trust between the two populations involved in the conflict.

6.3 Immunity

It is worth mentioning that the ICTR and gacaca courts try individuals irrespective of their constitutional mandate with regard to the prosecution of genocide. Indeed, immunity is considered an obstacle in the fight against impunity.

7 Sentencing

Neither the ICTR nor gacaca courts confer the death sentence; the heaviest penalty is life imprisonment. When abolishing the death penalty in 2007, Rwanda replaced it with life imprisonment with solitary confinement as its severest sentence. It is worth mentioning that the abolition of the death penalty was one the conditions set by the ICTR for the transfer of cases to Rwanda, including cases of genocide.

The genocide in Rwanda is peculiar due to the active involvement of the population. In fact, Rwanda's political and military leaders may be considered as having conceived the genocide, while a large number of the

(5)any person who committed the offence of rape or sexual torture, together with his or her accomplice.
(6)The Prosecutor General of the Republic shall publish at least twice a year, a list of offenders in the first category forwarded by the *Gacaca* Cell Courts.

Second category:
(1) a notorious murderer who distinguished himself or herself in his or her location or wherever he or she passed due to the zeal and cruelty employed, together with his or her accomplice ;
(2) any person who tortured another even though such torture did not result into death, together with his or her accomplice;
(3) any person who committed a dehumanising act on a dead body, together with his or her accomplice;
(4) any person who committed or is an accomplice in the commission of an offence that puts him or her on the list of people who killed or attacked others resulting into death, together with his or her accomplice;
(5) any person who injured or attacked another with the intention to kill but such intention was not fulfilled, together with his or her accomplice;
(6) any person who committed or aided another to commit an offence against another without intention to kill, together with his or her accomplice.

Third category:
A person who only committed an offence related to property. However, when the offender and the victim come to a settlement by themselves, settle the matter before the authorities or before the witnesses before commencement of this law, the offender shall not be prosecuted.

population implemented it.[20] Thus, the large scale of the genocide may be attributable to the large number of the population involved.

The ICTR opted for selective justice by prosecuting those individuals bearing the greatest responsibility in the genocide, whereas the gacaca courts have opted for the categorisation of individuals based on the gravity of their involvement in the genocide. In addition, at the ICTR genocide sentences are based on circumstances surrounding the convicted (aggravating and mitigating circumstances) whereas, in gacaca courts, besides taking into consideration the surrounding circumstances (mitigating and aggravating) the sentences are pronounced based on the category to which the accused belongs to.

Thus, article 72(1) of Organic Law 13/2007 of 19 May 2007 provides for life imprisonment for an individual belonging to the first category and who refuses to confess, plead guilty, repent and ask for forgiveness or whose confession, guilty plea, repentance or request for forgiveness was dismissed. The provision seems to compel individuals to confess their guilt. Article 72(2) provides for a prison sentence ranging from 25 to 20 years for individuals belonging to the first category but who have pleaded guilty, confessed, repented and asked for forgiveness once convicted. These provisions may create confusion for gacaca judges (who do not have any formal legal training) when they have to establish whether or not an accused has pleaded guilty, asked for forgiveness, repented or confessed. This is due to the similarity in meaning of the different terms. In my opinion, the legislator should have avoided repeating words which are so similar in meaning.

In addition, it is very difficult for a judge to establish whether an accused has *repented* after pleading guilty. This is because that person might plead guilty during the proceedings whereas repentance, as a long process, happens only after the proceedings have been concluded.

The same law provides for community service for individuals belonging to the second category who have confessed and who had spent half of their sentences in prison.

An interesting question that arises is whether the categorisation of individuals based upon the gravity of their involvement is in compliance with the principle of equality before the law as a human rights and constitutional principle.

20 See JB Lyakaremye *Les juridictions 'Gacaca' ou un pis-aller à l'insoluble problématique de la répression du génocide au Rwanda* http://www.page-rwanda.ca/JusticeTextes Gacaca.html (accessed 5 March 2010).

8 Reparations

Reparations may be defined as the embodiment of a society's recognition, remorse and atonement for harm inflicted.[21] Genocide victims, like any other victims of human rights violations, need reparation to repair actual damage suffered by a human rights violation.[22] Reparation may be either moral or material or both.[23] In the case of genocide, it is regrettable that neither the ICTR nor gacaca courts provide material reparation for the victims.

However, some may argue that the restitution of property is a form of reparation and that, therefore, gacaca courts have been providing material reparation because they provide for the restitution of property stolen or destroyed during the genocide.[24]

9 Conclusion

The chapter has analysed the prosecution of the crime of genocide in the ICTR and in gacaca courts. The ICTR and gacaca courts both have jurisdiction over genocide; the main difference lies in the lack of a definition of the crime in the gacaca law. Other differences between the two institutions are: judges from the ICTR are highly trained in law, whereas *gacaca* judges do not have any formal legal training. The gacaca judges' understanding of genocide remains limited to case law and therefore they are unlikely to develop jurisprudence on the matter. In addition, sentences in *gacaca* courts relate to convictions based on categories of criminal responsibility. Furthermore, gacaca courts are able to impose community service as a sentence for certain catgories of offenders, while the ICTR Statute does not provide for such a sanction.

21 See N Roht-Ariaza 'Reparations decisions and dilemma' (2004) 27 *Hastings International and Comparative Law Review* 157.

22 See LJ Laplante 'On the indivisibility of rights: Truth commissions, reparations and the right to development' (2007) 10 *Yale Human Rights and Development Law Journal* 147; art 2 ICCPR.

23 n 19 above.

24 S Vandeginste 'Réparation pour les victimes de génocide, de crimes contre l'humanité et des crimes de guerre au Rwanda' http://www.ier.ma/IMG/pdf/reparationRwanda.pdf (accessed 1 April 2010).

CHAPTER 11

PROSECUTING PIRACY IN THE HORN OF AFRICA: THE CASE OF KENYA

*Osogo Ambani**

1 Introduction

The usual state of insecurity in the Horn of Africa has now navigated into the waters – the Indian Ocean. According to the International Maritime Organization (IMO)[1] pirates successfully attacked 27 sea vessels off the East African coast and attempted 33 others in 2007.[2] A year later, in 2008, the atrocities escalated to 111 attacks in the same region.[3] In 2009, 47 vessels and nearly 300 crew members were captured in the same black spot, that is, the Gulf of Aden.

Pirates have seemingly enhanced their art occasioning profound risks and losses. 'By most accounts, the Somali pirates have been, by and large, very successful at their infamous venture'.[4] Middleton has conducted a reliable study of the situation of piracy at the coast of Somalia.[5] According to this analysis, pirates are regularly demanding and receiving million-dollar ransom payments and are becoming more aggressive and assertive. It is, indeed, estimated that shipping companies have already suffered

* LL.B(Nairobi); LL.M(Pretoria); Lecturer, Catholic University of Eastern Africa, Kenya. The author is indebted to Annet Mbogoh for her support during the research and Robert Gitonga for his insights which enriched the study immensely.

1 Initially known as the Intergovernmental Marine Consultative Organization (IMCO), IMO was established to provide 'for cooperation among Governments in areas ... affecting shipping in international trade'. The organization was set up by the Convention on the Intergovernmental Maritime Consultative Organization of 6 March 1948.

2 See Report of the International Expert Group on Piracy off the Somali coast, Workshop commissioned by Special Representative of the UN Secretary General to Somali 10 – 21 November 2008, p 13.

3 See RK Panjab 'The pirates of Somalia: Opportunistic predators or environmental prey?' (2010) *William and Mary Environmental Law & Policy Review* 378.

4 Panjab (n 3 above) 378.

5 See 'Piracy in Somalia: Threatening global trade, feeding local wars', Chatham House, Briefing paper. October 2008.

losses in excess of one hundred million dollars.[6] There is also chance that Somali pirates could become agents of international terrorist networks. 'Income' from such ransoms is already helping to pay for the war in Somalia, including suspect organisations such as Al-Shabaab. On the humanitarian front, piracy is making aid deliveries to drought-stricken Somalia ever more difficult and costly. The World Food Programme (WFP) has had to seek Canada's escort during her deliveries. Due to the danger and cost of piracy, insurance premiums for the Gulf of Aden have gone up by over 40% compelling shipping to avert the Gulf of Aden/Suez Canal and divert around the Cape of Good Hope.[7] This has a likelihood of adding considerably to the costs of manufactured goods and oil often transported via the same route. Even more critical, piracy might cause a major environmental disaster in the Gulf of Aden if a tanker is sunk or run aground or set on fire. The apparent use of ever more powerful weaponry makes this increasingly likely.

This situation clearly deserves (legal) amelioration. However, efforts in that direction have suffered a number of pitfalls from lack of political will, to jurisdictional problems right to certain capacity challenges. Kenya, a not very developed legal system, has been the epicenter of the prosecution of Somali pirates, occasioning even more challenges. When it all began, Kenya had yet to pass the necessary anti-piracy legislation, and it has been argued that Kenya's corrupt judicial system cannot be trusted to conduct free and fair trials.[8]

This chapter studies both the international legal framework regulating piracy, and Kenya's domestic system, which has almost singularly been entrusted with the task of prosecuting pirate cases off the coast of Somalia. Thus, the offence of piracy (its definition and suppression) is traced first to international law. Kenya's municipal framework as well as attempts at prosecuting the crime in the legal system is then reviewed before making certain suggestions aimed at forestalling the prevailing crisis.

2 The international crime of piracy: The standard and the Kenyan practice

The most relevant instrument for the suppression of piracy is the United Nations Convention on the Law of the Sea of 1982 (UNCLOS). The Preamble to the treaty expresses hope that the codification and development progressively of the law of the sea

6 M Silva 'Somalia: State failure, piracy, and the challenge to international law' (2010) 50 *Virginia Journal of International Law* 566.
7 RTT News, http://www.rttnews.com (accessed on 12 April 2010).
8 Silva (n 6 above) 573.

> will contribute to the strengthening of peace, security, cooperation and friendly relations among all nations in conformity with the principles of justice and equal rights and will promote the economic and social advancement of all peoples of the world in accordance with the purposes and principles of the UN as set forth in the Charter.

The consequent suppression of piracy within the same instrument is thus in line with this expectation.

UNCLOS defines the offence of piracy in fairly similar terms with a much earlier Treaty, the High Seas Convention of 1958 (HSC). This definition describes piracy as

> (a) Any illegal acts of violence or detention, or any act of depredation, committed for private ends by the crew or the passengers of a private ship or a private aircraft, and directed
>
> (i) On the high seas, against another ship or aircraft, or against persons or property on board such ship or aircraft;
>
> (ii) Against a ship, air craft, persons or property in a place outside the jurisdiction of any State.
>
> (b) Any act of voluntary participation in the operation of a ship or of an aircraft with knowledge of facts making it a pirate ship or aircraft; and
>
> (c) Any act of inciting or of intentionally facilitating an act described in subparagraph (a) or (b).[9]

Piracy could also be committed by a warship, government ship or government aircraft whose crew has mutinied.[10] For a ship or aircraft to be considered pirate, it has to be 'intended by the persons in dominant control to be used for the purpose of committing one of the acts referred to in article 101'.[11]

Kenya's novel Merchants and Shipping Act[12] – by dint of section 371 as read together with 369(1) – adopts the above definition in its entirety, placing the legal system in consonance with the international standard. Before the enactment of this fairly nascent legislation, the Penal Code[13] merely stated that 'any person who, in territorial waters or upon the high seas, commits any act of piracy *jure gentium* is guilty of the offence of

9 Art 101 of UNCLOS.

10 Art 102.

11 Art 102. According to Panjab, if this definition and especially the term 'depredation' are anything to go by, then two kinds of piracy occur off the coast of Somalia.

> First, there is the well-known, highly publicized, and terrifying piracy committed by Somalis against foreign ships. Second there is an equally threatening form of piracy-over-fishing without licenses or compensation and, worse, dumping of nuclear and other forms of toxic waste into Somali waters – being perpetrated by ships from a significant number of foreign nations.

12 Chapter 4, Laws of Kenya. The law was enacted in 2009.

13 Sec 69 of the Penal Code, Chapter 63, Laws of Kenya, was repealed by the Merchants Shipping Act which sought to consolidate all laws relating to matters of the sea.

piracy'.[14] In addition, piracy would crystallize where any person who, being the master, an officer or a member of the crew of any ship and a citizen of Kenya – (a) unlawfully runs away with the ship; or (b) unlawfully yields it voluntarily to any other person; or (c) hinders the master, an officer or any member of the crew in defending the ship or its complement, passengers or cargo; or (d) incites a mutiny or disobedience with a view to depriving the master of his command.[15] As shown below, this definition fell below UNICLOS' standards, was largely problematic and inadequate in addressing modern-day piracy. This is not however, to suggest that the international threshold is ideal: At least four limitations are evident even in UNCLOS' definition. Firstly, the offence of piracy can only be perpetrated on the high seas or outside the jurisdiction of any state. Illegal acts of piracy committed inside the territorial waters of a country are not envisioned. In this respect, UNCLOS has been criticized for failing to contemplate the emergence of failed states such as Somalia and failing to address the situation when an act of piracy occurs within a country's territorial waters, or in waters of a neighboring country, rather than on the high seas.[16] At best, illegal acts in territorial waters are considered 'sea robbery' and are dealt with by municipal law.[17] Under Kenya's Merchants Shipping Act, for example, 'armed robbery against ships'

> [m]eans any unlawful act of violence or detention or any act of depredation, or threat thereof, other than an act of piracy directed against persons or property on board such as ship within territorial waters or waters under Kenya's jurisdiction.

Although UNCLOS excludes the Exclusive Economic Zone (EEZ) from being counted as part of the high seas for other purposes,[18] article 58(2) qualifies this exemption by providing that articles 88 to 115 and other pertinent rules of international law apply to the EEZ as long as these are not incompatible with its very essence. This makes it plain that the provisions of the high seas regime (including all provisions on piracy) are applicable to EEZ in so far as they are not incompatible with UNCLOS provisions on the same.[19] Judge Gaswaga of Seychelles is in agreement that

> the Exclusive Economic Zone (EEZ) – stretching for up to 200 nautical miles past the territorial seas – is essentially concerned with resources. The law of the coastal state does not apply in the EEZ, and it does not have general enforcement rights. Other than as regards resources, EEZ's are counted as the high seas.[20]

14 Sec 69.
15 Sec 69(2).
16 Silva (n 6 above) 575.
17 Silva (n 6 above) 570.
18 Art 86.
19 'Piracy and legacy: Reconciling public and private interests', International law Discussion Group and Africa Programme.
20 *The Republic v Mohamed Ahmed Dahir & 10 Others, Supreme Court of Seychelles,* P 57.

It follows that the coastal state enjoys economic rights in the EEZ while at the same time provisions on the crime of piracy simultaneously apply.

Secondly, the offence of piracy becomes operative only when illegal or violent acts are committed. What amounts to an illegality remains subject of speculation for it is unclear whether the determination of 'illegal acts' is derived from municipal or international law.

Further, as it has been pointed out, 'the essence of piracy under international law is that it must be committed for private ends'.[21] However, the public/private distinction is not always obvious. Often, private interests take political manifestations and ramifications belying the broader distinction. It has, for instance, been argued that 'illegal acts committed for political rather than private ends also fall outside the international law definition of piracy'.[22] Shaw agrees stating that 'any hijacking or takeover for political reasons is automatically excluded from the definition of piracy'.[23] Another opinion would be that the distinction should advisably be between private/public and not private/political. In this sense, what is public is that which is sanctioned by a State. Any other item belongs to the realm of 'private'. Indeed, there is now case law indicating that politically motivated acts of protests can constitute piracy.[24] Strictly speaking a war ship or government vessel cannot commit piracy unless the passengers (naturally military officials) have mutinied.

Finally, UNCLOS' definition only covers attacks committed from a private vessel against another vessel. Going by this understanding, seizure of vessel by its own passengers does not amount to piracy. The consequence of this limitation is to exclude certain acts of 'terrorism' from the regime of the crime of piracy.

3 Prosecuting piracy: A Kenyan perspective

International law does not just define the offence under review but equally has explicit provisions on the power of search and seizure of pirate ships and pirates.[25] States are required to 'cooperate to the fullest possible extent in the repression of piracy on the high seas or in any other place outside the jurisdiction of any state'. It is in pursuance of this mandate that the UN Security Council recently called for the deployment of 'vessels and military

21 MN Shaw *International law* (1998) 423.
22 Silva (n 6 above) 570.
23 Shaw (n 21 above) 423.
24 See *Castle John v NV Mabeco* (Belgium, Court of Cassation, 1986) 77 International Law Reports 537
25 See UNCLOS arts 105 – 110.

aircraft in accordance with international law'[26] in the repression of piracy in the East African coast.

Once captured, there is a genuine expectation that the seizing state shall penalize those arrested. It is instructive however, that UNCLOS does not place express responsibility on the seizing state to specifically prosecute arrested suspects. It simply empowers 'the courts of the State which carried out seizure' to determine the penalties to be imposed including 'the action to be taken with regard to the ships, aircraft or property subject to the rights of third parties acting in good faith'.[27] Commenting on a similiar question earlier, the International Law Commission took the position that 'the State must be allowed certain latitude as to measures it should take to this end in any individual case'.[28] Such discretionary penalties may include prosecution.

It would seem, from the practice, that the decision to prosecute arrested suspected pirates is mostly a difficult one. This often is because of a number of attendant challenges relating to jurisdiction; associated risks and fears and capacity problems. In this respect, Kenya's recent attempt at prosecuting Somali pirates is particularly illustrative.

3.1 Jurisdictional problems

Jurisdictional problems arise first because international law cedes jurisdiction to many parties even in a single instance. Although UNCLOS recognizes jurisdiction only for the State which seizes the pirate,[29] through other criteria, international law may yield jurisdiction to many and different states. Under the Convention for the Suppression of Unlawful Acts of Violence Against the Safety of Maritime Navigation (the SUA Convention),[30] which proscribes certain unlawful acts *inter alia* amounting to piracy,[31] States are required to take necessary measures to establish

26 Resolution 1838 of the UN Security Council.

27 Art 19 of the High Seas Convention 1958; Article 105, UNCLOS. According to Shaw: The fact that every state may arrest and try persons accused of piracy makes that crime quite exceptional in international law, where so much emphasis is placed upon the sovereignty and jurisdiction of each particular state within its territory.

28 (1956) II *Yearbook of International Law Commission*, 282.

29 Art 105.

30 Adopted in 10 March 1988; entered into force on 1 March 1992.

31 Arts 3 of the SUA Convention reads:

> Any person commits an offence if that person unlawfully and intentionally: (1) Seizes or exercises control over a ship by force or threat thereof or any other form of intimidation; or (2) Performs an act of violence against a person on board a ship if that act is likely to endanger the safe navigation of that ship; or (3) Destroys a ship or causes damage to a ship or its cargo which is likely to

jurisdiction when such offence is committed: against or on board a ship flying the flag of the State at the time the offence is committed; in the territory of that State, including its territorial sea; and, finally, by a national of the State.[32]

A State may also establish jurisdiction over any such offence when: It is committed by a stateless person whose habitual residence is in that State or during its commission a national of that State is seized, threatened, injured or killed, or it is committed in an attempt to compel that State to do or abstain from doing any act.[33] Further, under the customary international law principle of universal jurisdiction, just any other state has jurisdiction to try heinous international crimes such as piracy.

> The basis for this is that the crimes involved are regarded as particularly offensive to the international community as a whole ... Universal jurisdiction over piracy has been accepted under international law for many centuries and constitutes a long-established principle of the world community.[34]

Piracy is in fact the original universal jurisdiction crime, and it has been an inspiration for the modern expansion of universal jurisdiction.[35] It is the oldest crime to which universal jurisdiction applies.[36] Apart from piracy, such jurisdiction can only be exercised over the most heinous crimes such as genocide, crimes against humanity and war crimes.[37] Citing Lowe, Write has argued that piracy may not be exactly heinous: 'the rationale for universal jurisdiction is that by definition piracy occurs on the high seas

endanger the safe navigation of that ship; or (4) Places or causes to be placed on a ship, by any means whatsoever, a device or substance which is likely to destroy that ship, or cause damage to that ship or its cargo which endangers or is likely to endanger the safe navigation of that ship; or (5) Destroys or seriously damages maritime navigational facilities or seriously interferes with their operation, if any such act is likely to endanger the safe navigation of ship; or (6) Communicates information which he knows to be false, thereby endangering the safe navigation of ship; or (7) Injures or kills any person, in connection with the commission or the attempted commission of any of the offences set forth in subparagraphs (a) to (f).
Any person also commits an offence if that person: (1) attempts to commit any of the offences set forth in paragraph 1; or (2) abets the commission of any of the offences set forth in paragraph 1 perpetrated by person or is otherwise an accomplice of a person who commits such an offence; or (3) Threatens, with or without a condition, as is provided for under national law, aimed at compelling a physical or juridical person to do or refrain from doing any act, to commit any of the offences set forth in paragraph 1, subparagraphs (b), (c) and (e), if that threat is likely to endanger the safe navigation of the ship in question.

32 Art 6(1).
33 Art 6(2).
34 Shaw (n 21 above) 470.
35 E Kontorovich & S Art 'An empirical examination of universal jurisdiction for piracy' (2010) 104 *American Journal of International Law* 437.
36 YM Dutton 'Bringing pirates to justice: A case for including piracy within the jurisdiction of the international criminal court' (2010) 11 *Chicago Journal of International Law* 201.
37 J Write 'Retribution but no recompense: A critique of the torturer's immunity from civil suit' (2010) 30 *Oxford Journal of Legal Studies* 159.

and it is easy to avoid the jurisdiction of any state'.[38] The SS Lotus case arrived at the same position, except perhaps that it seems to suggest that the 'universal jurisdiction' lies with the state that captures the pirates. As Moore J held:

> [b]y [the] law of nations … [as a matter of] universal jurisdiction, under which the person charged with the offence may be tried and punished by any nation into whose jurisdiction he may come … [The pirate] is treated as an outlaw, as the enemy of all mankind – *hostis humani generis –whom any nation may in the interest of all capture and punish*.[39]

Thus, numerous states have jurisdiction to both arrest and punish pirates so long as they have been apprehended on the high seas or within the territory of the state concerned.

The implication of these broad jurisdictional criteria is that a State which seizes a vessel, one whose ship is the target of piracy, one who's national is suspected for committing piracy, that in which a stateless person is habitually resident, and the victims' State may all simultaneously claim jurisdiction. Not to mention just any other member of the international community capturing the pirates and seizing the doctrine of universal jurisdiction. Such multi-faceted approach to jurisdiction should ordinarily cause confusion and conflicting claims to jurisdiction. It is perhaps why in the face of escalating piracy off the coast of Somali the UN Security Council called upon 'all States, and in particular flag, port and coastal States, States of the nationality of victims and perpetrators of piracy and armed robbery, and other States with relevant jurisdiction under international law and national legislation', to cooperate in determining jurisdiction.[40] This could have been an effort at averting jurisdictional conflicts.

In practice however, jurisdiction over pirate cases – especially off the coast of Somalia - has not been treated as a trophy. It has hardly been contested. In fact, most states are unwilling to prosecute such cases. Silva has lamented that 'although the Security Council resolutions authorize the pursuit of pirates into Somali waters, most nations have been reluctant to take pirates into custody for prosecution in their own domestic courts.'[41] In April 2009, for instance, Dutch Naval Forces captured and released 7 Somali pirates, a happening that illustrates their reluctance to resort to prosecution.[42] Another account has noted:

38 Write (n 37 above) 159.
39 *SS Lotus* (*France v Turkey*), 1927 PCIJ (ser. A), No 9 at 70. Emphasis added.
40 Resolution 1816, UN Security Council, paragraph 11.
41 Silva (n 6 above) 576.
42 E Labott 'Clinton says releasing pirates sends wrong signal', CNN, 20 April 2009.

> As the piracy problem escalated in 2008, patrolling nations caught hundreds of pirates. Unwilling to bring them back to their countries for trial, the patrolling vessels destroyed their firearms and equipment but released them.[43]

To date, only four non-Western states – China, India, Kenya and Yemen – have used universal jurisdiction to prosecute piracy.[44] Kenya, which is perhaps the only State that readily accepted and prosecuted Somali pirates,[45] has at certain times wavered. At some point, Kenya's Foreign Affairs Minister, Moses Wetangula, was quoted as saying; 'for the last two weeks we have declined to accept captured pirates from some of our friendly countries and told them to try it elsewhere'.[46] The official further stated: 'We discharged our international obligation. Others shied away from doing so. And we cannot bear the burden of the international responsibility'.[47] Kenya's own Attorney General has wondered: 'why then are these countries afraid to prosecute the pirates arrested by their naval forces in the high seas?'[48]

Jurisdictional problems may also arise because of conflict between national and international law. It is possible that national law may provide for a different jurisdictional criterion from that stipulated at the international level.[49] This scenario has operated in Kenya. Prior to the enactment of the Merchant Shipping Act in 2009, the Penal Code did enunciate a restricted jurisdiction for all crimes including piracy. Section 5 of this law which also relates to piracy provides that national courts have criminal jurisdiction extending to every place within the State, including territorial waters - but not beyond. Further the Penal Code stipulates that municipal courts could only seize jurisdiction where the suspected criminals are Kenyans. There was, it follows, real danger that without purposeful reading of statute, courts of law were likely to avert adjudicating over offences committed in the high seas or those involving non-Kenyans.

This predicament did arise in the case of *R v Hassan M Ahmed and 9 Others.*[50] The defendants were accused of jointly attacking and detaining an Indian vessel, *MV Safina Al Bisarat 275 – 280* off the coast of Somali. They allegedly attacked the crew and demanded $50 000 and a satellite

43 Kontorovich & Art (n 35 above) 437.
44 As above.
45 As pointed out elsewhere herein, in July 2010 Seychelles convicted Somali pirates.
46 See RTT News, http://www.rttnews.com (accessed on 12 April 2010).
47 RTT News, http://www.rttnews.com (accessed on 12 April 2010).
48 See F Mukinda & A Shiundu, 30 March 2010. Daily Nation news, available at http://allafrica.com, (accessed 24 April 2010).
49 Shaw (n 21 above) 470 where it is stated: Piracy under international law (or piracy *jure gentium*) must be distinguished from piracy under municipal law. Offences that may be characterized as piratical under municipal laws do not necessarily fall within the definition of piracy in international law, and thus are not susceptible to universal jurisdiction (depending of course upon the content and form of international conventions),
50 Criminal Case No 434 of 2006.

phone. They took over the ship for five days during which they also attempted an attack on three others. The suspects were eventually seized by the United States Navy officers and delivered to Kenya for trial. The accused persons were charged with piracy under the aforementioned section 69 of the Penal Code. The tribunal of first instance found them guilty and sentenced them to 7 years imprisonment.

They appealed the decision. On appeal, the litigants argued that municipal courts lacked jurisdiction both because the alleged offence was committed in the high seas and also since the parties were not Kenyans. The appeal judge held that

> [e]ven if the Penal Code had been silent on the offence of piracy, I am of the view that the Learned Principal Magistrate would have been guided by the United Nations Convention on the Law of the Sea (UNCLOS) ...[51]

The judge further observed that

> [e]ven if the Convention had not been ratified and domesticated, the Learned Principal Magistrate was bound to apply international norms and instruments since Kenya is a member of the civilized world and is not expected to act in contradiction to expectations of member states of the United Nations.[52]

The Court ruled in favour of a 'supposed' spirit of the international threshold, even where this was beyond the scope of municipal law. International law provisions on the offence of piracy were upheld, despite the fact that Kenya was mostly reputed as a dualist state.[53] In dualist states, international law does not take immediate effect until it has gone through incorporation or transformation.

A similar situation obtained in *Mohamud A Kheyre and 6 Others*[54] where the accused were again charged with piracy contrary to section 69(1) as read with section 69(3) of the Penal Code. The particulars of the case were that on 11 February 2009, armed with offensive vessels, the accused persons attacked a vessel, *MV Polaris*, in the high seas in the Indian Ocean. They were seized by US Navy officers patrolling the Gulf of Aden and handed over to Kenyan authorities. Yet again, the defense objected to Kenya's jurisdiction arguing that the actors were not Kenyan nationals or habitually resident there, and, further still, that the offences were committed outside the borders of the State. The Court took the opinion that when Parliament legislated against piracy, it must have been fully aware that the offence is normally committed in the high seas and that the

51 At 10.
52 At 11.
53 The original judicial authority for this principle (dualism) in Kenya was expressed in the case of *Okunda v Republic* [1970] EA 512. This state of affairs has however been reversed by the 2010 Constitution which at article 2(6) recognizes international law as a source of law.
54 Case No 791 of 2009.

provision was meant to ensure international tranquility. It was further the Court's position that the use of the words '*jure gentium*' in the municipal description of the offence implied intention to be bound by international law. Thus, it mattered less whether that the accused persons were Kenyan or foreign.

What however, requires to be highlighted is the fact that the courts in both instances may have misrepresented the position of international law – and UNCLOS in particular. As stated above, under UNCLOS, jurisdiction is the prerogative of the seizing state. There are however exceptions under international law so that the flag ship state, the State in whose territory the offence is committed, the State whose nationals or self is victimized may claim jurisdiction. Going by this position, there is no way Kenya, which has hardly had any connection with the acts of piracy, could claim jurisdiction, except by taking advantage of the concept of universal jurisdiction. Even then, as stated in the SS Lotus case, linkage to the offence or offenders might be necessary before a State can seize the concept of universal jurisdiction. Usually, it is the seizing state which ordinarily has the universal jurisdiction.

3.2 Risks and fears

It has been stated above that many states are unwilling to take over and prosecute cases of piracy. Among the reasons for this laxity is another explanation why prosecuting piracy remains the path not taken – fear of the risks involved.

> The apparent reasons for this refusal to accept these judicial burdens are many: for example, ... concerns about the safety and impartiality of local judges, ... and fears that if convicted, the pirates will be able to remain in the country where are prosecuted.[55]

In Kenya, for instance, Government officials claim that prosecuting piracy exposes the State to attack by the 'terrorist sympathizers' of the Indian Ocean pirates.

There are equally concerns that after serving their jail terms or where prosecution aborts, the released pirates may lodge genuine claims to either asylum or other status posing even greater security threats. According to Kenya's Attorney General 'prosecution is one thing, but what happens if they are acquitted or they serve out their terms? These are crucial national security questions we are looking at'.[56]

55 Dutton (n 36 above).
56 Silva (n 6 above) 573.

3.3 Capacity problems

Any legal system hoping to prosecute suspected pirates ought, as a condition precedent, to have sufficient capacity. Such an undertaking calls for, amongst others, solid judicial and prison systems. The legal system in question should further have the necessary resources to gather and organize evidence – even across the borders – for effective and timely prosecution. Such is no mean task. For instance, it is hard to find the shipping crew in one place to give evidence. Indeed, 'shipping crews are constantly on the move, and it is very inconvenient to bring them to a specific place at a specific time to testify in court'.[57] It is equally not beyond pirates 'to kill all crew members and leave no witnesses to their crimes'.[58] There is in addition need for expertise both in international criminal law as well as in the presentation of evidence for prosecution purposes. Even more critical, in the case of Somali pirates, language challenges have often prompt up, sometimes leading to the compromising entitlements such as those of accused persons. The challenge was manifest in Seychelles'' case, *The Republic v Mohamed Ahmed Dahir & 10 Others, Supreme Court of Sychelles,* where the defence complained that the accused were not explained their constitutional rights – to counsel, to remain silent and to be informed of the reasons for their arrest and detention in a language understood by them – before being arrested. The Court's response is instructive:

> Of course it was impracticable to provide a lawyer to the accused while at sea. Even if counsel were to be assigned at the time there was no Somali/English interpreter in the country to assist him and the police as well as the court until the United Nations Office on Drugs and Crime (UNODC) procured one from overseas, '… *as soon as it was reasonably practicable thereafter*', in line with Article 18 (3) of the Constitution.[59]

The infrastructural capacity defined above is hardly available in Kenya, which, in early 2009, signed agreements with the United States and the United Kingdom allowing for the extradition of suspected pirates for prosecution in Kenya.[60] The legal system has many challenges. To begin with, the judicial system suffers from the crisis of backlog of cases, a dilemma that threatens to cripple the entire apparatus. By December 2009, the cases pending before the Court of Appeal in Nairobi and its circuit stations were estimated at 2,372, the High Court stations at 115,344 and magistrates' courts at 792,297 making a total of 910,013. Of the cases in the magistrates' courts, 144,963 were classified as criminal cases, 398,136 as traffic cases and the rest as civil cases. The said report defines backlog as

57 Panjab (n 2 above) 450.
58 Panjab (n 2 above) 450.
59 *The Republic v Mohamed Ahmed Dahir & 10 Others, Supreme Court of Sychelles, Criminal Side No 51 of 2009.* Judgment of D Gaswaga dated 26 July 2010.
60 The Extradition (Contiguous and Foreign Countries) Act, chapter 76, Laws of Kenya, Revised Edition, 2009. The treaties are contained in a Schedule to the Act.

cases pending for over five years.[61] According to the Judiciary's own report, case backlog is due to a number of factors. These include shortage of judicial officers and staff, inadequate number of courts and infrastructure, inappropriate rules of procedure, court vacations, and jurisdictional limits on magistrates' courts and mechanical management of court records and proceedings.[62]

Adding the unique and brittle prosecution of piracy to the already stretched system only worsens the situation. By the end of March 2010, the prison system had custody of well over 53 000 prisoners, yet the Attorney General reportedly revealed that the State had more than 100 (precisely 118) suspected pirates in custody and some serving up to 20-year prison sentences,[63] adding salt to the injury. Corruption and incompetence are equally not inconsistent with Kenya's judicial and prison systems.

Kenya's 'courage' to prosecute pirates thus requires international support and cooperation if it has to succeed. The now outmoded Security Council Resolution 1816 anticipated this requirement when it called for cooperation in the

> [p]rosecution of persons responsible for acts of piracy and armed robbery off the coast of Somalia, consistent with applicable international law ... and render assistance by, among other actions, providing disposition and logistics assistance with respect to persons under their jurisdictions and control, such victims and witnesses and persons detained as a result of operations ...[64]

In similar vein, Security Council's Resolution 1851 called upon states to make special agreements with other nations in the region to facilitate prosecution of piracy.[65] It also encouraged the creation of an international cooperation system and a center for the sharing of information. It further held that for twelve months following the adoption of Resolution 1846

> [s]tates and regional organizations cooperating in the fight against piracy and armed robbery at sea off the coast of Somalia for which advance notification has been provided by the TFG to the Secretary-General may undertake all necessary measures that are appropriate in Somalia, for the purpose of suppressing acts of piracy and armed robbery at sea, pursuant to the request of the TFG ...

In reality however, this support has not been forthcoming, at least in the case of Kenya, prompting a government official to decry: 'We have declined to accept captured pirates ... because some of them promised to

61 Report on the Synchronized Survey of Pending Cases in Kenyan Courts (December 2009) as cited by the Final Report of the Task Force on Judicial Reforms, P 33.
62 Final Report of the Task Force on Judicial Reforms, P 33.
63 Mukinda & Shiundu, Daily Nation, 30 March 2010.
64 Para 11.
65 SC Res. 1851, P 3, U.N. Doc. S/RES/1851 (Dec. 16, 2008)

support us. They did not support us. Others supported us but not well enough'.[66]

4 Conclusion

Kenya has been at the centre of prosecuting the now rampant cases of piracy off the coast of Somalia. However, these efforts have met with real challenges. Some of these relate to an inadequate international and (earlier) municipal legislative framework, jurisdictional problems, a number of risks, lack of capacity, amongst others.

There is thus need for the reviewing of the law to expand the scope of piracy. Jurisdictional problems should be at the centre of such review. At the very least these efforts ought to make sure that virtually all civilized states have legislation proscribing piracy in the modern sense of the offence. Further, the capacity of states/forums chosen for the prosecution of pirates should first be evaluated. Even then support from the international community is necessary to make the entire effort a success. Support in this regard may involve material support in which case the establishment of trusts and funds might be necessary. Cooperation may also be in the form of sharing intelligence to aid both the seizing and prosecution of piracy. If possible, the shipping fraternity could come together to support and facilitate efforts at suppressing piracy. In the end, it might help society to work towards the stabilization of Somalia and all other failed or failing states.

66 Associated Press, available at http://news.yahoo.com/9/ap/privacy (accessed on 24 April 2010).

PART IV: IMPLEMENTATION OF THE ROME STATUTE IN AFRICA

CHAPTER 12

POSITIVE COMPLEMENTARITY AND THE FIGHT AGAINST IMPUNITY IN AFRICA

*Benson Olugbuo**

1 Introduction

On 17 July 1998 the Rome Statute was adopted at the plenipotentiary conference, sponsored by the United Nations (UN).[1] The treaty entered into force on 1 July 2002,[2] resulting in the establishment of the International Criminal Court (ICC). As of November 2010, 114 state parties have ratified the Rome Statute, of which 31 are from the African continent.[3] The ICC has jurisdiction over persons most responsible for international crimes: genocide; war crimes; crimes against humanity and the crime of aggression.[4] Currently, there are five situations before the ICC and all of them are from Africa.[5] However, there are other situations under

* LL.B (Nigeria); LL.M (Pretoria); PhD Candidate, Teaching & Research Assistant, (Cape Town); Solicitor and Advocate of the Supreme Court of Nigeria.

1 Rome Statute of the International Criminal Court, UN Doc A/CONF 183/9 of 17 July 1998. For background on the establishment of the ICC, see generally R Lee (ed) *The International Criminal Court – The making of the Rome Statute: Issues - negotiations - results* (1999); C Bassiouni (ed) *The Statute of the International Criminal Court: A documentary history* (1998); A Cassese (ed) *The Rome Statute of the International Criminal Court: A commentary* (2002); F Lattanzi and W Schabas (eds) *Essays on the Rome Statute of the International Criminal Court* (1999).

2 Art 126 Rome Statute.

3 Seychelles became the 31st African state to deposit its instrument of ratification with the UN on 10 August 2010 and the Republic of Moldova became the 114th state party to the Rome Statute of the ICC on 12 October 2010. See UN Treaty Collection http://treaties.un.org/pages/ViewDetails.aspx?src=TREATY&mtdsg_no=XVIII-10&chapter=18&lang=en (accessed 13 November 2010).

4 The Review Conference of the Rome Statute held in Kampala, Uganda from 31 May - 11 June 2010 adopted a definition of the crime of aggression. However, the ICC will have jurisdiction over the crime subject to a decision to be taken after 1 January 2017 by the same majority of states parties as is required for the adoption of an amendment to the Statute. See Assembly of States Parties (ASP) resolution RC/Res 6 adopted at the 13th plenary meeting 11 June 2010, http://www.icc-cpi.int/iccdocs/asp_docs/Resolutions/RC-Res.6-ENG.pdf (accessed 15 September 2010).

5 The Situations in Central African Republic (CAR), Democratic Republic of the Congo (DRC), Sudan, Uganda and Kenya.

analysis by the ICC Prosecutor.[6]

The ICC was called the 'missing link' in international justice by former UN Secretary-General, Kofi Annan.[7] Supporters of the ICC have argued that its presence alone serves as a deterrent to would-be dictators and their collaborators and also helps to end impunity for gross human rights violations.[8] However, the apparent attention to cases in Africa[9] has resulted in negative sentiments regarding the court on the continent. It has been argued by some African leaders that the ICC is a Western tool deployed against African states,[10] while it has also been seen as a post-colonial justice system targeting weak states in Africa.[11]

This chapter examines the extent to which the ICC can ensure justice, promote peace, and end ongoing conflict in Africa by employing positive complementarity to further the work of the ICC in Africa. In the second section of the discussion it introduces the principle of complementarity and outlines its drafting history. The chapter looks at the current divergent and convergent views on complementarity; the meaning of positive complementarity; and the outcome of the Review Conference of the Rome Statute on positive complementarity. The third section explores voices from the field in relation to the events unfolding in the Democratic Republic of the Congo (DRC), Sudan and Uganda. The benefits of national prosecution of crimes using the complementarity principle are discussed, and it is argued that positive complementarity offers an opportunity for the ICC and national judicial institutions to hold accountable those responsible for serious crimes of concern to the international community.

6 The Office of the Prosecutor is currently conducting a preliminary analysis of the situations in Afghanistan, Georgia, Guinea, Côte d'Ivoire, Colombia and Palestine. See ICC 'Office of the Prosecutor' http://www.icc-cpi.int/Menus/ICC/Structure+of+the+Court/Office+of+the+Prosecutor/ (accessed 15 September 2010).

7 Kofi Annan's Press conference in Rome, Italy, following the 60th ratification of the Rome Statute on 11 April 2002 http://www.iccnow.org/documents/KofiAnnanPressConf11April02.pdf (accessed 15 September 2010).

8 M Ellis 'The International Criminal Court and its implication for domestic law and national capacity building' (2002) 15 *Florida Journal of International Law* 215, 223.

9 Of the five situations currently before the ICC, three (Uganda, DRC and CAR) were through self-referrals under art 14 of the Rome Statute; the situation in Darfur was through the UN Security Council (UNSC) acting under Chapter VII of the UN Charter and under art 13 of the Rome Statute; Kenya is through the *proprio motu* powers of the Prosecutor under art 15 of the Rome Statute.

10 D Kezio-Musoke 'Kagame tells why he is against ICC charging Bashir' *Daily Nation* 3 August 2008 http://allafrica.com/stories/200808120157.html (accessed 15 September 2010).

11 M Mamdani *Saviours and Survivors: Darfur, politics, and the war on terror* (2009) 284.

2 Complementarity principle and international justice

2.1 Origin of the concept in the Rome Statute

The ICC operates on the principle of complementarity that makes it the duty of every state to exercise its criminal jurisdiction over those responsible for international crimes.[12] This is unlike the International Criminal Tribunal for Yugoslavia (ICTY),[13] the International Criminal Tribunal for Rwanda (ICTR)[14] and the Special Court for Sierra Leone (SCSL),[15] which have primacy over national jurisdictions on the prosecution of international crimes. The complementarity principle, recognised as the hallmark of the Rome Statute, is not peculiar to the treaty as its origin predates negotiations leading to the adoption of the Rome Statute.[16] The ICC is expected to complement and not supplant the prosecution of international crimes by national jurisdictions.[17]

The principle of complementarity is based not only on respect for the primary jurisdiction of states, but also on practical considerations of efficiency and effectiveness, since states will generally have the best access to evidence, witnesses, and resources to carry out proceedings.[18] Before the adoption of the Rome Statute in 1998, some international treaties had indirectly made reference to the principle of complementarity by encouraging prosecution at the national level. These treaties include the Geneva Convention for the Amelioration of the Condition of the Wounded and Sick in Armed Forces in the Field,[19] the International Convention on the Suppression of the Punishment of the Crime of

12 Arts 1 and 17 Rome Statute; M Benzing 'The complementarity regime of the International Criminal Court: International criminal justice between states sovereignty and the fight against impunity' (2003) 7 *Max Planck Yearbook of United Nations Law* 591, 592.

13 UNSC Res 827 of 25 May 1993 establishing the International Criminal Tribunal for the former Yugoslavia.

14 UNSC Res 955 of 8 November 1994 establishing the International Criminal Tribunal for Rwanda.

15 UNSC Res 1315 of 14 August 2000 establishing the Special Court for Sierra Leone.

16 M El-Zeidy 'The principle of complementarity: A new machinery to implement international criminal law' (2003) 23 *Michigan Journal of International Law* 869, 896.

17 M Newton 'Comparative complementarity: Domestic jurisdiction consistent with the Rome Statute of the International Criminal Court' (2001) 167 *Military Law Review* 20, 26.

18 R Cryer *et al An introduction to international criminal law and procedure* (2007) 127.

19 Art 49 Geneva Convention for the Amelioration of the Condition of the Wounded and Sick in Armed Forces in the Field, entered into force on 21 October 1950.

Apartheid,[20] and the Convention on the Prevention and Punishment of the Crime of Genocide.[21]

The current provision of the complementarity principle in the Rome Statute has its origin in the 1994 International Law Commission (ILC) Draft Statute,[22] generally seen as the cornerstone for the construction of the notion of complementarity as currently provided in the Rome Statute.[23] The 1994 ILC Draft provides in its preamble that the '[ICC] is intended to be complementary to national criminal justice systems in cases where such trial procedures may not be available or may be ineffective'.[24] The ILC Draft also proposed circumstances under which an ICC investigation or prosecution may be inadmissible.[25] The complementarity principle went through several changes during the Preparatory Committee (PrepCom) meetings convened by the UN.[26] However, some of the thorny issues surrounding the complementarity principle were agreed upon before the Rome Conference. For example, states were interested in the relationship between the proposed court and national courts and were hesitant to accept any compromise proposal without knowing the legal relationship between the two.[27] According to John Holmes, '[t]he uniqueness of the legislative history concerning the complementarity regime is that most of the issues were largely resolved in the Preparatory Committee prior to the Rome Conference'.[28] This shows that states were actually interested in how the ICC would affect their sovereignty and also

20 Art 4(b) International Convention on the Suppression and Punishment of the Crime of Apartheid UN Doc A/9030 (1974) entered into force on 18 July 1976. The Apartheid Convention was adopted by the General Assembly on 30 November 1973, by 91 votes in favour, four against (Portugal, South Africa, the United Kingdom and the United States) and 26 abstentions. It came into force on 18 July 1976. It has been ratified by 107 states; J Dugard 'Convention on the Suppression and Punishment of the Crime of Apartheid' http://untreaty.un.org/cod/avl/pdf/ha/cspca/cspca_e.pdf (accessed 15 September 2010).

21 Arts 5 and 6 Convention on the Prevention and Punishment of the Crime of Genocide, entered into force on 12 January 1951.

22 The Draft Statute for an International Criminal Court was adopted by the ILC at its forty-sixth session in 1994, and was submitted to the General Assembly as a part of the ILC's Report covering the work of that session (1994 ILC Draft).

23 M El-Zeidy *The principle of complementarity in international criminal law: Origin, development and practice* (2008) 126.

24 Para 3 1994 ILC Draft.

25 Art 35 1994 ILC Draft provides that '[t]he Court may, on application by the accused or at the request of an interested State at any time prior to the commencement of the trial, or of its own motion, decide, having regard to the purposes of this Statute set out in the preamble, that a case before it is inadmissible on the ground that the crime in question:

> (a) Has been duly investigated by a State with jurisdiction over it, and the decision of that State not to proceed to a prosecution is apparently well-founded;
> (b) Is under investigation by a State which has or may have jurisdiction over it, and there is no reason for the Court to take any further action for the time being with respect to the crime; or
> (c) Is not of such gravity to justify further action by the Court.'

26 The *ad hoc* Committee that drafted the ILC Draft in 1994 was replaced by the Preparatory Committee in 1996.

27 El-Zeidy (n 23 above) 127.

28 J Holmes 'Principle of complementarity' in Lee (n 1 above) 43.

wanted to ensure that the ICC would not take over genuine efforts by national judicial institutions to make their citizens accountable for crimes committed in their jurisdiction.

In furtherance of the complementarity principle, the Chief Prosecutor of the ICC stated that '[t]he effectiveness of the International Criminal Court should not be measured by the number of cases that reach it. On the contrary, complementarity implies that the absence of trials before this Court, as a consequence of the regular functioning of national institutions, would be a major success'.[29] This is generally seen as a core activity of the ICC to ensure that states are able to hold their nationals accountable and to offer help and assistance where necessary to achieve the desired goal of complementarity and prosecutions at the national level.

Furthermore, the Office of the Prosecutor (OTP) sees its engagement in the fight against impunity as not only the prosecution of mass atrocities but also encouraging and facilitating national judicial institutions to act effectively in cases of crimes within the jurisdiction of the ICC. This was clearly stated by the OTP:[30]

> A major part of the external relations and outreach strategy of the Office of the Prosecutor will be to encourage and facilitate States to carry out their primary responsibility of investigating and prosecuting crimes. In any assessment of these efforts, the Office will take into consideration the need to respect the diversity of legal systems, traditions and cultures. The Office will develop formal and informal networks of contacts to encourage States to undertake State action, using means appropriate in the particular circumstances of a given case.

However, recent developments have shown that the OTP may have abandoned this approach and is pursuing the prosecution of crimes within the jurisdiction of the ICC. This has resulted in criticism of the OTP's *modus operandi*, as it appears the court may have abandoned its complementary task of ensuring that states hold their nationals accountable.[31] Encouraging and facilitating states to carry out their responsibilities not only entail prosecution, but also involve other proactive activities involving both the ICC and national judicial institutions aimed at oiling the wheels of complementarity for the smooth

29 ICC 'Statement made by Mr Luis Moreno-Ocampo during the ceremony for the solemn undertaking of the Chief Prosecutor of the International Criminal Court 16 June 2003' http://www.icc-cpi.int/NR/rdonlyres/D7572226-264A-4B6B-85E3-2673648B4896/143585/030616_moreno_ocampo_english.pdf (accessed 21 September 2010).

30 ICC 'Paper on some policy issues before the Office of the Prosecutor' September 2003, http://www.icc-cpi.int/NR/rdonlyres/1FA7C4C6-DE5F-42B7-8B25-60AA962ED8B6/143594/030905_Policy_Paper.pdf (accessed 21 September 2010) (OTP Policy Paper).

31 W Burke-White 'Proactive complementarity: The International Criminal Court and national courts in the Rome system of international justice' (2008) 49 *Harvard International Law Journal* 53, 55.

administration of international justice. This opportunity has to be fully explored as the complementarity regime of the Rome Statute also serves as a catalyst for domestic judicial reform .[32]

The OTP stands to gain when it acts as a partner with state parties in the prevention and prosecution of crimes, as it is obvious that it would have to ride on the back of states to achieve its prosecutorial policies and contribute to ending impunity for international crimes. This is because the ICC does not have a police force or military firepower to ensure the arrest and surrender of those it has indicted for international crimes and would rely on states to achieve its objectives.[33] The OTP should be on the forefront of contributing to the development of effective national justice systems capable of trying those who commit mass atrocities at the national level.[34] This process, coupled with OTP's limited focus on prosecution, will have far-reaching effects.

2.2 Divergent and convergent views on complementarity

It has been noted that the complementarity principle gives states primary jurisdiction over crimes committed by their nationals or in their territories.[35] However, there is currently controversy as to whether the complementarity test in the Rome Statute is a two or three prong test.[36] It has been argued that the ICC has jurisdiction over a case when there are no national proceedings or a state is 'unwilling or unable genuinely' to prosecute its nationals.[37] The argument is further reinforced by the OTP where it supports the three-prong test by stating that prosecution can take place when '[t]here is no impediment to the admissibility of a case before the Court where no state has initiated any investigation. There may be cases where inaction by states is the appropriate course of action'.[38] Some scholars have also expressed their support for this legal position.[39]

32 W Burke-White 'Complementarity in practice: The International Criminal Court as part of a system of multilevel global governance in the Democratic Republic of Congo' (2005) 18 *Leiden Journal of International Law* 557, 568.

33 C Jalloh 'Regionalizing international criminal law?' (2009) 9 *International Criminal Law Review* 445, 457.

34 J Turner 'Nationalizing international criminal law' (2005) 41 *Stanford Journal of International Law* 1.

35 M du Plessis 'Complementarity: a working relationship between African states and the International Criminal Court' in M du Plessis (ed) *African guide to international criminal justice* (2008) 129.

36 Art 17 Rome Statute.

37 D Robinson 'The mysterious mysteriousness of complementarity' (2010) 21 *Criminal Law Forum* 67, 68.

38 OTP Policy paper (n 30 above) 5.

39 J Stigen *The relationship between the International Criminal Court and national jurisdiction* (2008) 199; J Kleffner *Complementarity in the Rome Statute and national criminal jurisdiction* (2008) 104. For a review of books on the complementarity principle, see I Stegmiller 'Complementarity thoughts' (2010) 21 *Criminal Law Forum* 159 – 174.

In *Prosecutor v Dyilo,*[40] the Pre-Trial Chamber of the ICC stated that because the DRC was not acting in relation to the specific charge of conscription of child soldiers, it was not exercising its jurisdiction for the purpose of complementarity and therefore held the case to be admissible. The Chamber was of the view that national proceedings must encompass both the person and the conduct which is the subject of the case before the court.[41] The decision and its interpretation of article 17 of the Rome Statute, adding a third prong test of 'inactivity' or 'inaction' beyond 'unwilling and unable genuinely', have been criticised by scholars.[42] It has been argued that 'inaction, while is in itself consistent with article 17, has led to outcomes that are inconsistent with the intention of the drafters in adopting the complementarity mechanism: [that is], keeping the ICC as a court of last resort while encouraging national jurisdiction to exercise their primary duty to prosecute'.[43]

These criticisms notwithstanding, the decisions of the Pre-Trial Chambers regarding the three prong test have recently been confirmed by the Appeals Chamber that 'inactivity' is a basis for the intervention of the court in the interpretation of article 17 of the Rome Statute. The Appeals Chamber stated that the case of Germain Katanga was admissible as Congolese courts had not filed any charges against Katanga relating to the Bogoro massacre of February 2003. [44]

Beyond the drafting inelegance or otherwise in article 17 is the proposition that the OTP can achieve more through the promotion of positive complementarity. The ICC should use positive complementarity to leverage its activities in relation to obvious shortcomings in enforcing its mandate and managing the huge expectations to deliver justice to those who are victims and survivors of mass atrocities. It is obvious that the ICC as presently constituted lacks the clout, resources, and the manpower to be the world's international criminal law enforcer.[45] This would be done where possible, through collaboration and effective engagement with national governments.

40 *Prosecutor v Dyilo* ICC-01/04-01/06 Decision on the Prosecutor's Application for a Warrant of Arrest, 10 June 2006.

41 As above, paras 37 – 39.

42 W Schabas 'Prosecutorial discretion *v* Judicial activism' (2008) 6 *Journal of International Criminal Justice* 731, 757; A Sheng 'Analyzing the International Criminal Court complementarity principle through a Federal Court lens' (2006) *Berkeley Electronic Press* http://law.bepress.com/expresso/eps/1249 (accessed 15 September 2010) 5.

43 N Jurdi 'Some lessons on complementarity for the International Criminal Court Review Conference (2009) 34 *South African Yearbook of International Law* 28, 30.

44 *Prosecutor* v *Katanga and Chui* ICC-01/04-01/07 OA 8 Judgment on the Appeal of Mr Germain Katanga against the Oral Decision of Trial Chamber II of 12 June 2009 on the Admissibility of the Case, 25 September 2009.

45 Burke-White (n 31 above) 53 - 54.

2.3 Understanding positive complementarity

Positive complementarity is defined by the OTP as a proactive policy of cooperation aimed at promoting national proceedings.[46] It is regarded as a managerial concept that governs the relationship between the court and domestic jurisdictions on the basis of three cardinal principles: the idea of a shared burden of responsibility; the management of effective investigations and prosecutions; and the two-pronged nature of the cooperation regime.[47] It is a process which actively encourages investigation and prosecution of international crimes within the court's jurisdiction by national jurisdictions. States can do so 'where there is reason to believe that such states may be able or willing to undertake genuine investigations and prosecutions ...'.[48] On the other hand, the Assembly of States Parties (ASP) Report of the Bureau on complementarity refers to positive complementarity as:[49]

> [A]ll activities/actions whereby national jurisdictions are strengthened and enabled to conduct genuine national investigations and trials of crimes included in the Rome Statute, without involving the Court in capacity building, financial support and technical assistance, but instead leaving these actions and activities for States, to assist each other on a voluntary basis.

The definition has been criticised as limiting the role of the ICC as an institution. The intention is for states to reduce the amount of money spent on the ICC.[50] This is because the ASP had initially envisaged a role for the ICC in the application of positive complementarity in its activities.[51] In its Prosecutorial Strategy (2009 to 2012), the OTP stated that it would operate on four fundamental principles: positive complementarity; focused investigations and prosecutions; addressing the interests of victims; and maximizing the impact of the OTP's work.[52] The OTP argues that it has 'adopted a positive approach to complementarity, meaning that it encourages genuine national proceedings where possible; relies on national and international networks; and participates in a system of

46 ICC 'Prosecutorial Strategy 2009 ? 2012' 1 February 2010, http://www.icc-cpi.int/NR/rdonlyres/66A8DCDC-3650-4514-AA62-D229D1128F65/281506/OTPProsecutorialStrategy20092013.pdf (accessed 15 September 2010) (OTP Strategy 2009 -2012).

47 C Stahn 'Complementarity: A tale of two notions' (2008) 19 *Criminal Law Forum* 87, 113.

48 W Burke-White 'Implementing a policy of positive complementarity in the Rome system of justice' (2008) 19 *Criminal Law Forum* 59, 62.

49 Para 16 Report of the Bureau on stocktaking: Complementarity, http://www.icc-cpi.int/iccdocs/asp_docs/ASP8R/ICC-ASP-8-51-ENG.pdf (accessed 15 September 2010).

50 M Wierda 'Stocktaking: Complementarity' International Centre for Transitional Justice Briefing Paper, May 2010.

51 Paras 24 – 25 Report of the Bureau on the Strategic Planning Process of the International Criminal Court, ICC-ASP/5/30, 20 November 2006, www.icc-cpi.int/iccdocs/asp_docs/library/asp/ICC-ASP-5-30_English.pdf (accessed 15 September 2010).

52 Para 15 OTP Strategy 2009 – 2012 (n 46 above).

international co-operation'.[53] Regarding positive complementarity, the OTP intends to 'encourage genuine national proceedings where possible, including in situation countries, relying on its various networks of co-operation, but without involving the Office directly in capacity building or financial or technical assistance'.[54]

In analysing the need for positive complementarity, it is important to highlight some provisions of the Rome Statute that support this view. Under part 9 of the Rome Statute, which provides for 'International Cooperation and Judicial Assistance', the ICC 'may, upon request, cooperate with and provide assistance to a State Party conducting an investigation into or trial in respect of conduct which constitutes a crime within the jurisdiction of the Court or which constitutes a serious crime under the national law of the requesting State'.[55] The OTP is also given the opportunity to 'seek for additional information from States' regarding crimes that fall under the jurisdiction of the ICC.[56]

The Prosecutor can defer an investigation at the request of the state to allow the state to conduct its own investigations and trials.[57] Furthermore, the OTP can encourage states parties to investigate and prosecute crimes and may at any time reconsider a decision to initiate an investigation or prosecution based on new facts or information which may be related to the ability of the state concerned to hold its nationals accountable.[58] These provisions in the Rome Statute recognise the role of the ICC in promoting positive complementarity.[59]

Positive complementarity is an important tool in the fight against impunity and should not be ignored for several reasons. The ICC can only try a few of those who bear responsibility for crimes of international concern. If there are no effective national judicial mechanisms, there will be serious issues of impunity which could undermine any success recorded by the ICC. National judicial institutions also offer the best places to try these crimes, as they would serve as a deterrent to others and give victims an opportunity to participate and closely follow the proceedings at the national level. Furthermore, positive complementarity will ensure the development of national judicial systems in the prosecution of international crimes.

53 Para 58 OTP's Report on the activities performed during the first three years (June 2003 – June 2006) 14 September 2006, http://www.icc-cpi.int/NR/rdonlyres/D673DD8C-D427-4547-BC69-2D363E07274B/143708/ProsecutorialStrategy20060914_English.pdf (accessed 15 September 2010).

54 Para 17 OTP Strategy 2009 – 2012 (n 46 above).

55 Art 93(10) Rome Statute.

56 Art 15 Rome Statute.

57 Art 18 Rome Statute.

58 Art 53 Rome Statute.

59 Burke-White (n 48 above) 67.

2.4 The Review Conference and positive complementarity

The Review Conference of the Rome Statute of the ICC, which took place from 31 May to 11 June 2010 in Kampala, Uganda, offered an opportunity for participants and those interested in international justice generally to review the activities of the ICC since 2002 and chart a way forward for the future engagements of the court. The official Review Conference was divided into two major parts. The first was a stocktaking exercise: co-operation; complementarity; peace and justice and the impact of the Rome Statute on victims and affected communities. The second part was the adoption of the definition of the crime of aggression[60] and proposed amendments to articles 8[61] and 124[62] of the Rome Statute. However, there were additional meetings organised by non-governmental organisations (NGOs), civil society organisations (CSOs) and government officials to coincide with the Review Conference.[63]

Prior to the start of the Review Conference, CSOs had convened an international symposium on the ICC stocktaking process from 27-28 May 2010 in Kampala. The NGOs issued a *communiqué* in which they recommended that state parties to the Rome Statute should urgently adopt laws implementing the Rome Statute and that the ICC should submit an annual report on its activities to the ASP to catalyse national investigation and prosecution efforts.[64] At its seventh plenary meeting, held on 3 June 2010, the Review Conference conducted a stocktaking exercise on the issue of complementarity during which several participants reported on their experiences relating to the investigation and prosecution of crimes at the national level. Subsequently, a resolution was adopted on 8 June 2010, calling on the ICC, states parties and other stakeholders, including international organisations and CSOs, to explore additional ways in which

60 See n 4 above.

61 The Review Conference amended art 8 to include the prohibition of 'employing poison or poisoned weapons; asphyxiating, poisonous or other gases, and all analogous liquids, materials or devices; bullets which expand or flatten easily in the human body, such as bullets with a hard envelope which does not entirely cover the core or is pierced with incisions' in any conduct that took place in the context of and was associated with armed conflict not of an international character'. See Resolution RC/Res5 adopted at the 12th plenary meeting, on 10 June 2010, http://www.icc-cpi.int/iccdocs/asp_docs/Resolutions/RC-Res.5-ENG.pdf (accessed 11 August 2010).

62 The Review Conference retained art 124 and decided to review its provisions during the 14th session of the Assembly of States Parties. See Resolution RC/Res 4, adopted at the 11th plenary meeting on 10 June 2010, available at http://www.icc-cpi.int/iccdocs/asp_docs/Resolutions/RC-Res.4-ENG.pdf (accessed 11 August 2010).

63 Eg, Human Rights Network of Uganda set up a Peoples' Space at the conference centre where NGO events were organised throughout the duration of the Review Conference.

64 *Communiqué* of the International Symposium on the Stocktaking Process convened at Hotel Africana, Kampala, from 27 – 28 May 2010 by the Human Rights Network of Uganda, Uganda Coalition on the International Criminal Court and the International Commission of Jurists, http://www.iccnow.org/documents/CommuniqueFinal30May2010.pdf (accessed 10 September 2010).

to enhance the capacity of national jurisdictions to investigate and prosecute serious crimes of concern to the international community.[65]

3 Positive complementarity and voices from the field

3.1 Democratic Republic of the Congo and positive complementarity

The Democratic Republic of the Congo (DRC) signed the Rome Statute on 8 September 2000 and ratified the treaty on 11 April 2002. On 19 April 2004, the DRC referred the situation to the prosecutor of the ICC who announced an intention to open investigation on 23 June 2004. The ICC is investigating crimes committed from 1 July 2002 when the Rome Statute entered into force.

Shortly after the DRC ratified the Rome Statute, the Congolese Parliament amended the country's Military Criminal Codes, and granted military courts exclusive jurisdiction over international crimes.[66] As a monist state, international instruments ratified by the DRC apply directly to the country as long as these are not contrary to law and custom.[67] While the Preamble to the revised Code acknowledges that the DRC had ratified the Rome Statute, it did not adopt the Statute's definitions of genocide, war crimes, and crimes against humanity. Instead, the Code proposed alternate, unclear definitions.[68] Military courts in the DRC have exclusive jurisdiction over genocide, war crimes and crimes against humanity, even if the perpetrator is a civilian.[69] There have been concerns about military courts and their jurisdiction over civilians as it violates the Principles and Guidelines on the Right to a Fair Trial and Legal Assistance in Africa.[70] It is believed that the Rome Statute Bill currently before the DRC Parliament (as of November 2010) will resolve this problem as it would transfer jurisdiction over international crimes to national courts and make

65 Assembly of States Parties Resolution RC/Res 1 adopted at the 9th plenary meeting on 8 June 2010; http://www.icc-cpi.int/iccdocs/asp_docs/Resolutions/RC-Res.1-ENG.pdf (accessed 11 August 2010).

66 Loi 023/2002 du 18 Nov 2002 portant Code Judiciaire Militaire and Loi 024/2002 du 18 Nov 2002 portant Code Pénal Militaire.

67 Arts 153 and 215 Constitution of Democratic Republic of Congo, 2006.

68 M Adjami and G Mshiata 'Democratic Republic of the Congo: Impact of the Rome Statute and the International Criminal Court' International Centre for Transitional Justice Briefing Paper, May 2010 (ICTJ DRC Briefing Paper).

69 International Centre for Transitional Justice (ICTJ) 'The Democratic Republic of Congo must adopt the Rome Statute implementation law' April 2010; http://www.ictj.org/static/Factsheets/ICTJ_DRC_RomeStatuteBill_fs2010.pdf (accessed 10 September 2010).

70 Principle L(c) of the Principles and Guidelines on the Right to a Fair Trial and Legal Assistance in Africa, adopted in 2001; M Wetsh'okonda Koso 'Military justice and human rights: An urgent need to complete reforms' Open Society Initiative for Southern Africa (2010) 44.

provision for victims' participation and due process guarantees in domestic proceedings in the DRC.[71]

Despite these limitations, the military courts have proceeded to adjudicate over crimes committed in the DRC. The military court of the garrison of Haut-Katanga, Katanga Province, on 5 March 2009 convicted the Mai Mai commander Gédéon Kyungu Mutanga and twenty other Mai Mai combatants for crimes on major charges, including crimes against humanity.[72] According to Human Rights Watch (HRW), '[t]he military trial was also significant because the judges applied the definition of crimes against humanity as found in the Rome Statute of ICC [...] and its application by the military court illustrates the ICC's impact beyond its own trials in The Hague'.[73]

Furthermore, the military courts have also invoked the provisions of the Rome Statute in cases like *Mutins de Mbandaka,*[74] *Songo Mboyo,*[75] *Bongi,*[76] *Kahwa*[77] and *Bavi,*[78] involving crimes under the Rome Statute.[79] In these cases, victims participated as either witnesses or through their legal representatives and some of them who were interviewed were happy to see that the perpetrators of the crimes were brought to justice by the DRC government.[80]

In furtherance of the principle of positive complementarity, the OTP can assist the DRC national judicial system to prosecute crimes under the Rome Statute. The strengthening of the DRC legal system and sharing of case files related to crimes committed in the DRC could be an opportunity for the court to build the capacities of national systems. The case of Thomas Lubanga Dyilo serves as an illustration.

71 ICTJ (n 69 above).
72 Report of the Secretary-General of the UN to the General Assembly on Children and armed conflict, A/64/742–S/2010/181 64th session Agenda item 65(a), Promotion and protection of the rights of children, para 26, http://www.reliefweb.int/rw/RWFiles2010.nsf/FilesByRWDocUnidFilename/EGUA-85NMA2-full_report.pdf/$File/full_report.pdf (accessed 10 September 2010).
73 HRW Press Release 'DR Congo: Militia leader guilty in landmark trial: Crimes against humanity conviction an important step for justice' 10 March 2009, http://www.hrw.org/en/news/2009/03/10/dr-congo-militia-leader-guilty-landmark-trial (accessed 10 September 2010).
74 TMG de Mbandaka *Affaire Mutins de Mbanaka* 12 January 2006, PR 086/05 (First tribunal); TMG de Mbandaka, Affaire *Mutins de Mbandaka*, 20 June 2006, RP 086/05 - RP 101/06 (Appeal tribunal) and CM de l'Equateur, Affaire *Mutins de Mbandaka*, 15 June 2007, RPA 615/2006 (Final appeal).
75 TMG de Mbandaka, as above, Affaire *Songo Mboyo,* 12 April 2006, RP 084/05 (first tribunal) and CM de l'Equateur, Affaire *Songo Mboyo,* 7 June 2006, RPA 014/06 (Appeal tribunal).
76 TMG de l'Ituri Affaire *Bongi*, 24 March 2006, RP 018/06.
77 TMG de l'Ituri Affaire *Kahwa*, 2 August 2006, RP 039/06.
78 TMG de l'Ituri Affaire *Bavi*, 19 February 2007, RP 101/06.
79 For a discussion of the cases and the direct application of the Rome Statute in DRC see Avocats Sans Frontieres 'The application of the Rome Statute of the International Criminal Court by the courts of Democratic Republic of the Congo' (2009) (ASF DRC Report).
80 ICTJ DRC Briefing Paper (n 69 above).

On 19 March 2005, DRC issued an arrest warrant against Thomas Lubanga Dyilo, charging him with the crime of genocide[81] and crimes against humanity,[82] including the crimes of murder and illegal detention.[83] He was detained in the DRC when the ICC arrest warrant was issued and Thomas Lubanga Dyilo was charged with the war crimes of recruitment and enlistment of children as child soldiers. In its decision to issue an arrest warrant against Thomas Lubanga Dyilo, the Pre-Trial Chamber stated:[84]

> [F]or the purpose of the admissibility analysis of the case against Mr Thomas Lubanga Dyilo, the Chamber observes that since March 2004 the DRC national justice system has undergone certain changes, particularly in the region of Ituri where a Tribunal de Grande Instance has been re-opened in Bunia. This has resulted inter alia in the issuance of two warrants of arrest by the competent DRC authorities for Mr Thomas Lubanga Dyilo in March 2005 for several crimes, some possibly within the jurisdiction of the Court, committed in connection with military attacks from May 2003 onwards and during the so-called Ndoki incident in February 2005. Moreover, as a result of the DRC proceedings against Mr Thomas Lubanga Dyilo, he has been held in the Centre Pénitentiaire et de Rééducation de Kinshasa since 19 March 2005. Therefore, in the Chamber's view, the Prosecution's general statement that the DRC national judicial system continues to be unable in the sense of article 17(1) (a) to (c) and (3) of the Statute does not wholly correspond to the reality any longer.

Under positive complementarity, the OTP would have encouraged the DRC government to include the crime of conscription and the enlistment of child soldiers in the charge sheet against Thomas Lubanga Dyilo.[85] This is because at the time the OTP made application for the arrest of Thomas Lubanga Dyilo, the DRC national justice system was working and the state was meeting its international obligation in terms of addressing impunity.[86] The court only proceeded against Thomas Lubanga Dyilo because the DRC did not indict him on the conscription and enlistment of child soldiers.[87]

The OTP is beginning to appreciate the need for positive complementarity in its activities. For example, in September 2008, the OTP announced the opening of a third case in the DRC, focusing on alleged crimes committed in Kivu provinces by a multiplicity of

81 Art 164 DRC Military Code.

82 Arts 166 - 169 DRC Military Code.

83 *Prosecutor v Dyilo* (n 40 above) Decision on the Prosecutor's Application for a Warrant of Arrest, art 58 para 33.

84 *Prosecutor v Dyilo* (n 40 above) para 36.

85 N Jurdi 'The prosecutorial interpretation of the complementarity principle: Does it really contribute to ending impunity on the national level?' (2010) 10 *International Criminal Law Review* 73, 90.

86 W Schabas 'Complementarity in practice: Some uncomplimentary thoughts' (2008) 19 *Criminal Law Forum* 5, 25.

87 *Prosecutor v Dyilo* (n 40 above) para 37.

perpetrators and groups. In relation to its investigation and in furtherance of the principle of positive complementarity, the OTP plans to 'facilitate investigations by [DRC] judiciary and contributions to "*dossiers d'instruction*" against perpetrators'.[88] It is argued that this assistance should not be limited to the DRC but several other places where there are conflicts and the involvement of the ICC will involve minimal cost and there would be value-added results. The domestic implementation of the Rome Statute and the overhaul of the criminal justice system in the DRC and other countries in Africa should be seen as a vital component of positive complementarity as it will give states the ability to have national procedures to hold accountable persons who commit crimes under the Rome Statute.

3.2 The Darfur conflict and positive complementarity

The conflict in Darfur has attracted local, regional and international condemnations and led the Secretary General of the UN to set up an International Commission of Inquiry on Darfur to investigate mass atrocities committed in the Darfur region of Sudan.[89] The UN Darfur Report stated that, though the Government of Sudan (GoS) had not pursued a policy of genocide,[90] single individuals, including government officials, may have entertained genocidal intent and that it would be for a competent court to make the determination on a case-by-case basis.[91] The report further stated that 'international offences as crimes against humanity or large scale war crimes may be no less serious and heinous than genocide'[92] and recommended that the situation be referred to the ICC.[93]

The report further stated that 'the Security Council must act not only against the perpetrators but also on behalf of the victims'[94] and suggested the establishment of a Compensation Commission designed to grant reparation to the victims of the crimes in Darfur, whether or not the

88 ICC 'Report of the Activities of the Court to the Assembly of States Parties' Eighth Session, para 40, ICC-ASP/8/40, 21 October 2009, http://www.icc-cpi.int/NR/rdonlyres/30DEDD3C-0053-4230-AE19-C14932E0BF7A/0/ICCASP840ENG.pdf (accessed 26 August 2010).

89 UN 'Report of the International Commission of Inquiry on Darfur to the United Nations Secretary-General', Pursuant to Security Council Resolution 1564 of 18 September 2004, 25 January 2005 http://www.un.org/News/dh/sudan/com_inq_darfur.pdf (accessed 20 September 2010) (UN Darfur Report).

90 Para 518 UN Darfur Report.

91 Para 520 UN Darfur Report.

92 Para 642 UN Darfur Report.

93 Para 569 UN Darfur Report.

94 Para 649 UN Darfur Report.

perpetrators of such crimes have been identified.[95] On 31 March 2005 the Security Council of the United Nations referred the Darfur situation to the ICC.[96]

On 7 June 2007, the Sudanese government announced the establishment of the Special Criminal Court for Events in Darfur (SCCED) in response to the announcement by the OTP about the opening of investigations in Darfur.[97] The jurisdiction of SCCED included acts constituting crimes under the Sudanese Penal Code and charges relating to violations cited in the report of the Commission of Inquiry and, any charges pursuant to any other law, as determined by the Chief Justice of Sudan.[98] Furthermore, in November 2005, Sudan established two additional chambers for the SCCED and created special investigative committees to oversee the activities of SCCED. These include the Judicial Investigations Committee, the Special Prosecutions Commissions, the Committees Against Rape, the Unit for Combating Violence Against Women and Children and the Committee on Compensation.[99] These were aimed at addressing the crimes in Darfur.[100] The decree which established the SCCED was amended in November 2005 to include 'international humanitarian law' in the jurisdiction of the SCCED while two additional seats were established for Nyala and El Geneina.[101] The cases brought before the SCCED did not reflect the international crimes committed in Darfur and the SCCED has been seen as a ploy by Sudan to circumvent the ICC jurisdiction.[102]

95 Paras 570 and 649 UN Darfur Report. It is, however, interesting to note that though the case is currently before the ICC, nothing substantial has been done to alleviate the suffering of the victims and survivors who bear the brunt of the ongoing atrocities in Darfur. Millions have been displaced and currently live in squalor camps in Darfur and Chad with little or no meaningful humanitarian assistance from the Sudanese government and the international community.

96 UNSC Res 1593 (2005) adopted on 31 March 2005 with 11 votes in favour and 4 abstentions from Algeria, Brazil, China, United States.

97 See Letter dated 18 June 2005 from the Charge d'affaires a.i of the Permanent Mission of the Sudan to the UN addressed to the President of the Security Council S/2005/403, 22 June 2005; http://daccess-dds-ny.un.org/doc/UNDOC/GEN/N05/395/89/PDF/N0539589.pdf?OpenElement (accessed 11 September 2010). See also UN Office for the Coordination of Humanitarian Affairs - Integrated Regional Information Networks (IRIN) 'Sudan: Judiciary challenges ICC over Darfur cases' 24 June 2005, http://www.reliefweb.int/rw/RWB.NSF/db900SID/KKEE-6DNSU2?OpenDocument (11 September 2010).

98 Art 5 Decree Establishing the Special Criminal Court on the Events in Darfur, 7 June 2005; reprinted in UN Doc S/2005/403.

99 ICC 'Third Report of the Prosecutor of the International Criminal Court to the U.N. Security Council Pursuant to UNSCR 1593 (2005)' 14 June 2006, http://www.icc-cpi.int/library/cases/OTP_ReportUNSC_3-Darfur_English.pdf (accessed 21 September 2010).

100 S Baldo 'Sudan: Impact of the Rome Statute and the International Criminal Court' June 2010 ICTJ Briefing on the Review Conference, 3 (ICTJ Sudan Briefing Note).

101 O Elagab 'The Darfur Situation and the ICC: An appraisal' (2008) 1 *Journal of Politics and Law* 43, 51.

102 HRW 'Lack of conviction: The Special Criminal Court on the Events in Darfur' June 2006.

In 2009, Sudan amended its Criminal Act of 1991 through the efforts of the Arab League, introducing international crimes into the Sudanese penal code.[103] Despite these developments there are still flaws in the Sudanese criminal justice system. The Armed Forces Act of 2007, while criminalising serious violations of international humanitarian law and human rights law, also provides for immunity to members of the armed forces which can only be waived by the President. The Sudanese Criminal Procedure Act (CPA) prohibits investigations and proceedings outside Sudan for any citizen that may have committed the crimes in the amended 2009 Criminal Act of 1991. The CPA also prohibits anyone in Sudan from assisting in the extradition of any Sudanese for the prosecution of war crimes, crimes against humanity and genocide.[104]

In relation to the ICC investigations in Darfur, on 27 April 2007, the Pre-Trial Chamber I issued an arrest warrant for 51 counts of crimes against humanity and war crimes against Ahmad Mohammed Harun (Mohammed Harun) and Mohammed Ali Abd-Al-Rahman (Ali Kushayb) for the crimes committed by the Sudanese Armed Forces (SAF) and the Janjaweed militia.[105] Sudan refused to co-operate with the court and, instead, promoted Mohammed Harun to be the Minister of State for Humanitarian Affairs from Minister of State for the Interior of Government of Sudan.[106] On 14 July 2008, the OTP applied for an arrest warrant against President Omar Hassan Al Bashir for 10 charges of genocide, crimes against humanity and war crimes.[107]

The OTP argues that Al Bashir used state apparatus to commit massive crimes in Darfur. On 4 March 2009, Pre-Trial Chamber I issued an arrest warrant for Al Bashir for five counts of crimes against humanity, including the crimes of extermination, rapes and killings, and two counts of war crimes, intentionally directing attacks against a civilian population as such or against individual civilians not taking part in hostilities and pillaging. The Court did not retain the genocide charges. The OTP appealed against this decision on 6 July 2009 and the Appeals Chamber, on 3 February 2010, decided that the Pre-Trial Chamber I applied an erroneous standard of proof and directed the Pre-Trial Chamber I to decide on the correct standard of proof whether a warrant of arrest should be issued against Al Bashir for genocide.

103 Para 15 OTP's statement to the United Nations Security Council on the situation in Darfur, the Sudan, pursuant to UNSCR 1593 (2005) 4 December 2009, http://www.icc-cpi.int/NR/rdonlyres/BA525867-5B58-4CDD-B6CF-8105181658D6/281343/UNSecurityCouncilStateFINAL1.pdf (accessed 21 September 2010).

104 ICTJ Sudan Briefing Note (n 102 above) 3.

105 *The Prosecutor v Harun ('Ahmad Harun') and Abd-Al-Rahman ('Ali Kushayb')* ICC-02/05-01/07.

106 ICC 'Situations and Cases: Darfur, Sudan' http://www.icc-cpi.int/menus/icc/situations%20and%20cases/situations/situation%20icc%200205/related%20cases/icc%200205%200107/darfur_%20sudan?lan=en-GB (accessed 21 September 2010).

107 *Prosecutor v Al Bashir, Case ICC-02/05-01/09.*

On 12 July 2010, the Pre-Trial Chamber I held that 'on the basis of the standard of proof as identified by the Appeals Chamber [...] there are reasonable grounds to believe that Al Bashir acted with *dolus specialis/* specific intent to destroy in part the Fur, Masalit and Zaghawa ethnic groups'.[108] The Chamber subsequently issued a second arrest warrant against Al Bashir.[109]

Sudan has consistently resisted the authority and jurisdiction of the ICC over its nationals and claims, amongst other things, that the UNSC Resolution 1593 is flawed[110] and that the indictment and issuance of arrest warrants against Sudanese officials are violations of the Vienna Convention on the Law of Treaties[111] and customary international law relating to the immunity of state officials in the case of Al Bashir.[112] However, scholars and activists are quick to point out that although Sudan is not a state party to the Rome treaty, by virtue of the fact that the situation was referred to the ICC by the Security Council acting under Chapter VII of the Charter of the United Nations, Sudan as a member of the UN is bound to co-operate with the ICC.[113]

From the statements made by the OTP to the UN Security Council, it appears that Sudan initially co-operated with the ICC on the investigations both in Uganda and Sudan.[114] The OTP stated that 'previous cooperation demonstrates that when willing, the Sudanese authorities are able to provide diverse forms of cooperation'.[115] This can be illustrated by the fact that the OTP and the Sudanese government signed an agreement on 2

108 *Prosecutor v Al Bashi* Second Decision on the Prosecution's Application for a Warrant of Arrest 12 July 2010.

109 As above..

110 International Crisis Group (ICG) 'Sudan: Justice, peace and the ICC' 17 July 2009, Africa Report 152, 10.

111 Art 34 Vienna Convention on the Law of Treaties, 1969, adopted on 23 May 1969 and entered into force on 27 January 1980.

112 P Gaeta 'Does President Al Bashir enjoy immunity from arrest?' (2009) 7 *Journal of International Criminal Justice* 315, 316; C Jalloh 'The African Union and the International Criminal Court: The summer of our discontent(s)' *JURIST - Forum* 6 August 2010, http://jurist.org/forum/2010/08/the-african-union-and-the-international-criminal-court-the-summer-of-our-discontents.php (accessed 13 September 2010); R Cryer 'Prosecuting the Leaders: Promises, Politics and Practicalities' (2009) 1 *Göttingen Journal of International Law* 45, 64.

113 S William and L Sherif 'The arrest warrant for President Al Bashir: Immunities of incumbent heads of state and the International Criminal Court' (2009) 14 *Journal of Conflict and Security Law* 71, 80; D Akande 'The Legal Nature of Security Council Referrals to the ICC and its Impact on Al Bashir's Immunities' (2009) 7 *Journal of International Criminal Justice* 333, 342; D Akande 'The Bashir indictment: Are serving heads of state immune from ICC prosecution?' *Oxford Transitional Justice Research Working Paper Series* 30 July 2008; D Akande 'The jurisdiction of the International Criminal Court over nationals of non-state parties: Legal basis and limits' (2003)1 *Journal of International Criminal Justice* 618 – 650.

114 ICC 'Eleventh Report of the Prosecutor of the International Criminal Court to the UN Security Council Pursuant to UNSC 1593 (2005)' http://www.icc-cpi.int/NR/rdonlyres/A250ECCD-D9E5-433B-90BB-76C068ED58A3/282160/11thUNSCReportENG1.pdf (accessed 4 September 2010) (OTP UNSC Report 11).

115 Para 23 OTP UNSC Report 11.

October 2005 on the arrest of the leaders of the Lord's Resistance Army (LRA) who were objects of ICC arrest warrants. In November 2005 representatives of the ICC visited Khartoum to discuss matters relating to both the LRA and the situation in Darfur.[116]

The co-operation between the ICC and Sudan resulted in mutual exchanges in relation to judicial records and other documents relating to article 53 of the Rome Statute. Reports of the Sudanese National Commission of Inquiry and Ministry of Defence were also discussed. Sudanese officials were interviewed in Khartoum under article 55 of the Rome Statute as potential witnesses, and five missions were undertaken to Khartoum, the last sometime between January and February 2007.[117]

However, the government severed an official communication and co-operation with the OTP in April 2007 and embarked on a spirited campaign to discredit the ICC with the backing of the Arab League[118] and the African Union (AU).[119] In July 2008, some African and Arab members of the UNSC supported by China and Russia proposed a deferral of ICC investigations under article 16 of the Rome Statute. This was done in a draft resolution to renew the mandate of the AU-UN Hybrid Operation in Darfur (UNAMID) on the grounds that the ICC arrest warrant was a threat to peace in Sudan.[120] The proposal was dropped from the resolution adopted to extend UNAMID because of a lack of support and consensus amongst members of the Security Council.[121]

It appears that the problem of prosecuting those responsible for crimes in Sudan is a lack of political will and not necessarily the inability of the Sudanese government to hold its nationals accountable. According to the OTP,[122]

> The ability of the Sudanese judicial system to carry out proceedings has been demonstrated *inter alia* by the decision, announced on 6 May by [...] Justice Minister Abdel-Basit Sabdarat, to prosecute those responsible for investment fraud up to $175 million in North Darfur. Minister Sabdarat announced that 58 suspects had been taken into custody and would face criminal charges, including two ex-police officers. The case shows that [Sudanese] authorities can prosecute serious crimes where there is willingness to do so. The

116 As above.

117 Para 25 OTP UNSC Report 11.

118 BBC 'Arab leaders back "wanted" Bashir' 30 March 2009, http://news.bbc.co.uk/2/hi/7971624.stm (accessed 13 September 2010).

119 BBC 'African Union in rift with court' 3 July 2009,http://news.bbc.co.uk/2/hi/8133925.stm (accessed 13 September 2010).

120 ICTJ Sudan Briefing Note (n 102 above) 5; UNSC 'Report of the UNSC 5947th Meeting on July 31 2008' SC/9412, http://www.un.org/News/Press/docs/2008/sc9412.doc.htm (accessed 13 November 2010).

121 UNSC Resolution 1828 (2008), S/RES/1828 (2008) adopted by the Security Council at its 5947th meeting on 31 July 2008.

122 Para 52 OTP's UNSC Report 11.

Prosecution hopes to see similar action for war crimes, crimes against humanity and genocide.

The issue that needs to be addressed is how positive complementarity may be used to ensure that Sudan is willing and able to hold its nationals accountable. A close study of Resolution 1593 shows that the Security Council had also envisaged positive complementarity in the prosecution of those responsible for international crimes in Sudan. For example, it '*encourages* the Court, as appropriate and in accordance with the Rome Statute, to support international co-operation with domestic efforts to promote the rule of law, protect human rights and combat impunity in Darfur'.[123] Furthermore, the resolution calls on the court and the AU to 'discuss practical arrangements that will facilitate the work of the Prosecutor and of the Court, including the possibility of conducting proceedings in the region, which would contribute to regional efforts in the fight against impunity'.[124]

The OTP is therefore under an obligation to ensure that any process aimed at the prosecution of crimes in Sudan is successful to the extent possible and should work in collaboration with the African Union (AU) to ensure that there is no impunity in Sudan. Under positive complementarity the ICC should continue to encourage genuine investigations and prosecutions of crimes in Sudan and also monitor the activities of the AU in Sudan to ensure that there is compliance with Resolution 1593.

Regarding other efforts to end the Darfur conflict, the Peace and Security Council (PSC) of the AU on 21 July 2008 called for the formation of a body, the AU High-Level Panel on Darfur (AUPD).[125] This decision was endorsed by the 12th Ordinary Session of the Assembly of Heads of State and Governments of the AU in February 2009. The AUPD[126] convened its inaugural meeting in Addis Ababa in March 2009, followed by several other consultations, and submitted its report on 29 October 2009 to the 207th PSC meeting at the level of Heads of State and Government in Abuja, Nigeria.[127]

The AU accepted the report, endorsed it as its official policy and

123 UNSC Res 1593, 31 March 2005, S/RES/1593 (2005) http://daccess-dds-ny.un.org/doc/UNDOC/GEN/N05/292/73/PDF/N0529273.pdf?OpenElement (accessed 4 September 2010).

124 Para 9 UNSC Res 1593.

125 AU 'Introductory Note by the Chairperson of the Commission' during the Peace and Security Council 207th Meeting at the Level of Heads of State and Government, 29 October 2009, Abuja, Nigeria.

126 Members of the AUPD included Thabo Mvuyelwa Mbeki, Gen Abdulsalami Abubakar (Rtd), Pierre Buyoya, Ahmed Maher El Sayed, Judge Florence Ndepele Mwachande Mumba, Kabir Abdulfatah Mohammed and Rakiya Omaar.

127 AU 'Report of the African Union High-Level Panel on Darfur' PSC/AHG/2(CCVII) 29 October 2009, http://www.sudantribune.com/spip.php?article32905 (accessed 21 September 2010) (AU Darfur Report).

established the AU High Level Implementation Panel (AUHIP)[128] to assist in the implementation of all aspects of the AUPD recommendations.[129] The OTP has stated that it is ready to assist the AUHIP in its activities.[130] It appears AUHIP activities may have been hampered by the rejection of the Darfur hybrid tribunal by Sudan.[131] On a positive note, Sudan informed AUHIP of its commitment to its programme of action as it seems the setting up of the Darfur hybrid tribunal is not a priority in the current dispensation.[132]

The AU Darfur Report argues that the conflict in Darfur is a result of the culmination of repressive policies carried out by both previous and current governments of Sudan and defines the conflict as 'Sudan's crisis in Darfur'.[133] The conflict is a result of years of neglect and gross human rights abuses by Sudan coupled with the competition for power, land and scarce resources in the region. The Report further stated that current actions are not adequate and fall below the minimum thresholds of individual criminal responsibility and recommended the setting up of a Hybrid Court for Darfur.[134] The AUPD argues that Sudan has the opportunity to show its willingness to end impunity in Darfur and rightly states:[135]

> [S]hould Sudan make genuine efforts to address the crimes in Darfur, the judges of the ICC would be required to evaluate those steps to consider whether they meet the requirements of Article 17. The final determination of this issue, however, is for the judges of the ICC alone.

Despite the setting up of the AUHIP and the co-operation offered by the OTP, it appears the war of attrition between the ICC and the AU may not

128 Members of AUHIP are Thabo Mbeki, Pierre Buyoya and Abdulsalami Abubakar.
129 AU 'Report of the Chairperson of the Commission on the Activities of the African Union High–Level Implementation Panel on Sudan' PSC/PR/2(CCXXXV) Peace and Security Council 235th Meeting, Addis Ababa, 2 July 2010 http://www.ausitroom-psd.org/Documents/PSC2010/235th/Report/ReportAUHIP.pdf (accessed 13 September 2010).
130 Para 21 Statement of the Prosecutor of the International Criminal Court to the UNSC on the situation in Darfur, Sudan, pursuant to UNSC 1593 (2005).
131 'Sudan reiterates rejection of Darfur hybrid courts' *Sudan Tribune* 1 November 2009, http://www.sudantribune.com/spip.php?article32973 (accessed 4 September 2010).
132 AUHIP's Programme of Action revolves around the following nine areas: (i) helping to accelerate the process towards the resolution of the conflict in Darfur; (ii) helping to ensure the implementation of the CPA; (iii) assisting the parties to address post=referendum issues; (iv) working with the government of Sudan and with the government of Southern Sudan, Sudanese political parties and other stakeholders, to develop a national consensus about the challenges facing the country, including making unity attractive; (v) working with Southern Sudan political parties to develop a consensus about the challenges facing Southern Sudan; (vi) working with the GoSS and others to address the issue of inter-communal conflict in Southern Sudan; (vii) helping to ensure the April 2010 general elections are free and fair; (viii) helping to ensure that Sudan's neighbours support Sudan's conflict-resolution process; (ix) and helping to co-ordinate international action on Sudan.
133 Para 2 AU Darfur Report.
134 Para 246 AU Darfur Report.
135 Para 255 AU Darfur Report.

abate soon as evidenced by recent events. During the Fifth Ordinary Session of the Assembly of Heads of State and Governments of the AU held from 25 to 27 July 2010 in Kampala, the AU in a resolution expressed its disappointment that the UN Security Council had not acted upon its request to defer the proceedings initiated against Omar Al Bashir in accordance with article 16 of the Rome Statute which allows the Security Council to defer cases for one year.[136] The AU further reiterated its decision that AU member states shall not co-operate with the ICC in the arrest and surrender of Omar Al Bashir.[137] Member states of AU were urged to balance, where applicable, their obligations to the AU with their obligations to the ICC.[138] They were also required to speak with one voice to ensure that the proposed amendment to article 16 of the Rome Statute which would allow the UN General Assembly to take over the power of the Security Council to defer cases for one year in cases where the Security Council has failed to take a decision within a specified time-frame.[139] Furthermore, the AU rejected, in the interim, the request by the ICC to open a liaison office to the AU in Addis Ababa, Ethiopia.[140]

The rejection of the establishment of an ICC liaison office is a missed opportunity as this would have been a good opportunity for consensus building between the ICC and the AU.[141] The relationship between the ICC and the AU has degenerated due to a lack of trust and effective communication between the two institutions and the misunderstanding of the role of the ICC in the fight against impunity. The OTP needs to continue the positive relationship with the AUHIP to ensure that efforts aimed at accountability in Sudan are not backtracked. It is also evident that the involvement of the ICC in the Darfur conflict may have contributed to the changes going on currently in the Sudanese legal system. Whether these changes will lead to the prosecution of those responsible for international crimes in Darfur is something that has to be monitored closely. The OTP is encouraged to make effective use of positive complementarity to ensure that there is a synergy of collaboration between all actors working for accountability in Sudan. The use of positive complementarity will not limit the statutory authority of the ICC to investigate and to prosecute international crimes where the court has jurisdiction and where national governments fail to undertake genuine

136 Para 4 AU Decision on the Progress Report of the Commission on the Implementation of Decision Assembly/AU/Dec 270 (XIV) on the Second Ministerial Meeting on the Rome Statute of the International Criminal Court Doc Assembly/AU/10(XV), http://www.africa-union.org/root/UA/Conferences/2010/juillet/Summit_2010_b/doc/DECISIONS/Assembly%20AU%20Dec%20289-330%20(XV)%20_E.pdf (accessed 19 August 2010) (AU ICC Decision).

137 Para 5 AU ICC Decision.

138 Para 6 AU ICC Decision.

139 Para 7 AU ICC Decision.

140 Para 8 AU ICC Decision.

141 D Akande *et al* 'An African expert study on the African Union concerns about article 16 of the Rome Statute of the ICC' *Institute for Security Studies Policy Paper* (2010) 23.

prosecutions themselves.[142] If effectively deployed and used, it will assist states, including the Sudan, to develop an ability to hold citizens accountable and thereby ensure that the ICC truly becomes a court of last resort.

3.3 The northern Uganda conflict and positive complementarity

The northern Uganda conflict is one of the longest-running conflicts in East Africa and has been raging for two decades.[143] The Lord's Resistance Army (LRA) has its origin in the Holy Spirit Movement led by Alice Auma Lakwena, and is a combination of forces allied against the National Resistance Movement (NRM) of President Museveni.[144] Alice promised her soldiers powers of invincibility if they obeyed her spiritual rules. However, the firepower of the Uganda Peoples' Defense Force (UPDF) defeated them at a battle near Kampala in 1987. Alice fled to Kenya and Joseph Kony, who is said to be related to Alice, took over the remaining soldiers and transformed it into the LRA.[145] Though some have claimed that the LRA has no official political agenda in its war with the government of Uganda, it succeeded in bringing economic activities in northern Uganda to a standstill.

The LRA has for over two decades attacked civilians and undermined the cultural values of the Acholi and other ethnicities in northern Uganda by killing and maiming innocent civilians, raping and abducting children and turning them into sex-slaves and 'death squads.'[146] The LRA allegedly operated from Sudan and there were allegations that Sudan supported the LRA. In return, Sudan accused Uganda of supporting the Sudan Peoples' Liberation Army/Movement (SPLA/M).[147] Both the LRA and Uganda People's Defence Force are known to have committed several human rights abuses during the northern Uganda conflict.[148]

There have been several processes aimed at bringing an end to the conflict in northern Uganda. The Ugandan government promulgated the

142 Burke-White (n 31 above) 53, 72.

143 T Allen *Trial justice: The International Criminal Court and the Lord's Resistance Army* (2006) 25 – 27.

144 HRW 'The scars of death: Children abducted by the Lord's Resistance Army in Uganda' 1 September 1997, http://www.hrw.org/en/reports/1997/09/18/scars-death (accessed 11 August 2010) (HRW Uganda Report).

145 HRW Uganda Report 80.

146 L Keller 'Achieving peace with justice: The International Criminal Court and Ugandan alternative justice mechanisms' (2008) 23 *Connecticut Journal of International Law* 209, 233.

147 F Nyakairu 'Are resurgent Ugandan rebels backed by Khartoum?' *AlertNet* 10 September 2009 http://www.alertnet.org/db/an_art/55866/2009/08/10-130728-1.htm (accessed 10 August 2010).

148 Z Lomo and L Hovil 'Behind the violence: The war in Northern Uganda' (2004) 99 *Institute for Security Studies Monograph* 45.

first Amnesty Statute in 1987, targeting armed rebellions against the government.[149] In 1998, the government introduced another Amnesty Bill.[150] The Amnesty Bill was criticised by several people including the Acholi Religious Leaders Peace Initiative (ARLPI). They argued that the Bill was not inclusive and discriminated against some combatants willing to lay down arms. The ARLPI subsequently presented a memo to the government calling for unconditional amnesty to all combatants who agreed to lay down their arms and embrace peace.[151] The Amnesty Act, passed in 2000, applied to conflicts that commenced on or after 26 January 1986 and also had a life-span of six months which could be extended by the Minister of Internal Affairs under statutory notice.[152]

On 16 December 2003, Uganda referred the situation concerning the LRA to the ICC.[153] There were criticisms about the referral because it failed to mention the culpability of the government in the abuses in northern Uganda and the ICC was urged to investigate all sides in the conflict.[154] The OTP subsequently announced that the ICC would investigate all parties to the northern Uganda conflict.[155] Opposition rose against the referral from northern Ugandans who saw the ICC as an obstruction to peace and reconciliation.[156] Despite several pleas and threats from those in charge of the peace negotiations, the prosecutor went ahead and charged the top leadership of the LRA with several crimes under the Rome Statute and requested warrants of arrest.[157] The Pre-Trial Chamber judges agreed with him and issued warrants of arrest against top commanders of the LRA.[158]

The referral put the LRA in the spotlight and in a difficult position. This made them agree to peace negotiations with the Ugandan

149 B Afako 'Reconciliation and justice: 'Mato oput' and the Amnesty Act, 2002' http://www.c-r.org/our-work/accord/northern-uganda/reconciliation-justice.php (accessed 11 August 2010).

150 Bill 13 *Uganda Government Gazette* 58 XCL 22 September 1998.

151 Afako (n 153 above).

152 Art 18 Amnesty Act 2000.

153 ICC 'President of Uganda refers situation concerning the Lord's Resistance Army (LRA) to the ICC' ICC-20040129-44 http://www.icc-cpi.int/menus/icc/press%20and%20media/press%20releases/2004/president%20of%20uganda%20refers%20situation%20concerning%20the%20lord_s%20resistance%20army%20_lra_%20to%20the%20icc?lan=en-GB (accessed 11 August 2010).

154 HRW 'ICC: Investigate all sides in Uganda' 4 February 2004 http://www.hrw.org/en/news/2004/02/04/icc-investigate-all-sides-uganda (accessed 11 August 2010).

155 ICC 'Prosecutor of the International Criminal Court opens an investigation into Northern Uganda' ICC-OTP-20040729-65 http://www.icc-cpi.int/menus/icc/press%20and%20media/press%20releases/2004/prosecutor%20of%20the%20international%20criminal%20court%20opens%20an%20investigation%20into%20nothern%20uganda?lan=en-GB (accessed 11 August 2010).

156 A Little 'Balancing accountability and victim autonomy at the International Criminal Court' (2007) 38 *Georgetown Journal of International Law* 363, 376.

157 The Prosecutor applied for the warrants of arrest on 5 May 2005. See International Criminal Court ICC-02/04-01/05 *Prosecutor v Kony, Otti, Odhiambo and Ongwen*.

158 The warrants of arrest were issued under seal on 8 July 2005 and unsealed on 13 October 2005 for security reasons and to ensure the protection of victims.

government.[159] In 2006, the LRA and Ugandan government embarked on peace negotiations, brokered by the Vice-President of the Government of Southern Sudan (GoSS), Riek Machar.[160] According to the International Crisis Group (ICG), '[t]he Juba process was initially hailed as historic for good reasons. Started in June 2006, it produced five signed protocols in 21 months, designed to conclude 22 years of conflict and guarantee the disarmament and reintegration of one of the worst human rights abusing insurgencies ever'.[161] Between June 2006 and July 2008 the LRA and the Ugandan government agreed on five main items of the peace process agenda:[162]

> (1) Comprehensive solutions to the conflict, including special attention to the economic recovery of the north, positions for northerners in the government and a fund to pay reparations to conflict victims;
>
> (2) Accountability and reconciliation, including mechanisms for creation of a special division of the High Court to try the most serious crimes and promotion of truth telling and traditional justice mechanisms;
>
> (3) A permanent cessation of hostilities agreement;
>
> (4) Disarmament, demobilisation and reintegration (DDR) principles for processing and resettling former combatants in Uganda; and
>
> (5) An agreement on implementation and monitoring mechanisms, requiring the government, after the [Final Peace Agreement] is signed and during a transitional period in which the LRA is to fully assemble, to ask the UN Security Council to adopt a resolution deferring all investigation and prosecution of LRA leaders by the International Criminal Court (ICC) for up to a year.

The Ugandan government and the LRA later signed the Annexure on Accountability and Reconciliation which enabled the government to establish the War Crimes Division (WCD) of the High Court of Uganda.[163] However, despite assurances about his safety and the need to conclude the negotiations by signing the final peace agreement, Joseph Kony did not turn up on 10 April 2008 as earlier anticipated. He cited the ICC indictment as a reason for his failure to conclude the peace deal. This apparent drawback notwithstanding, the Ugandan government proceeded to put into place mechanisms aimed at ensuring that the national judicial

159 International Crisis Group (ICG) 'Northern Uganda: Seizing the opportunity for Peace' Africa Report N°124 – 26 April 2007 http://www.crisisgroup.org/en/regions/africa/horn-of-africa/uganda/124-northern-uganda-seizing-the-opportunity-for-peace.aspx (accessed 11 August 2010).

160 ICG 'Peace in Northern Uganda?' *Africa Briefing* 13 September 2006 http://www.crisisgroup.org/~/media/Files/africa/horn-of-africa/uganda/B041%20Peace%20in%20Northern%20Uganda.ashx (accessed 20 September 2010).

161 ICG 'Northern Uganda: The road to peace, with or without Kony' *Africa Report* 146 – 10 December 2008 http://www.crisisgroup.org/en/regions/africa/horn-of-africa/uganda/146-northern-uganda-the-road-to-peace-with-or-without-kony.aspx (accessed 11 August 2010).

162 As above.

163 British Broadcasting Corporation 'Uganda sets up war crimes court' 26 May 2008 http://news.bbc.co.uk/2/hi/africa/7420461.stm (accessed 11 August 2010).

system is able to deal with the northern Ugandan conflict by setting up the WCD. On 10 March 2010, the Parliament of Uganda passed the Rome Statute of the International Criminal Court 2006 Bill[164] into law, thereby incorporating provisions of the Rome Statute into Uganda's domestic legal system.[165] President Museveni subsequently signed the bill into law shortly before the commencement of the Review Conference.[166] The Ugandan government recently charged Thomas Kwoyelo – a former LRA commander – before the WCD.[167]

The knotty issue that is yet to be resolved is whether the WCD is an answer to Uganda's initial inability to hold members of the LRA accountable and whether the government can use the International Criminal Court Act of 2010 to try individuals for crimes committed in northern Uganda in the WCD in contravention of the constitutional provision of non-retroactivity.[168] It has been argued that if a credible war crimes court is established in Uganda, the ICC may decide to declare the LRA case inadmissible.[169] By creating the WCD, Uganda is taking steps to institute accountability mechanisms that the ICC was created to promote through the process of positive complementarity.[170] It is therefore argued that the ICC should support the effective running of the WCD, thereby assisting in the development of a strong national judicial system in Uganda.

Can Uganda possibly prosecute members of the LRA with the current state of the criminal justice system? Would the prosecution be seen as shielding members of the LRA from the ICC? With the referral of the conflict to the ICC, Uganda automatically submitted its jurisdiction over members of the LRA to the ICC. But under the Rome Statute it can bring an application to suspend the activities of the court based on challenges to the jurisdiction of the ICC or admissibility of a case.[171] It would be up to the decision of the ICC judges if there are reasonable grounds to believe

164 'MPs Pass ICC Bill' *New Vision* 10 March 2010 http://allafrica.com/stories/201003110195.html (accessed 11 August 2010).

165 ICG 'LRA: A regional strategy beyond killing Kony' *Africa Report* – 28 April 2010 http://www.crisisgroup.org/en/publication-type/media-releases/2010/africa/lra-a-regional-strategy-beyond-killing-kony.aspx (accessed 11 August 2010).

166 The International Criminal Court Act 2010 *Uganda Gazette* 39 CIII, 25 June 2010, assented to on 25th May 2010 http://www.beyondjuba.org/policy_documents/ICC_Act.pdf (accessed 10 November 2010).

167 W Anyol 'Former LRA commander sent to war court' *The New Vision* 6 September 2010 http://www.newvision.co.ug/D/8/13/731176 (accessed 14 September 2010).

168 Art 28 (7) Constitution of Uganda, 1995, provides that '[n]o person shall be charged with or convicted of a criminal offence which is founded on an act or omission that did not at the time it took place constitute a criminal offence'.

169 A Dworkin 'The Uganda-LRA war crimes agreement and the International Criminal Court' 25 February 2008 http://www.crimesofwar.org/onnews/news-uganda2.html (accessed 11 August 2010).

170 W Rist 'Why Uganda's new war crimes court is a victory for the ICC' 29 May 2008 http://jurist.law.pitt.edu/forumy/2008/05/why-ugandas-new-war-crimes-court-is.php (accessed 11 August 2010).

171 Arts 17 & 19 Rome Statute.

that Uganda can hold the LRA accountable for crimes committed in northern Uganda.

The ratification and domestic implementation of the Rome Statute and the setting up of the WCD of the High Court of Uganda should be seen as part of fulfilling Uganda's mandate under the complementarity principle and should be supported by the international community. Under positive complementarity, the OTP can help the WCD by sharing evidence it has on the LRA to help in prosecuting members of the LRA. The court may also adopt a hybrid model of adjudication where its judges and prosecutors collaborate with those at the national level in the adjudication of international crimes.[172] It is further suggested that the WCD should have international judges who should not necessarily be ICC judges. Judges of the WCD can also benefit from the experiences of the ICC as visiting professionals at the seat of the court in The Hague.[173] The Ugandan criminal justice system should make provisions for victims' participation in its proceedings and accord them the same rights as provided under the Rome Statute. The Registrar of the ICC could be supportive in this regard by offering expertise on the experiences of the ICC in relation to the protection of witnesses and their participation in proceedings before the ICC.[174]

4 Conclusion

The ICC and African states need to do more to reassure each other that they are willing and able to work together to end impunity in Africa. The ICC cannot on its own ensure that those who are responsible for international crimes are held accountable. African leaders should know that an era of impunity without accountability is fast becoming a thing of the past.[175] Both the ICC and AU member states would gain form an effective international criminal justice system and national judicial systems capable of holding persons accountable for mass atrocities.[176]

172 Turner (n 34 above) 2.

173 The ICC currently offers visiting professional placements to persons who have extensive academic and/or professional expertise in an area of work relevant to or related to the Court. See 'Visiting Professional Placements' http://www.icc-cpi.int/Menus/ICC/Recruitment/Internships+and+Visiting+professionals/The+Internships+and+Visiting+Professionals+Programme.htm (accessed 11 August 2010).

174 S Arbia 'The Three Year Plans and Strategies of the Registry in respect of complementarity for an effective Rome statute system of international criminal justice' prepared for the Consultative Conference on International Criminal Justice, 9 – 11 September 2009, UN Headquarters, New York, http://www.internationalcriminaljustice.net/experience/papers/session2.pdf (accessed 12 August 2010).

175 O Oko 'The challenges of international criminal prosecutions in Africa' (2007-2008) 31 *Fordham International Law Journal* 343, 412.

176 Jalloh (n 33 above) 445, 452.

The 31 African states that have signed and ratified the Rome Statute did not do so under duress or compulsion but under what could be seen as a genuine effort to tackle human rights atrocities endemic in Africa. The current allegations by African leaders that the ICC prosecutions would destabilise the continent is one that needs to be discussed on its merits.

In proposing positive complementarity in the fight against impunity, it should be noted that the principle of complementarity applies even when the case is before the ICC. There is no difference whether the case before the ICC is by self referral, *proprio motu* or through Security Council referral.[177] The OTP and states could therefore learn from each other in relation to mutual cooperation and assistance. The OTP should maximise the positive complementarity regime offered by both the Rome Statute and Resolution 1593 to co-operate with the AUHIP in its activities in Darfur. Likewise, developments in the DRC and Uganda offer synergies of co-operation that can be maximised by the OTP to ensure that states hold their nationals accountable. According to Judge Sang-Hyun Song, President of the ICC,[178]

> in a national setting, effective positive complementarity requires both a good legal framework and necessary capacity in terms of skills and resources for investigations, prosecutions and trials ... [t]he ICC itself is of course glad to support the strengthening of national capacity by acting as a catalyst and a facilitator where possible.

Through positive complementarity, the OTP will be seen as having a broader role of ending impunity by encouraging national jurisdictions to undertake their own investigations and prosecutions of international crimes.[179] Encouraging states to undertake prosecutions at the national level should not be seen as the only goal or success of positive complementarity. Rather, it should be used primarily by the OTP as a policy tool to maximise the impact of the ICC and this remains subject to the overarching imperative of effective and expeditious justice.[180]

177 R Cryer 'Sudan, Resolution 1593, and international criminal justice' (2006) 19 *Leiden Journal of International Law* 195, 220.

178 ICC 'Keynote remarks by Judge Sang-Hyung Song, President of the International Criminal Court at the ICTJ retreat on complementarity' Greentree Estate, New York, 28 October 2010, http://www.icc-cpi.int/NR/rdonlyres/01E1CD2E-8B10-4E67-83E3-011C499B49B9/282629/101028PresidentSong.pdf (accessed 10 November 2010).

179 Burke-White (n 48 above) 59, 61.

180 Stahn (n 47 above) 87, 109.

CHAPTER 13

IMPLEMENTATION OF THE ROME STATUTE IN MALAWI AND ZAMBIA: PROGRESS, CHALLENGES AND PROSPECTS

*Mwiza Nkhata**

1 Background

The establishment of the International Criminal Court (ICC or the Court) has been hailed as 'the most innovative and exciting development in international law since the creation of the United Nations'.[1] The approval, in July 1998, of the Rome Statute of the International Criminal Court (the Rome Statute or the Statute) by a conference of diplomatic plenipotentiaries has been ranked among 'the most significant events in the global fight against impunity'.[2] As dictated by article 126, the Rome Statute entered into force on 1 July 2002 after the treaty's ratification by 60 state parties.[3] The Court, which is the first permanent, treaty based,

* LL.B (Hons) (Malawi); PGCHE LL.M; LL.D (Pretoria). Lecturer, Faculty of Law, University of Malawi.

1 W Schabas *An introduction to the international criminal court* (2004) 25. Du Plessis and Ford posit that the creation of the ICC has been of enormous practical and symbolic significance and has given institutional form to the vision of ending impunity – M du Plessis & J Ford 'Introduction' in M du Plessis & J Ford (eds) *Unable or unwilling: Case studies on domestic implementation of the ICC Statute in selected African countries* (2008) ISS Monograph Series 141 1. Kreß asserts that 'The establishment in Rome of the ICC in July 1998 constitutes the culmination of a momentous historical development whereby a system to repress crime under general international law was combined with the essentially preventive collective security system under the UN Charter. In future, these two systems have the potential to form two central pillars of a world order defined by peace' – C Kreß 'The International Criminal Court as a turning point in the history of international criminal justice' in A Cassese (ed) *The oxford companion to international criminal justice* (2009) 143.

2 B Murungi 'Implementing the international criminal court statute in Africa: Some reflections' (2001) 7 *East African Journal of Peace and Human Rights* 136. The ICC represents a unique opportunity for addressing impunity but also faces equally unique challenges if it has to fulfill its mission – See P Kastner 'The ICC in Darfur – Saviour or spoiler?' (2007) 14 *ILSA Journal of International and Comparative Law* 145 153-156. See also O Oko 'The challenges of international criminal prosecutions in Africa' (2008) 31 *Fordham International Law Journal* 343.

3 See http://www.icc-cpi.int/Menus/ICC/About+the+Court/ (accessed 16 March 2010).

international criminal court, is based in The Hague and was established, as the Preamble to the Rome Statute indicates, principally to bring an end to impunity for the perpetrators of the most serious crimes of concern to the international community.[4] As of 2010, 114 countries were state parties to the Rome Statute and 31 of these states were African.[5] In light of the preceding, it could be said that over half of the states on the African continent have 'endorsed' the ICC.

A dominant theme that runs through the Rome Statute is that the ICC is created as a court of last resort and will only act to complement domestic jurisdictions.[6] The ICC regime was not designed to replace domestic legal systems.[7] Basically, this means that the Court will not admit a case before it if the matter is already under investigation or being prosecuted in a national jurisdiction – except where the concerned state is unwilling or unable to carry out genuine investigations or prosecutions.[8] This is known as the complementarity principle. The complementarity principle is based not just on the respect for the primary jurisdiction of states with regard to international crimes but also on practical considerations of efficiency and effectiveness.[9] It must be apparent that states will generally have the best access to evidence, witnesses and the resources necessary for the efficacious conduct of proceedings.[10]

It must be noted that while the principle of complementarity allows the ICC to function without unnecessarily antagonising states with respect to the preservation of their sovereignty, it could also be, and arguably already has been, a source of stress and strain between the ICC and state parties. Complementarity requires that state parties properly delineate the parameters within which the complementarity must be exercised. This also means that apart from signing and ratifying the Rome Statute, state parties must domestically determine the particular manner in which they would want to give meaning to the Statute's complementarity regime.

The discussion in this chapter focuses on two countries that are both parties to the Rome Statute – Malawi[11] and Zambia[12] – and attempts to

4 As above.
5 See http://www.icc-cpi.int/Menus/ASP/states+parties/ (accessed 16 March 2010).
6 Para 10 Preamble; art 1 Rome Statute.
7 BC Olugbuo 'Implementing the International Criminal Court Treaty in Africa: The role of non-governmental organisations and government agencies in constitutional reform' in KM Clarke & M Goodale (eds) *Mirrors of justice: Law and power in the post-cold war era* (2010) 106, 124-125.
8 See art 17 Rome Statute.
9 R Cryer *et al An introduction to international criminal law and procedure* (2007) 127.
10 As above.
11 Malawi signed the Rome Statute on 3 March 1999. It deposited its instrument of ratification on 19 September 2002 – http://www.icc-cpi.int/Menus/ASP/states+parties/African+States/Malawi.htm (accessed 16 March 2010).
12 Zambia signed the Rome Statute on 17 July 1998. It deposited its instrument of ratification on 13 November 2002 – http://www.icc-cpi.int/Menus/ASP/states+parties/African+States/Zambia.htm (accessed 16 March 2010).

discern the progress that these two countries have made in implementing the Rome Statute. The chapter also explores the challenges that these countries are facing in implementing the Rome Statute and also provides an indication of the prospects for the domestication of the Statute in these two countries. Having regard to the current prominence of the debate on the Court and Africa, the chapter begins with a brief discussion of the position of Africa with regards to the Court. The chapter then explores the general question on the need for domestication of the Rome Statute before going into a discussion of the progress, challenges and prospects for the domestication of the Statute in the two countries under discussion.

2 Africa and the International Criminal Court

The role of the ICC in Africa has generated much comment and mixed reaction among a broad spectrum of Africans.[13] Considerable bad publicity has marred the relations between Africa and the ICC in recent months. While five of the situations currently under investigation by the Court are all from Africa, it is arguable that a general African animosity towards the Court may have been heightened by the Security Council's referral of the situation in the Darfur to the Court and the subsequent indictment of the Sudanese President Omar Al Bashir. The indictment of the Sudanese President, particularly, has resulted in criticism from some quarters of the ICC as a 'Western tool, designed to subjugate leaders of the African continent and advance an imperialist agenda'.[14] Similarly, the exercise of *proprio motu* powers of the Prosecutor in relation to the Kenyan situation has resulted into much criticism. The three African situations under investigation by the ICC – Uganda, the Democratic Republic of the Congo (DRC) and the Central African Republic (CAR)[15] – have not caused as much uproar, arguably, because these situations are before the ICC as a result of referrals by the state parties concerned.[16]

The current tensions between some African countries and the ICC, unfortunately, have the propensity of undermining and blemishing

13 MJ Adriko 'The obligations of state parties under the Rome Statute' Workshop organised by Uganda Coalition on the International Criminal Court, Entebbe 5-6 September 2008, http://www.apilu.org/Presentation_made_by_Adrilo_Moses_on_the_domestication_of_the_Rome_Statute_in_Africa.pdf (accessed 16 March 2010).

14 Coalition for the International Criminal Court 'Africa and the International Criminal Court' http://coalitionfortheicc.org/documents/Africa_and_the_ICC.pdf (accessed 17 March 2010).

15 See http://www.icc-cpi.int/menus/icc (accessed 9 September 2010). Notably, on 31 March 2010 the Pre-Trial Chamber II granted the prosecution authorisation to open an investigation *proprio motu* in the situation of Kenya - http://www.icc-cpi.int/Menus/ICC/Situations+and+Cases/ (accessed 9 September 2010).

16 These referrals can be made under art 14 of the Rome Statute. Although art 15 of the Rome Statute grants the Prosecutor the ability to initiate investigations on his own, the Office of the Prosecutor has generally encouraged states parties to refer situations for investigation to the Court – 'Paper on some policy issues before the Office of the Prosecutor' http://www.amicc.org/docs/OcampoPolicyPaper9_03.pdf (accessed 16 March 2010).

Africa's involvement in the establishment and subsequent operation of the Court. In the first place, it is important to recall that African states played a central role in the adoption of the Rome Statute.[17] It must be noted in this regard, that African countries were especially active during the negotiations for the establishment of the Court and they made detailed and extensive contributions during the negotiation process.[18] For example, Southern African states, Malawi included, played a very important role in the negotiations leading to the establishment of the ICC.[19] Further, at least 47 African states were represented during the drafting of the Rome Statute and many of the African countries were members of the Like-Minded Group that pushed for the adoption of the Statute.[20] Strikingly, Africa remains the most heavily represented region in the Court's membership, in terms of state party ratification of the Statute.[21] The African involvement in the drafting process, one could plausibly argue, entails that the final product and the framework it creates is as much a product of the African contribution as it is of the other state parties that participated in the drafting. A fact often glossed over is that Africa is also well represented in the Court's hierarchy and by implication, in its operations.[22] It is thus rather erroneous to quickly dismiss the ICC as a Western tool established for imperialistic purposes. Additionally, the widespread ratifications of the Statute by African countries must signify, at the very least, Africa's 'endorsement' of the ICC and the processes that it stands for.[23]

Perhaps the most high-profile manifestation of African countries' unease with the work of the ICC was the adoption by the African Union of a decision whereby members of the AU were urged not to co-operate

17 J Dugard 'Africa and international criminal law: Progress or marginalization?' (2000) 94 *American Society of International Law Proceedings* 229 230.

18 AMICC 'Africa and the International Criminal Court' http://www.amicc.org/docs/Africa%20and%20the%20ICC.pdf (accessed 16 March 2010).

19 BC Olugbuo 'Implementation of the Rome Statute in Africa: An analysis of the South African legislation' (2004) 1 (1) *Eyes on the ICC* 219 220.

20 Coalition for the International Criminal Court (n 14 above).

21 As above.

22 Five of the Court's current judges are African: Fatoumata Dembele Diarra (Mali); Akua Kuenyehia (Ghana); Daniel David Ntanda Nsereko (Uganda); Joyce Aluoch (Kenya); and Sanji Mmasenono Monogeng (Botswana).There are also several Africans that occupy high-level positions at the Court, for example, Deputy Prosecutor Fatou Bensouda (The Gambia), Deputy Registrar Didier Preira (Senegal).

23 Concededly, the dynamics of treaty signature and ratifications in Africa are pretty complex. It is a fact that African states invariably lead in the signing and ratification of international treaties while their compliance with most of the treaties is often abysmal. The reasons for the lack of compliance are multifarious but do not necessarily stem from a lack of will to comply with the treaty obligations. Some states simply do not have the resources and expertise to ensure compliance with the treaties. See C Odinkalu 'Back to the future: The imperative of prioritising for the protection of human rights in Africa' (2003) 47 *Journal of African Law* 1 24.

with the ICC in the execution of the warrant for the arrest of Al Bashir.[24] The precise legal implications of the AU's decision, especially in so far as it affects the obligations of state parties to the Rome Statute, are clearly beyond the scope of the present chapter. Suffice it to note that there is an evident disagreement among AU members themselves on whether to co-operate with the ICC on the Al Bashir Warrant or not.[25] This disagreement has been manifested by statements made on behalf of other countries, for example, South Africa and Botswana, who have indicated that they would, in effect, execute the warrant should Al Bashir be within their territories.[26] This disagreement by African states, this chapter argues, serves to confirm the fact that African countries are duly cognisant of the existence of the ICC and the obligations that the Rome Statute creates for them. The refusal by some states to blindly follow the AU resolution, it is further argued, demonstrates the willingness of some African countries to respect their obligations under the Rome Statute.[27]

Although the indictment of the Sudanese President has invariably inflamed tensions between African countries and the ICC, it is also important to note that the ICC remains highly relevant to Africa. Several reasons have been proffered that justify the relevance of the ICC to Africa, among them are the following:[28] firstly, Africa has had a disproportionate share of conflicts which has invariably also set the stage for the commission of some of the crimes that the Rome Statute addresses. The three situations that have been referred to the ICC by Uganda, DRC and CAR are perfect examples of some of the violations that accompany most conflicts in Africa. The referrals on Uganda and the DRC also exemplify the huge cost that impunity has made the African continent bear. Secondly, and related to the first point, the perpetual prevalence of conflict in some African

24 Decision on the meeting of African state parties to the Rome Statute of the International Criminal Court (ICC) Doc Assembly/AU/13 (XIII) http://www.africa-union.org/root/AU/Conferences/2009/july/summit/decisions/ASSEMBLY%20AU%20DEC%20243%20-%20267%20(XIII)%20_E.PDF (accessed 16 March 2010). Strangely, in 2005 the Prosecutor reported to the Security Council that the Court had, in principle, reached a co-operation agreement with the AU and the agreement had been finalised and only awaited execution – Second Report of the Prosecutor of the International Criminal Court, Mr Luis Moreno Ocampo, to the Security Council Pursuant to UNSC 1593 (2005) 13 December 2005, http://www.icc-cpi.int/NR/rdonlyres/2CFC1123-B4DF-4FEB-BEF4-52E0CAC8AA79/0/LMO_UNSC_ReportB_En.pdf (accessed 16 March 2010).

25 There seems to be a measure of ambivalence in the AU's position with respect to the ICC. Olubguo notes that while one of the key commitments in the AU's Strategic Plan is the ratification of the Rome Statute by all African countries, very little has been done towards the attainment of this goal. As a matter of fact there is no department within the AU that coordinates the drive towards ratification – BC Olugbuo (n 7 above) 128.

26 See, eg, BR Dinokopila 'The prosecution and punishment of international crimes in Botswana' (2009) 7 *Journal of International Criminal Justice* 1077-1085.

27 It was reported that Al Bashir was unable to travel to South Africa for the inauguration of President Jacob Zuma because South Africa had indicated that it would honour its obligations under the Rome Statute and execute the warrant for the arrest of Al Bashir if he had travelled to South Africa; see Institute for Security Studies 'South Africa reaffirms its support for the ICC' http://www.polity.org.za/article/south-africa-reaffirms-its-support-for-the-icc-2009-09-09 (accessed 16 March 2010).

28 AMICC (n 18 above).

countries has tended to weaken the states' capacities to effectively and efficaciously investigate and prosecute the crimes within their own territories. It is also arguable that the three referrals that have been made to the ICC are premised on a candid appreciation of the limitations that the referring states would face if they were to investigate and prosecute the matters themselves. Thirdly, and connected to the second point, it is often the case that in weak states, the competing demands on national resources do not allow for the allocation of sufficient resources to investigate and prosecute the offences in question. The most common deficiencies in this connection are the lack of finances and personnel. Lastly, bearing in mind the fact that the ICC is established as a court of last resort, its relevance for Africa is pronounced in those instances where other means of resolving the conflict have been tried but failed. It is clear, for example, that various reconciliation mechanisms, including amnesties, have been tried and failed in the DRC, CAR and Uganda. It is for such situations that the ICC retains great relevance as an instrument that can bring about an end to impunity.

It must, therefore, be clear from any analysis of the developments surrounding the ICC and Africa that the Court is not necessarily picking on African states for persecution and victimisation in an imperialistic manner. Those that emphasize the fact that the Court is only investigating African situations deliberately fail to concede the fact that the Court is also investigating situations in Colombia, Afghanistan and Georgia, among others.[29] Needless to state that, should the evidence from these investigations meet the necessary threshold, the Court will be obliged to issue warrants and commence prosecutions. Only if the Court fails to proceed in, for example, Afghanistan, Georgia and Colombia, in spite of massive evidence of the commission of the Rome Statute's crimes, would it be plausible to argue that the Court is picking on African Countries. It, therefore, behoves African countries, as active participants in the creation of the edifice that is the International Criminal Court, to continue supporting the Court in all manner possible. It is within this spirit that one must understand the resolution adopted by the African Commission on Human and Peoples' Rights in which it urged member states of the AU (then OAU) to ratify the Rome Statute urgently.[30] It is also important that in its Resolution the African Commission on Human and Peoples' Rights also urged member states of the AU to rapidly incorporate the Rome Statute into their domestic systems.

29 Coalition for the International Criminal Court (n 14 above).
30 ACHPR /Res 59 (XXXI) 02: Resolution on the Ratification of the Statute of on the International Criminal Court by OAU Member States (2002).

3 Is there need for the domestication of the Rome Statute?

Clearly, the crimes that the Rome Statute deals with can be dealt with in any country, irrespective of either the nationality of the perpetrator or where they were committed, under the principle of universal jurisdiction.[31] The framework created by the Rome Statute envisages that state parties will, in the due course of events, domesticate the Statute.[32] The principle of complementarity, which is one of the principles on which the Court's regime is founded, highlights the need for state parties to adopt measures for the domestication of the Statute. At the core of the complementarity principle is the requirement that state parties must, wherever possible, be allowed to deal with all the international crimes within their domestic legal systems.[33] Where the state is unable to deal with the offences within the domestic legal system it must have in place mechanisms and processes that would allow for the arrest and surrender of those suspected of having committed international crimes to the Court.[34] The Court does not, therefore, in any way attempt to usurp the jurisdiction of domestic courts but merely aims to complement them and remains a court of last resort. Domestication, evidently, is an obligation that all state parties assume upon ratifying the Rome Statute.[35]

While African states have been at the forefront in ratifying the Rome Statute, the progress on domestic implementation of the Statute has been rather slow.[36] The result is that while Africa has the highest number of ratifications of the Rome Statue per continent, it also has the least implementing legislation in place.[37] Concededly, draft implementing legislation exists in several African countries but only a few countries have

31 The principle of universal jurisdiction allows a municipal court to exercise jurisdiction over an international crime irrespective of the place where the crime was committed or the nationality of the perpetrator. The national court thus acts as the agent of the international community in the prosecution of an enemy of all mankind in whose punishment all states have an equal interest – *Attorney General of the Government of Israel v Eichmann* 36 ILR 277 298-304. True universal jurisdiction, however, applies only in the case of crimes under customary international law i.e. piracy, slave-trading, war crimes, crimes against humanity, genocide and torture – J Dugard *International law: A South African perspective* (2005)156-157.

32 This understanding clearly informs the entire cooperation regime that the Statute establishes under its Chapter IX.

33 R Cryer *et al* (n 9 above) 127-128.

34 M du Plessis & J Ford 'Overview of the general nature of Rome Statute implementation obligations' in M du Plessis & J Ford (eds) *Unable or unwilling: Case studies on domestic implementation of the ICC Statute in selected African countries* (2008) ISS Monograph Series 141 11.

35 Murungi argues that the obligations that state parties assume under the Rome Statute necessarily require that they adopt implementing legislation in order to fulfil the obligations – BK Murungi (n 2 above) 137.

36 O Bekou & S Shah 'Realising the potential of the International Criminal Court: The African experience' (2006) *Human Rights Law Review* 499 501.

37 BC Olugbuo (n 7 above) 127.

passed domesticating statutes to date.[38] The slow progress on the domestic implementation of the Rome Statute, Dugard claims,[39] may be evidence of a common African pattern. As Dugard further explains, African countries on the one hand, have often played a constructive and progressive role in the development of new norms and institutions at the international level. On the other hand, Africa has noticeably lagged behind in the domestic implementation of these norms and also in the establishment of institutions to support the institutions created at the international level.

While Dugard's argument may have merit, it is important to bear in mind, as Odinkalu argues, that Africa's slow pace of domestication may largely be connected to a lack of capacity in most African states.[40] Bekou and Shah identify three reasons that, supposedly, affect the rate of domestication of the Rome Statute in Africa.[41] Firstly, the authors posit that implementation is slow because the drafting and subsequent passing of implementing legislation is inherently a time-consuming process that may sometimes also depend on the prevailing political will. This has meant that while some countries have come up with draft implementing legislation this has often remained in draft form for what is clearly an inordinate period of time. Secondly, the authors argue that the complexities involved in drafting implementing legislation have also slowed down domestication in some countries. Some countries, it is contended, simply do not have the resources and the expertise to properly engage in the domestication process. In the absence of external help such countries are unlikely to make any significant progress on domestication anytime soon. Thirdly, Bekou and Shah also argue that the delay in domesticating the Statute could simply be because some countries assume that domestication is not necessary because they follow the monist tradition. This perception, however, is not very correct.[42] Needless to state that the subtleties of the Rome Statute and the manner in which monism is applied in practice necessarily require that some steps towards domestication be undertaken even in monist states.

While the general principles of treaty interpretation – notably *pacta sunt*

38 These countries are South Africa, Kenya, Uganda, Senegal, Burkina Faso, Niger and Burundi. Draft domesticating legislation exists in about twenty African countries and the process of adopting it is almost complete in a few of the twenty countries - http://coalitionfortheicc.org/documents/Africa_and_the_ICC.pdf (accessed 17 March 2010).

39 J Dugard (n 17 above) 229.

40 C Odinkalu 'Back to the future: The imperative of prioritising for the protection of human rights in Africa' (2003) 47 *Journal of African Law* 1 24.

41 Bekou & Shah (n 36 above) 502-505.

42 Monism, as Brownlie notes, is represented by a number of jurists whose theories diverge in significant aspects. This, obviously, has implications for the practical application of the doctrine – I Brownlie *Principles of public international law* (2008) 31-33.

servanda[43] – offer persuasive reasons for states to adopt laws domesticating the Rome Statute, the obligation to adopt implementing legislation principally stems, as earlier pointed out, from the Rome Statute itself and there are several reasons specific to the Rome Statute that make it imperative for state parties to domesticate the Statute. Before delving into the factors specific to the Rome Statute that require states to adopt implementing legislation it is important to appreciate some general points about the domestication of the Rome Statute.

Obviously, implementation strategies will vary from one legal system to the other.[44] The big distinction here is between dualist and monist states, but even within dualist states, for example, different strategies may have to be adopted. Some states may decide to merely amend their existing legislation while others may decide to adopt new legislation altogether. Whatever the approach adopted, two points seem to be key to a successful implementation strategy. Firstly, successful domesticating legislation must address all the issues regarding implementation in a manner that deals with the individual state's concerns.[45] This requires that a state's implementing legislation must attempt to reconcile or resolve all the peculiarities of its system with the edifice created by the Rome Statute. A conscious effort must be undertaken to resolve all the existing and potential incompatibilities between provisions of domestic statutes and the Rome Statute. Secondly, the provisions in the Rome Statute provide an indication about the basic requirements that all implementing legislation must comply with. In devising implementing legislation, therefore, a state cannot purport to detract from the standards that are embodied in the Statute; if anything, the state can only attempt to enhance the vibrancy of its implementing regime in line with the ideals of the Statute. The minimum standards that implementing legislation must comply with are those in the Statute itself.

The supervening justification for states to domesticate the Rome Statute emerges from the nature of the system that the Statute creates. One immediately notes that the criminal justice system that is set up by the Rome Statute relies heavily on national legal systems.[46] States parties retain the primary role of investigating and prosecuting all international

43 'Every treaty in force is binding upon the parties to it and must be performed by them in good faith' - art 26 Vienna Convention on the Law of Treaties, 1969, http://untreaty.un.org/ilc/texts/instruments/english/conventions/1_1_1969.pdf (accessed 17 March 2010).

44 Among the common approaches are: the amendment of constitutions and other laws, the adoption of new legislation, the purposive interpretation of the Constitution and other laws – BC Olugbuo 'Domestic implementation of the Rome Statute of the International Criminal Court: A comparative analysis of strategies in Africa' LLM Dissertation, University of Pretoria, https://repository.up.ac.za/upspace/bitstream/2263/1069/1/olugbuo_bc_1.pdf (accessed 29 March 2010).

45 Bekou & Shah (n 36 above) 506.

46 JB Terracino 'National implementation of ICC crimes: Impact on national jurisdictions and the ICC' (2007) 5 *Journal of International Criminal Justice* 421.

crimes within their jurisdiction and the presence of national laws that are adequate both in substance and procedure is crucial to a functional international criminal justice system. To properly achieve this, it is argued, states need to domesticate the Rome Statute.[47] The complementarity that informs almost every aspect of the Court's work cannot be properly achieved if state parties do not domesticate the Rome Statute.

The necessity of domestication can be fully appreciated by analysing a few issues that may arise in the interaction between a state party and the Court. Firstly, since the Court is designed as a court of last resort, most prosecutions must, ideally, still take place in the domestic legal system. The Court, however, only assumes relevance with respect to the crimes listed in article 5 of the Rome Statute and generally only with regard to those that bear the greatest responsibility for the commission of the crimes in issue. This means that the domestic jurisdiction must inevitably deal with all the other perpetrators of crimes whose involvement in the criminal enterprise is not very grave. The domestic jurisdiction, however, cannot properly deal with the matter unless its legal system either already contains definitions about the crimes in article 5 of the Statute or where it has incorporated these offences into its domestic law. Secondly, to apprehend persons for the commission of the offences under the Rome Statute, the offences themselves must be fully recognised in the particular country. Needless to repeat that the Court does not possess a police force and will inevitably rely on its members to effect the arrests; however, these arrests can only be achieved if the offences are recognised in the laws of the state party.[48] Thirdly, and related to the second reason, the entire co-operation regime that the Court so desperately needs to succeed will be emptied of meaning if state parties do not proceed to domesticate the Statute. This is because the domestic framework for co-operation with the ICC in the various states, though building on the provisions in the Statute, must, principally, be constructed by domestic legislation.

In spite of the legal obligations that ratification of a treaty connotes,[49] domestication is critical for complementarity and co-operation between the Court and the state party concerned.[50] To achieve meaningful cooperation under the Statute state parties must, necessarily, domesticate

47 As above, 422.

48 This is also true of the regime for the enforcement and execution of the Court's judgments under Part X of the Statute. The success of the entire regime is dependent on state co-operation and state co-operation will be enhanced with domestication of the Rome Statute.

49 Under art 18 of the Vienna Convention on the Law of Treaties a state must refrain from acts that may defeat the object and purpose of the treaty where it has expressed its consent to be bound by the treaty.

50 See especially arts 86 & 88 Rome Statute.

and fully implement the Rome Statute.[51] State parties must endeavour to provide detail and specifics to the complementarity and co-operation that underlies the entire ICC regime. This can only be achieved by means of a domesticating statute as the Rome Statute itself merely presents the broad parameters within which complementarity and co-operation must be achieved. For African countries, the domestication of the Rome Statute acquires special significance as one of the principles on which the African Union functions is the right of the Union to intervene in a member state if crimes similar to those in article 5 of the Rome Statute are being committed.[52] The commitment to act against genocide, war crimes and crimes against humanity, arguably, is thus already present among African countries. This commitment must, however, be met with consistent action by African states. In the main, domestication of the Rome Statute provides a country with the means by which it can become a part of the broader international criminal justice project and to do so in an orderly fashion.

4 Malawi and the International Criminal Court

Although Malawi has been a party to the Rome Statute since 2002, very little has been done towards the domestication of the Statute. In the following section, the chapter shall chart the progress, challenges and the way forward on the question of the domestication of the Rome Statute in Malawi. This shall be done by analysing the current framework for the prosecution and punishment of international crimes in Malawi. Admittedly, there are numerous issues over which the Malawian framework for prosecuting and punishing international crimes intersects with the Rome Statute's framework. The discussion in this section, however, focuses on the following areas, by way of illustration: sources of law and the place of international law in Malawi; official immunities; the law on extradition and surrender of suspects; and the effect of the bilateral immunity agreement with the United States of America.

4.1 Current framework for prosecuting and punishing international crimes

4.1.1 Sources of criminal law and the place of international law in Malawi

The principal source of criminal law in Malawi remains the Penal Code.[53] The Penal Code is Malawi's most comprehensive catalogue of criminal

51 F Bensouda 'Introduction to the Rome Statute and the role of African countries in the drafting process' Presentation at Workshop on the International Criminal Court: A Rome Statute's implementing legislation for Malawi, 26-27 February 2010, Lilongwe, Malawi.

52 See art 4(h) Constitutive Act of the African Union -http://www.au2002.gov.za/docs/key_oau/au_act.htm (accessed 17 March 2010).

53 Ch 7:01 Laws of Malawi.

offences. Procedurally, the Criminal Procedure and Evidence Code[54] provides for the manner in which all criminal trials in Malawi must be conducted.[55] What is immediately clear is that the regime of criminal law in Malawi, like that of most countries, is territorial in nature. In essence, the criminal law of Malawi only regulates conduct that has been committed in Malawi. Additionally, however, the criminal law of Malawi also regulates conduct that has been committed partly within Malawi and partly outside Malawi where the perpetrator of the conduct happens to be within the jurisdiction.[56]

Ideally, therefore, Malawian courts can try crimes under the Rome Statute should the perpetrator be found in Malawi and where it is proved that the offence was committed in Malawi or partly in Malawi and partly outside Malawi. The preceding, however, presumes that the offences in the Rome Statute are already recognised and legislated for under Malawian law. The actual situation, however, reveals a mixed and somewhat confused picture. Genocide, crimes against humanity and war crimes are not specifically dealt with in any Malawian statute.[57] Concededly, the Constitution does state in section 17 that 'acts of genocide are prohibited and shall be prevented and punished'. Since the adoption of the Constitution, however, no legislation has been adopted to provide further detail to section 17 of the Constitution.[58] Section 17 thus remains a mere exhortatory statement with regard to Malawi's position on genocide. This means that while the prohibition of genocide is recognised in Malawian law there is no framework for dealing with any conduct that may be

54 Ch 8:01 Laws of Malawi.

55 All offences must be tried in accordance with the provisions of the Criminal Procedure and Evidence Code except where a statute exists and provides for a different procedure – sec 6 Criminal Procedure and Evidence Code.

56 Sec 5 Penal Code: 'When an act which, if wholly done within the jurisdiction of the court, would be an offence against this code, is done partly within and partly beyond the jurisdiction, every person who within the jurisdiction does or makes any part of such act may be tried and punished under this code in the same manner as if such act had been done wholly within the jurisdiction.' Sec 66 Criminal Procedure and Evidence Code: 'Every court has authority to cause to be brought before it any person who is in Malawi and is charged with an offence committed within Malawi or partly within and partly beyond Malawi or which according to law may be dealt with by it and to deal with the accused according to its jurisdiction.'

57 Admittedly, Malawi is a party to the Geneva Conventions of 1949 but this is clearly not enough for dealing with the crimes under the Rome Statute – see Geneva Conventions Act Ch 12:03 Laws of Malawi. Under sec 4(1) of the Geneva Conventions Act Malawian courts may exercise universal jurisdiction over grave breaches of the Geneva Conventions but in practice no Malawian court has ever invoked this provisions – FE Kanyongolo *Malawi: Justice sector and the rule of law* (A review by AfriMAP and Open Society Initiative for Southern Africa) (2006) 33.

58 Constitutions normally provide in very general and broad terms. It is left to legislatures to pass specific legislation that gives full meaning to the provisions in a constitution.

classified as genocide.[59]

One may argue that these *lacunae* may be addressed by having recourse to international law, as this is recognised as a source of law in Malawi.[60] While international law is a valid source of law in Malawi, it is important to realise that a blanket recourse to it does not avert the necessity of domesticating the Rome Statute. Malawi is a dualist state and while customary international law, except where it is inconsistent with the Constitution is automatically binding on Malawi, all other treaties require a domesticating statute before they can form part of the laws of Malawi.[61] This means that even though Malawi is a party to the Rome Statute the Statute will not be part of the laws of Malawi until Malawi passes a domesticating statute. It is through the mechanism of a domesticating statute that Malawi would then provide for the specifics about its relationship with the Court. As earlier intimated the multitude of obligations that the Rome Statute creates will only be fully and meaningfully resolved if Malawi domesticates the Rome Statute.

In relation to the sources of criminal law and the place of international law in Malawi *vis-à-vis* the International Criminal Court, the following – to mention but a few – emerge: the Rome Statute is not part of the laws of Malawi – admittedly, Malawi as a state party has the obligation to comply with its provisions – and thus its provisions have no direct applicability before any Malawian court. The crimes that the Rome Statute covers are not, with the partial exclusion of genocide, expressly recognised in Malawi. In the case of the partial recognition of genocide, not only is there no definition in Malawian law of this offence, no procedures exist for the proper handling of this offence should there be a case alleging its commission in Malawi. Although the Constitution mandates Malawian courts to have regard, where applicable, to current norms of public international law and comparable foreign case law in interpreting the

59 As a state party to the Rome Statute one would hope that the definition of genocide in the Statute would be highly persuasive in understanding genocide in Malawi, even in the absence of a definition in Malawian law. Strangely, Malawi is not a party to the Genocide Convention of 1948. For a list of the state parties to the Genocide Convention, see http://treaties.un.org/Pages/ViewDetails.aspx?src=TREATY&mtdsg_no=IV-1&chapter=4&lang=en (accessed 29 March 2010).

60 Sec 211 Constitution of the Republic of Malawi.

61 Sec 211 of the Constitution provides for the application of international law in Malawi. This provision, however, is not free from ambiguity. Practice in Parliament has further confused matters and it is now no longer clear as to how international treaties are to come into force in Malawi. As Kanyongolo notes, poor wording of sec 211 or not, there is no specific legislation in Malawi that sets out the appropriate procedure for incorporation of international law – FE Kanyongolo (n 57 above) 33-34. One hopes that the Malawi Supreme Court of Appeal has clarified the issue in *In the matter of Chifundo James (a female infant)* MSCA Adoption Appeal 28 of 2009 (unreported).

Constitution,[62] this recourse cannot resolve the glaring *lacunae* that we have just pointed out.

4.1.2 The law on official immunities

Official immunities generally provide for exemptions from investigation and prosecution over conduct that would otherwise render one liable to prosecution and investigation. These immunities will often arise as a result of a person's position at the time of the commission of the alleged offence. The office of head of state and most diplomatic and consular positions accord varying degrees of immunity from prosecution and investigation to their holders. The Rome Statute, however, presents a radical departure from the 'traditional' position on immunities. In as far as offences under the Rome Statute are concerned, immunities have been rendered obsolete.[63] The effect is that one cannot raise official immunity as a bar to an investigation or prosecution by the Court.

Article 27 of the Rome Statute – which bars official immunities – has very serious implications for many African countries, especially those that have constitutional provisions guaranteeing immunity to their heads of state. This apparent tension between municipal constitutions' provisions on immunity and the Rome Statute, however, has also been the subject of serious discussion among some European state parties to the Statute.[64] It is notable that, he irrelevance of official capacity as provided in article 27 has been declared to be incompatible with the domestic constitutions of, for example, Belgium,[65] France[66] and Luxembourg.[67] In spite of the tensions that article 27 supposedly generates it is clear that all state parties to the Statute are under an obligation to realign their domestic provisions to give effect to article 27. As will be demonstrated below, the evolving law on official immunities actually supports a limited version of immunity which fundamentally differs from the provisions in most domestic laws.

Having regard to provisions in Malawi's laws that provide for immunity, it will be important to properly reconcile the Rome Statute's position on immunity with local law during the domestication process. For example, under section 91(2) of the Constitution of Malawi, President cannot be charged with any criminal offence during the subsistence of his/

62 Sec 11(2)(c) Constitution of the Republic of Malawi.

63 Art 27 Rome Statute.

64 For a fuller discussion of the positions of some European countries with respect to art 27 of the Statute, see BC Olugbuo (n 44 above) 21-22 & 27-30.

65 See Opinion of the Council of State of 21 April 1999 on a legislative proposal approving the Rome Statute on the International Criminal Court Parliamentary Document 2-239 (1999/2000) 94.

66 See Decision 98-408 DC of 22 January 1999 (Treaty on the Statute of the International Criminal Court) *Journal officiel* 24 January 1999 1317.

67 See Opinion of the Council of State on the draft laws concerning the approval of the Rome Statute on the International Criminal Court 4 May 1999, 44.088.

her term in office. To the credit of the Malawian Constitution, section 91(3) opens the way for holding ex-presidents to account for any acts committed by them outside of their official capacities.[68] Further, under the Immunities and Privileges Act,[69] various protections are offered to consular and diplomatic staff in Malawi. These privileges necessarily mean that persons occupying diplomatic positions may not be brought to account before Malawian courts for actions done by them while in office. It is unlikely, however, that the immunities under the Immunities and Privileges Act cover war crimes, crimes against humanity and genocide.

In relation to immunities, it is important to note that while the Malawian Constitution seems to provide blanket immunities to, for example, the President, emerging international practice recognise a more limited immunity.[70] Emerging jurisprudence strongly suggests two things.[71] Firstly, there can be no immunity with regard to the crimes that the Court deals with. Secondly, immunity is only with regard to the official acts of the person concerned. This means that there can be no immunity with regard to activities that are patently illegal. The fact that international law seems to recognise a more limited version of immunity while the Constitution of Malawi recognises a broader immunity is one of the issues that can only properly be resolved through a domestication statute. On the face of it, the provisions of the Constitution must reign supreme.[72] However, one must recall that international law is only applicable in Malawi if its stipulations do not conflict with any local law.[73] While the Malawian courts will strive to avoid a clash between local law and international law, where such a clash occurs local law will always prevail. Irrespective of the provisions in Malawi's laws it is clear that should, by way of illustration, a former head of state for Malawi find himself before the ICC, such a person will not be allowed to raise his/her immunity for offences under the Rome Statute. In the main the resolution of this issue raises the perennial debate about the superiority of either municipal law or international law, especially when considered from a municipal perspective. It should be stated that each regime retains superiority within its own sphere of influence.[74]

68 Sec 91(3) states thus: 'After a person has vacated the office of President, he or she shall not be personally liable for acts done in an official capacity during his or her term of office but shall not otherwise be immune.'

69 Ch 16:01 Laws of Malawi. The Immunities and Privileges Act also achieves a domestication of the Vienna Convention on Diplomatic Relations of 1961.

70 The turning point in international law seems to be the Treaty of Versailles which lifted the immunity of a head of state for 'a supreme offence against international morality and the sanctity of treaties' – art 227 of the Treaty of Versailles, 1919. For the Treaty of Versailles, see http://net.lib.byu.edu/~rdh7/wwi/versailles.html (accessed 29 March 2010).

71 In *R v Bow Street Metropolitan Stipendiary Magistrate: Ex Parte Pinochet Ugarte (No 3)* [1999] 2 WLR 872; [1999] 2 All ER 97 (HL).

72 Sec 5 Constitution of the Republic of Malawi.

73 *In the matter of Chifundo James* (A female infant) (n 61 above).

74 I Brownlie (n 42 above) 33.

4.1.3 The law regulating extradition and surrender

The ICC has neither a police force nor a prison service. In order to effect arrests of suspects it relies on the co-operation of the state parties to the Rome Statute.[75] Even in the execution of sentences of imprisonment, the ICC relies on state parties to provide the correctional facilities.[76] While by signing and ratifying the Rome Statute state parties have undertaken to co-operate with the Court in the arrest and surrender of all suspects, the actualisation of this co-operation, in most states, requires further clarification. This is largely because most of the state parties already have legislation that details when they can conduct an extradition and at whose request it may be processed. Clearly, while the practice of extraditing offenders is not novel it is the surrender to the ICC that presents its own unique challenges.

In Malawi the extradition of offenders is regulated by the Extradition Act.[77] This Act outlines the procedures that must be followed in the event there is a request for the extradition of an offender. Several features of the Extradition Act actually bring out the need for an Act to domesticate the Rome Statute in Malawi. Firstly, although the Extradition Act does allow for the surrender of offenders outside of Malawi, it is notable that the Act proceeds on the presumption that a request for the surrender must have been made by a government. This necessarily means that a request for the surrender of a fugitive from the ICC would not fall for resolution within the Act's framework. Secondly, Malawi's co-operation for the purposes of the Extradition Act is only extended to countries that are referred to, under the Act, as 'designated countries.'[78] The Extradition (Designated Countries) Order, made under the Extradition Act, lists down all the countries with which Malawi has entered into extradition arrangements. Needless to state, the ICC is not among the countries listed in the Order. Even though the Minister may enter into arrangements the result of which would be the extension of the countries on the list, it is worth noting that the Act supposes that such an arrangement can only be made with another country and not an international organisation.[79] Thirdly, the Extradition Act also presupposes that one would be extradited only where the offence concerned is also an offence not only in the country where the offender is sought to be extradited but also under the laws of Malawi.[80] Having regard to the fact that war crimes, genocide and crimes against humanity have yet to be specifically legislated for in Malawi it is difficult to imagine how

75 See eg art 89 Rome Statute.
76 See art 103 Rome Statute.
77 Ch 8:03 of the Laws of Malawi.
78 A designated country is basically a country with which Malawi has entered into an extradition agreement.
79 Sec 3 Extradition Act.
80 Sec 5 Extradition Act.

Malawi could co-operate with the Court on requests for extradition and surrender.

The discord between Malawi's extradition law and its obligations under the Rome Statute makes it imperative for the country not only to domesticate the Statute but also to synchronise its law on extradition with its obligations under the Statute. Such a deliberate act would harmonise Malawi's laws with its obligations under the Rome Statute and thus give greater meaning to the complementarity and co-operation that underlie the Statute. A 'quick-fix' solution to the problem would be to effect amendments to the Extradition Act so that the ICC would be brought within the aegis of the Act. However, having regard to the enormity of the issues which the extradition arrangement with the ICC must cover it is advisable that this issue be comprehensively addressed in domesticating legislation. As matters stand, there is a chasm between Malawi's obligations under the Statute and the manner in which these ought to be fulfilled in practice.[81] An innovative way to circumvent the problem is to acknowledge the 'qualitative difference' between extradition and 'surrender'.[82] The Rome Statute supports the concept of surrender and not extradition. Technically, therefore, states that 'surrender' suspects to the ICC may not be held to contravene their own domestic laws barring extradition of suspects.

4.1.3 Effect of the bilateral immunity agreements with the USA

Although the United States of America (USA) signed the Rome Statute in 2000 it subsequently 'unsigned' the treaty.[83] This means that the USA is not a party to the Rome Statute. In spite of this, the USA has been, since the Rome Statute entered into force, actively courting state parties, and even non-state parties, to the Rome Statute and negotiating bilateral immunity agreements supposedly under the aegis of article 98 of the Rome Statute.[84] The effect of these bilateral immunity agreements, which are

81 Complications that may arise as a result of such a gap have already been manifested in Malawi. In 2003 Malawi arrested suspected Al Qaeda terrorists and surrendered them to the USA without following proper procedures. The government proceeded to co-operate with the Americans on the surrender of the suspects even though the suspects' lawyers had applied for and been granted bail by the High Court. By the time the High Court granted bail the suspects were already out of the country – see 'Arrest of terror suspects sparks religious animosity' http://www.newsfromafrica.org/newsfromafrica/articles/art_1036.html (accessed 29 March 2010) and 'Malawi terror suspects in Sudan' http://news.bbc.co.uk/2/hi/africa/3092973.stm (accessed 29 March 2010).

82 BC Olugbuo (n 19 above) 224.

83 http://www.iccnow.org/?mod=usaicc (accessed 22 March 2010).

84 For most developing countries aid incentives have been used by the USA to secure their signatures for the bilateral immunity agreement. Strangely, the USA has threatened and in some cases cancelled proposed aid because countries were slow to sign up to the bilateral immunity agreements. This is strange because withholding aid actually reduces the capacity of the concerned state to contribute in the global fight against terror – DH Cotton & GO Odongo 'The magnificent seven: Africa's response to US article 98' (2007) 7 *African Human Rights Law Journal* 1 5-8.

either reciprocal or non-reciprocal, is to effectively remove USA citizens and military personnel from the jurisdiction of the ICC. The agreements prohibit the surrender to the ICC of a broad scope of persons including current or former government officials, military personnel and US employees including contractors and nationals. Notably, these bilateral immunity agreements do not include an obligation to subject the persons concerned to investigation and prosecution should a state surrender them to the USA and not the ICC. Malawi, it must be stated, entered into a bilateral agreement with the USA in September 2003.[85]

The precise effect of the bilateral immunity agreements remains hotly contested. From the American perspective, the agreements are framed within the principle of complementarity on which the ICC is founded. The underlying assumption seems to be that the USA would want to retain primary jurisdiction over all its citizens with respect to crimes under the Statute irrespective of where the offences were committed. The other perspective, however, argues that the bilateral immunity agreements are contrary to international law and the Rome Statute itself.[86] It remains to be seen how Malawi will marry its obligations under the Rome Statute with those that it has undertaken under the bilateral immunity agreement. Again, the direction that the country will take on the matter will best be manifested in the provisions of legislation that domesticates the Rome Statute.

Importantly, however, the fact that a country has entered into a bilateral immunity agreement with the USA does not mean that such a country cannot adopt domesticating legislation. It then becomes a matter for the domesticating state to balance the obligations that it has under the two instruments in a manner that does not defeat the purpose of either instrument. Therein lies the potential conflict between the bilateral immunity agreements and the Rome Statute. The only emerging solace at present seems to be that the position of the USA on the Rome Statute may be changing and the protection of USA citizens under the bilateral immunity agreements may, in future, be limited to acts done by USA citizens in their official capacities.

85 http://www.ll.georgetown.edu/guides/documents/Malawi03-131.pdf (accessed 22 March 2010). The agreement between Malawi and the USA is rather in the form of an executive agreement, it may nevertheless fall under the definition of a treaty under art 2 of the Vienna Convention on the Law of Treaties.

86 From this perspective it is generally argued that the bilateral immunity agreements seriously threaten the existence and effectiveness of the court – DDN Nsereko 'Triggering the jurisdiction of the International Criminal Court' (2004) 4 *African Human Rights Law Journal* 256 262.

4.2 Existing challenges and the way forward

In as far as Malawi's obligations under the Rome Statute are concerned, the biggest challenge remains the lack of implementing legislation. It is hard to imagine how Malawi can effectively give meaning to both the complementarity and co-operation principles under the Rome Statute without legislation that defines how this must be achieved. For example, as earlier highlighted, Malawi's provisions on extradition and official immunities are not in line with the Rome Statute. These inconsistencies necessarily mean that there would be serious conflicts and contradiction should, for example, there be a need for Malawi to surrender a suspect to the ICC.[87] Needless to state that at the moment there would be no 'basis' for Malawi to surrender any suspect to the ICC. Under the current framework any attempted surrender may be challenged for illegality. The need to harmonise the immunity regime under the Statute with domestic legislation also offers another compelling reason why Malawi must take deliberate steps to domesticate the Rome Statute.

On a positive note, it is encouraging to learn that Malawi has expressed its commitment to the adoption of legislation domesticating the Rome Statute.[88] The country recognises that the promulgation of implementing legislation is an essential step in the process of co-operation and complementing the work of the ICC.[89] Perhaps unwittingly, Malawi's assumption of the Chairmanship of the African Union (AU) in 2010 has thrust its position on the Rome Statute into the limelight. It is arguably in this vein that Malawi's Deputy-Minister of Foreign Affairs stated that Malawi, as Chair of the AU, will lead by example in domesticating the Rome Statute.[90] Domesticating the Rome Statute will be Malawi's clearest statement of its intention to be part of the global community that is

87 The lack of Rome Statute implementing legislation brings to mind the dilemma that Malawi once faced when a hijacked plane was landed at Chileka Airport in Blantyre when the country had no legislation on hijacking. The result was that the offenders were tried on a series of other 'lesser' offences, eg, demanding property with menaces with intent to steal the same, wrongful confinement of people and being in possession of explosives without permit – see *Republic v Kamil & Yaghi* 1971-72 ALR Mal 358. Such a situation must not be allowed to happen again.

88 Keynote address by Honourable AG Mtendere, Deputy Minister of Foreign Affairs on behalf of A Peter Mutharika, Minister of Justice and Constitutional Affairs during the opening of the Workshop on the International Criminal Court and implementing legislation for Malawi, 26-27 February 2010, Lilongwe, Malawi. Rather dishearteningly is the fact that it has been reported that Malawi indicated it had commenced the process of enacting cooperating legislation in 2002 - http://coalitionfortheicc.org/documents/ICCAfrica_Issue1_Jun06_en.pdf (accessed 25 March 2010).

89 As above.

90 Keynote address by Honourable AG Mtendere. The Malawi Law Society has also recommended that government should adopt a clear strategy to ensure a timely adoption of the implementing legislation. See also International Bar Association 'Legal profession of African Union's new Chair stands firm on commitment to the adoption of Rome Statute implementing legislation' http://www.ibanet.org/Article/Detail.aspx?ArticleUid=26B7E703-E35E-40EC-90F0-8F4B8F352774 (accessed 23 March 2010).

committed to fighting impunity. It remains to be seen how expediently Malawi will match its verbal commitment with concrete action.

As Malawi contemplates the domestication of the Rome Statute it is important to realise that the process of domestication itself may, admittedly, be long and tedious. It is a process in which a deliberate attempt to involve all stakeholders must consciously be undertaken, especially having regard to the need to synchronise the subtleties of the Rome Statute with domestic law. This process must build on existing foundations and progress already made to further clarify the complementarity and co-operation between Malawi and the Court. For example, a determination will have to be made whether to incorporate article 5 of the Rome Statute in the domesticating statute to be passed or include this in the Penal Code. It is worth noting that the amended Penal Code has already attempted to include some elements of the crimes under the Rome Statute and for this reason it may be sensible to keep all the crimes under the Penal Code while reserving all other issues for the implementing legislation.[91]

Related to the above, to properly involve all stakeholders in the drafting of implementing legislation there is the obvious need of harnessing the full potential of civil society in the country. Civil society's network across the country ought to be utilised to galvanise a broad-based discussion over all issues pertaining to the Rome Statute and Malawi. This would help confer legitimacy on the entire process of domestication. It is important to note, as Dugard has argued, that some of the animosity in Africa about the ICC may be as a result of a failure by civil society to generate awareness about the Court and the need to pass domesticating legislation.[92] It is thus incumbent on the government of Malawi to take deliberate steps to engage all stakeholders in the process of crafting implementing legislation.

5 Zambia and the International Criminal Court

Largely as a result of a common colonial history, Zambia's legal system bears significant similarities to that of Malawi. This means that Zambia faces challenges that are broadly similar to Malawi in domesticating the Rome Statute. Most of the general points that were made in connection with Malawi are thus relevant for Zambia as well. These two countries, however, have not made similar progress on the implementation of the Rome Statute and in the following section the chapter will discuss the

91 The Malawi Law Commission completed its review of the Penal Code in 2000. The recommendations have yet to be passed by parliament and may, in the light of the passage of time, have to be reviewed again before parliament can enact them – Malawi Law Commission *Report on the review of the Penal Code* (2000).

92 J Dugard (n 17 above) 229 230.

progress, prospects and challenges to the domestication of the Rome Statute in Zambia. A similar thematic emphasis to that adopted for the discussion on Malawi shall be followed.

5.1 Current framework for prosecuting and punishing international crimes

5.1.1 Sources of criminal law and the place of international law in Zambia

As is the case in Malawi, the Zambian Penal Code Act[93] is the country's most comprehensive catalogue of prohibited conduct in the country. It outlines all the offences for which one is liable to be arrested and tried in Zambian courts. The jurisdiction of Zambian courts, for the purposes of the offences under the Penal Code Act, is limited by Zambia's territorial reach.[94]

Again, as is the case in Malawi, even though the Penal Code's reach is, strictly speaking territorial, it also applies to regulate criminal conduct that is committed partly within Zambia and partly outside of Zambia.[95] Furthermore, if a citizen of Zambia engages in conduct outside Zambia which would be against the Penal Code Act if committed in Zambia, he or she is dealt with as if the conduct had been perpetrated in Zambia.[96] Notably, the Zambian Penal Code Act does not legislate for any of the crimes covered under the Rome Statute. Arguably, there are offences under the Penal Code Act that bear slight resemblances to the offences under the Rome Statute. Among these offences would be, firstly, the prohibition of the promotion of tribal war under section 46 of the Penal Code Act. The second is the prohibition towards the demonstration of hatred, ridicule or contempt for persons because of their race, tribe, place of origin or colour in section 70 of the Penal Code Act. However, although one may be persuaded to include these offences under the umbrella of war crimes and crimes against humanity, respectively, it is worth noting that the severity which offences need to attain before they fall under the Rome Statute is absent in the above offences as codified in Zambia. For example, under section 70 of the Penal Code Act the offence is punishable with only two years imprisonment upon conviction. This means that the offence is clearly treated as a misdemeanor.[97] This lack of severity, it is argued, would generally remove the offences from the ambit of the International Criminal Court.

93 Ch 87 Laws of Zambia.
94 Sec 5 Penal Code Act, Ch 87 Laws of Zambia.
95 Sec 6(2) Penal Code Act.
96 Sec 6(1) Penal Code Act.
97 See sec 4 Penal Code Act.

The procedure for the trial of all offences under the Penal Code Act is outlined in the Criminal Procedure Code Act.[98] Section 3 of the Criminal Procedure Code Act confirms that all offences under the Penal Code Act, unless the contrary is stipulated, can be tried by the High Court of Zambia.[99] The provisions of Part IV of the Criminal Procedure Code also confirm the territorial limits of the jurisdiction of the courts of Zambia. Under section 65 of the Code it is the presence of an accused person within the jurisdiction of a court after having committed an offence within Zambia which makes one liable to the jurisdiction of Zambian courts. Although the Criminal Procedure Code Act provides extensive detail about how criminal trials in Zambia must be conducted, just as is the case in Malawi, the challenge is that the Rome Statute offences are not formally codified in any Zambian statute. This means that there is a grave *lacuna* in terms of how Zambia would deal with Rome Statute crimes should there be an allegation that these have been committed in Zambia. This would, obviously, affect Zambia's compliance with its obligations, as a state party, under the Rome Statute.

Again, one may argue that Zambia could address these *lacuna* by relying on international law and the principle of universal jurisdiction. Although this may appear an innovative way of surmounting this legislative gap, the same complications that the chapter highlighted in the case of Malawi are also largely applicable here. Zambia, it must be recalled, is also a dualist state. This means that the Rome Statute and its provisions will not become part of the laws of Zambia until a domesticating statute has been passed. In the absence of a domesticating statute, notably, Zambia still has obligations under the Rome Statute but the Statute does not have the force of domestic law in the country. Domestically, therefore, the provisions of the Rome Statute are practically irrelevant before the Zambian courts. The point to highlight here is that for a state to properly fulfil its obligations under the Rome Statute it needs to domesticate the Rome Statute. Without domestication, the concerned state will find many of its domestic laws at odds with provisions in the Rome Statute in many aspects.

5.1.2 Law on official immunities

Zambia, just like Malawi, will also have to conduct a proper review of its laws on official immunities if it is to properly fulfil its obligations under the Rome Statute. The Zambian Constitution provides for the immunity of the person holding the office of President even though this is not in the same breadth as in Malawi.[100] The Zambian Constitution, seemingly, recognises that this immunity is not absolute. Although no civil or criminal

98 Ch 88 Laws of Zambia.
99 See also sec 5 Criminal Procedure Code Act.
100 See sec 43 Constitution of Zambia.

proceedings may be commenced against a sitting President, the National Assembly can by resolution allow proceedings to proceed against a former President where it determines that such proceedings are not contrary to the interests of the state.[101] This in essence means that the Zambian National Assembly can waive the immunity that normally attaches to the office of the President. It is under the preceding arrangement that the Zambian National Assembly proceeded to lift the immunity of the former head of state, Frederick Chiluba, paving the way for his trial on corruption charges.[102]

Further immunities in Zambian law are provided in the Diplomatic Immunities and Privileges Act.[103] As the short title to this Act indicates, this is an Act that is meant to give effect to the Vienna Convention on Diplomatic Relations and to provide for the immunities, privileges and capacities of certain organisations and persons. In furtherance of the preceding purpose the Act lists the provisions of the Vienna Convention on Diplomatic Relations which have the force of law in Zambia.[104] The Diplomatic Immunities and Privileges Act generally protects all diplomatic agents and diplomatic premises from interference by the law enforcement agencies of Zambia.

In spite of Zambia's extensive provisions on official immunity, one must realise that by signing up to the Rome Statute, Zambia has contracted to comply with a regime that, in essence, makes irrelevant all the elaborate provisions on official immunity. This is particularly true where the people sought to be conferred with the immunity are suspected of committing the offences listed in the Rome Statute. It is largely as a result of such inconsistencies that the need to properly domesticate the Rome Statute arises. Through the mechanism of domestication Zambia would then take a conscious effort to properly resolve this manifest inconsistency between provisions of its local law and its obligations under the Statute. While Zambia, like Malawi, may be stalling in harmonising its laws on official immunities, it is important to recognise that should a Zambian national be charged with Rome Statute offences, such a national would not be able to raise the immunity provided in local law as a defence.

5.1.3 The law regulating extradition and surrender

As highlighted earlier in the chapter, the ICC relies on state parties to effect arrests and also facilitate the surrender of suspects to it for the purposes of

101 Sec 43(3) Constitution of Zambia.

102 The Zambian National Assembly removed former President F Chiluba's immunity in 2002. He was subsequently tried and acquitted of corruption charges. See, 'Zambians jubilate over lifting of Chiluba's immunity' at http://www.encyclopedia.com/doc/1P2-13314964.html (accessed 25 March 2010).

103 Ch 20 of the Laws of Zambia.

104 Sec 3(1) and the First Schedule to the Diplomatic Immunities and Privileges Act.

trial. While the Rome Statute itself has elaborate provisions regulating how the Court must co-operate with state parties for the purposes of the surrender of suspects, most of the states parties in Africa have yet to realign their local laws to comply with the Statute. Zambia is one such state.

The principal statute which regulates the extradition and surrender of suspects in Zambia is the Extradition Act.[105] It is clear from a reading of the Act that the extradition that the Act seeks to regulate is between Zambia and other countries and that no provision is made for the processing of extradition requests from an international organisation.[106] Further, the Extradition Act necessarily requires that the conduct for which extradition is sought be criminal both in Zambia and the requesting state.[107] The provisions of the Extradition Act are, arguably, supplemented by the Mutual Legal Assistance in Criminal Matters Act.[108] This piece of legislation, according to its long title, is meant to provide for the implementation of treaties of mutual legal assistance in criminal matters. Under the Act, legal assistance in criminal matters is rendered by Zambia to the countries listed in the Order made by the Minister under section 5. The ICC is not listed in the Order.[109] While the Mutual Legal Assistance in Criminal Matters Act may supplement the provisions and procedures under the Extradition Act, it is important to note that nothing in the Mutual Legal Assistance in Criminal Matters Act can be interpreted to authorise the extradition or arrest or detention with a view to extradition of any person.[110] This means that for purposes of extradition and surrender the principal framework remains that in the Extradition Act.

The above position highlights several complications that are likely to arise should there be an immediate need for Zambia to honour a request to surrender a suspect to the ICC. In the first place, the fact that there is no formal framework for co-operation between Zambia and the Court would create delays and complexities before Zambia could honour such a request. In the absence of such a framework Zambia would have to either quickly enact domesticating legislation or negotiate an *ad hoc* co-operation agreement with the Court. In the second place, the entire regime for extradition of offenders in Zambia is practically irrelevant in as far as co-operating with the ICC is concerned. The ICC is not among the entities that the Act recognises as deserving co-operation under the Act and neither

105 Ch 94 of the Laws of Zambia.
106 The countries with which Zambia can co-operate with for extradition purposes are broadly divided into commonwealth countries and foreign countries and there is the explicit assumption that the extradition arrangement will convey reciprocal obligations and benefits – see, generally, secs 3 & 45 of the Act. Again an innovative way to look at the issue is to think of Zambia as 'surrendering' suspects under the aegis of the Rome Statute rather than extraditing under its own laws.
107 Sec 4 of the Act; sec 17 Extradition Act.
108 Ch 98 Laws of Zambia.
109 See The Mutual Legal Assistance in Criminal Matters (Specified States) Order, Statutory Instrument 95 of 1996.
110 Sec 4(2) Mutual Legal Assistance in Criminal Matters Act.

would the offences under the Rome Statute meet the requirements under the Act – strictly speaking, the crimes in the Rome Statute have not been domestically recognised as criminal offences under Zambian law. This would mean that since the conduct for which extradition is sought is not criminal in Zambia, co-operation would not necessarily be forthcoming. Such complexities, among others, again, highlight the need for the adoption of a domesticating statute that would properly clarify all issues relating to the co-operation between Zambia and the ICC.

5.1.4 Effect of bilateral immunity agreements with the USA

Like Malawi and many other countries, Zambia signed a bilateral immunity agreement with the USA.[111] The situation with regard to Zambia's obligations under the Rome Statute closely mirrors that of Malawi. There is a pressing need for Zambia to deliberately reconcile its obligations under the bilateral immunity agreement with its obligations under the Rome Statute. Again, the best mechanism for achieving this would be the passing of a domesticating statute which outlines all of Zambia's obligations under the Statute in clear detail.

5.2 Existing challenges and the way forward

Zambia signed the Rome Statute on 17 July 1998 and it deposited its instrument of ratification on 13 November 2002.[112] In August 2004 at a workshop on the implementation of the Rome Statute, the Zambian Minister of Justice, George Kunda, intimated that Zambia had began the process of reviewing its laws in preparation of passing implementing legislation.[113] Not much progress, however, was made in the time after that ministerial commitment. In 2006 during a workshop organised by the Coalition for the International Criminal Court and Zambia's national coalition, the then Minister of Justice again pledged to start the implementation process.[114] The subsequent Presidential and Parliamentary Elections, allegedly, slowed down the process. It is now alleged that Zambia has some form of draft implementing legislation in the pipeline.[115]

111 Zambia signed the agreement on 1 July 2003, http://www.iccnow.org/?mod=country&iduct=192 (accessed 25 March 2010).

112 http://www.icc-cpi.int/Menus/ASP/states+parties/African+States/Zambia.htm (accessed 23 March 2010).

113 Coalition for the International Criminal Court *ICC-Africa* 5 http://coalitionfortheicc.org/documents/ICCAfrica_Issue1_Jun06_en.pdf (accessed 23 March 2010).

114 http://www.iccnow.org/?mod=country&iduct=192 (accessed 26 March 2010).

115 http://asiapacific.amnesty.org/library/Index/ENGIOR400412006?open&of=ENG-385 (accessed 23 March 2010). It is more likely, however, that the process of preparing implementing legislation in Zambia is still in its very early stages and what currently exists might be no more than White Paper within the Attorney-General's office – Interview with Prof M Hansungule, 26 March 2010.

Having draft legislation in place can be equated to a serious manifestation of intent to comply with the Rome Statute. As pointed out in the case of Malawi, the process of coming up with draft implementing legislation and finally passing it into law can be long and tedious and so it seems to be the case with Zambia. While Zambia must be commended for initiating the process of coming up with the draft legislation, it needs to take the final step and transform the draft into binding legislation before it can fully comply with its obligations under the Rome Statute. Only when this legislation is in force can it be said that Zambia has properly aligned itself to fulfil its obligations under the Rome Statute. This would also properly align Zambia to co-operate with the Court in line with the Statute while at the same time allowing the Court to complement Zambia's efforts towards eradicating impunity.

In the process of pushing for the final adoption of the Rome Statute implementing legislation, Zambia ought to fully utilise the potential of civil society. This would enable, not only for there to be widespread sensitisation of the legal regime that Zambia has decided to subject itself to, but would also ensure that there is a broad-based consultation on the issues concerned. A thorough consultation on the draft legislation would, in the event the legislation is used to extradite Zambian nationals in future, for example, lessen the animosity that the populace in Zambia would have towards the court.

6 Conclusion

From the discussion in this chapter it must have emerged quite clearly that states must move beyond mere ratification and take concrete steps towards domestication of the Rome Statute if they have to properly fulfil their obligations under the Statute. The case for domestication of the Rome Statute, as was demonstrated earlier in the chapter, is highly compelling and flows, principally, from a state party's signature and/or ratification of the Statute. For all those states that have signed and/or ratified the Rome Statute domestication must come as a matter of course.

The situation in both Malawi and Zambia exemplifies the numerous huddles that state parties that have signed and/or ratified the Rome Statute, but not domesticated it, are likely to find themselves in. It is immaterial that there may not immediately be suspected war criminals or genocidaires in the two countries under discussion. Should, for example, an instance arise where either Malawi and Zambia are required to surrender a suspect to the ICC, myriad issues would arise that would complicate any purported surrender. As a matter of fact, any surrender of suspects and many other forms of co-operation with the ICC in Zambia and Malawi, at the current state of law, are likely to be challenged for legality. In all this, it must be constantly recalled that the efficacy and vibrancy of the ICC is dependent on the enthusiasm of states in implementing the Statute's provisions in domestic law. It is for this reason that Malawi and Zambia both need to take urgent steps to domesticate the Rome Statute.

CHAPTER

14 IMPLEMENTATION OF THE ROME STATUTE IN SOUTH AFRICA

*Lee Stone**

1 Introduction

South Africa has always been a fervent supporter of a permanent international criminal court. From the commencement of the negotiations towards the Rome Statute establishing the International Criminal Court, South Africa assumed a leadership role and was influential in drafting the Rome Statute.[1] Since 1993 South Africa had participated in efforts to establish the ICC when the International Law Commission (ILC) had presented a draft statute to the General Assembly's Sixth Committee for consideration. Subsequently, South Africa was frequently invited to participate in the meetings of the bureau of the conference and was thus a member of the Drafting Committee of the Rome Conference and co-ordinated the formulation of significant parts of the Rome Statute, including part 4.[2]

South Africa's prominent position within the Southern African Development Community (SADC) was also apparent during the negotiation, ratification and implementation of the Rome Statute. SADC's consultative meetings were held between 1995 and 1997 to explore the benefits and implications of establishing an ICC. Thereafter, a conference of SADC member states was held from the 5 to 9 July 1999 in Pretoria, South Africa. During this conference, a Model Enabling Act, Ratification

* LL.B (Free State); LL.M (Pretoria); Diploma in the Justiciability of Socio-Economic and Cultural Rights (Åbo); Attorney of the High Court of South Africa and Senior Lecturer, Faculty of Law, Howard College Campus, University of KwaZulu-Natal, Durban.

1 M du Plessis 'International criminal courts, the International Criminal Court, and South Africa's implementation of the Rome Statute' in J Dugard *International law: A South African perspective* (2006) 177. See also C Blair and M du Plessis 'Africa's obstruction of justice' http://www.guardian.co.uk/commentisfree/2009/jul/18/darfur-bashir-african-union-icc (accessed 18 December 2009).

2 H Jallow & F Bensouda 'International criminal law in an African context' in M du Plessis (ed) *African guide to international criminal law* (2008) Institute for Security Studies 43.

Kit, was adopted.[3] If one looks at the scheme of South Africa's implementing legislation, it is clear that this Model Enabling Act informed South Africa's own implementing legislation. Moreover, South Africa's implementing legislation serves as a model for other African states, both in terms of substance and procedure.[4]

South Africa signed the Rome Statute on 17 July 1998 and ratified it on 27 September 2000, becoming the 23rd state party. Within South Africa, an inter-departmental committee was established to determine whether the Rome Statute was constitutional and could thus be domesticated. Finding the Rome Statute constitutional, an explanatory memorandum was attached to the Rome Statute and it was submitted to Cabinet and then to Parliament. This implementing legislation, referred to as 'Implementation of the Rome Statute of the International Criminal Court Act 27 of 2002' (ICC Act) was signed into law in August 2002.

South Africa's endorsement of the ICC is thus beyond question, subject of course, to the proviso that a State Party should be afforded the first opportunity to see that justice is served. This is in accordance with the understanding that international criminal law is intended to be enforced and international crimes are supposed to be prosecuted at the domestic level since domestic prosecutions are seen to have more legitimacy than international prosecutions of international crimes.[5] It is not surprising, therefore, that South Africa is admired for its conscientious approach to upholding principles of international criminal law, the rule of law and ending impunity.

South Africa has not signed the Agreement on Privileges and Immunities and the public has rejected signing a Bilateral Immunity Agreement with the USA. By ratifying the Rome Statute and incorporating its provisions, South Africa has illustrated its political willingness to pursue national prosecutions if and when necessary.[6] In this regard, the Preamble to the ICC Act affirms South Africa's commitment to bring 'persons who commit such atrocities to justice ... in a court of law of the Republic in terms of its domestic law where possible'. By virtue of the process of implementing the Rome Statute domestically, South Africa has also set an example to other African States,[7] albeit that South Africa's rather ambiguous relationship concerning the indictment of Sudanese

3 See the ICC Ratification Kit – Model Enabling Act www.radicalparty.org/tribunal/ICC_southafrica_model.htm (accessed 18 December 2009).

4 A Katz 'An act of transformation: The incorporation of the Rome Statute of the ICC into national law in South Africa' (2003) 12 *African Security Review* 27.

5 Cryer *et al An introduction to international criminal law and procedure* (2009) 54.

6 A Marschik 'The politics of prosecution: European national approaches to war crimes' in TLH McCormack & GJ Simpson (eds) *The law of war crimes* (1997) 100.

7 M du Plessis 'South Africa's implementation of the ICC Statute: An African example' (2007) 5 *Journal of International Criminal Justice* 461.

President Omar Al Bashir has served to impair South Africa's reputation as an ardent adherent to the rules of international law to some extent.

Prior to the ICC Act, South Africa had no municipal legislation on the subject of war crimes or crimes against humanity. The principle of *nullum crimen sine lege* would most probably have constituted an impediment to the prosecution of international crimes recognised by customary international law in South African domestic courts[8] as prosecutions are unlawful and invalid in the absence of domestic legislation specifically penalising conduct amounting to grave breaches of customary international law.[9] Therefore, the ICC Act ensures that the jurisdiction of South African courts to prosecute ICC crimes is not inhibited and that the South African government co-operates with the court.

Impetus has been given to South Africa's ability to investigate and prosecute international crimes by virtue of the establishment of the Priority Crimes Litigation Unit (also known as the Hawks), which is dedicated entirely to ensuring the effectiveness of South Africa's implementing legislation. Accordingly, ICC legislation gives South African authorities the power to investigate and prosecute acts of genocide, crimes against humanity and war crimes, no matter where those acts have been committed. This applies even if the perpetrators are not South African nationals. In order to give meaningful effect to the Rome Statute, the ICC Act has three aims: First, it intends to do justice to the complementarity scheme built into the Rome Statute whereby states are expected to prosecute individuals within their national jurisdictions for crimes the ICC ultimately has jurisdiction over. Secondly, it endeavours to ensure that South Africa is able to co-operate fully with the ICC, and thirdly, it enacts into South African domestic law the substantive offences the ICC may assert jurisdiction over, being the core crimes of genocide, crimes against humanity, and war crimes.[10]

2 The domestication of the Rome Statute in South Africa

The South African government prioritised the domestication of the Rome Statute in South Africa. The procedural prescripts for such domestication were complied without any delay. In this regard, an inter-departmental committee was established to determine whether the Rome Statute is

8 Du Plessis (n 1 above) 196.
9 See *S v Basson* 2007 (3) SA 582 (CC) where the court found it unnecessary 'to consider whether customary international law could be used … as the basis in itself for a prosecution under the common law' (para 172, fn 147).
10 Du Plessis M 'Bringing the International Criminal Court home – the implementation of the Rome Statute of the International Criminal Court Act 2002' (2003) 16 *South African Journal of Criminal Justice* 2.

constitutional. The necessity for this is provided for in section 231(4) of the Constitution of the Republic of South Africa, which provides:

> An international agreement becomes law in the Republic when it is enacted into law by national legislation, unless it is inconsistent with the Constitution or an Act of Parliament.

Having found the Rome Statute to be consonant with the Constitution with no amendments being required, the committee engaged in a process of carefully considering the multitude of political and legal aspects that could have an impact on the effective functioning of the Rome Statute within South Africa. Finding no fundamental impediments, South Africa incorporated the Rome Statute into its domestic law by way of the ICC Act.

The ICC Act entered into force on 18 July 2002. What is interesting is that the ICC Act adopted the Rome Statute in its entirety as a schedule to the Act. For this reason, the term 'rules' in the ICC Act is defined to mean the Rules of Procedure and Evidence referred to in article 51 of the Rome Statute, thereby allowing South African Courts to have regard to the relevant substantive and procedural provisions,[11] thus ensuring consistency between the prosecutions that take place at the domestic level and before the ICC. Further proof of the ICC Act's conformity with the Rome Statute is that the ICC Act incorporates the Rome Statute's definitions of the core crimes as well as the elements which make up the crimes of genocide, war crimes, and crimes against humanity. Section 1 of the ICC Act defines a 'crime' to mean the crime of genocide, crimes against humanity and war crimes. A 'war crime' is defined to mean any conduct referred to in Part 3 of the Rome Statute. These crimes now form part of South African law through the Act.[12] An obvious benefit of this situation is that the domestic courts' jurisdiction cannot easily be ousted by the ICC and as such, the ICC would be prevented from intervening in future cases until and unless it becomes clear that South Africa is unable or unwilling to prosecute a suspected perpetrator of an international crime.[13]

While the ICC Act does not contain the general principles of criminal law as set out in articles 22 to 33 of the Rome Statute, it is submitted that this is not fatal as these general principles will find application in any domestic trial under the ICC Act. An accused would therefore be entitled to the ordinary defences and protections that are guaranteed under South

11 See Katz (n 4 above) 27 and du Plessis (n 10 above) 14. This enables state parties to conduct a prosecution of such crimes domestically should they elect to do so (and to remove any possibility that the crimes for which surrender is sought, cannot be found in national law).

12 Du Plessis (n 1 above) 197.

13 Cryer (n 5 above) 63.

Africa's progressive Constitution[14] which contains an extensive list of rights to which arrested, detained and accused persons are entitled.[15]

The ICC Act is forward-looking in that it provides for the amendment of domestic laws, such as the Criminal Procedure Act 51 of 1977 and the Military Discipline Supplementary Measures Act 16 of 1999. Such amendments will bring them in conformity with the definition of crimes under the Rome Statute and deals with several other co-operation issues such as arrest and surrender of persons and prosecution of offences against the administration of justice in terms of the Rome Statute. As such, the ICC Act provides for interpretations and definitions consistent with the South African Constitution and the Rome Statute.[16]

3 Analysis of the implementation of the International Criminal Court Act

3.1 Complementarity

The 'complementarity' obligation placed on South African courts is emphatically stated in the ICC Act. Section 3 of the Act defines as one of its objects:

> The enabling, as far as possible and in accordance with the principle of complementarity, the national prosecuting authority of the Republic to adjudicate in cases brought against any person accused of having committed a crime in the Republic and beyond the borders of the Republic in certain circumstances.

When coming to a decision about the prosecution of a perpetrator of an international crime listed in the Rome Statute, section 5(3) requires the National Director of Prosecutions to recognise South Africa's obligation under the principle of complementarity to exercise jurisdiction over and prosecute persons accused of having committed an ICC crime. Therefore, prosecutors and courts in South Africa are now in a position to investigate, prosecute, try and sentence those persons guilty of the heinous conduct that gives rise to these crimes.[17]

Article 86 describes the general duty on states to co-operate fully with the ICC in the investigation and prosecution of crimes. Article 87(7) goes

14 Du Plessis (n 7 above) 464.

15 See sec 35 of the Constitution of the Republic of South Africa, 1996.

16 See *inter alia*, BC Olugbuo 'Domestic implementation of the Rome Statute of the International Criminal Court: A comparative analysis of strategies in Africa' Unpublished LLM Thesis, University of Pretoria, (2003) 39, available at http://www.up.ac.za/dspace/bitstream/2263/1069/1/olugbuo_bc_1.pdf (accessed 18 December 2009).

17 Katz (n 4 above) 27. See also Du Plessis (n 7 above) 461.

further to provide that the failure to co-operate can, amongst others, lead to a referral of the state to the Security Council. The two provisions read in conjunction imply that complementarity obliges South African courts to investigate and prosecute the ICC offences of crimes against humanity, war crimes and genocide (and perhaps soon, the crime of aggression) at the national level and only if the courts at the national level are unwilling or unable to investigate or prosecute, may the ICC intervene in order to indict those who are alleged to have committed such crimes.[18] The threat of a referral to the Security Council is seen to compel a state party to undertake its obligations to the full extent possible.

3.2 Core crimes and the elements

As far as subject-matter jurisdiction of the ICC is concerned, the Rome Statute codifies the elements which make up the crimes of genocide, war crimes, and crimes against humanity. States party to the Rome Statute are obliged to take steps to prohibit, as a matter of national or domestic law, the crimes or conduct described in the statute.[19] Since the ICC Act has incorporated the Rome Statute's definitions of the core crimes through a schedule appended to the Act, part 1 of Schedule 1 of the Act follows the wording of article 6 of the Rome Statute in relation to genocide, part 2 of the Schedule mirrors article 7 of the Statute in respect of crimes against humanity, and part 3 does the same for war crimes as set out in article 8 of the Statute.[20]

Notwithstanding the incorporation of the definitions of international crimes, neither the ICC Act nor Schedule 1 refers specifically to article 9 of the Rome Statute on Elements of Crimes.[21] This is potentially fatal since the Elements of Crimes are vital to the effective enforcement of the ICC Act as they aid the interpretation and application of the definitions of the international crimes falling within the jurisdiction of the Rome Statute. However, it may be argued that since the three crimes are incorporated into the Act, the South African courts should be able to take judicial notice of the elements of the crimes within the parameters of section 35 of the Constitution. Alternatively, these Elements of Crimes should be

18 Du Plessis (n 1 above) 200.

19 M du Plessis 'Complementarity and Africa: The promises and problems of international criminal justice' (2008) 17 *African Security Review* 157.

20 Du Plessis (n 10 above) 14.

21 'Finalized Draft Text of the Elements of Crimes' (PCNICC/2000/INF/3/Add.2). The Elements of Crimes is a document adopted in June 2000 by the Preparatory Commission for the International Criminal Court.

incorporated into the ICC Act by way of an amendment Act of Parliament.[22]

3.3 Jurisdiction

Section 4(1) of the ICC Act creates jurisdiction for a South African court over ICC crimes by providing that:

> [d]espite anything to the contrary in any other law of the Republic, any person who commits a crime as described in the Rome Statute, is guilty of an offence and liable on conviction to a fine or imprisonment.

This is the traditional principle of territoriality. Extra-territorial jurisdiction (which deems a crime to have been committed on the territory notwithstanding that it did not take place there) is provided for in section 4(3) of the Act, which states that the jurisdiction of a South African court will be triggered when a person commits an ICC crime outside the territory of the Republic,[23] on condition that he or she falls within the confines of one or more of the following possibilities:

> (a) that person is a South African citizen; or
>
> (b) that person is not a South African citizen but is ordinarily resident in the Republic;[24] or
>
> (c) that person, after the commission of the crime, is present in the territory of the Republic (irrespective of whether or not they are a South African citizen or have a close and substantial connection with South Africa);[25] or
>
> (d) that person has committed the said crime against a South African citizen or against a person who is ordinarily resident in the Republic (the so-called passive personality principle, conferring jurisdiction over an individual who causes harm to one of its citizens abroad).

In the circumstances, the ICC Act grants relatively expansive jurisdiction to South African courts with regard to crimes provided for under the Rome Statute.

22 It has been contended by du Plessis (see n 1 above at 136) that these Elements of Crimes should be incorporated by way of regulations into South Africa law. However, as a result of the separation of powers doctrine these Elements of Crimes cannot merely be 'added' by way of ministerial regulations since original legislation – which the ICC Act is – cannot be amended by regulations which constitute subordinate legislation, by the relevant Minister.

23 Du Plessis (n 1 above) 198. See also M du Plessis 'Goldstone's Gaza Report shows courage' *Cape Times* 8 October 2009, available at http://www.mediareviewnet.com/index.php/200910081262/Opinion-Article/Goldstone-s-Gaza-Report-Shows-Courage.php (accessed 20 December 2009).

24 This is referred to as the active and passive personality principle based on the nationality of the offender or the victim.

25 This is in conformity with the principle of universal jurisdiction, whereby a state acquires jurisdiction to prosecute the perpetrators of crimes of concern to the international community on the basis that these perpetrators are common enemies of mankind.

3.4 Immunities and privileges

In accordance with article 27 of the Rome Statute, chapter 2 of the ICC Act excludes immunity from prosecution conferred by constitutions to heads of state or government and officials. The Act also provides for the immunity and functioning of the Courts' personnel. The purpose of the privileges and immunities of the officials of the Court, its personnel and officials and those participating in proceedings of the Court is to safeguard the integrity and autonomy of the Court. On the basis of fundamental principles of international law, as a treaty-based international organisation, the Court and its officials will need to have sufficient diplomatic status to carry out their responsibilities. When it comes to immunity of heads of state, section 4(2)(a) of the ICC Act provides:

> notwithstanding any other law to the contrary, including customary and conventional international law, the fact that a person ... is or was a head of State or government, a member of a government or parliament, an elected representative or a government official ... is neither (i) a defence to a crime; nor (ii) a ground for any possible reduction of sentence once a person has been convicted of a crime.

In terms of the Act, South African courts are mandated to prosecute a perpetrator of an international crime, irrespective of their 'official status' as head of state. Support for an argument that section 4(2)(a) has done away with immunity comes from the Constitution itself as section 232 provides that '[c]ustomary international law is law in the Republic unless it is inconsistent with the Constitution or an Act of Parliament'. In addition, section 233 of the Constitution is pertinent as it provides that,

> [w]hen interpreting any legislation, every court must prefer any reasonable interpretation of the legislation that is consistent with international law over any alternative interpretation that is inconsistent with international law.

While this may be interpreted to mean that the customary international law barrier to prosecuting individuals enjoying immunity may be invoked, this position must be juxtaposed with a consideration of the practical realities: acting under the complementarity scheme of the Rome Statute, South African courts are accorded the same power to 'trump' the immunities which usually attach to officials of government as the ICC has by virtue of article 27 of the Statute.[26] As such, the South African government's obligation to end impunity will not be relinquished merely on account of an accused person raising the argument that they are

[26] See Du Plessis (n 7 above) 15.

immune by virtue of their official capacity.[27] The situation concerning the arrest warrant for Omar Al Bashir, the Sudanese President, places the issue of immunity into sharp focus and is discussed further below.

Even in the unlikely event that a court in South Africa refuses to prosecute a head of state or other official, section 5(6) of the ICC Act states that a decision by the National Director 'not to prosecute a person under this section does not preclude the prosecution of that person in the International Criminal Court'. Furthermore, article 98(1) of the Rome Statute entails that states parties have a duty of co-operation with the court, requiring such states to arrest and surrender to the court persons charged with an ICC crime.[28] However, article 98(1) regulates the operation of immunity by providing that a state is not obliged to hand over an individual to the court if doing so would be 'inconsistent with its obligations under international law with respect to the State or diplomatic immunity of a person ... of a third State, unless the Court can first obtain the cooperation of that third State for the waiver of the immunity'. Article 98(1) would thus apply to an official whose state has not waived their immunity through article 27, thus requiring the ICC to seek a waiver with respect to such an official. Thus, South Africa would be prohibited from extraditing an accused person who may find him or herself on South African territory but who is a national of a non-party State.

3.5 Procedural considerations and applicable law

Article 88 of the Rome Statute is a provision carrying substantial import as it obliges states to ensure that the procedures and powers to enable all forms of co-operation contemplated in the statute are in place nationally.

27 With regard to immunity, amnesties and pardons could have similar results. See J Dugard 'Possible conflicts of jurisdiction with truth Commissions' in A Cassese *et al* *The Rome Statute of the International Criminal Court: A Commentary (vol II)* (2002) 699. In the South African context, art 53(2)(c) of the ICC Statute gives the Prosecutor discretion to refuse prosecution at the instance of a state or the Security Council where, after investigation, he concludes that 'a prosecution is not in the interests of justice, taking into account all circumstances'. It is envisaged that this provision would become applicable in the context of a country where amnesty has been granted either by a truth commission or by the outgoing or incoming government as a political act of reprieve. Amnesties which are analogous to the South African amnesties granted by the quasi-judicial amnesty committee functioning as part of a Truth and Reconciliation Commission process established by a democratically elected government may well constitute a bar to prosecution by the ICC. However, states are not permitted to grant amnesty for the crimes of genocide, torture and 'grave breaches' under the Geneva Conventions.

28 See Du Plessis (n 1 above) 207. While it has previously been debated whether this obligation would arise in the case of a head of state of a state which is not a party to the Rome Statute, it has been proven that non-ratification of the Rome Statute is insufficient reason to prevent a head of state from being prosecuted as other mechanisms, such as a Resolution taken by the UN Security Council could entail that a head of state (such as Sudanese President Hassan Omar Al Bashir) is prosecuted.

While the ICC Act has not incorporated part 3 of the Rome Statute which includes what it described as 'general principles of criminal law', section 2(a) of the ICC Act states that applicable law for any South African court hearing any matter arising under the ICC Act includes 'conventional international law, and in particular the Statute'. The implication of this is that those defences and grounds for liability (such as superior orders, mistake of fact or law, *nullum crimen sine lege*, command responsibility, mental illness, intoxication, self-defence and duress) contained in the Rome Statute become applicable in South Africa.[29]

Of special significance is the non-applicability of a statute of limitations within South Africa. This reflects the provisions of article 29 of the Rome Statute. South Africa has realised this provision by effecting an amendment to section 18 of the Criminal Procedure Act 51 of 1977. Section 39 of the ICC Act therefore indirectly states that the right to institute a prosecution for crimes of genocide, war crimes and crimes against humanity is a right which does not prescribe.[30]

3.5.1 Procedure for domestic prosecutions

Section 5 of the Act regulates domestic prosecutions and is a rather complex process of engagement between a variety of government departments and officials. Section 5(1) of the ICC Act requires that the consent of the National Director of Public Prosecutions must be obtained before any prosecution may be instituted against a person accused of having committed a crime. The Act further provides in section 5(4) that after the National Director has consented to a prosecution, an appropriate High Court must be designated for that purpose. This provision bears testimony to the importance attached to prosecutions of international crimes. The designation of such a court must be provided in writing by the 'Cabinet member responsible for the administration of justice ... in consultation with the Chief Justice of South Africa and after consultation with the National Director [of Public Prosecutions]'.

In the event that the National Director of Public Prosecutions declines to prosecute – that is, the South African authorities prove to be unable or unwilling to prosecute – section 5(5) compels the National Director to inform the Director-General of Justice and provide full reasons for that decision. Consonant with the principle of complementarity, the Director-General is then obliged to forward the decision, together with reasons, to the Registrar of the ICC in The Hague.[31] An unjustified refusal will result in international responsibility of South Africa for its failure to comply with its obligations under the ICC Statute. The ICC then bears the onus of

29 Du Plessis (n 10 above) 15.
30 As above 16.
31 Du Plessis (n 1 above) 200.

deciding whether to prosecute the suspect or not. The ICC will invariably proceed if it concludes that South Africa's decision not to prosecute was motivated purely by a desire to shield the individual concerned from prosecution.[32]

It is envisaged that the usual trial procedure for a criminal trial in the High Court will be followed and in accordance with section 4(1) of the ICC Act the High Court is permitted to impose any competent sentence which it would otherwise have been entitled to impose in terms of its domestic criminal sentencing jurisdiction, including life imprisonment;[33] imprisonment; a fine; reparations (monetary compensation);[34] and correctional supervision.[35]

Notwithstanding the broad discretion conferred on domestic courts to investigate and prosecute international crimes, section 2 of the ICC Act constrains these powers by requiring that a South African court shall apply the Constitution and the law when prosecuting a person allegedly responsible for a core crime. Moreover, the Act provides in section 2(a) that applicable law for any South African court hearing any matter arising under the Act includes 'conventional international law; and in particular the Rome Statute'. Therefore, the general principles of international criminal law will invariably find application before a South African court.

3.5.2 Prosecutions before the ICC

In pursuit of co-operation between the ICC and the South African government, the ICC Act provides an elaborate procedure to ensure that perpetrators of international crimes are prosecuted. In order to invoke the procedures for a prosecution before the ICC, it is imperative that suspected/accused persons are brought before the ICC. Article 89 of the Rome Statute thus provides that:

32 See art 17(2)(a) of the Rome Statute.

33 The appropriateness of a sentence of life imprisonment is mediated by the provisions of art 77(1)(b) of the Rome Statute which provides that life imprisonment is reserved for when it is 'justified by the extreme gravity of the crime and the individual circumstances of the convicted person'. Therefore, in the South African context, life imprisonment is deemed to be a competent sentence in terms of sec 4(1) of the ICC Act although the Act does not set out the circumstances when such a sentence will be appropriate.

34 According to art 75(2) of the Rome Statute, the ICC is empowered to address the issue of reparations to victims, and may 'make an order directly against any convicted person' specifying reparations. According to sec 25(2) and (3) of the ICC Act, this order of a fine or reparations has the effect of a civil judgment and therefore must be registered with a court having jurisdiction within South Africa. Sec 26 goes on to provide that the Director-General of Justice and Constitutional Development thereafter has the responsibility of paying over to the ICC any amount realized in the execution of the sentence or the order, and from that must be subtracted any expenses incurred by the Republic in executing the order.

35 Du Plessis (n 1 above) 200.

> The Court may transmit a request for the arrest and surrender of a person … to any state on the territory of which that person may be found and shall request for the cooperation of that state in the arrest and surrender of such a person.

4 Arrest, surrender, extradition and transfer

Trials *in absentia* are not permitted by the Rome Statute so the ICC is dependent on the co-operation and assistance of national authorities to secure the attendance of accused individuals. Article 59 of the Rome Statute deals with 'arrest' and 'surrender' proceedings in the custodial state.[36] Significantly, upon ratification of the Rome Statute, states accept that there are no grounds for refusing ICC requests for arrest and surrender. However, should a conflict arise between South Africa and the ICC regarding arrest and surrender, then under section 10(2) of the ICC Act the magistrate may at any time during the inquiry 'postpone that inquiry for purposes of consultation between the relevant authorities of the Republic and the Court as contemplated in Article 97 of the Statute'.

4.1 Arrest

The ICC Act envisages two types of arrest: one in terms of an existing warrant issued by the ICC, and another in terms of a warrant issued by South Africa's National Director of Public Prosecutions. In both scenarios the warrant (whether endorsed or issued) must be in the form and executed in a manner that is compatible with that which exists in respect of warrants of arrest under existing South African law.[37]

With respect to an arrest in terms of a warrant issued by the ICC, in order to obtain such a warrant and surrender from the ICC the Prosecutor would have to have convinced a Pre-Trial Chamber of the court (consisting of three judges) that there were 'reasonable grounds to believe' the suspect had committed a core crime.[38] Thereafter, in terms of section 8 of the ICC Act, when South Africa receives a request from the ICC for the arrest and surrender of a person for whom the ICC has issued a warrant of arrest, it must refer the request to the Director-General of Justice and Constitutional Development with the necessary documentation to satisfy a local court that there are sufficient grounds for the surrender of the person to The Hague.[39] This request must be submitted along with the 'material supporting the request' to a magistrate who must endorse the ICC's warrant of arrest for execution in any part of the Republic (section 8(2)).[40]

36 Katz (n 4 above) 27- 28. Surrender is the term used in the ICC Act.
37 Du Plessis (n 1 above) 201.
38 Du Plessis (n 10 above) 9.
39 Sec 8(1). See Du Plessis (n 1 above) 201.
40 See art 89 of the Rome Statute. See Du Plessis (n 1 above) 201.

Section 9 concerns an arrest in terms of a warrant issued by the National Director of Public Prosecutions. According to section 9(1) the Director-General of Justice is mandated to receive a request from the ICC for the provisional arrest of a person who is suspected or accused of having committed a core crime, or has been convicted by the ICC. The Director-General is then obliged to immediately forward the request to the National Director of Public Prosecutions, who must then apply for the warrant before a magistrate.[41]

A request from the ICC for the arrest and surrender of a person is to be referred to the Director-General of the Department of Justice. The Director-General shall immediately forward the request to a magistrate who must endorse the warrant of arrest for execution in any part of South Africa. Section 10(1) of the ICC Act then stipulates that after being arrested, the arrestee is to be brought 'before a magistrate in whose area of jurisdiction he or she has been arrested or detained, within 48 hours after that person's arrest or on the date specified in the warrant for his or her further detention'. The South African authorities after that become engaged in what is known as the 'surrender' ('delivery') of an arrestee to the ICC.[42]

According to section 10(1)(a) to (c) of the ICC Act, the magistrate holding the inquiry is to consider the evidence adduced and must establish three issues.[43] The first issue is whether the warrant applies to the person in question; second, whether the person has been arrested in accordance with the procedures laid down by domestic law, and third, whether the rights of the person have been respected. If the magistrate is satisfied that the three requirements have been complied with, he or she must issue an order committing the person to prison pending his or her surrender to the ICC ('a committal order'). It is important to note that section 10(5) of the ICC Act provides that the magistrate does not issue an order of surrender but rather an order of committal to prison.[44]

4.2 Surrender

There is a qualitative difference in nature between 'surrender' and 'extradition'. Article 102 of the Rome Statute provides that 'surrender' means the delivering up of a person by a state to the Court, while 'extradition' means the delivering up of a person by one statue to another as provided by treaty, convention or national legislation.

41 Du Plessis (n 1 above) 201.
42 As above, 202.
43 Katz (n 4 above) 28.
44 As above.

When it comes to a request by the ICC for the surrender of a person, the process set out in the ICC Act is similar to that contained in the Extradition Act 67 of 1962 with a number of significant differences with a view towards streamlining the process. The rationale for this streamlined process is to facilitate the surrender of a person in a far quicker and easier way than compared to the extradition of a person to a foreign state. While the intention may have been admirable, Katz criticises the surrender provisions in the ICC Act and submits that it may not have been successful after all[45] based *inter alia* on the fact that there is no provision for any competent authority, whether a court or the executive branch of government, to issue an order of surrender.[46]

Katz reveals that upon a closer analysis of the arrest and surrender provisions, it seems that the scheme of arrest and surrender to the ICC provided for in the South African legislation to give effect to the Statute is somewhat defective. He goes on to state that the situation is invariably as a result of the attempt to reflect the compromise on the issue of extradition and as a result South Africa may not be able to comply with its obligations to assist the ICC in securing the attendance of a person before it.[47] According to Katz, the provision in the ICC Act dealing with the removal of persons – section 11(1) – refers to any person in respect of whom an order to be surrendered has been given under section 10(5). Section 10(5) does not refer to 'an order to be surrendered'. No other section refers to an order to be surrendered. Accordingly, the ICC Act does not properly, or at all, provide South African authorities with the necessary power to respond to a request for surrender by the ICC. This anomaly is explained by the attempt to utilise only parts of the extradition process without a full consideration of the effect of leaving out the other parts and a failure to appreciate that there is a fundamental difference between surrender and extradition.

In the first place, no mention is made of the double criminality rule which is central to extradition procedures; and of possibly even more importance is the fact that there is no requirement in the ICC Act that a *prima facie* case be shown against the suspect.[48] The magistrate is only required to be satisfied that the person may be surrendered to the court: (a) for prosecution for the alleged crime; (b) for the imposition of a sentence by the court for the crime in respect of which the person has been convicted; or (c) to serve a sentence already imposed by the court.[49] In addition, the magistrate must find that the ICC has a genuine interest in the surrender of the arrestee. However, there is little indication in the Act as to what level of proof must be proffered by the prosecution to prove these

45 As above.
46 As above 25.
47 As above 28 - 29.
48 Du Plessis (n 10 above) 9.
49 Du Plessis (n 1 above) 202.

additional requirements, such as, whether the court must inquire if there is evidence to justify his trial for the offence he is alleged to have committed although it is submitted that information required for the original warrant of arrest would provide the material supporting the request for surrender.[50]

Section 10(8)(b) provides that any person against whom an order of committal to prison has been made has a right of appeal to a High Court, which must be exercised within seven days after the date of the order. The appeal must deal exclusively with the requirements set out in section 10(1)(a) to (c).

4.3 Extradition

The Extradition Act 67 of 1962 regulates the extradition of a person from South Africa to a foreign state. Once a request for extradition has been received, discretion is conferred on the Minister of Justice to determine whether the extradition should proceed. If extradition is deemed appropriate, a hearing is held before a magistrate. The Magistrate's Court is responsible only for establishing whether the person is extraditable and not the issue in respect of which extradition is being sought. In the event that a magistrate rejects the application for an extradition order, there is no right of appeal and the matter is closed. However, if a magistrate approves of an extradition order being granted, the executive branch of government (with the Minister of Justice being the only authority with the power to fulfil this role) is required to decide whether an extradition order should be made.[51]

5 Co-operation with the ICC and assistance in terms of article 93 of the Rome Statute

The Rome Statute requires state parties to assist the ICC by co-operating in relation to investigations and prosecutions. Such assistance is subject to the domestic law of the Republic and the Statute. Section 14 of the ICC Act is modelled on article 93 of the Rome Statute and provides for the areas of co-operation,[52] being:

(a) the identification and whereabouts of persons or the location of items;

(b) the taking of evidence, including testimony under oath, and the production of evidence, including expert opinions and reports necessary to the Court;

(c) the questioning of any person being investigated or prosecuted;[53]

50 Du Plessis (n 7 above) 468.
51 Katz (n 4 above) 28.
52 Du Plessis (n 1 above) 203.

(d) the service of documents, including judicial documents;[54]

(e) facilitating the voluntary appearance of persons as witnesses or experts before the Court;[55]

(f) the temporary transfer of persons in custody for purposes of identification or for obtaining testimony or other assistance;

(g) the examination of places or sites, including the exhumation and examination of grave sites;

(h) the execution of searches and seizures;[56]

(i) the provision of records and documents, including official records and documents; the protection of victims and witnesses and the preservation of evidence;

(j) the identification, tracing and freezing or seizure of proceeds, property and assets and instrumentalities of crimes for the purpose of eventual forfeiture, without prejudice to the rights of *bona fide* third parties;[57] and

(k) any other type of assistance which is not prohibited by law, with the view to facilitating the investigation and prosecution of crimes within the jurisdiction of the Court.

With respect to the examination of witnesses, this is regulated by sections 15, 16, 17, 18 and 19 of the ICC Act and provides for the procedure for the examination of witnesses before a magistrate, the rights and privileges of the witness, the offences which a witness might commit, and the procedure by which the attendance of a witness might be secured in proceedings before the ICC.[58]

6 Declaration of the seat of the ICC within South Africa and associated measures of assistance

Section 6 of the ICC Act provides that, consequent upon a request by the ICC, the president may declare any place in the Republic to be the seat of

53 Regard must be had to the provisions of sec 35 of the South African Constitution and art 55 of the Rome Statute which guarantee certain rights to a person under investigation, such as the right against self-incrimination, the right to remain silent, and the right to legal assistance.

54 This is regulated by sec 21 of the ICC Act.

55 Sec 20 of the ICC Act regulates the transfer of a prisoner to the ICC for the purposes of giving evidence or to assist in an investigation.

56 This is regulated by sec 30 of the ICC Act. This is limited specifically to requests made by the ICC and for investigations related to the ICC.

57 The making of forfeiture and confiscation orders is regulated in sec 14(k), 22(1) and 27(1). This provision is modelled on art 93(1)(k) of the Rome Statute which provides for the 'identification, tracing and freezing or seizure of proceeds, property ... [etc] for the purposes of eventual forfeiture'. Once a restraint order has been 'registered' by the relevant Registrar of the High Court, the ICC Act provides that the order has the effect of a restraint order made by that High Court under the Prevention of Organised Crime Act 121 of 1998. According to sec 28(1) of the ICC Act, where a confiscation order has been `registered', the order has the effect of a civil judgment of the court at which it has been registered.

58 Du Plessis (n 1 above) 204.

the ICC. This fact will then be proclaimed in the Government Gazette. Various privileges and immunities apply to this court. In the first instance, the court is accorded such rights and privileges of a South African court of law in the Republic as may be necessary to enable it to perform its functions (section 7(1)). Section 7(2) then goes on to provide that the judges, the prosecutor, the deputy prosecutors and the registrar of the court, while performing their functions in the Republic, enjoy the same immunities and privileges that are accorded to a representative of another state or government in terms of section 4(2) of the South African Diplomatic Immunities and Privileges Act 37 of 2001. The immunities include immunity from the criminal and civil jurisdiction of the courts of the Republic, and the privileges enjoyed are those which (a) a special envoy or representative enjoys in accordance with the rules of customary international law; or (b) are provided for in any agreement entered into with a state, government or organisation whereby immunities and privileges are conferred upon such special envoy or representative.

Section 7(3) provides that the deputy-registrar, the staff of the office of the prosecutor and the staff of the registry of the court enjoy the privileges and facilities necessary for the performance of their functions in the Republic as may be published by proclamation in the *Government Gazette* as provided for in section 7(2) of the Diplomatic Immunities and Privileges Act of 2001. Furthermore, the Minister of Foreign Affairs may, after consultation with the Minister of Justice, confer immunities and privileges on any other member of the staff of the court or any person performing a function for purposes of the ICC Act. Such immunities and privileges are conferred by the Minister of Foreign Affairs publishing a notice in the Government Gazette, on such conditions as he or she deems necessary (section 7(4)). Section 7(5) provides that any person who is accorded immunities or privileges in terms of the ICC Act must have his or her name entered into a register as contemplated in section 9(1) of the Diplomatic Immunities and Privileges Act 2001.

7 Enforcement of sentences

State parties are obliged to share the responsibility of enforcing sentences of imprisonment, in accordance with principles of equitable distribution. This is unequivocally provided for in article 103(3)(a) of the Rome Statute and Rule 201 of the Rules of Procedure and Evidence. States are required to indicate their willingness to allow convicted prisoners to serve their sentences within their domestic penal institutions, although the Netherlands may have to perform this task if no state offers its prison services (article 103(4)).[59] In order to give effect to this enforcement scheme, section 31 of the ICC Act provides that the Minister of

59 Du Plessis (n 1 above) 205.

Correctional Services must consult with the Cabinet and seek the approval of Parliament with the aim of informing the ICC whether South Africa can be placed on the list of states willing to accept sentenced persons. Section 32 goes on to provide that if the Republic is placed on the list of states and is designated as a state in which an offender is to serve a prison sentence, then such person must be committed to prison in South Africa. The provisions of the Correctional Services Act 111 of 1998 and South African domestic law then apply to that individual. The sentence of imprisonment may only be modified at the request of the ICC, after an appeal by the prisoner to, or review by, the court in terms of section 32(4)(b) of the Rome Statute which mirrors article 110(2) of the Rome Statute which states that the ICC 'alone shall have the right to decide any reduction of sentence'.[60]

A competent sentence could include forfeiture of proceeds, property and assets derived directly or indirectly from that crime, without prejudice to the rights of bona fide third parties but only in addition to imprisonment (article 77(2)(a)). Reparations are also an option in terms of section 75, which provides that the ICC is empowered to address the issue of reparations to victims, and may 'make an order directly against any convicted person' specifying reparation.[61] This will most probably take the form of monetary compensation. Sections 25 and 26 of the ICC Act make provision for the execution of such fines and compensation orders within the Republic: sections 25(2) and 25(3) state that such orders must be 'registered' with a court in the Republic having jurisdiction. Once the order has been registered, that sentence or order 'has the effect of a civil judgment of the court at which it has been registered', and the Director-General of Justice must pay over to the ICC any amount realised in the execution of the sentence or the order, minus any expenses incurred by the Republic in the execution thereof.[62]

8 Effective implementation and enforcement of the ICC Act by way of regulation-making

In order to ensure that the ICC Act functions as originally intended, section 38 of the ICC Act empowers the Minister of Justice to make regulations regarding the ICC Act when necessary. Section 1 of the Act

60 Du Plessis (n 1 above) 206. Notwithstanding this provision, du Plessis has poignantly stated that it is doubtful that South Africa will be placed on the list of states available for enforcement of duty in light of the poor state of prisons in South Africa, which have in fact been described as being in breach of national law and international standards. Eg, the Judicial Inspectorate of Prisons reported at the end of 2000 that prisons were severely overcrowded, with some at 200% occupancy rate, and that a third of the prison population who were awaiting trial were detained under inhumane conditions. Earlier reports by groups such as Human Rights Watch show that 'South African prisons are places of extreme violence, where assaults on prisoners by guards or fellow inmates are common and often fatal.

61 See art 75(2) Rome Statute.

62 Sec 26 ICC Act.

accordingly provides that such regulations would be included as part of the Act.[63] To date, the Minister has only made regulations providing for such aspects as the obtaining of evidence; restraint orders; sentences; compensatory orders; and confiscation orders.[64]

9 Recent developments illustrating the effect of implementation of the Rome Statute in South Africa

The adoption of a progressive implementing Act on the ICC has ensured that South Africa plays a leading role on the continent and is at the cutting edge of developments concerning the interpretation, implementation and enforcement of the Rome Statute.[65] This momentum and South Africa's good repute have unfortunately suffered a decline in recent months due to South Africa's apparent 'amnesia' concerning the obligations it had voluntarily undertaken.

Du Plessis prophetically stated in 2004 that the true test for the ICC Act will come when an international criminal makes his or her appearance on our territory.[66] Notwithstanding the perception that South Africa is committed to the fight against impunity, South Africa has recently found itself mired in controversy concerning its external position on the ICC since it has been criticised for sacrificing the ideals of international justice on the altar of political expediency.[67] In particular, South Africa's recent position on the ICC has not been a model of clarity.[68] Events turning on fundamental principles of international criminal law whereupon South Africa was expected to take decisive action can be classified under the following broad discussion issues: South Africa's response to the article 98 Bilateral Immunity Agreements imposed by the United States of America; attempts to arrest ZANU-PF officials who had been accused of committing crimes against humanity in Zimbabwe and who were subsequently on South African territory; South Africa's [ambiguous] position with regards to the international arrest warrant issued by the ICC for Sudanese President Omar Al Bashir; the 'Gaza docket'; and South Africa's controversial proposal concerning an amendment to article 16 of

63 Du Plessis (n 1 above) 198 at fn 138.

64 Regulations made under sec 38 of the Implementation of the Rome Statute of the International Criminal Court Act Act 27 of 2002, published in Government Notice R 1089 of 16 August 2002 (*Government Gazette* 23761).

65 C Gevers 'Gaza docket: SA must tighten policies on international criminal justice' *Business Day* 20 August 2009 http://www.businessday.co.za/articles/Content.aspx?id=79073 (accessed 18 December 2009).

66 Du Plessis (n 7 above) 15.

67 C Gevers 'SA's bold proposal shows up the flaws in the Rome compromise' *Business Day* 29 December 2009 http://www.businessday.co.za/articles/Content.aspx?id=90453 (accessed 4 January 2010).

68 M du Plessis 'Recent cases and developments: South Africa and the International Criminal Court' 2009 (3) *South African Journal of Criminal Justice* 443.

the Rome Statute to the effect that the provision allowing for the UN Security Council to delay proceedings before the court be amended to allow for the UN General Assembly to do so in the event that the Council fails to act.

9.1 South Africa's response to the article 98 Bilateral Immunity Agreements imposed by the United States of America

On 12 July 2002, the UN Security Council unanimously adopted Resolution 1422. This resolution granted immunity from prosecution by the ICC to UN peacekeeping personnel from countries that were not party to the ICC. The Resolution was passed at the insistence of the United States, which threatened to veto the renewal of all UN peacekeeping missions unless its citizens were shielded from prosecution by the ICC. In response to the Resolution, South Africa joined with Canada, Brazil, and New Zealand in submitting a letter of opposition to the Resolution alleging that the Council's pursuit of the matter, despite the clear opposition of the international community, was 'damaging international efforts to combat impunity, the system of international justice, and the collective ability to use these systems in the pursuit of international peace and security'. South Africa's stance was a challenge to the legitimacy of the Council's arrogating to itself the right to interpret and change the meaning of treaties.

This Resolution was valid for a period of one year and it was subsequently renewed for a further year by Resolution 1487. In his capacity as South Africa's Ambassador to the UN, Dumisani Kumalo condemned the renewal of the Resolution by stating that the adoption of Resolution 1487 cast a shadow on the integrity of the ICC Statute, the Criminal Court, and the application of international law'.[69]

In the context of Resolutions 1422 and 1487, the United States started systematically adopting Bilaterial Immunity Agreements (otherwise known as article 98 agreements) with state parties to the ICC. The purpose of the Bilateral Immunity Agreements is to prevent the states concerned from transferring through whatever procedure, without the consent of the United States, any 'current or former [g]overnment officials, employers (including contractors), or military personnel or nationals' of the United States either to the ICC or to a third state or entity with the purpose of eventual transfer to the ICC. Although pressured to do so, South Africa refused to sign an article 98 agreement. The United States set a deadline of 31 June 2003 for the conclusion of the agreement and simultaneously threatened that should South Africa refuse to sign the agreement, military

[69] See M du Plessis 'South Africa's response to America's hostility towards the International Criminal Court' (2005) 30 *South African Yearbook of International Law* 112.

aid to the value of 7.2 million US dollars provided by the United States would be suspended. South Africa refused to sign and was accordingly black-listed by the United States on 1 July 2003. The official government statement for the deliberate refusal to sign the agreement was South Africa's 'commitment to the humanitarian objectives of the ICC and the country's international obligations'. South Africa's steadfast position signified a victory for South Africa's adherence to the principles of international criminal law and it is such conduct which set South Africa apart as a leader in the quest for ending impunity for crimes against humanity, war crimes and genocide.

9.2 Zimbabwean officials accused of committing crimes against humanity

South Africa's former respected position came under scrutiny in 2008 when a dossier was submitted to the National Prosecuting Authority concerning South Africa's obligations under the ICC Act.[70] The substance of this dossier concerned 18 Zimbabwean human rights violators who had allegedly committed crimes against humanity during the run-up to the 2008 elections. The rationale for the dossier was to urge the National Prosecuting Authority to institute prosecutions where they had previously refused on account of a decision taken by the police not to investigate the allegations. The Southern African Litigation Centre and the Zimbabwe Exiles Forum appealed the decision and sought an order setting aside the decision not to prosecute these perpetrators and, moreover, to have these human rights violators arrested in the event they travel to South Africa.

The ostensible motive behind the submission of the dossier was to prevent South Africa from becoming a haven for those who commit crimes against humanity. This case is ongoing and has not yet resulted in litigation or prosecutions.[71]

9.3 South Africa's reaction to the international arrest warrant issued against Sudanese President Omar Al Bashir and South Africa's legal obligations if Omar Al Bashir were to arrive in South Africa

In 2009 an arrest warrant against Sudanese President Omar Al Bashir was issued after the UN Security Council decided to refer the crimes committed in Sudan to the ICC for investigation and possible prosecution. Al Bashir stands accused of crimes against humanity and war crimes committed in the Darfur conflict by government officers and soldiers. However, at its

70 The dossier was composed of a legal opinion compiled by Advocates Wim Trengove, Gilbert Marcus and Max du Plessis.

71 Du Plessis (n 68 above) 442.

February 2009 Summit, the AU Assembly adopted a decision expressing its 'deep concern' regarding the indictment (*sic*) of Al Bashir, and mandating the AU Commission to dispatch a high-level delegation to the UN Security Council to advocate for the deferral of proceedings under article 16.[72] Notwithstanding the AU's decision, on 4 March 2009, ICC judges confirmed the international arrest warrant for Sudan's president. On 3 July 2009, at the AU Summit of Heads of State and Government held in Libya, the Sirte Declaration was passed (with South Africa's full support) which resolved that African states would defy the arrest warrant issued by the ICC for Al Bashir. In particular, this resolution categorically states that member states have refused to co-operate in the arrest and surrender of the Sudanese president. It is believed that the recent discontent with the ICC can be traced to the suggestion that 'the ICC is a hegemonic tool of Western powers which is targeting or discriminating against Africans because its first cases flow from this continent'.[73] The reluctance to comply with the arrest warrant for Al Bashir is in line with the criticism that the Court's work is undermining peace efforts or conflict resolution processes. Furthermore, an objection has been voiced that the ICC has deigned to proceed against a sitting head of state of a country that is not a party to the Rome Statute.[74]

South Africa's position was widely condemned[75] until the Ministry of International Relations and Cooperation confirmed the government's commitment to the rule of law. However, by this time the South African government was embarrassed by the fact that Botswana had shown exceptional leadership by maintaining a principled position on the obligations in the Rome Statute while South Africa was vacillating between wilful disobedience to its own voluntary obligations and respect for the ICC as an institution which it had helped create. Incidentally, the government's reversion to a commitment to the rule of law coincided with an international arrest warrant for Al Bashir being endorsed by a Pretoria magistrate.[76]

72 *Decision on the application by the International Criminal Court (ICC) Prosecutor for the indictment of the President of the Republic of the Sudan* Assembly/AU/Dec 21 Addis Ababa 1-3 February 2009.

73 Du Plessis (n 68 above) 443. This complaint implicates questions about head of state immunity under customary international law and the extent to which the Rome Statute's provisions which strip that immunity can be made applicable to President Al Bashir.

74 Du Plessis (n 68 above) 442.

75 This criticism against the South African government's approach took the form of a statement dated 15 July 2009 signed by several South African civil society organization and many concerned individuals calling upon President Jacob Zuma to honour South Africa's treaty obligations by cooperating with the ICC in relation to the warrant of arrest issued for President Omar Al Bashir. The General Council of the Bar of South Africa also issued a statement (GCB Circular No 111/09, 15 July 2009) criticising the government's apathetic approach to our obligations under the Implementation of the Rome Statute of the ICC Act and our Constitution. See du Plessis (n 68 above) 444.

76 This information is obtained from the report by Dr Ayanda Ntsaluba, Director-General of the Department of International Relations and Cooperation for the period January to December 2009 (on file with author).

The Department of International Relations and Cooperation was at pains to provide an explanation as to why the AU had reached the decision it did and why South Africa latterly distanced itself from such decision. According to Dr Ntsaluba, the Director-General of the Department of International Relations and Cooperation, it appears that the AU Decision was based on the *Yerodia* case, a decision by the International Court of Justice, which held that the indictment of a Foreign Minister of the Democratic Republic of Congo by Belgium in terms of its domestic law, was in violation of Belgium's obligations in terms of the international law applicable to immunities.[77] Ntsaluba emphasised that the finding in the *Yerodia* case was not applicable and that it was further held in the *Yerodia* case that an incumbent or former Minister of Foreign Affairs may be subject to criminal proceedings before certain international criminal courts, when such courts have jurisdiction (such as the ICC clearly does).[78]

Article 27 of the Rome Statute (which informs section 4(1) of the ICC Act) must be read with reference to article 98 of the Rome Statute which creates a situation which aims to stop the Court from proceeding with a request for surrender in the following circumstances:

> The Court may not proceed with a request for surrender or assistance which would require the requested State to act inconsistently with its obligations under international law with respect to the State of diplomatic immunity of a person or property of a third State, unless the Court can first obtain the cooperation of that third State for the waiver of the immunity; or pursuant to which the consent of a sending State is required to surrender a person of that State to the Court, unless the Court can first obtain the cooperation of a sending State for the giving of consent for the surrender.

However, section 4(1) of the ICC Act ousts the applicability of other domestic laws in respect of an accused, with the result that the immunity from prosecution that Al Bashir would normally have enjoyed in terms of the Diplomatic Immunities and Privileges Act 37 of 2001 is not applicable, and Al Bashir is not immune from prosecution. Thus, while the academic weight of authority is that Al Bashir's immunity had been removed by the Rome Statute, a definitive ruling from the ICC concerning the relationship between article 27 and article 98 would be welcomed so as to prevent a repeat of the situation in which South Africa found itself.

9.4 South Africans allegedly implicated in war crimes during Operation Cast Lead in Gaza

On 3 August 2009 the Solidarity Alliance and the Media Review

77 *DRC v Belgium (Yerodia Case)*, ICJ, 2006.

78 Report by Dr Ayanda Ntsaluba, Director-General of the Department of International Relations and Cooperation (n 76 above).

Network[79] used South Africa's ICC Act to present a 3500-page docket to the National Prosecuting Authority and the Hawks (South Africa's new Priority Crimes Unit). The dossier alleges that certain individuals, including members of the Israeli army who fought in Operation Cast Lead, are guilty of international crimes during the Gaza offensive and it thus advocates for an investigation in South Africa of foreign nationals and South Africans allegedly implicated in war crimes during the operation. In parallel with their South African request, the complainants handed the dossier over to the ICC's prosecutor in early September. What is particularly interesting about the request for an investigation into the conduct of the Israeli soldiers is that Israel is not a member State of the ICC,[80] and yet the Israeli soldiers are acutely aware of the legal consequences which are likely to ensue for their conduct which amounts to crimes against humanity and war crimes. They have been fortunate thus far not have been subjected to these consequences.[81]

9.5 Proposed amendment to article 16 (deferral of investigation or prosecution) of the Rome Statute

Article 121(1) of the Rome Statute reads:

> After the expiry of seven years from the entry into force of this Statute, any State Party may propose amendments thereto. The text of any proposed amendment shall be submitted to the Secretary-General of the United Nations, who shall promptly circulate it to all States Parties.

South Africa has taken cognisance of article 12 and made an ambitious proposal concerning amendment to the ICC's deferral regime contained in article 16.[82] Article 16 provides:

> No investigation or prosecution may be commenced or proceeded with under this Statute for a period of 12 months after the Security Council, in a resolution adopted under Chapter VII of the Charter of the United Nations, has requested the Court to that effect; that request may be renewed by the Council under the same conditions.

To put this into context, article 16 was designed to cover those situations where the Security Council, in pursuit of the restoration of international

79 These two organisations instructed a team of leading international lawyers, headed by Professor John Dugard, to settle the docket.

80 UN Secretary-General Ban Ki-Moon has lent his full support to the prosecution of those who have committed violations of international human rights law in Gaza. See Siun, Gaza Update: 300 Human Rights Groups Request War Crimes Prosecution of Israel, 20 January 2009 http://cebo.org/labels/UNWRA.html (accessed 7 February 2010).

81 Du Plessis (n 23 above).

82 The amendment was tabled by South Africa for consideration at the 8th Assembly of States Parties in The Hague in November 2009 and has also been placed on the agenda for the 9th Assembly of States Parties in New York to be held in 2010.

peace of security, requests the ICC to suspend the investigation or prosecution of a government or armed group leader or other high-standing official involved in peace negotiations. It is worth noting that, in its present form, article 16 reflects a compromise[83] reached during the drafting process whereby the role of the Security Council has been severely curtailed. Consequently, what article 16 entails is that the Security Council (in its capacity as the guardian of international peace and security) should take preventive action through a resolution under Chapter VII of the UN Charter requesting that no investigation or prosecution is commenced for a renewable period of twelve months rather than having the power to authorise an investigation or prosecution. In order to take effect a deferral will require the approval of nine of the members of the Council and the lack of a contrary vote by any of the five permanent members.[84]

In the recent past South Africa has made every effort to exert political pressure on the Security Council in order to 'persuade' it to exercise its power of deferral to halt proceedings against Sudanese President Al Bashir for a year. When these attempts proved fruitless, South Africa proposed an amendment to article 16 by relying on the controversial Uniting for Peace Resolution, adopted by the UN General Assembly in 1950 to break a deadlock over the Korean War.[85] Due to an inability on the part of African states to agree on a common strategy concerning the submission of the proposed amendment to article 16, South Africa agreed to introduce the proposals in Plenary and it was left to the remaining African states to decide on whether or not to support them. In the end very few African states took the floor to support the recommendations.[86] Nevertheless, this recommendation was endorsed by the Assembly of the AU in January 2010[87] and as such, it remains on the agenda for the Assembly of States Parties to be held in New York in 2010.

South Africa's argument in favour of an amendment to article 16 is premised on the fact that the current set-up of the ICC is flawed, and

83 It is pertinent to state that the content of art 16 was opposed by a number of African states, including South Africa, at the Rome Conference in 1998 but for purposes of ensuring that the Rome Statute would become operative, many states sacrificed their ideals and voted in favour of the Statute.

84 See L Conderelli & S Villalpando 'Referral and deferral by the Security Council' in Cassese *et al* (eds) *The Rome Statute of the International Criminal Court: A commentary Vol I* (2002) 646.

85 It was the Uniting for Peace Resolution (GA Res 377 (1950)) wherein the General Assembly declared that it had residual authority to take steps to maintain or restore peace and security when the Council failed to exercise its primary responsibility in this regard 'because of a lack of unanimity of the permanent members'. See the case of *Certain Expenses of the United Nations* (Advisory Opinion) 1962 ICJ Rep 151 where the legality of this resolution was confirmed by the ICJ.

86 See 'Report of the Commission on the Outcome and Deliberations of the 8th Session of the Assembly of States Parties to the Rome Statute of the ICC held at The Hague, Netherlands from 16 to 26 November 2009' in 'Report on the Ministerial Meeting on the Rome Statute of the ICC (Annex II)' Assembly/AU/Dec 245 (XIII) January 2010.

87 'Decision on the Report of the Second Meeting of States Parties to the Rome Statute of the International Criminal Court (ICC)' Doc Assembly/AU/8(XIV).

repeats the hierarchical and unjust structure of the international system.[88] At the centre of the current regime of the court are the UN Security Council's referral and deferral powers: article 16 is the 'negative' component of the council's relationship with the court, the 'positive' one being article 13, which allows the council to proactively refer a matter to the court. The proposed amendment purports to grant the General Assembly authority to supplant the Security Council when the latter refuses to be moved by calls to defer investigations before the ICC. Furthermore, it attempts to establish a secondary responsibility in the assembly for the maintenance of international peace and security in the event of Security Council inaction.[89]

10 Conclusion

South Africa is a dualist state. Accordingly, an act of transformation of the international treaty into the domestic system has to be promulgated so that obligations undertaken could be lawfully be given effect to. South Africa has successfully achieved this objective and has been confronted with situations in which its implementing legislation has been put to the test. These recent events turning on South Africa's commitment to international criminal law delineate the two main functions of the ICC Act: to allow our local courts and police service to co-operate with the ICC in apprehending suspects indicted by the ICC (such as Al Bashir); and to ensure we fulfil our treaty obligations domestically to investigate individuals (for example those named in the Gaza docket) — who are South African or come within our jurisdiction — suspected of war crimes, genocide, or crimes against humanity. This second function is strictly in accordance with the principle of complementarity which obliges member states to act domestically by investigating and prosecuting these crimes or, if unwilling or unable to do so, surrendering suspects to The Hague for prosecution.

Although South Africa is regarded as an excellent example of commitment to the principles of international human rights law, the recent confusion surrounding the South African government's equivocation on our voluntarily-undertaken commitments calls for a coherent and co-ordinated policy on international criminal justice within government.[90]

88 The result entrenches the Great Powers exception granted to permanent Security Council members by giving the council the sole discretion to refer and defer matters to the court.

89 Gevers (n 67 above).

90 Gevers (n 65 above).

SELECTED BIBLIOGRAPHY

Books

Allen, T *Trial justice: The International Criminal Court and the Lord's Resistance Army* (2006) Zed Books: London/New York

Ankumah, E and Kwakwa E (eds) (2005) *African perspectives on international criminal justice* Africa Legal Aid: Accra/Pretoria

Ball, H (1999) *Prosecuting war crimes and genocide: The 20th century experience* Martinus Nijhoff: Leiden/Boston

Bassiouni, M (2009) *The pursuit of international criminal justice: A world study on conflicts, victimization, and post conflict justice* Intersentia: Antwerp

Bassiouni, M (ed) (2002) *Post-conflict justice* Transnational Publishers: New York

Bassiouni, M (1999) *Crimes against humanity in international criminal law* Martinus Nijhoff: Leiden/Boston

Bassiouni, M (ed) (1998) *The Statute of the International Criminal Court: A documentary history* Transnational Publishers: New York

Brandon B and Du Plessis M (eds) (2005) *The prosecution of international crimes: A practical guide to prosecuting ICC crimes in Commonwealth States* Commonwealth Secretariat: London

Broomhall, B (2003) *International justice and the International Criminal Court: Between state sovereignty and the rule of law* Oxford University Press: New York

Cassese, A (2003) *International criminal law* Oxford University Press: New York

Cassese, A *et al* (eds) (2002) *The Rome Statute of the International Criminal Court: A commentary (vol I)* Oxford University Press: New York

Cassese, A *et al* (eds) (2002) *The Rome Statute of the International Criminal Court: A Commentary (vol II)* Oxford University Press: New York

Clarke, K and Goodale, M (eds) (2010) *Mirrors of justice: Law and power in the post-Cold War era* Cambridge University Press: Cambridge

Cryer, R *et al* (2007) *An introduction to international criminal law and procedure* Cambridge University Press: Cambridge

De Than, C and Shorts, E (eds) (2003) *International criminal law and human rights* Sweet & Maxwell: London

Du Plessis, M (ed) (2008) *African guide to international criminal justice* Institute for Security Studies: Pretoria

El-Zeidy, M (2008) *The principle of complementarity in international criminal law: Origin, development and practice* Martinus Nijhoff: Leiden/Boston

Horst, F *et al* (eds) (2001) *International and national prosecutions of crimes under international law: Current developments* Berlin Verlag Arno Spitz: Berlin

Kittichaisaree, K (2001) *International criminal law* Oxford University Press: New York

Kuper, L (1982) *Genocide: Its political use in the twentieth century* Yale University Press: New Haven

Lattanzi, F & Schabas, W (eds.) (1999). *Essays on the Rome Statute of the International Criminal Court* Fagnano Alto: il Sirente

Lattimer M and Sands P (2003) *Justice for crimes against humanity* Hart Publishing: Oregon

Lee, R (ed) (1999) *The International Criminal Court – The making of the Rome Statute: Issues – negotiations – results* Kluwer Law International: The Hague

Mamdani, M (2009) *Saviours and Survivors: Darfur, politics, and the war on terror* Pantheon Books: New York

McAdams J (ed) (1997) *Transitional justice and the rule of law in New Democracies* University of Notre Dame Press: Notre Dame

Menon, V (ed) (2008) *War crimes and law* Icfai University Press: Hyderabad

Meron, T (1989) *Human rights and humanitarian norms as customary law* Oxford University Press: Oxford/New York

Morris, V & Scharf, M (1995) *An insider guide to the International Criminal Tribunal for former Yugoslavia* Transnational Publishers: New York

Mugwanya G (2007) *The crime of genocide in international law: Appraising the contribution of the UN Tribunal for Rwanda* (2007) Cameron May: UK

Neier A (1998) *War crimes: Brutality, genocide, terror, and the struggle for justice* Times Books:

Robertson, G (2002) *Crimes against humanity: The struggle for global justice* (2002) 403-426 Penguin Books: London

Schabas, W (2007) *An introduction to the International Criminal Court* Cambridge University Press: Cambridge

Schabas, W (2000) *Genocide in international law: The crime of crimes* Cambridge University Press: Cambridge

Schabas, W (2000) *Genocide in international law* Cambridge University Press: Cambridge

Sluiter, G and Vasiliev, S (eds) (2009) *International criminal procedure: Towards a coherent body of law* Cameron May: UK

Stigen, J (2008) *The relationship between the International Criminal Court and national jurisdiction* Martinus Nijhoff: Leiden/Boston

Tronvoll, K et *al* (eds) (2009) *The Ethiopian Red Terror trials: Transitional justice challenged* James Currey: New York

Van Schaack, B and Slye, R (2007) *International criminal law and its enforcement: Cases and materials* Foundation Press: New York

Waddel, N and Clark, P (*eds*) (2008) *Courting conflict? Justice, peace and the ICC Africa* Institute for Security Studies: Pretoria

Wilson R (2001) *The politics of Truth and Reconciliation in South Africa: Legitimizing the post-Apartheid state* Cambridge University Press: New York

Journal articles

Akande, D 'The legal nature of Security Council referrals to the ICC and its impact on Al Bashir's immunities' (2009) 7 *Journal of International Criminal Justice* 333

Akande, D 'The jurisdiction of the International Criminal Court over nationals of non-state parties: Legal basis and limits' (2003) 1 *Journal of International Criminal Justice* 618

Aversano, D 'Can the Pope be a defendant in American courts? The grant of head of state immunity and the judiciary's role to answer this question' (2006) 18 *Pace International Law Review* 495

Bagaric, M 'Scientific proof that human enjoy punishing wrongdoers: The implications for punishment and sentencing' (2005) 1 *International Journal of Punishment and Sentencing* 98

Bako, P 'Does traditional conflict resolution lead to justice? – The *Mato Oput* in Northern Uganda' (2009) 3 *Pretoria Student Law Review* 103

Bassiouni, M 'From Versailles to Rwanda in seventy-five years: The need to establish a permanent international criminal court' (1997) 10 *Harvard Human Rights Journal* 11

Bassiouni, M 'Searching for peace and achieving justice: The need for accountability' (1996) 59 *Law and Contemporary Problems* 9

Bekou, O & Shah, S 'Realising the potential of the International Criminal Court: The African experience' 2006 (6) *Human Rights Law Review* 499

Benzing, M 'The complementarity regime of the International Criminal Court: International criminal justice between states sovereignty and the fight against impunity' (2003) 7 *Max Planck Yearbook of United Nations Law* 591

Burke-White, W 'Complementarity in practice: The International Criminal Court as part of a system of multilevel global governance in the Democratic Republic of Congo' (2005) 18 *Leiden Journal of International Law* 557

Burke-White, W 'Proactive complementarity: The International Criminal Court and national courts in the Rome system of international justice' (2008) 49 *Harvard International Law Journal* 53

Burke-White, W 'Implementing a policy of positive complementarity in the Rome system of justice' (2008) 19 *Criminal Law Forum* 59

Burns, P 'An international criminal tribunal: The difficult union of principle and politics' (1994) 5 *Criminal Law Forum* 341

Cassese, A 'The Special Court and international law: The decision concerning the Lomé Agreement amnesty' (2004) *Journal of International Criminal Justice* 1130

Cayley, T 'The prosecutor's strategy in seeking the arrest of Sudanese President Al Bashir on charges of genocide' (2008) 6 *Journal of International Criminal Justice* 829

Chirwa, D 'The implications of the emerging jurisprudence in international criminal law for penal regimes in post-independent Africa' (2004) 17 *South African Journal of Criminal Justice* 193

Chitiyo, K and Devlin, L'The International Criminal Court and Africa' (2008) 28 *The Royal United Services Institute Newsbrief* 69

Ciampi, A 'The proceedings against president Al Bashir and the prospects of their suspension under article 16 ICC Statute' (2008) 6 *Journal of International Criminal Justice* 885

Clark, T 'The prosecutor of the International Criminal Court, amnesties, and the "interests of justice": Striking a delicate balance' (2005) 4 *Washington University Global Studies Law Review* 389

Cryer, R 'Prosecuting the leaders: Promises, politics and practicalities' (2009) 1 *Göttingen Journal of International Law* 45

Cryer, R 'Sudan, Resolution 1593, and international criminal justice' (2006) 19 *Leiden Journal of International Law* 195

Danne, M 'Constructing a hierarchy of crimes in international criminal law sentencing' (2001) 87 *Virginia Law Review* 419

Du Plessis, M 'Recent cases and developments: South Africa and the International Criminal Court' (2009) 3 *South African Journal of Criminal Justice* 443

Du Plessis, M 'South Africa's implementation of the ICC Statute: An African example' (2007) 5 *Journal of International Criminal Justice* 461

Du Plessis, M 'South Africa's response to American hostility towards the International Criminal Court' (2005) 30 *South African Yearbook of International Law* 112

Du Plessis, M 'Bringing the International Criminal Court home – the implementation of the Rome Statute of the International Criminal Court Act 2002' (2003) 16 *South African Journal of Criminal Justice* 2

Edelenbos, C 'Human rights violations: A duty to prosecute?' (1994) 7 *Leiden Journal of International Law* 5

Elagab, O 'The Darfur Situation and the ICC: An appraisal' (2008) 1 *Journal of Politics and Law* 43

Ellis, M 'The International Criminal Court and its implication for domestic law and national capacity building' (2002) 15 *Florida Journal of International Law* 215

El-Zeidy, M 'The principle of complementarity: A new machinery to implement international criminal law' (2003) 23 *Michigan Journal of International Law* 869

Fox, H 'State immunity and the international crime of torture' (2006) 2 *European Human Rights Law Reports* 142

Gaeta, P 'Does President Al Bashir enjoy immunity from arrest?' (2009) 7 *Journal of International Criminal Justice* 315

Gaeta, P 'Is the practice of "self-referrals" a sound start for the ICC?' (2004) 2 *Journal of International Criminal Justice* 951

Gavron, J 'Amnesties in light of developments in international law and the establishment of the International Criminal Court' (2002) 51 *International & Comparative Law Quarterly* 91

Greenawalt, A 'Complementarity in crisis: Uganda, alternative justice, and the International Criminal Court' (2009) 50 *Virginia Journal of International Law* 108

Greenawalt, A 'Rethinking genocidal intent: The case of a knowledge-based interpretation' (1999) *Columbia Law Review* 2259

Haile-Mariam, Y 'The quest for justice and reconciliation: The International Criminal Tribunal for Rwanda and the Ethiopian High Court' (1998-99) 22 *Hastings International and Comparative Law Review* 679

Henham, R 'Developing contextualized rationales for sentencing in international criminal trials: A plea for empirical research' (2007) 5 *Journal of International Criminal Justice* 757

Henham, R 'Conceptualising access to justice and victims' rights in international sentencing' (2004) 13 *Social Legal Studies* 29

Hoening, P 'The dilemma of peace and justice in Northern Uganda' (2008) Vol 14 *East African Journal of Peace and Human Rights* 338

Howland, T 'Learning to make proactive human rights interventions effective: The Carter Center and Ethiopia's Office of the Special Prosecutor' (2000) 18 *Wisconsin International Law Journal* 419

Huigens, K 'On commonplace punishment theory' (2005) *University of Chicago Legal Forum* 437

Jackson, M 'The customary international law duty to prosecute crimes against humanity: A new framework' (2007) 16 *Tulane Journal of International and Comparative Law* 117

Jalloh, C 'Regionalising international criminal law' (2009) 9 *International Criminal Law Review* 445

Jalloh, C 'The contribution of the Special Court for Sierra Leone' (2007) 15 *African Journal of International and Comparative Law* 173

Jordan, J 'Paust, applicability of international criminal laws to events in the former Yugoslavia' (1994) 9 *American Journal of International Law & Policy* 499

Jurdi, N 'Some lessons on complementarity for the International Criminal Court Review Conference (2009) 34 *South African Yearbook of International Law* 28

Jurdi, N 'The prosecutorial interpretation of the complementarity principle: Does it really contribute to ending impunity on the national level?' (2010) 10 *International Criminal Law Review* 73

Katz, A 'An act of transformation: The incorporation of the Rome Statute of the ICC into national law in South Africa' (2003) 12 *African Security Review* 27

Kastner, P 'The ICC in Darfur – Saviour or spoiler?' (2007) 14 *ILSA Journal of International and Comparative Law* 145

Keller, L 'Achieving peace with justice: The International Criminal Court and Ugandan alternative justice mechanisms' (2008) 23 *Connecticut Journal of International Law* 209

Kress, C 'The Darfur Report and genocidal intent' (2005) Vol 3 *Journal of International Criminal Justice* 562

Kress, C 'Self-referrals' and 'waivers of complementarity' (2004) 2 *Journal of International Criminal Justice* 944

Leibman, L 'From Nuremberg to Bosnia: Consistent application of international law' (1994) 42 *Cleveland State Law Review* 705

Little, A 'Balancing accountability and victim autonomy at the International Criminal Court' (2007) 38 *Georgetown Journal of International Law* 363

Mallory, J 'Resolving the confusion over the head of state immunity: The defined right of kings' (1986) 86 *Columbia Law Review* 169

Maqungo, S 'The establishment of the International Criminal Court: SADC's participation in the negotiations' (2000) 9 *African Security Review* 42

McHugh, J 'Utilitarianism, punishment, and ideal proportionality in penal law: Punishment as an intrinsic evil' (2008) 10 *Journal of Bentham Studies* 1

Megret, F 'The politics of international criminal justice' (2002) 13 *European Journal of International Law* 1262

Moellendorf, D 'Amnesty, truth and justice: AZAPO' (1997) 13 *South African Journal on Human Rights* 283

Mugwanya, G 'Criminal justice through international criminal tribunals: Reflections on some lessons for national criminal justice systems' (2006) 6 *African Human Rights Law Journal* 59

Murungi, B 'Implementing the international criminal court statute in Africa: Some reflections' (2001) 7 *East African Journal of Peace and Human Rights* 136

Murungu, C 'Judgment in the first case before the African Court on Human and Peoples' Rights: A missed opportunity or a mockery of international law in Africa?' (2010) 3 *Journal of African and International Law* 187

Naqvi, Y 'Amnesty for war crimes: Defining the limits of international recognition' (2003) 85 *International Review of the Red Cross* 583

Nmehielle, V & Jalloh, C 'The legacy of the Special Court for Sierra Leone' (2006) 30 *The Fletcher Forum of World Affairs* 109

Newton, M 'Comparative complementarity: Domestic jurisdiction consistent with the Rome Statute of the International Criminal Court' (2001) 167 *Military Law Review* 20

Nicol-Wilson, M 'The realisation of the right to bail in the Special Court for Sierra Leone: Problems and prospects' (2007) 7 *African Human Rights Law Journal* 506

Nsereko, D 'Triggering the jurisdiction of the International Criminal Court' (2004) 4 *African Human Rights Law Journal* 256

Oko, O 'The challenges of international criminal prosecutions in Africa' (2008) 31 *Fordham International Law Journal* 343

Pion-Berlin, D 'To Prosecute or pardon? Human rights decisions in the Latin American Southern Cone (1993) 15 *Human Rights Quarterly* 105

Robinson, D 'The mysterious mysteriousness of complementarity' (2010) 21 *Criminal Law Forum* 67

Robinson, D 'Serving the interest of justice: Amnesties, truth commissions and the International Criminal Court' (2003) 14 *European Journal of International Law* 481

Roht-Arriaza, N & Gibson, L 'The developing jurisprudence on amnesty' (1998) 20 *Human Rights Quarterly* 843

Roht-Arriaza, N 'State responsibility to investigate and prosecute grave human rights violations in international law' (1998) 78 *California Law Review* 451

Romero, J 'The Special Court for Sierra Leone and the juvenile soldier dilemma' (2004) 2 *North-western University Journal of International Human Rights* 8

Sadat, L 'Exile, amnesty and international law' (2006) *Notre Dame Law Review* 955

Schabacker, E 'Reconciliation of justice and ashes: Amnesty commissions and the duty to punish human rights offenses' (1999) 12 *New York International Law Review* 1

Scharf, M 'The amnesty exception to the jurisdiction of the International Criminal Court' (1999) 32 *Cornell International Law Journal* 507

Schey, P *et al* 'Addressing human rights abuses: Truth commissions and the value of amnesty' (1997) 19 *Whittier Law Review* 325

Sinclair, I 'The law of sovereign immunity: Recent developments' (1980) 2 *Hague Recueil des Cours* 113

Stewart, D 'Immunity and accountability: More continuity than change?' (2005) 99 *American Society International Law Proceedings* 227

Schabas, W 'Prosecutorial discretion *v* judicial activism' (2008) 6 *Journal of International Criminal Justice* 731

Schabas, W 'Complementarity in practice: Some uncomplimentary thoughts' (2008) 19 *Criminal Law Forum* 5

Schabas, W 'Sentencing by international tribunals: A human rights approach' (1997) 7 *Duke Journal of Comparative and International Law* 461

Terracino, J 'National implementation of ICC crimes: Impact on national jurisdictions and the ICC' (2007) 5 *Journal of International Criminal Justice* 421

Tiba, F 'The Mengistu genocide trial in Ethiopia' (2007) 5 *Journal of International Criminal Justice* 513

Turner, J 'Nationalizing international criminal law' (2005) 41 *Stanford Journal of International Law* 1

William, S and Sherif, L 'The arrest warrant for President Al Bashir: Immunities of incumbent heads of state and the International Criminal Court' (2009) 14 *Journal of Conflict and Security Law* 71

Reports

AU 'Report of the Chairperson of the Commission on the Activities of the African Union High–Level Implementation Panel on Sudan' PSC/PR/2(CCXXXV) Peace and Security Council 235th Meeting, Addis Ababa, 2 July 2010

Report on the Ministerial Meeting on the Rome Statute of the ICC (Annex II)' Assembly/AU/Dec 245 (XIII) January 2010

AU Report of the African Union High-Level Panel on Darfur' PSC/AHG/2(CCVII) 29 October 2009

Report of the Activities of the Court to the Assembly of States Parties' Eighth Session, para 40, ICC-ASP/8/40, 21 October 2009

Report on the Work of the Office of the High Commissioner for Human Rights in Uganda, UN Doc A/HRC/4/49/Add2, 12 February 2007

Report of the Secretary-General on the Establishment of a Special Tribunal for Lebanon, delivered to the Security Council, UN Doc S/2006/893 (15 November 2006)

Third Report of the Prosecutor of the International Criminal Court to the U.N. Security Council Pursuant to UNSCR 1593 (2005)' 14 June 2006

Report of the Special Rapporteur on torture and other cruel, inhuman or degrading treatment or punishment, Manfred Nowak, UN Doc E/CN 4/2006/6 (23 December 2005)

UN 'Report of the International Commission of Inquiry on Darfur to the United Nations Secretary-General', Pursuant to Security Council Resolution 1564 of 18 September 2004, 25 January 2005

Eleventh Report of the Prosecutor of the International Criminal Court to the UN Security Council Pursuant to UNSC 1593 (2005)

UN Secretary-General's Report on the Rule of Law and Transnational Justice in Conflict and Post-Conflict Situations, s/2004/616

Report of the Truth and Reconciliation Commission of Sierra Leone (2004)

Report on Guatemala by the Expert, Mr Hector Gros Espiell, prepared in accordance with para 9 of UN Commission on Human Rights Resolution 1989/74, 46 UN ESCOR Comm'n on Hum Rts, paras 48, 49, 57, 66(c) UN Doc E/CN 4/1990/45

Report on Haiti by the Expert, Mr Philippe Texier, prepared in conformity with UN Commission on Human Rights Resolution 1989/73, 46 UN ESCOR Comm'n on Hum. Rts, paras 55, 61, 67, 87, 91, 102, 106(c) & (e), UN Doc E/CN 4/1990/44

Report of the Working Group on Enforced or Involuntary Disappearances, 45 UN ESCOR Comm'n on Hum Rts 85 para 312, UN Doc E/CN 4/1989/18

Report presented by Mr S Amos Wako, United Nations Special Rapporteur on Summary and arbitrary executions, pursuant to Economic and Social Council Resolution 1987/60 (E/CN 4/1988/22, 19 January 1988)

Final Report on the situation of human rights in El Salvador submitted to the Commission on Human Rights by Mr Jose Antonio Pastor Ridruejo in fulfilment of the mandate conferred under Commission resolution 1986/39, 43 UN ESCOR Comm'n on Hum Rts 13 para 60, UN Doc E/CN4/1987/21

Report prepared by the Special Rapporteur on the situation of human rights in Chile in accordance with para 11 of the Commission on Human Rights Resolution 1983/38 of 8 March 1983, UN Doc A/38/385 para 341 (1983)

Report of the Working Group on a Draft Convention Against Torture and Other Cruel, Inhuman or Degrading Treatment or Punishment, 36 UN ESCOR Comm'n on Hum Rts 11 para 61, UN Doc E/CN 4/1367 (1980)

Report of the Working Group on Enforced or Involuntary Disappearances, 47 UN ESCOR Comm'n on Hum Rts 86

Report of the Committee of Eminent African Jurists on the Case of Hissene Habré

Report of the Secretary-General of the UN to the General Assembly on Children and armed conflict, A/64/742–S/2010/181 64th session Agenda item 65(a), Promotion and protection of the rights of children

TABLE OF CASES

Permanent Court of International Justice

Greco-Bulgarian Communities case, 1930 P.C.I.J. (Ser.B) No. 17

Polish Nationals in Danzig case, 1931 P.C.I.J (Ser. A/B) No 44

SS Lotus (*France v Turkey*) (1927) PCIJ Rep. Ser. A, No. 10

International Court of Justice

Asylum Case (Colombia v Peru), Judgment, 20 November 1950, ICJ Reports (1950) 126

Barcelona Traction, Light and Power Co. Ltd (Belgium v Spain), 1970 I.C.J. 3

Case Concerning Certain Criminal Proceedings in France (Republic of the Congo v France), Provisional Measures, Order of 17 June 2003, ICJ Reports (2003) 102

Case Concerning Military and Paramilitary Activities In and Against Nicaragua, (Nicaragua v USA), Judgment, 27 June 1986, ICJ Reports (1986)

Case Concerning Questions of Interpretation and Application of the 1971 Montreal Convention Arising from the Aerial Incident at Lockerbie (Libyan Arab Jamahiriya v United States) 1992 I.C.J. 114, 160-81 (Apr. 14) (Weeramantry, J., dissenting)

Case Concerning Questions Relating to the Obligation to Prosecute or Extradite (Belgium v Senegal), Request for the Indication of Provisional Measures, Order of 28 May 2009, ICJ General List No.144

Case Concerning the Arrest Warrant of 11 April 2000 (The Democratic Republic of Congo v Belgium), 2002 ICJ Reports, 14 February 2002

Legal Consequences for States of the Continued Presence of South Africa in Namibia (South West Africa) notwithstanding Security Council Resolution 276, 1971 I.C.J. 66 (June 21)

North Sea Continental Shelf (Federal Republic of Germany v Denmark; Federal Republic of Germany v Netherlands), Judgment, 20 February 1969, ICJ Reports (1969)

Reservation to the Convention on the Prevention and Punishment of the Crime of Genocide, 1951 I.C.J. 15

Right of Passage Over Indian Territory (Portugal v India), 1960 I.C.J. 123, 135 (Apr. 12)

International Military Tribunal at Nuremberg

Nuremberg Judgment, *International Military Tribunal,* 1946, reprinted in (1947) 41 *American Journal of International Law* 172, 221

The United States of America, the French Republic, the United Kingdom of Great Britain and Northern Ireland, and the Union of Soviet Socialist Republics v Hermann Wilhelm Goring et al, Order of the Tribunal Granting Postponement of Proceedings Against Gustav Krupp Von Bohlen, 15 November 1945, I Trial of the Major War Criminals, 143

International Criminal Court

Prosecutor v Al Bashir, Decision on the Prosecution's Application for a Warrant of Arrest against Omar Hassan Al Bashir, Case No. ICC-02/05-01/09, Public Reducted Version, Pre-Trial Chamber I, 4 March 2009

Prosecutor v Harun ('Ahmad Harun') and Abd-Al-Rahman ('Ali Kushayb') ICC-02/05-01/07

Prosecutor v Dyilo ICC-01/04-01/06, Decision on the Prosecutor's Application for a Warrant of Arrest 10 June 2006

Prosecutor v Katanga and Chui, ICC-01/04-01/07 OA 8, Judgment on the Appeal of Mr Germain Katanga against the Oral Decision of Trial Chamber II of 12 June 2009 on the Admissibility of the Case, 25 September 2009

Prosecutor v Al Bashir, Case No. ICC-02/05-01/09, Decision on the Prosecution's Application for a Warrant of Arrest against Omar Hassan Ahmad Al Bashir, 3 April 2009

Prosecutor v Al Bashir, Case No. ICC-02/05-01/09, Second Decision on the Prosecution's Application for a Warrant of Arrest, (Public), 12 July 2010

Prosecutor v Al Bashir, Case No. ICC-02/05-01/09, Warrant of Arrest for Omar Hassan Ahmed Al Bashir, 4 March 2009

Prosecutor v Al Bashir, Case No. ICC-02/05-01/09-OA, Judgment on the Appeal of the Prosecutor Against the Decision on the Prosecutor's Application for a Warrant of Arrest Against Omar Hassan Ahmad Al Bashir, 3 February 2010

International Criminal Tribunal for the former Yugoslavia

Prosecutor v Blagojević and Jokić, Judgment of 17 January 2005 (TC)

Prosecutor v Blaškić, Case No.IT-95-14-PT, *Decision on the Admissibility of the Request for Review by the Republic of Croatia of an Interlocutory Decision of a Trial Chamber (Issuance of Subpoenae Duces Tecum) and Scheduling Order*, 29 July 1997(AC)

Prosecutor v Blaškić, (Case No. IT-95-14-AR 108bis), *Judgment on the Request of the Republic of Croatia for Review of the Decision of Trial Chamber II of 18 July 1997*, 29 October 1997(AC)

Prosecutor v Blaškić, Case No. IT-95-14, *Judgment on the Request of the Republic of Croatia for Review of the Decision of Trial Chamber II of 18 July 1997*, 29 October 1997 (TC)

Prosecutor v Blaškić, Case No.IT-95-14-PT, *Decision on the Objection of the Republic of Croatia to the issuance of Subpoenae Duces Tecum*, 18 July 1997(TC)

Prosecutor v Delalić, Case No. IT-96-21-T, Order on the Prosecution's Request for a Formal Finding of the Trial Chamber that the Accused Landzo is Fit to Stand Trial, 23 June 1997 (TC)

Prosecutor v Erdemović, Case No. IT-96-22-S, Sentencing Judgment, 5 March 1998 (TC)

Prosecutor v Kristić, Case No.IT-98-33-A, Appeals Judgment, 19 April 2004, (AC)

Prosecutor v Kristić, Case No.IT-98-33-A, Decision on Application for Subpoenas, 1 July 2003 (AC)

Prosecutor v Kunarać, Case No. IT-96-23 & IT-96-23/I-A, Judgment, 12 June 2002 (AC)

Prosecutor v Kunarać, Kovać and Vuković, Case No. IT-96-23 –T and IT-96-23/1-T, Judgment, 22 February 2001(TC)

Prosecutor v Kuperškić et al, Case No. IT-95-16-T, Judgment of 14 January 2000 (TC)

Prosecutor v Milošević, Decision on Preliminary Motions, Decision of 8 November 2001(TC)

Prosecutor v Stakić, Case No. IT-97-24-A, Judgment (AC)

Prosecutor v Vaslajević, Case No. IT-98-32-A, Appeal Judgment, 25 February 2004, (AC)

Prosecutor v Brdanin and Talić, Case No. IT-99-36-T, *Subpoena ad Testificandum*, 17 July 2003 (TC)

Prosecutor v Celebici, Case No. IT-96-21-A, 20 February 2001(AC)

Prosecutor v Talic, Case No. IT-99-36/1-T, Decision regarding Fitness of the Accused to Stand Trial, 29 April 2003 (TC)

Prosecutor v Strugar, Case No. IT-01-42-T, *Subpoena ad Testificandum*, 28 June 2004 (TC)

Prosecutor v Halilović, Case No.IT-01-48-AR73, Decision on the Issuance of Subpoenas, 21 June 2004 (AC)

Prosecutor v Halilović, Case No. IT-01-48-T, Decision on Prosecution's Motion for Issuance of a Subpoena Ad Testificandum and Order for Lifting *Ex Parte* Status, 8 April 2005 (TC)

Prosecutor v Milošević, Case No. IT-02-54-T, Decision on Assigned Counsel Application for Interview and Testimony of Tony Blair and Gerhard Schroder, 9 December 2005 (TC)

Prosecutor v Milošević, Case No. IT-02-54-T, *Request for Binding Order to be Issued to the Government of the United Kingdom for the Cooperation of a Witness pursuant to Rule 54bis*, 18 August 2005 (TC)

Prosecutor v Milošević, Case No. IT-02-54-T, Decision on the Prosecution's Application for Issuance of a *Subpoena ad Testificandum* for Witness K33 and Request for Judicial Assistance Directed to the Federal Republic of Yugoslavia, 5 July 2002 (TC)

Prosecutor v Blagojević, Case No. IT-02-60-T, Order In re Defence's Request for the Issuance of *Subpoenas ad Testificandum*, Orders for Safe Conduct and an Order for the Service and Execution of the Subpoenas and Orders for Safe Conduct, 5 May 2004 (TC)

Prosecutor v Tadic, Case IT-94-1-T, Decision on Jurisdiction, 2 October 1995 (TC)

Prosecutor v Tadić, Case No. IT-94 1 A-R72, Decision on the Defence Motion for Interlocutory Appeal on Jurisdiction, 2 October 1995

Prosecutor v Tadić, Case No. IT-94-1-AR72, Decision on the Defence Motion for Interlocutory Appeal on Jurisdiction, 2 October 1995 (AC)

Prosecutor v Tadic, Case No.IT-94-1-A, Judgment of the Appeals Chamber, Jurisdiction, 15 July 1999(AC)

Prosecutor v Martić, Case No. IT-95-11-PT, Decision on the Prosecution's Additional Filing Concerning 3 June 2005 Prosecution Motion for Subpoena, 16 September 2005 (TC)

Prosecutor v Furundžija, Case No. IT-95-17/1-T, 10 December 1998, (TC)

Prosecutor v Kupreškić et al, Case No. IT-95-16, 14 January 2000, (AC)

Prosecutor v Jelišić, Case No. IT-95-10-A, Judgment, 5 July 2001, (AC)

Prosecutor v Strugar, Case No. IT-01-42-A, Judgment, 17 July 2008, (AC)

Prosecutor v Aleksovski, Case No. IT-95-14/1-A, Judgment, 24 March 2000 (AC)

Prosecutor v Kunarać et al, Case No. IT-96-23 and IT-96-23/1-T, Judgment, 22 February 2001, (TC)

Prosecutor v Karadžić, Case No.IT-95-5/18-PT, Decision on Appellant Radovan Karadžić's Appeal Concerning Holbrooke Agreement Disclosure, ICTY Appeals Chamber, 6 April 2009 (AC)

Prosecutor v Karadžić, Case No.IT-95-5/18-PT, Appeal of the Decision Concerning Holbrooke Agreement Disclosure, 28 January 2009 (AC)

Prosecutor v Karadžić, Case No.IT-95-5/18-PT, Decision on the Accused's Holbrooke Agreement Motion, 8 July 2009 (TC)

Prosecutor v Tordorović, Case No. IT-95-9/1-S, Sentencing Judgment, 31 July 2001(TC)

Prosecutor v Celebici, Case No. IT-96-21, Judgment, 16 November 1998 (TC)

International Criminal Tribunal for Rwanda

Barayagwiza v Prosecutor, Case No. ICTR-97-19 (AC), Judgment, 3 November 1999

Gacumbitsi v Prosecutor, Case No. ICTR-2001-64-A, Judgment, 7 July 2006(AC)

Kambanda v Prosecutor, Case No. ICTR 97-23-A, Judgment, 19 October 2000 (AC)

Prosecutor v Kajelijeli, Case No. ICTR-98-44A-T, Judgment and Sentence, 1 December 2003 (AC)

Prosecutor v Kambanda, Case No. ICTR-97-23-S, Judgment and Sentence, 4 September 1998, (TC)

Prosecutor v Karemera et al, Case No.ICTR-98-44-T, Decision on Defence Motion for Issuance of Subpoena to Witness T, Trial Chamber of ICTR, 8 February 2006 (TC)

Prosecutor v Karemera et al, Decision on Nzirorera's *Ex Parte* Motion for Order for Interview of Defence Witnesses NZ1, NZ2, Trial Chamber of ICTR, 12 July 2006 (TC)

Prosecutor v Karemera, Case No. ICTR-98-44-AR73.10, Decision on Nzirorera's Interlocutory Appeal Concerning His Right to be Present during Trial, 5 October 2007 (TC)

Prosecutor v Karemera, Ngirumpatse and Nzirorera, Case No. ICTR-98-44-T, *Decision on Joseph Nzirorera's Motions for Subpoena to Leon Mugesera and President Paul Kagame,* 19 February 2008 (TC)

Prosecutor v Kayishema and Ruzindana, Case No. ICTR-95-1-A, Judgment (Reasons), 1 June 2001 (AC)

Prosecutor v Kayishema and Ruzindana, Case No. ICTR-95-1-T, Judgment and Sentence, 21 May 1999, (TC)

Prosecutor v Muhimana, Case No. ICTR-95-1B-T, Judgment, 28 April 2005 (TC)

Prosecutor v Musema, Case No. ICTR-96-13-T, Judgment and Sentence, 27 January 2000, (TC)

Prosecutor v Nahimana et al, Case No. ICTR-99-52-T, Decision on Motion by the Defence in Accordance with Rule 74 bis, 20 February 2001 (TC)

Prosecutor v Nahimana et al, Case No. ICTR-99-52-T, Judgment and Sentence, 3 December 2003, (TC)

Prosecutor v Niyitegeka, Case No. ICTR-96-14-T, Judgment and Sentence, 16 May 2003, (TC)

Prosecutor v Ntakirutimana and Gerard Ntakirutimana, Case Nos. ICTR-96-10-A and ICTR-96-17-A, 13 December 2004 (AC)

Prosecutor v Rutaganda, Case No. ICTR-96-3, Judgment and Sentence, 6 December 1999, (TC)

Prosecutor v Rutaganda, Case No.ICTR-96-3-A, Judgment, 26 May 2003, (AC)

Prosecutor v Simon Bikindi (TC), Case No. ICTR-01-72-T, Judgment, 2 December 2008 (TC)

Prosecutor v. Gacumbitsi, Case No. ICTR-2001-64-T, Judgment, 19 June 2004 (TC)

Prosecutor v Kajelijeli, Case No. ICTR-98-44A-A, 23 May 2005 (AC)

Prosecutor v Kajelijeli, Case No. ICTR-98-44A-T, Judgment and Sentence, 1 December 2003, (TC)

Prosecutor v Ntakirutimana, ICTR-96-10-A & ICTR-96-17-A, ICTR Appeals Chamber, Judgment, 13 December 2004 (AC)

Prosecutors v Bagosora et al, Case No. ICTR-98-41-T, Decision on Request for Subpoenas of United Nations Officials, 'Request for Subpoenas of Kofi Annan, Iqbal Riza, Shaharyar Khan and Michel Hourigan Pursuant to Rule 54' of 25 August 2006, Trial Chamber I, Decision of 6 October 2006(TC)

Prosecutors v Bagosora et al, Decision on Request for a Subpoena, Trial Chamber of ICTR, 11 September 2006 (TC)

Rutaganda v Prosecutor, Case No. ICTR-96-3-A, Judgment, 26 May 2003 (AC)

Rwamakuba v Prosecutor, Case No. ICTR-98-44C-A, Decision on Appeal against Decision on Appropriate Remedy,13 September 2007 (AC)

Seromba v Prosecutor, Case No. ICTR-2001-66-A, Appeal Judgment, 12 March 2008 (AC)

Special Court for Sierra Leone

Amicus Brief in the Matter of David Anyaele and Emmanuel Egbuna v Charles Ghankay Taylor and Others, A submission from the Open Society Justice Initiative to the Federal High Court of Nigeria, Abuja Division, November 2004

Dissenting Opinion of Hon. Justice Bankole Thompson on Decisions on Motions by Moinina Fofana and Sam Hinga Norman for the Issuance of a Subpoena Ad Testificandum to H.E Alhaji Dr Ahmed Tejan Kabbah, President of the Republic of Sierra Leone, (Case No. SCSL-04-14-T)

Prosecutor v Norman, Case No. SCSL-04-14-AR 72, Decision on Preliminary Motion based on Lack of Jurisdiction (Child Recruitment), 13 May 2004

Prosecutor v Norman, Fofana and Kondewa, Case No. SCSL-04-14A, Decision on Prosecution Appeal Against the Trial Chamber's Decision of 2 August 2004 Refusing Leave to File an Interlocutory Appeal, 17 January 2005

Prosecutor v Norman, Fofana and Kondewa, Case No. SCSL-04-14-I, Decision on Motions for Judgment of acquittal Pursuant to Rule 98, 21 October 2005

Prosecutor v Norman, Fofana and Kondewa, Case No. SCSL-04-14-T, *Decision on Motions by Moinina Fofana and Sam Hinga Norman for the Issuance of a Subpoena Ad Testificandum to H.E Alhaji Dr. Ahmad Tejan Kabbah, President of the Republic of Sierra Leone*, Trial Chamber I, 13 June 2006

Prosecutor v Norman, Fofana and Kondewa, Case No. SCSL-04-14-T, Decision on Motions for Judgment of acquittal Pursuant to Rule 98, 21 October 2005

Prosecutor v Norman, Fofana and Kondewa, Case No. SCSL-04-14-T, Majority Decision on the Prosecution's Application for Leavc to File an Interlocutory Appeal Against the Decision on the Prosecution's Request for Leave to Amend the Indictment Against Samuel Hinga Norman, Moinina Fofana and Allieu Kondewa, 2 August 2004

Prosecutor v Norman, Fofana and Kondewa, Case No. SCSL-04-14-T, Reasoned Majority decision on Prosecution Motion for a Ruling on the Admissibility of Evidence, 24 May 2005

Prosecutor v Norman, Fofana and Kondewa, Civil Defence Forces (CDF) Trial, Case No. SCSL-04-14-I, 5 February 2004 (Indictment)

Prosecutor v Norman, Kallon and Kamara, Case Nos. SCSL-2004-14-AR 72(E), SCSL-2004-15-AR 72(E0, SCSL-2004-16-AR 72(E), Decision on Constitutionality and Lack of Jurisdiction, 13 March 2004

Prosecutor v Sesay, Kallon and Gbao, Case No. SCSL-04-15-PT, Decision on Prosecution request for Leave to Amend the Indictment, 6 May 2004

Prosecutor v Sesay, Kallon and *Gbao,* Case No. SCSL-04-15-T, Trial Chamber I, 30 June 2008

Prosecutor v Sesay, Kallon and Gbao, Case No. SCSL-04-15-T, Trial Chamber, Judgment Summary, 25 February 2009

Prosecutor v Sesay, Kallon and Gbao, Case No.SCSL-04-15-1-A, Judgment, Appeals Chamber, 25 October 2009

Prosecutor v Sesay, Kallon and Gbao, Revolutionary United Front (RUF) Trial, Case No. SCSL-04-15-PT, 13 May 2004 (Indictment)

Prosecutor v Taylor, Case No. SCSL-03-01-I, Decision on Immunity from Jurisdiction, Appeals Chamber, 31 May 2004

Prosecutor v Taylor, Case No. SCSL-2003-01-I, (Indictment), 3 March 2003.

Prosecutor v Taylor, Case No.SCSL-2003-01-I, Decision on Immunity from Jurisdiction, 31 May 2004

Extra-ordinary Chambers in the Courts of Cambodia

Criminal Case File No. 002/14-08-2006, Investigation No. 002/19-2007-ECCC/OCIJ, (Khieu Samphan), *Provisional Detention Order*, 19 November 2007

Extra-ordinary Chambers in the Courts of Cambodia, Criminal Case File No. 002/14-08-2006, Investigation No. 002/19-09-2007, ECCC-OCIJ, *Police Custody Decision*, 12 November 2007

Extra-ordinary Chambers in the Courts of Cambodia, Criminal Case File No. 002/14-08-2006, Investigation No. 002/19-09-2007, ECCC-OCIJ, *Provisional Detention Order*, 14 November 2007

The Iraq Surpeme Criminal Tribunal

Prosecutor v Saddam Hussein Al-Majid et al, Defendants' Preliminary Submission Challenging the Legality of the Special Court, 21 December 2005.

Inter-American Court of Human Rights

Consuelo et al v Argentina, Case 10.147, 10.181, 10.240, 10.262, 10.309, 10.311, Inter-Am. C.H.R., Report No. 28/92, OEA/Ser.L/V/II.83, doc. 14 P1 (1993)

Gary Hermosilla et al v Chile, Case 10.843, Inter-Am. C.H.R., Report No. 36/96, OEA/Ser.L/V/II.95, doc. 7 rev. p.46 (1997)

Mascre Las Hojas v El Salvador, Case 10.287, Report No. 26/92, Inter-Am. C.H.R., OEA/Ser.L/V/II.83, doc. 14 p83, conclusion p5c (1993)

Velasquez Rodriquez Case, Inter-Am. Ct. H. R. (Ser. C) No. 4, (1998) (Judgment)

European Court of Human Rights

France, Norway, Denmark, Sweden and The Netherlands v Turkey 8 *Eur. Hum. Rts Rep.* 205, 213 (1985)

Ireland v United Kingdom, 25 Eur. Ct. H. R. (ser. A) (1978)

Tas v Turkey, 33 Eur. H.R. Rep. 15 PPHI-H3 (2000)

X and Y v Netherlands, 91 European Court Human Rights Law Reports. (ser. A) 1985) (judgment)

The African Court on Human and Peoples' Rights

Michelot Yogogombaye v The Republic of Senegal, Application No. 001/2008, 15 December 2009, African Court on Human and Peoples' Rights, Judgment

The Court of Justice of the West African Community

Arrêt CEDEAO/ECOWAS Ruling: *Habré c République du Senegal*, 18 Novembre 2010

The African Commission on Human and Peoples' Rights

Amnesty International and Others v Sudan (2000) AHRLR 296 (ACHPR)

Commission Nationale des Droits de l'Homme et des Libertes v Chad (2000) AHRLR 66 (ACHPR 1995)

Constitutional Rights Project and Others v Nigeria (2000) AHRLR 227 (ACHPR 1999)

Malawi African Association and Others v Mauritania (2000) AHRLR 149 (ACHPR 2000)

Media Rights Agenda and Others v Nigeria (2000) AHRLR 200 (ACHPR 1998)

United Nations Committee against Torture

Souleymane Guengueng et Autres C/ Senegal, Communication No.181/2001: Senegal. 19/05/2006.*CAT/C/36/D/181/2001*

Decision on Admissibility, dated November 23, 1989, Regarding Communications nos 1/1988, 2/1988 and 3/1988 (*O.R., M.M. and M.S. v Argentina*), Report of the Committee Against Torture, U.N.

GAOR, 45th Sess., Supp. No. 44, at annex VI, U.N. Doc. A/45/44, (1990)

United Nations Human Rights Committee

Baoboeram v Surinam, Comm. Nos. 146/1983 and 148-154/1983, 40 U.N. GAOR Supp. (No. 40) Annex X, para 13.2, U.N. Doc. A/40/40 (1985)

Bleir v Uruguay, Comm. No. 107/1981, 38 U.N. GAOR Supp. (No.40) Annex XXII, U.N. Doc. A/38/40 (1983)

Dermit v Uruguay, Comm. No. 84/1981, 38 U.N. GAOR Supp. (No. 40) Annex IX, para. 11, U.N. Doc. A/38/40 (1983)

Muteba v Zaire, Comm. No. 124/1982, 39 U.N. GAOR Supp. (No. 40) Annex XIII, U.N. Doc. A/39/40 (1984)

Quinteros v Uruguay, Comm. No. 107/1981, 38 U.N. GAOR Supp. (No. 40) Annex XXII, U.N. Doc. A/38/40 (1983)

National Jurisdictions

Democratic Republic of Congo

TMG de Mbandaka, Affaire Mutins de Mbandaka, 12 January 2006, PR 086/05 (first tribunal)

TMG de l'Ituri, Affaire *Bongi*, 24 March 2006, RP 018/06

Affaire *Songo Mboyo,* 12 April 2006, RP 084/05(first tribunal)

CM de l'Equateur, Affaire *Songo Mboyo,* 7 June 2006, RPA 014/06 (appeal tribunal)

TMG de Mbandaka, Affaire *Mutins de Mbandaka*, 20 June 2006, RP 086/05 - RP 101/06 (Appeal tribunal)

TMG de l'Ituri, Affaire *Kahwa*, 2 August 2006, RP 039/06

TMG de l'Ituri, Affaire *Bavi*, 19 February 2007, RP 101/06

CM de l'Equateur, Affaire *Mutins de Mbandaka*, 15 June 2007, RPA 615/2006 (final appeal)

Uganda

Jowad Kezaala v Attorney General, Constitutional Petition No. 24 of 2010

Israel

Attorney-General of Israel v Adolf Eichmann, (1968) 36 ILR 18 (District Court of Jerusalem)

Attorney-General of Israel v Adolf Eichmann, (1968) 36 ILR 227 (Supreme Court of Israel)

South Africa

Azanian Peoples Organization (AZAPO) v President of the Republic of South Africa 1996 (4) SA 671 (CC)

S v Johannes Velde van der Merwe, Adriaan Johannes Vlok, Christoffel Lodewikus Smith, Gert Jacobus Louis Hosea and Hermanus Johannes van Staden, Plea and Sentencing Agreement in Terms of Section 105A of Act 51 of 1977 (as amended), 17 August 2007

State v Basson 2005 SA 30/03 (CC)

Ethiopia

General Embibel Ayele v Special Prosecutor, Criminal Appeal File No 34459, Federal Supreme Court, (Tir 16, 2000 e.c.)

Special Prosecutor v Col Haile-Mariam and 173 Others, Preliminary Objections, Criminal File No.1/87, Decision of Meskerem 29, 1988 EC (GC)

Special Prosecutor v Col. Mengistu Haile-Mariam & Others, Federal High Court, First Criminal Division, Ruling on Prelimenary Objections, 9 October 1995

Special Prosecutor v Colonel Mengistu Haile-Mariam & others, Federal Supreme Court, Appeals Judgment, Criminal File No 30181, 26 May 2008

Senegal

Court of *Cassation,* Judgment No. 14 of 20 March 2001, *Souleymane Guengueng et Autres c. Hissene Habré*

India

Jashir Singh v Vipin Kumar Jaggi, AIR 2001 SC 2734

United Kingdom

Mighell v The Sultan of Johore, [1894] 1 QB 149

R v Bow Street Metropolitan Stipendiary Magistrate, Ex Parte Pinochet (1998) 4 All ER 897 (HL)

United States

Brief for the United States, in Tachiona, on her own behalf and on behalf of her late Husband Tapfuma Chiminya Tachiona, et al; Petitioners v United States of America, On Petition for a Writ of Certiorari to the United States Court of Appeals for the Second Circuit, In the Supreme Court of the United States, No.05-879, April 2006

Filartiga v Pena Irala, 630 F.2d 876, 882-884 (2d Cir. 1980)

Presbyterian Church of Sudan v Talisman Energy Inc. 244 F. Supp. 2d 289, 306 (S.D.N.Y. 2003)

Tachiona v Mugabe, 169 F. Supp. 2d 259, 309 (S.D.N.Y.2001)

Tel-Oren v Libyan Arab Republic 726 F.2d 774, 795 (D.C. Cir. 1984)

The Schooner Exchange v McFadden (1812), 11 US 137-138

United States v Noriega, 808 F. Supp. 791 (SD Fla 1992)

SUBJECT INDEX

A

B

C

D

L

M

N

O

P

R

S

T

U

V

W